AUSPICIOUS WISDOM

THE TEXTS AND TRADITIONS
OF
ŚRĪVIDYĀ ŚĀKTA TANTRISM
IN
SOUTH INDIA

DOUGLAS RENFREW BROOKS

State University of New York Press

Published by
State University of New York Press, Albany

Printed in the United States of America

For information, address State University of New York Press, State University Plaza, Albany, NY 12246

Production by Christine M. Lynch
Marketing by Theresa A. Swierzowski

Library of Congress Cataloging-in-Publication Data

Brooks, Douglas Renfrew
Auspicious wisdom : the texts and traditions of Śrīvidyā Śākta Tantrism in south India / Douglas Renfrew Brooks.
p. cm. — (SUNY series in tantric studies)
Includes bibliographical references and index.
ISBN 0-7914-1145-1 (hard : alk. paper) . — ISBN 0-7914-1146-X (pbk. : alk. paper)
1. Śrīvidyā (Hindu cult) 2. Shaktism—India, South.
3. Tantrism—India, South. I. Title. II. Series.
BL1225.S73B76 1992
294.5'514—dc20

91-31730
CIP

10 9 8 7 6 5 4 3 2

tasmai śrīgurave namaḥ

The goddess Rājarājeśvarī *in situ* at the *Shri Rājarājeśvarī Peetham*, Rochester, New York. Image provided by the *Shri Rājarājeśvarī Peetham*. Photo courtesy of Douglas Renfrew Brooks.

CONTENTS

ACKNOWLEDGMENTS

For more than a decade Dr. G. Sundaramoorthy, Head of the Department of Sanskrit, Madurai-Kamaraj University has led me through the perils of Hindu studies and provided insights into Śrīvidyā that would otherwise be unobtainable. None of my work would be possible but for him.

Thomas B. Coburn graciously shared his own important work on the goddess traditions. To my colleagues at the University of Rochester, Edward Wierenga, Th. Emil Homerin, J. Andrew Overman, Deborah Lyons, Katherine Argetsinger, Karen Fields, and Dean A. Miller who tolerate my endless queries and read my drafts, I offer gratitude and friendship. William Scott Green's special contribution warrants particular mention. To work with him daily is a special privilege. Lesley M. Adams offered important help and constant encouragement.

The late Agehananda Bharati made a special contribution to this work. His constructive criticism, encouragement, and erudition advanced my understanding of religion. Those of us who study the Hindu Tantra will miss him terribly.

M. David Eckel has always provided me with a model of excellence for comparative studies in religion; his wisdom and his friendship are my constant source of inspiration.

I must also acknowledge Paul Müller-Ortega, the Tantric Studies Series Editor, and William D. Eastman, the Director of SUNY Press, whose interest in my work has made possible the two volumes that will appear in this series.

Śrī Meru Cakra. Image provided by the *Shri Rājarājeśvarī Peetham.* Photo courtesy of Douglas Renfrew Brooks.

ABBREVIATIONS
APPEARING IN PARTS 1 AND 2 AND IN THE BIBLIOGRAPHY

I. SANSKRIT AND TAMIL SOURCES

JT	*Jñānārṇava Tantra*
KKV	*Kāmakalāvilāsa*
KT	*Kulārṇava Tantra*
LSN	*Lalitāsahasranāma*
LTS	*Lalitātriśatī*
LTSB	*Lalitātriśatībhāṣya*
MBh	*Mahābharata*
NS	*Nityotsava*
NSA	*Nityāṣoḍaśikārṇava*
PKS	*Paraśurāmakalpasūtra*
RV	*Ṛg Veda*
SL	*Saundaryalaharī*
TA	*Tantrāloka*
TM	*Tirumanitiram* of Tirumūlar
TR	*Tripurārahasya*
TTU	*Tripurātāpinī Upaniṣad*
TU	*Tripurā Upaniṣad*
TUbhāṣya	*Tripurā Upaniṣadbhāṣya* of Bhāskararāya
TRT	*Tantrarāja Tantra*
VT	*Vāmakeśvara Tantra*
VVR	*Varivasyārahasya*
YH	*Yoginīhṛdaya*

II. OTHER ABBREVIATIONS

ABORI	Annals of the Bhandarkar Oriental Research Institute
ALS	Adyar Library Series
ASS/AnS	*Ānandāśrama* Sanskrit Series, Poona

Bharati	*The Tantric Tradition*
BEFEO	*Bulletin de l'Ecole Francaise d'Extrême-Orient*, Paris
CHI	Cultural History of India
CSS	Chowkhamba Sanskrit Series
Dyczkowski	*The Doctrine of Vibration*
Gnoli	*Luce delle Sacre Scritture*
Gonda	"The Indian Mantra"
GOS	Gaekwad Oriental Series
Heesterman	*The Inner Conflict of Tradition*
HT	*Hindu Tantrism*
HTSL	*Hindu Tantric and Śākta Literature*
IHQ	Indian Historical Quarterly
JAOS	Journal of the American Oriental Society
KSS	Kāśī Sanskrit Series
KSTS	Kashmir Series of Texts and Studies, Śrīnagar
Pandey	*Abhinavagupta: An Historical and Philosophical Study*
PEW	Philosophy East and West, Honolulu
PWSBT	Prince of Wales Saraswati Bhavan Texts, Varanāsī
Rastogi	*Krama Tantricism of Kashmir*
SBG	Saraswati Bhavan Granthamala
Śākta Upaniṣads	Translation and introduction by A. G. Krishna Warrier
Staal	"The Meaninglessness of Ritual"
WZKS	Wiener Zeitschrift für die Kunde Sud-und Ostasiens, Wien
ZDMG	Zeitschrift der Deutschen Morgenländischen Gesallschaft, Leipzig, Wiesbaden
ZMR	Zeitschrift für Missionwissenschaft und Religionswissenschaft, Münster, Westfalen

PREFACE

STUDYING GODDESS-CENTERED HINDU TANTRISM:

Take Śrīvidyā, for example

This book focuses on one example from the esoteric Tantric traditions of Hinduism.[1] The tradition is best known as Śrīvidyā or "Auspicious Wisdom," a pan-Indian goddess-centered or Śākta cult whose roots are traceable to the sixth century.[2] Śrīvidyā centers on the beneficent (*saumya*) mother goddess (*devī*) and flourishes today in both north and south India among women and men of many castes. Historically, it has always been limited to those who possess ritual literacy in Sanskrit.

This study of Śrīvidyā focuses on developments in south Indian traditions and argues for a distinctive south Indian form of the cult. To learn about Śrīvidyā one "had better ask not about its condition at a given point in history...but rather about its dynamics, its continuing processes, its 'progress' through time."[3] I do not propose an interest in Śrīvidyā's history for its own sake, but to understand how one might interpret contemporary realities. As Jacob Neusner has written, "Tradition serves as the mode of orientation toward present and future, as the way of interpreting existence, not because it tells us where we have been but because it explains who we are, what we are, where we are and should be."[4]

Few contemporary Hindus associate the word "Tantra" with themselves, their beliefs, practices, or traditions. For brahman caste "Vaidikas" this is especially true. These "high-caste" devotees imagine themselves the custodians of the so-called Vedic tradition. For them, "Tantra" suggests all that they are not: disdain for the Vedic and brāhmaṇic legacy, a corruption of age-old morality and ritual custom, and a preoccupation with sex and black magic.[5] To be a Vaidika and a Tantric seems to some of them incommensurate. Yet significant factions within the larger complex of Hindu Tantrism either claim to be both Vaidika and Tantric, or warrant this description.[6] On what basis are such claims made? Why do others warrant this description?

While only some within Hindu Tantrism seek out connections to brāhmaṇical Hinduism, those who do assume a complex matrix of historical, ideological, and ritual associations. We have not yet identified the stakes involved for Hindus who endorse, advocate, criticize, or disdain the term "Tantra" nor have we explored fully the implications of calling oneself, or being called, a "Tāntrika."

Instead of adopting a platform whose purpose is to reject or endorse Tantric views, we must begin to interrogate the various social and intellectual associations made with terms, texts, and traditions. Studying Hindu Tantra need not and should not be confused with recommending it. This study assumes a basic familiarity with the elements and structures that define Hindu Tantric traditions. These have been described in some detail in a number of reliable sources.[7]

We still know far too little about the beliefs and practices described in Tantric texts and almost nothing about the legacy of these traditions, either among past or contemporary Hindus. While Tantric esotericism makes it difficult for the uninvited, not all who perpetuate these traditions are unwilling to discuss them and not all texts are impenetrable. To consider critically the relationship between historical texts and the legacy of particular Tantrisms, we will need to develop models and methods that can describe *and* explain the transmission of tradition in both oral and written modes of discourse. For the more difficult task of comparing specific elements within Hindu Tantrism, or types of Hindu Tantric religion with other religions (including other forms of Hinduism), we will require a discourse that can account for phenomena in terms other than their own. That is, we will need to place the subject in the service of some other paradigm, question, or problem in the study of religion. One cannot begin to address comparison seriously until data are well-understood and methods for study are developed.

Śrīvidyā was created, elaborated, and perpetuated by Sanskrit-literate Hindus familiar with the most sophisticated forms of brāhmaṇic culture, that is, by male *smārta* brahmans, the self-appointed guardians of Vedic authority, ritual practice, culture, and custom.[8] Not a single historical Śrīvidyā writer finds a conflict of interests in being both Vaidika and Tāntrika. Many contemporary practitioners, however, either dispute or feel the need to clarify an association between Śrīvidyā and Tantra. Our examination of Śrīvidyā's ideology will not only demonstrate its relationship to Śākta Tantrism, it will clarify its position with regard to brāhmaṇic Hinduism. By first grounding ourselves in the study of text and past traditions, we will create a basis on which to build a future anthropological study that focuses on living interpretation and practice.

The present volume is committed primarily to the task of describing and analyzing Śrīvidyā's texts and traditions as they have been received in contemporary south India, particularly in Tamilnadu. I seek to establish the canonical boundaries of living south Indian Śrīvidyā and to identify the texts, concepts, and commentators that form the core of contemporary interpretation and practice. My goal is to distinguish the legacy of Śrīvidyā from its pure textual presentation and to elaborate the content of its theology so that it can be compared with other developments in Hindu Tantra and south Indian religion. I will not introduce new data in every chapter, though much of what is here has not be presented before.[9]

Śrīvidyā is among the few cults of Hindu Tantrism—whether they be Śiva-centered, Viṣṇu-centered, or Śakti-centered—in which a comparison of textual ideologies and prescriptions with living interpretations and practices is theoretically possible. Others lack either texts or a tradition of living interpreters.[10] Of the two areas in India in which Śrīvidyā has flourished most visibly, Kashmir and south India, only the latter remains a vital tradition.[11] Not all texts or commentators influential in south Indian tradition are of south Indian origin and some may not even be mentioned by contemporary south Indian practitioners. In fact, the two most important historical writers in south Indian Śrīvidyā were both north Indians by birth. South Indian Śrīvidyā creates its distinctive tradition principally in two ways. First, by adopting and then expanding the Kashmiri canon and second, by assimilating the ethics and ideologies of south Indian brahman culture.

The place of preeminence in south Indian Śrīvidyā is held by Bhāskararāya Makhin, an eighteenth-century Maharastran who settled in Tamilnadu sometime after 1841 under the patronage of Seforji of Thanjavūr. His advocacy of the most controversial and convention defying Tantric ritual practices and his encyclopedic knowledge of the Śrīvidyā canon make him one of the tradition's most formidable intellectuals. His remarkable career will be treated later in some detail.[12] Bhāskararāya's intellectual nemesis, Lakṣmīdhara, reputedly served in the court of the fifteenth-century Orissan king Pratapatarudra Gajapati. In contrast to Bhāskararāya, Lakṣmīdhara endorses only the arch-conservative views of the so-called Samayācāra, characterized by its rejection of all things objectionable to brahman customs and morals. While other writers, such as the Kashmiris, Amṛtānanda, Śivānanda, and Jayaratha, figure in the development of south Indian traditions, all matters of textual interpretation and authoritative practice eventually lead to Bhāskararāya and Lakṣmīdhara.

By claiming itself to be Tantric *and* Vedic, Śrīvidyā creates an opportunity to study a relationship of "proximate otherness," that rather problematic situation that occurs when two distinct, competing, and sometimes irreconcilable phenomena negotiate coexistence.[13] This study limits the examination of "proximate otherness" to the interpretation of texts and the construction of a canon of signs and ritual prescriptions. While contemporary practitioners' views are included, their comments are meant only to augment, clarify, or dispute the views of influential historical commentators. Our focus is not on the textual canon per se but on those portions of the canon that create the paradigms of contemporary practitioners.

Axiomatic to the study of esoteric Tantric texts is the necessity of oral interpretation by living initiates; too much in texts is obscured by difficult language or is designed to exclude the uninitiated. Undoubtedly, the highly personal and idiosyncratic nature of ethnography places limits on the interpretation of historical texts. However, there is no serious alternative for the study of Tantric esotericism; one cannot omit the anthropological study of living traditions without creating the potential for serious misunderstanding.[14] It would be a mistake to take the Tantric's prescriptions or descriptions—be they textual, oral, historical, or contemporary sources regarding theory or practice—without a critical eye towards their multiple interpretations and practices.

If contemporary Tantric tradition is any marker of the past, then what Tantrics say they do is not always what they appear to do. Further, Tantrics have never intended texts to function as autonomous authorities or as complete descriptions of instantiated practice or ideology. The Tantric's hermeneutical positions regarding textual and oral authorities are more complex than that. Tantric texts create paradigms and normative values that may or may not carry the weight of prescriptive injunctions; in every case, the presence of the living guru is assumed to be the final arbiter of tradition. The scholar must be careful not to weigh Tantric *writing* too heavily in the historical equation that determines a given tradition. Similarly, the input of living practitioners should not overdetermine the interpretation of text and history. While one must study the present in order to understand the past, present understandings may not produce reliable images of the past. This situation does not make Tantrics "unreliable" in the sense of being untrustworthy. Rather, it suggests the need for methods of study that account for the discrepancy between written and oral traditions and between texts and the theological interpretations that contemporary Tantrics create. While Tantrics may claim perfect knowledge, the historian of religion must assume that all knowledge about Tantrism is subject to revision.

This volume has three aims: (1) to create an exemplum of Hindu Śākta Tantrism that is well understood, (2) to introduce methods for its study, and (3) to place this exemplum in the service of a persistent question in the comparative study of religion: How am I to apply what the one thing shows me to the case of two things?[15] The first two aims consume Part One. Part Two creates a theoretical model for addressing the third. Rather than describe the particulars of Śrīvidyā rituals, I will suggest how Tantric rites might be compared ideologically and structurally with certain non-Tantric Vedic rituals and explained within the larger context of Hindu law (*dharma*) and society.

READING *AUSPICIOUS WISDOM*

This book was not written only for specialists in Indian religion or Tantric studies, though the subject is complex and, at times, technical. That which seems arcane, specialized, uninteresting, or even unimportant to some of us may be precisely what stirs the blood of others and compels them to write, think, discuss, and persist in reexamination. There are, I think, different choices readers will make about what is interesting about Śrīvidyā and this analysis.

In the introduction to Part One, I summarize briefly the criteria that identify Śrīvidyā as a form of Hindu Śākta Tantrism; my purpose is to map out Śrīvidyā's territory by locating it within the ideological and ritual parameters of Śākta Tantrism.[16] I also consider those hermeneutic principles within Śrīvidyā that develop from its associations with Kashmiri Tantra and Vedic brāhmaṇical tradition. A purely theoretical comparison to rabbinic Judaism is introduced to reconsider the principles of organization that govern Śrīvidyā's peculiar, but not unique, modes of discourse.

In chapter 1, Śrīvidyā is examined within the framework of Kaula Tantrism, a broadly construed theological tradition that can be circumscribed by applying a notion of canon as a human labor. In the study of canon making and exegesis, one observes how Śrīvidyā identifies itself through a process of limitation and the overcoming of that limitation through ingenuity.[17] As I will show, a redescription of Śrīvidyā's canon requires understanding the persistence that permits extending a written canon of texts and an oral canon of fixed signs over every facet of human existence. The centerpiece of this chapter is a detailed discussion of the interpretative differences that define Śrīvidyā in terms of other Kaula Tantrisms and divide Śrīvidyā from within.

Chapter 2 describes Śrīvidyā's first appearance in south India and begins the discussion of the content of its canon. Focusing on hitherto unexamined Tamil sources, I will introduce the earliest evidence of Śrīvidyā as an autonomous cult of Śākta Tantrism in south India.

Chapter 3 describes the texts that form Śrīvidyā's canon and the historical figures who set the agenda for Śrīvidyā in contemporary south India. The central theoretical issues raised here involve the relationship of the textual and non-textual canons to the oral tradition of interpretation.

Chapters 4, 5, and 6 examine the core of Śrīvidyā theology: the ideology, myth, and worship of the goddess Lalitā Tripurasundarī who manifests in three hierarchical forms. Chapter 4 begins with her "coarse" anthropomorphic or "physical" image (*sthūlarūpa*) in which she appears iconographically as a beneficent (*aghora*) and benign (*saumya*) mother goddess and as the wife of the god Śiva. Lalitā's iconography is examined and her origin myth retold and analyzed in light of other goddess traditions. At stake is the goddess's incipient identity and relationship to other goddesses, especially those important in south India.

Chapter 5 takes up the goddess's subtle or mantra form (*sūkṣmarūpa*) called the "*śrīvidyā*," from which the cult takes its most frequent self-designation. To analyze the mantra, I introduce a Peircian model of semeiotic analysis, which is also used to reconsider the formative principles of canon making. As I will show, Śrīvidyā augments its textual canon with a distinctive non-textual canon of signs. This combined canon creates the principal means by which Śrīvidyā defines itself and through which it formulates its world view. The discussion of Śrīvidyā's various mantras and interpretations is both detailed and technical. Contemporary practitioners are as unapologetic as the texts when it comes to insisting on the importance of mantra science (*mantraśāstra*).

Chapter 6 centers on the goddess's transcendent manifestation (*parārūpa*) as the aniconic *śrīcakra* or *śrīyantra*, a geometrical diagram at the center of which are nine interlocking triangles representative of the goddess's self-effulgent (*spurattā*) creation of the universe. The discussion of the *śrīcakra* precipitates a detailed consideration of Śrīvidyā theology and the stated goals of ritual worship.

The goddess's three forms when utilized collectively and systematically in ritual worship (*upāsana*) define Śrīvidyā as a discipline (*sādhana*) within Hindu Śākta Tantrism. My emphasis, however, is not on the rituals themselves, which will be described in some detail in a second volume on living practice and interpretation. Rather, my objective is to redescribe the theology presented in both speculative and liturgical sources and thereby set the stage for further consideration of the relationship between textual theory and actual practice.

There are two basic theoretical objectives behind these detailed descriptions of the goddess. First, I wish to demonstrate how Śrīvidyā's chief marks—icon, mantra, and yantra—are nonrepresentational, that is to say, not natural and sensory in derivation but cultural and social.[18] Second, I will make clear how Śrīvidyā's basic theological components form transitive categories that serve as maps and labels within a complex, self-referential system. Śrīvidyā conceives itself as a discipline (*sādhana*) that permits access and appropriation of dispositional and episodic types of power which form divinity's substantive essence. As Sir John Woodroffe observed nearly a century ago, the Tantric conceives the world as power (*śakti*). As the goddess's own self-effulgence, he believes the world is nothing but power to be harnessed.[19] We will examine how power (*śakti*) becomes the goddess worshiper's most important category for interpreting the relations that govern the world and why Śrīvidyā deems auspiciousness (*śrī*), the goddess's chosen mode of manifestation in the triadic Lalitā, to be power's most useful, concentrated, and life-giving self-expression. Prescinding from the adepts' presuppositions about the sacrality of Śrīvidyā's system of signs and behaviors, we will instead concentrate on the ways in which these objects or actions become sacred by having attention focused on them.[20]

In sum, Part One concentrates on the construction of Śrīvidyā's canon, its exegesis of that canon, and its theoretical and normative understanding of the texts and signs that bind together the written and oral traditions.[21]

Part Two stands apart as an interpretive theory of Śrīvidyā's Tantric ritual and can be read separately. Taking my cue from Jonathan Z. Smith's statement that, "Ritual is a means of performing the way things ought to be in conscious tension to the way things are," I will demonstrate that Śrīvidyā's contemplative disciplines do not simply recreate the ultimate unity of the cosmos or propose a method for realizing an "eternal return." Rather, Śrīvidyā's rituals address the creative tension of ontological disjunction, that is, the overwhelming sense that the world presents, in everyday situations, concerns and conflicts that require remediation. Ritual is designed to demonstrate that the disjunctive world of everyday experience *is* divine. Further, ritual gains force where incongruity is perceived and thought about.[22] In this respect, Śrīvidyā's Tantric rituals are not fundamentally different from certain Vedic rituals in crucial respects. As J. C. Heesterman has written:

> [The ritual] has nothing to say about the world, its concerns and conflicts. It proposes, on the contrary, a separate, self-contained world ruled exclusively by the comprehensive and exhaustive order of the ritual. It has no meaning outside of its self-contained system of rules to connect it to the mundane order.... The ritual is *adṛṣṭārtha*, without visible purpose or meaning other than the realization of its perfect order, be it only for the duration of the ritual and within the nar-

row compass of the ritual enclosure.... The ritual holds out to man the prospect of a transcendent world he creates himself on the condition that he submits to the total rule of the ritual injunction. But at the same time, the open gap between the transcendent order of the ritual and the mundane ambivalence of conflict and interest is all the more obvious.[23]

Part I

ŚRĪVIDYĀ TRADITION AND TEXTS

INTRODUCTION

> For knowledge to be fulfilled it must emanate from texts (*śāstra*), from investigation with a wise teacher, and directly from oneself.[1]
>
> —Abhinavagupta

IDENTIFYING ŚRĪVIDYĀ IN ŚĀKTA TANTRISM

Śākta Tantrism can be imagined as a river of concepts and practices formed by the convergence of tributaries. While one can identify currents within this river, one cannot always separate currents or prevent the mixing of tributary waters. The Śrīvidyā *sampradāya,* or the School of Auspicious Wisdom, is a major current within this river; within Śrīvidyā there are a variety of interior currents. While the literary and nonliterary sources that make up Śrīvidyā's canon appear after most of the other main tributaries of Śākta Tantrism have converged, Śrīvidyā's interior currents continue to be fed from both contiguous and disparate sources over the course of time and space.[2] In other words, there may be a variety of Śrīvidyās at any given time and in different places. Whether these may be fundamentally similar or completely dissimilar, they are related because they contribute to the formation of a categorical whole.[3] The image of Śrīvidyā as a river current in which there are interior currents depicts a tradition that will admit distinctions but disavows disparities.

Like the Hindu pilgrim who, in the footsteps of his ancestors, sojourns at holy fords (*tīrtha*) to reenact ancient rites, the scholar must develop a sense of identity and "sameness" that allows him to talk meaningfully about the "place" of the Śrīvidyā's interior currents as well as about the limitations of demarcating a place that does not stand still.

Texts form important parts of Śrīvidyā's historically dynamic current; they appear to mark place and time, and thereby create a sense of fixed location. In Tantrism, however, texts in the context of tradition cannot be treated as *things* anymore than currents can be extracted from rivers. Texts are *events* that can be mapped; maps are not territory.[4] It would be a mistake to consider Śrīvidyā's texts alone as determinative of either the theological or ritual agenda.[5] Texts are neither treated as autonomous or self-sufficient entities to be read silently nor are they to be engaged apart from the rules that govern their use. To depict Śrīvidyā, or any school of Hindu Tantrism, as principally a religion of textual exegesis oversimplifies the evidence.[6]

The sanctity of a Tantric text not only depends on its content and its particular uses, but on its perceived origin, reputed authorship, and associations. Similarly, the sanctity of other signs, icons, and objects depends both on their interpretations *and* their function within a systematic program of ritual behaviors. The "holiness" of a text is a situational rather than a substantive category.

From the Śrīvidyā adept's point of view, the world is "unfinished." Rituals are the crucial means by which one understands this persistent fact. Textual exegesis, therefore, is secondary to enacting ritual and is perceived to depend on it. In other words, those incapable of performing the presribed rituals are prima facie disqualified from other textual interpretations. Ritual is Śrīvidyā's primary mode of thinking, interpreting, and acting because ritual can transform reality's inherent power into personal power. The world may be divine in origin—a projection of Śiva and Śakti, just as the scriptures are—but the world gains significance when its configurations and associations are put within one's grasp.[7]

It is not surprising that Śrīvidyā's dominant textual genre is liturgy. The liturgies, however, imply rather than explain the rules and methods required to interpret the goddess's triadic manifestation. Narrative expositions are rare, limited primarily to the least restricted and most exoteric aspect of the goddess, her iconography and myth. The preferred method of theological exposition is *to name* the essential and then *to list* the names in order to specify that which reality actually consists of.

Every list of divine names is a set of mantras used ritually. The origin of the mantras is said to be the goddess's subtle form (*sūkṣmarūpa*) as the *śrīvidyā*. Thus, the names used in ritual need not be intelligible to everyone nor must the activity of naming be open and unbounded. Rather, such names gain their importance precisely because they are part of a closed and restricted system in which the gurus of the tradition, not the names or the rules governing them, control the content and the modes of discourse.

Naming and listing set apart Śrīvidyā's world in terms familiar and stable and, at the same time, technical and intelligible only within the structures of initiated interpretation. In this sense Śrīvidyā bears a striking resemblance to rabbinic Judaism:

> In its ritual and its writing levitical religion promulgated a synchronic vision of a centered, structured, hierarchical, and orderly reality. Its practitioners celebrated precision, lineage, precedent, and concreteness, and had an exceedingly low tolerance for uncertainty, confusion, and ambiguity.[8]

Śrīvidyā creates a curious circularity with respect to ritual. Texts account for matters that are performed in reference to specific traditions and can be understood only by those already familiar with the subject.[9] The texts rarely describe or explain Śrīvidyā tradition. Texts are composed for the sake of the subject only, though interpreters assert that their purpose is to create normative understanding.[10]

While Śrīvidyā treats texts as prescriptions, from a critical perspective they are descriptive. Frits Staal's remarks about Pāṇinian tradition apply well to Śrīvidyā's textual history. He writes that "grammarians try to derive correct forms, but the correctness of forms is already known from those who know the language. In fact, in the case of conflict, it is the speakers who decide."[11] The critical feature of Śrīvidyā's texts is that gurus decide and justify contents; the texts themselves largely order and list.[12] While the guru's authority is imperial, a text, like a mantra, is considered dangerous to persons unqualified to manage its inherent power.

Making a text intelligible or acquiring access to mantra power demands a highly disciplined activity and specialized knowledge.[13] Texts and names become sacred through a process of objectification that links them to divinities, demigods, and sages. However, this objectification must be certified by gurus who are bound to a system of behavioral injunctions and normative expectations.[14] Tantrics gurus are once again similar to levitical rabbis—both have sought to develop and sustain a sociology of knowledge that makes them indispensable.[15]

ŚRĪVIDYĀ AND SMĀRTA BRAHMANISM

In contemporary south India, Śrīvidyā has been dominated by members of the Vedic-oriented *smārta* brahman community who, in their canonical works, define their tradition precisely in terms of being not-Tantric.[16] This disparity, however, seems to be a one-sided argument. Śrīvidyā's Tantras do not necessarily consider their practices to be either anti-*smārta* or anti-Vedic. Contemporary *smārta* brahman Śrīvidyā adepts attempt to hold the two traditions together without permitting them to compete. For example, when both Tantric and *smārta* rites are deemed obligatory duties, questions arise about priority and necessity, if they are parallel and duplicating. Which rite should be first performed? Do both rites need be performed if they duplicate obligatory behaviors? How are potential conflicts between rites to be resolved? Based on what criteria and on whose authority are such decisions made? While these questions may seem technical, arcane, or even trivial to the non-initiate, they are the stuff of which brahman-dominated Tantric Śrīvidyā is made.

Most conflicts of interest between *smārta* brahmanism and Śrīvidyā Tantrism are resolved by gurus in lineage traditions. The most frequent method for avoiding disputes is to claim different criteria for membership in each community tradition. Since Tantric initiation is not considered a birthright of caste or restricted to males, Śrīvidyā Tantrics can distinguish their smārtaism from their Tantrism by employing a "dual norm."[17] Such a solution either keeps the two traditions distinct on the basis of qualification (*adhikāra*) or ritual obligation (*karma*), or it creates a system that distributes the fruits of each and so deems them complementary.

ORTHODOXY AND ORTHOPRAXIES IN ŚRĪVIDYĀ

All discussions and debates over ritual action and ideology are directed towards establishing notions of correct practice. Few contemporary south Indian Śrīvidyā practitioners have an interest in or knowledge of speculative texts and commentaries. It will only take a few, they say, to carry on these traditions of textual exegesis. Those indifferent to theological disputes or rigorous textual exegesis are similarly obsessive, only their preoccupation involves the execution of rituals. There is little reason to think that the situation has ever been much different: liturgical handbooks outnumber speculative treatises and commentaries by at least a hundred to one.[18] While the corpus of liturgies continues to grow, there is little parallel interest in commentaries, exegesis, or further speculation.[19]

Within lineage traditions, conflicts between ideologies and practices arise due to deviations in practice, changing circumstances in transmission, or lost skills or connections. Among contemporary practitioners, such disputes and discrepancies remain insignificant unless there are competing factions claiming a particular lineage legacy. For example, those practitioners who claim to be in the tradition of the eighteenth-century theologian Bhāskararāya agree that Umānandanātha was his immediate disciple. Not all will agree that Umānandanātha is the definitive interpreter of his work. Further, few of these lineages follow Bhāskararāya's or Umānanda's ritual prescriptions and fewer still wish to discuss the views of Rāmeśvara Sūri, a nineteenth-century descendent of Bhāskararāya, who harshly criticizes Umānanda. Contemporaries who wish to engage in polemics are willing to take uncompromising stands similar to Rāmeśvara's remarks about Umānanda. Yet such debates are the exception rather than the rule. The canon and customs of Śrīvidyā lineages other than one's own lineage are a priori uninteresting or untrustworthy. It is not simply what texts say or what people do that makes them interesting or authoritative, but rather how and through whom texts or customs are believed to originate or are transmitted.[20]

While gurus decide which ideas, practices, and distinctions should be of interest to their disciples, they cannot ignore texts considered to be divine in origin or divinely interpreted. Thus, while disciples regard their gurus as the arbiters of tradition and its final authority, gurus must defer to their own gurus, to their sense of tradition, and, ultimately, to the claims made in texts recognized as their own. Since Śrīvidyā gurus teach disciples according to individual needs and capabilities, the scope for difference in interpretation and practice is significant. Disciples of a single guru may practice rituals and interpret texts so differently that they may not perform the same rituals or use the same texts at all. Lineages may have no normative ritual liturgies or ideologies; whether they do depends on the guru's emphasis on and enforcement of conformity and continuity. Even when a guru's teaching takes on a written form, the text remains subject to "correct" oral interpretation.

The sanctity of texts, brought about by affirming divine origins and guru interpretation, brought with it "an unimpeachable authenticity and the power of authentication."[21] Tantric commentators identify scriptural passages with introductory formula such as "it is said," "thus it is suggested," "the scripture says," and set apart the text from commentary so that they may confirm or deny their own theological and ritual interpretations.[22] Further, texts are often pulled together from sundry sources and preinterpreted in ways that may not be integral to their contextual meaning. The technique reflects the guru's preoccupation with maintaining his own control over the discourse, be it textual or commentarial. By juxtaposing different scriptures strategically within their own commentaries on doctrine, ritual, or other texts and by using them rhetorically in common structures, Śrīvidyā gurus make the texts appear to speak within their own restricted spheres of reference and according to the implicit rules of oral and written discourse that they control.[23]

When Śrīvidyā commentators select passages to support their scriptural interpretations, they encase their world in anonymous, synchronic, and rhetorically disciplined structures of discourse.[24] Like many gurus from the time of the Upaniṣads forward, Śrīvidyā gurus do not wish to leave individual marks on the tradition. Rather, they value egoistic anonymity over individuality and a lean, disciplined scholastic discourse over polemic engagement with non-Tantrics. Eschewing discussion of the "outside" non-Tantric/non-*smārta* world which surrounds them, they center on their immediate sphere of interest in order to address other Tantric specialists.

While it is impossible to verify the authority of oral scriptural exegesis deemed indispensable for the "correct" transmission of tradition, we can examine how Śrīvidyā gurus use their written texts. The comparison to rabbinic literature is once again striking. Like rabbinic documents, Śrīvidyā's historical documents "present the restricted discourse of a small number of men who appear primarily engaged in observing, discussing, and analyzing ideas, opinions, and behaviors, sometimes those recounted in scripture, but most often those of one another."[25] In both cases, these religious virtuosi do *not* write texts that are unintelligible to their intended audience; instead, the esotericism of the texts is insured by the necessity of oral explication from within initiated ranks. Texts presume knowledge of them and a command of the *type* of discourse that is necessary to decode them.

Śrīvidyā's product, as it were, is set of shapes, signs, and artifacts that create paradigms of meaning that do not reflect the world as anyone can see it, but rather only as the Śrīvidyā Tantric can see it. There is little or nothing about the natural or cultural world that *resembles* the goddess, her mantra, or the *śrīcakra*. The Śrīvidyā guru does not aim to convert or include those who do not yet understand or connect themselves with the triadic divinity and her creation. Rather, texts impress upon initiates the costs of ignorance and the potential for power in those who *do* control them. Though they intend to restrict their subject and keep much of their tradition secret, Śrīvidyā gurus are keenly aware of the intellectual discourse and various forms of religious behavior surrounding them. Writing texts thus serves as a means by which gurus "establish the group's identity, objectify its existence, consolidate its picture of reality, and codify the discourse that gives the group its distinctive character."[26]

Śrīvidyā is as much an idiom to be mastered and controlled as it is a set of written texts within the canon of Śākta Tantrism. While contemporary adepts will contend that oral traditions have been maintained intact over centuries of transmission, we must be satisfied with examining the strategies used to perpetuate Śrīvidyā's distinctive idiom and point out the persistence of the written idiom in historical discourse. Śrīvidyā's written idiom tacitly implies the socially imbedded and acquired skills of language, behavioral convention, and aesthetic preference that characterize the expectations of the gurus' actual or expected audience.[27]

The "missing" oral component that accompanies texts appears to be represented consistently in the form and structure of the written idiom. Throughout their history Śrīvidyā writers produce a constant self-identifying idiom that remains preoccupied with a delimited body of signs, concepts, and words. Further, Śrīvidyā gurus deliberately choose to use a distinctive Tantric idiom when other types and styles of Sanskrit are known to them. Were one not aware, for example, that Bhāskararāya lived in a political India dominated by Muslim rulers and was born in a *smārta* brahman community in which Tantric practices were morally and intellectually suspect, one would never know these facts from his writing. This eighteenth-century writer's Śākta Tantric idiom more closely resembles that of eleventh-century Śrīvidyā gurus than it does any other style of Sanskrit language. Further, Bhāskararāya composed non-Tantric works in a non-Tantric idiom. Thus, the constancy of the written Tantric idiom, and the commentator's deliberate efforts to sustain it, suggest an oral discourse that obeys similar rules.[28]

As an idiom of intricate cultural constructions, Śrīvidyā is obsessed with itself. Historical texts, even without their oral counterparts, present palpable evidence of the gurus' culture. Further, Śrīvidyā's written idiom remains consistent with the idiom of oral discourse used by contemporary gurus in south India.[29] This is the case despite the fact that most do not read texts regularly. Since all the available evidence of historical Śrīvidyā's interpretation is *written*, our primary task will be to focus on the ways in which traditionalists seek closure of their idiom in order to establish control of the subject. The gurus primary exercise is one of description and exegesis of a canon that is assumed, like other forms of knowledge, to be a well understood and reified category.

Śrīvidyā as a theological idiom projects an aesthetic vision and an intellectual sensibility rather than a moral one. As a sacred discourse, Śrīvidyā understands itself not to be constrained by historical personalities or driven by fancies of idiosyncratic interpreters. The signs, images, and concepts that form the stable center of Śrīvidyā's system do not offer a neutral record of "what actually happened" in antiquity. Rather, they are demonstrative of the process of canon making and exegesis as a "labor of the intellect and the imagination that codifies a particular...conception of reality in a distinctive mode of discourse that both derives from and generates that conception."[30]

Chapter 1

Kula Tantrism and Śrīvidyā Tradition

ORAL AND WRITTEN TANTRIC TRADITION AND THE DEVELOPMENT OF TANTRIC CANONS

Tantric textual history is rooted in a diffusion of ideas that occurs in two distinct but interdependent modes of transmission: oral and written. Even texts that are internally coherent assume knowledge that has decended "from mouth to ear."[1] The task here is to identify the principles that have governed the process of textual composition in Śrīvidyā Tantrism and to consider the implications these principles have for the tradition's historical transmission. As we shall see, nowhere is case for a centuries-long oral tradition of ideas and practices preceding written traditions made more clear than in the earliest Śrīvidyā texts.

Śrīvidyā practitioners go to great lengths to locate their traditions in the hoary past or to make an important historical (or quasi-historical) associations. For example, proponents universally will claim Śrīvidyā to be the "original secret" (*ādirahasya*) teaching of the Vedas. Some will make even more contentious claims in order to establish a particular historical or ideological identity. For example, certain south Indian branches of Śrīvidyā claim to descend through the lineage of the non-dualist theologian Śaṅkara. In this respect, Śrīvidyā is exemplary of one of Tantrism's most persistent features: the process of assuming, synthesizing, and interpreting ideas, customs, and practices in order to claim suzerainty over them. The governing principle is that "older is better," so that the more "ancient" a text can be shown to be—in sense of being in proximity to Vedic texts, which are always considered ancient—the more valuable and reliable it becomes. From a critical perspective it is nearly impossible to assess the antiquity or origin of many Tantric ideas and practices—a subject to which we shall return. The Tantrics' interest in the antiquity of texts or ideas is usually to classify them "authentic" or obsolete. Śrīvidyā practitioners will acknowledge, and often commend, different types of experience by admitting that different interpretations have derived from regional traditions (*deśācāra*), schools of thought (*sampradāya*), or lineages (*paramparā*).

By the eighth or ninth-century writing had gained acceptance as a viable, if not inherently limited, mode of expression for Tantric ideas.

The creative tension between oral and written modes of transmission fostered the growth of exegetical writing based on oral explanations. While almost all written Tantric texts presume further oral exegesis, we can be less certain about the original mode of a text's presentation.

The uncertain development of particular Tantric ideologies, however, does not arise from modes of original presentation. Whether a text was first oral and then written is tangential to an ideology of doctrinal authority. The guru of a given lineage can sublate, edit, or interpret a given text as he sees fit. A text's authenticity in the eyes of the guru is ultimately more important than its mode of presentation; texts are always secondary authorities to gurus.

Further, the emergence of written texts does not necessarily clarify the origin or chronology of Tantric ideas and practices. Tantrics are not often interested in defending or defining strict denominational or sectarian lines, especially between Śaiva and Śākta identities. In Śrīvidyā, for example, commentators draw no hard and fast boundaries around the textual canon; there is no single list of texts that has reached closure despite some who claim otherwise. But aversion to accepting only textually generated lists of texts as canonical should not be confused with the absence of a canon. For example, the *Mālinīvijaya Tantra* takes no fixed sectarian positions and has been variously interpreted as an authoritative source of ideology and doctrine by both Śaivas and Śāktas. While the *Mālinīvijaya* is a mainstay of Kashmiri Śaivism, it also displays a clear tendency towards the importance of Śakti(s); it is quoted selectively by later Śākta writers, including those within Śrīvidyā. Thus, a notion of canon that proves useful for distinguishing the Tantric from the non-Tantric must consider not only texts but also persons and groups who appropriate words, signs, and icons as part of a body of oral and written instruction. How then might one differentiate between that which is within a given Tantric tradition's canon and that which is not?

Tantrics exhibit what Jonathan Z. Smith calls "sacred persistence," defined as the rethinking of each little detail in a text and the obsession with the significance and perfection of each little action.[2] In the sundry ways in which Śrīvidyā authors use texts we see a radical, almost arbitrary selection made from an incredible number of potential sources. But, as Smith notes, once a selection is made the most extraordinary attention is given to its refinement and interpretation. Scholars of Hindu Tantrism have tended to emphasize the "givenness" of the textual horizon and have prescinded from commenting further on the principles of reduction at work within specific traditions. While it remains difficult to determine why a given source is chosen by a given author, it would be a mistake to assume that all texts that apparently conform to ideological or prescriptive standards will be included in a given lineage's canon.[3] Written canons appear to be formed in terms of their relation to oral instructions from gurus.

The significance of the oral tradition in the development of Śrīvidyā canons is twofold. First, the content of a historical writer's instruction remains private and forever obscure: one does not know precisely what a Tantric has learned. Second, the oral tradition determines the selections included in a written canon. The written canon of a given lineage obtains final closure only when one can enumerate a complete list of sources rather than a mere catalog organized around a subject or principle. The canon presupposes the necessary presence of an interpreter "whose task it is continually to extend the domain of the closed canon over everything that is known or everything that exists *without* altering the canon in the process."[4]

Śrīvidyā Tantrics, like other intellectual elites, assume a familiarity with traditions and ideas that they do not feel the need to introduce. Śrīvidyā creates a totalistic and complete system of signs and icons which, in the absence of an explicit articulation of a written canon's closure, serves as a functional equivalent.[5] Rather than center on textual exegesis per se, Śrīvidyā gurus focus on sets of signs and icons which not only remain constant but are perceived to be unalterable.

Like the written canon, the canon of signs and icons suggests a set of implicit rules that govern interpretation.[6] To locate a Śrīvidyā practitioner in the context of the larger tradition requires both a circumscription of cited texts and attention to the specific signs and icons over which he or she persists. Śrīvidyā makes human experience intelligible within structures of fixed signs and icons, and oral and written words. The signs and icons, like the written words and oral interpretations, become canonical when they mediate the relationship between the perceived larger tradition and the individual perceptions of gurus and disciples.

Śrīvidyā's literary birth, like much of the Tantras, is without infancy and its earliest texts assume an intellectual history of immense complexity and variety. One should not assume a "missing" canon of early sources. In India the technology of writing is not essential for the creation of a textual canon or for an external, collective memory. The traditions of Vedic recitation and ritual provide ample evidence of a sophisticated tradition that is purely oral in origin. In the case of Śrīvidyā, we know precious little about the historical circumstances under which texts were written or why writing was adopted.[7] If the contemporary situation resembles the past, then we can be reasonably certain that fixed texts or portions of texts continued to be transmitted in oral form even after their composition, whether they were either originally oral or written.

Sometime after the ninth century there was an explosion of written Tantric texts. With the text came commentators who became autonomous authorities in the transmission of tradition. Written exegesis demanded certain literary skills in decoding and interpreting texts, signs, or icons whether or not there was an earlier oral text. Such skills required highly technical knowledge. Tradition dictated both limited access to manuscripts and the living guru to interpret signs and the interpretations.

The "fixed" elements in Śrīvidyā preceding written texts are its sacred signs and icons: the image Lalitā Tripurasundarī, the *śrīvidyā* mantra, and the *śrīcakra*. Thus, the oral canon does not require fixed oral texts or interpretations rendered in complex sentences transmitted orally. Rather, oral tradition is established by a stable of fixed signs and icons over which interpretations are lain in a particular linguistic idiom. Tantrics could stanch outsiders from their texts either by encoding their signs or disclaiming their efficacy if rent from the context of a guru's oral interpretations. The power of a given sign is therefore partly determined by its relationship with the living guru, rather than by the text or the sign per se. In practical terms, one could be left outside the idiom and therefore without access to the interpretive matrix necessary to control the canon.

The uneasiness expressed about the revelation of secrets in written form seems, from the perspective of historical hindsight, to be have been well-founded. Esoteric knowledge has certainly fallen into the hands of the uninitiated; written texts gained autonomy once outside their author's hands. Yet the written word also revolutionized the pace of interpretive developments. While a guru could disavow the veracity or efficacy of written words as inappropriate to his lineage, the technology of writing made the transmission of teachings far more sophisticated. The perceived negative consequences of writing secret interpretations or powerful mantras has hardly prevented Śrīvidyā gurus from using writing as a method for advancing their ideas or practices.

Jack Goody has pointed out, "Writing creates the possibility of the autodidact and makes the acquisition of information potentially less personal, less 'intensive.'"[8] Surely, Tantrics wished to prevent both autodidacts and the depersonalization of their traditions since either situation would undermine the central authority of the guru and diminish the importance of having to be personally empowered to use texts or powerful signs. Critical to Śrīvidyā's esotericism then is the underlying tension between the preservation and smooth transmission of copious technical information, and the perceived necessity of an oral culture through which the canon is interpreted. With the potential for the oral interpreter to comment on written words came new questions about the guru's role and authority.

Writing fostered conversation between texts and within the tradition and further advanced the importance of the oral traditions, which came to include written texts memorized and then subjected to oral exegesis. This situation is not unique to Śrīvidyā or to Tantrism; as Goody has shown in his studies of the interface between written and oral cultures in Islamic traditions and elsewhere the situation is not even unique to India.[9]

Though Śrīvidyā texts and commentaries are interpreted exclusively within lineages, gurus and writers remain concerned about the putative continuity of the larger tradition (*sampradāya*). Written texts thus become markers by which Śrīvidyā gurus can acknowledge and codify differences within the larger tradition.[10] However, it is not always possible to determine from written texts alone if theories or rituals have historical instantiations.[11] Some liturgical texts, for example, appear to be written for reasons other than the performance of the liturgy.[12] Thus, ritual literature was sometimes written to advance either theoretical concerns about practice and the interpretation of doctrine, or to distinguish one specialized formulation from another. The dependence of ritual liturgies on theoretical works seems more difficult to establish, though theology is also clearly a means by which differentiation within the tradition is established.

At stake for Śrīvidyā gurus and practitioners who identify themselves with particular texts or writers are not only matters of abstract ideology, but larger political interests. Identifying with particular views, practices, or interpretations could shift allegiances, split lineages, and have consequences on one's community life as a caste Hindu. Thus, privacy and esotericism were used not only to maintain traditional secrets but also to insulate those whose views or practices might create controversy within their larger social community. Certain conservative brahmans, for example, would not wish to be associated with texts, traditions, or practices that violate normative social codes.

Interestingly, the effort to distinguish lineages, theologies, and practice was sometimes accompanied by a tendency for inclusion. An affirmation of one's own position did not necessarily mean a rejection of others. Once included into the idiom, the connection between the original source of a given concept, person, or text is made entirely secondary to its use within the exegetical system. Contemporary Śrīvidyā Śāktas exhibit the inclusive tendency by frequently referring to themselves also as Śaivas and *smārtas*. At the same time, they maintain distinctive doctrines (or sometimes interpretations of shared doctrines) and offer distinctive interpretations of signs and icons that might find their way into others' systems.

While this inclusive tendency may be applied inconsistently, it is not incongruous with historical traditions. Śrīvidyā Tantrics appropriate concepts and values articulated in other systems without concerning themselves with what others may say about the consequences of embracing these views. This disregard for intellectual territorial boundaries is especially evident when Śrīvidyā is brought closer to accepted forms of conventional Vedic/*smārta* ritual practice and the *advaita* Vedānta of Śaṅkarācārya. For example, the influential Bhāskararāya ignores the apparent inconsistency between the adoption of Kashmiri Śaiva non-dualism in Śrīvidyā texts and his interest in Śaṅkara's absolute non-dualism (*kevalādvaita*), despite the lack of common ground between the two systems on important matters of ideology and practice.[13]

An "authentic" interpretation of text or ideology does not depend either on arguments or the claim that the ideas were originally espoused by Śrīvidyā thinkers. Rather, the governing principle is coherent presentation *within the confines of the discourse.*

The mere absence of an early written reference does not necessarily preclude the possibility that a particular concept is not part of an older oral source. This view is commonly made by contemporary practitioners who wish to establish the preeminence of their traditions. For example, it is asserted that Śrīvidyā accepts a common Śākta position on the creation of the universe through sound (*śabdabrahman*). It may also be admitted that this theory was adopted from Kashmiri Śaivites who, in turn, may have systematized much older concepts.[14] And yet by bringing these speculations into a ritual practice surrounding the use of a yantra, the *śrīcakra*, Śrīvidyā's proponents can claim to have the "original" projection of creation. This is because the ideology behind the *śrīcakra* may be of common human origin, but the cakra itself is not. Śrīvidyā writers never say the *śrīcakra* is their unique property or a human innovation. Rather, the yantra is a sacred and divine artifact that reflects the process of creation and the universe's transcendent, self-created form (*svarūpa*). Human beings can disagree about the *śrīcakra*'s significance and, to some extent, the details of its appearance but they cannot trespass the theological boundary that affirms its divine origin.[15]

ŚRĪVIDYĀ: GODDESS WORSHIP IN THE ŚRĪKULA TANTRAS

Śrīvidyā's influence beyond the confines of Tantric Śāktism is evident from as early as the fourth or fifth centuries and predates its first systematic literary presentations in the eleventh or twelfth centuries.[16]

The characteristic feature of Śrīvidyā's so-called Śrīkula canon of Tantras is the focus on the goddess in her beneficent (*saumya* or *aghora*), benign and motherly form. The supreme Devī, called principally by the names Lalitā, Śrī, or Tripurasundarī contrasts sharply with the terrifying forms (*ghora*) of Kālī, Durgā, or Caṇḍī who provide the focus of the Kālīkula Tantras.[17] Holding the preeminent theological position within the system as the supreme principle in its dynamic and creative aspect, Lalitā, the supreme Śakti is always closely connected to her consort Śiva, her necessary complement, who represents the sentient and eternal reality. Though not the center of theological speculation, Śiva retains his indispensable role as the one who explains the secrets of the Tantra to Śakti.

The Śrīkula Tantras also include other genres of literature not formally under the rubric of Tantra. Such texts gain their authority by making claims for divine origins. These include sectarian Śākta Upaniṣads, various hymns (*stotras*), praises (*stavas*), and protective charms (*kavacas*), which are distinct from most ritual and exegetical materials considered to be strictly human in origin. These sources are "Tantric" inasmuch as they reflect Tantric concepts and values and discuss subjects of similar concern.

Śrīkula literature includes much that is tangential or irrelevant to Śrīvidyā practice. While some Śrīkula works focus on Śrīvidyā's distinctive triadic theology and the rituals associated with it, others have little or nothing to do with these concepts and focus instead on other deities, rites, or theological concepts.[18] The Śrīkula is not identical to Śrīvidyā.

Śrīvidyā is also mentioned in Tantric sources outside Śrīkula literature. In mantra treatises, such as the *Mantramahodadhi*, the *śrīvidyā* mantra is included as part of the broader discussion of mantras and ritual performance.[19] Portions of these sources are also part of Śrīvidyā's textual canon.[20] Some non-Śrīkula texts, or portions of text, are authoritative because of their regional impact. Thus, a text, or portions of a text, may gain entrance into a lineage's canon by virtue of local popularity, by the practice locally of its teaching, or by local regard for an author or subject.[21]

Śrīvidyā's votaries have been, and continue to be, involved with gods and rites other than Lalitā, the *śrīvidyā*, and *śrīcakra*. They are especially renown for their expertise in astrology and in Vedic sacrifice.[22] Such interests are often explained by appealing to the idea that all expressions of knowledge and power derive from Śrīvidyā practices. This criterion of reduction can thus be used to distinguish those within Śrīvidyā from those who may appropriate some aspect of its ideology or ritual.

Historically renown writers, who are only marginally involved with Śrīvidyā are sometimes invoked to lend importance or bolster arguments. For example, the great Kashmiri philosopher Abhinavagupta (c. 1000 *c.e.*), who was likely unaware of Śrīvidyā's theoretical and practical elements, is invoked by later Śrīvidyā writers as an authority.[23] While historical and contemporary Śrīvidyā writers may express deference to the views of such tangential authorities, they do not necessarily consider such authorities to be initiates. In other words, the tradition acknowledges a difference between "insiders" and "outsiders" but treats each source and figure individually regarding its potential value and degree of authority.

The earliest written texts of the Śrīkula treat Śrīvidyā votaries as a spiritual elite in a rather unstructured hierarchy of religious possibilities. Other theological positions are often accepted as provisionally valid and only occasionally rejected outright. Further, there is remarkably little dialogical exchange or confrontation in these texts. The usual pattern of position and counterposition common to Indian philosophical discourse is rare.

Exchanges between Śrīvidyā writers are marked by varying degrees of tolerance, especially regarding highly charged theological, practical, and social issues such as the inclusion of the five prohibited substances (*pañcamakāra*) in ritual or the practice of sexually explicit "meditation on the aspect of desire" (*kāmakalādhyāna*).[24] In one noteworthy case the dispute centers on the interpretation of a guru's works by disciples within separate lineages.[25] But little mention is made of anyone other than those who can bolster one's own position. Śrīvidyā texts present yet another instance in Indian history of a specialized group arguing and discussing matters without regard for anyone outside its limited sphere of interests. What is most significant, however, is the extent to which the influence of Śrīvidyā traditionalists is felt outside these limited circles.

ŚRĪVIDYĀ WITHIN AND BEYOND KULA TANTRISM

The identification of Śrīvidyā with the so-called *kula* Tantric tradition and the propensity of some writers to call themselves "Kaula Tantrics," requires investigation. The meaning of "*kula*," and derivative terms, both differs within Śrīvidyā's sectarian sources and in other traditions. In the most general sense, *kula* means a "family" or, as Agheananda Bharati has suggested, a "clan."[26] This translation, however, only begins to suggest the term's wide variety of meanings and applications.[27]

Abhinavagupta offers a variety of historical and theological explanations of *kula* and Kaulism. He attributes its founding with the legendary Macchanda, usually dated no later than the fifth century.[28]

As a marker for ideological or sectarian distinctions, the term *"kula"* is not particularly useful. Nearly all Śākta Tantric texts refer to themselves as *"kula"* until the sixteenth century. With the introduction of the so-called Samaya Śrīvidyā tradition by Lakṣmīdhara, *"kula"* takes on new and distinctive meanings. Even before Lakṣmīdhara, however, any technical meanings the term *"kula"* might have had for Kashmiri Śaivites are insignificant to Śrīvidyā traditionalists.

In contemporary south India the term "kaula" is associated with the ritual use of the *pañcamakāras* and other elements of anti-brāhmaṇical Tantrism. However, even as late as the early nineteenth-century Śākta/Śaiva texts use "Kaula" without negative evaluation—with the exception of Lakṣmīdhara who maintains the inferiority of Kaula views in contrast to his Samaya interpretations and the inappropriateness of Kaula rituals for twice-born Śrīvidyā adepts. The refinements in the meaning of the term *"kula"* and its derivatives—especially *kaula* and *kaulika*—made for the purposes of juxtaposing the Kaula position with that of Pratyabhijñā and Krama in Kashmiri traditions are not discussed in Śrīvidyā texts.

In contrast, the term *"kula"* has caused most Śrīvidyā writers little difficulty. All Śrīvidyā writers before Lakṣmīdhara, and the majority after him, refer to themselves as *kulācārins*, those who "practice according to the *kula*." Thus, as far as Śrīvidyā is concerned we should, as Harvey Alper has put it, treat Kaula lineages not as schools but rather "preceptorial lines."[29]

In *Tantrāloka*, chapter 28, Abhinavagupta mentions ten early teachers of the *kula* system; it is evident that Kaula, even from the earliest times, meant both Śiva- and Śakti-centered worshipers.[30] Śrīvidyā's earliest historical commentators who identify themselves as Kaulas do not use the term *"krama,"* which, as N. Rastogi has noted, refers to a distinct Kashmiri Śākta tradition. The position of the Kashmiri *krama* system familiar to Abhinavagupta and viewed in opposition to Kaulism by Jayaratha does little to sort out the relationship of Śrīvidyā to the *kula*.[31] The *krama*, despite being Śākta-oriented, receives no separate mention in the works of Śrīvidyā commentators. To its earliest historical commentators, Śrīvidyā is a *kula* tradition and the *kula*/Śaiva and *krama*/Śākta distinction obviously did not pose any significant interpretive problem. *Kula* did not mean strictly Śaiva anymore than *krama* meant to include all Śāktas. What then does it mean to call oneself a "Kaula" when both Abhinavagupta the Śaivite philosopher and Bhāskararāya the Śākta Śrīvidyā follower use the term to refer to themselves? A satisfactory answer depends on an appreciation of the term's multivalent meanings and its historical contexts.

In general, *kula* and Kaulism refers to the primary streams of Tantrism characterized by certain principles, values, and norms of religious practice.[32] They include the elements of ritual most frequently disputed inside and outside Tantric circles: the "five m's" (*pañcamakāra*), the worship of the female organ in the so-called *kāmakalā* meditation, and the inclusion of persons from all castes and both sexes as active ritual participants.[33]

Kaulism remains largely identified with Śrīvidyā even after the emergence of distinctive sub-schools. Bhāskararāya, for example, ignores Lakṣmīdhara when he defines the terms "Kaula" and "Samaya," though it is plainly evident that he is aware of Lakṣmīdhara's distinction. Further, Kaula Śrīvidyā writers deem sources authoritative without invoking the term "Kaula" or the canon proposed by K. C. Pandey so long as the texts support and, to some extent, broaden the scope of Śrīvidyā's ideological or ritual agenda.

To give just one instance of the intellectual distance that separates strands of Kaula Tantric tradition, one need only refer to Abhinavagupta who lists many of the sources of *kula* tradition in the twenty-ninth chapter of the *Tantrāloka*.[34] None of these are significant in Śrīvidyā. Conspicuously absent from Abhinavagupta's list is the foremost of Śrīkula Tantras, the *Vāmakeśvara Tantra*, despite its being known in Kashmir from the ninth century and its self designation as a *kula* source.[35] Śākta-centered traditions appear only as sub-schools of the Śaiva *kula* where, if Abhinavagupta is any indication, the focus lay primarily on the worship of various aspects of Śiva.

As Paul Müller-Ortega has recently shown, Abhinavagupta relates *kula* to the locus of divinity within the body. Müller-Ortega writes, "It is clear that the Kaula tradition teaches the primary importance of the body as the essential tool of sādhana.... The term *kula*, starting from a basic meaning of group, comes to mean the Embodied Cosmos, which encompasses the entire range of the manifest reality."[36] He goes on to say, "The Kaula lineage neither reviles nor tortures the body to achieve enlightenment. Rather, the tradition worships the body as a vessel of the Supreme. Indeed, the central tool for enlightenment is the body."[37] Given Müller-Ortega's remarks about Abhinavagupta's understanding of *kula*, it is little wonder that Śrīvidyā adepts have, with only a few exceptions, identified themselves as Kaulas.

Pandey's summary of the Kaula canon allows us to consider its relationship to Śrīvidyā. Śrīvidyā authors mention all the Tantras that Pandey lists though only two, the *Nityāṣoḍaśikārṇava* and the *Tantrarāja Tantra* are specifically concerned with the particulars of Śrīvidyā.[38] The *Kulārṇava Tantra*, one of the earliest Kaula Tantras cited by

Śrīvidyā commentators, treats Kaulism as identical to Tantrism and is far more concerned with extolling the greatness of Kaula principles than with Śrīvidyā per se.[39] In this sense, *Kulārṇava Tantra* is indicative of the majority of sources adopted by Śrīvidyā traditionalists but likewise reflects the tendency of all Indian commentators to use texts to advance their own particular agendas.[40]

In the *Tantrāloka* (35.373–374) Abhinavagupta maintains that the Trika, the Śiva-centered tradition he codifies, is the essence of the Kaula as fragrance is to a flower. Jayaratha, however, on *Tantrāloka* 38.51 says that *kula* stands for Śakti which is called "*nityā*" (literally "eternal" but perhaps a reference to the sixteen *nityā*s made prominent within Śrīvidyā). This suggests a closer link to Śākta-oriented traditions and would offer a justification for Jayaratha's choosing to comment on the *Nityāṣoḍaśikārṇava* portion of the *Vāmakeśvara Tantra*. Pandey is correct when he asserts that *kula* tradition is not another name for Abhinavagupta's *pratyabhijñā* system; he, too, subscribes to the opinion that it is a broader term indicating the basic principles set forth in the Tantras and the *Tantrāloka*.[41]

According to contemporary south Indian practitioners, the issue of how Śrīvidyā differs from the Śrīkula Tantras should be resolved at the level of specific lineages. At this level, the matter becomes a subject for anthropological study.[42] Within Śrīvidyā, the heart of the issue involves the rejection of certain Kaula principles, particularly the *pañcamakāras*, by those who harbor caste and religious sentiments that prohibit their inclusion in scripture. Those who reject these perceived "Kaula elements" either edit out controversial points or reject outright any text that includes them. Contemporary adherents of the Samaya sub-school are at the forefront of dissociating such ideas in Śrīkula Tantras with Śrīvidyā. In contemporary Śrīvidyā, and in noteworthy contrast to the position of historical exegetes, the Kaula/Samaya distinction is at the heart of all significant factionalism within Śrīvidyā.

At issue in Śrīvidyā's Kaula/Samaya split is more than the question of which texts belong in the written canon and which signs and icons should be the subject of interpretation. Rather, the differences center on normative ethical values and ritual conduct. The most generic meaning of the term "kula" is one of the first cited by Bhāskararāya in his *Saubhāgyabhāskara* on the *Lalitāsahasranāma*. The path is called "Kaula," he says, because it is connected with a family (*kula*). It refers to what is obtained in a lineage and through one's own family.[43] Thus, Śrīkula refers to the family of the beneficent goddess.

What may seem confusing or imprecise in Bhāskararāya is more likely a reflection of Śrīvidyā's penchant for layers of meanings woven into complex, interrelated patterns. On *Lalitāsahasranāma*

(*LSN*) n. 91, Bhāskararāya gives a simple Tantric sense to *kula*, he says that the *kula* means the succession from the supreme Śiva to one's own guru and that it refers to a way of life (*ācāra*) rather than the position in society in which one is born.[44] In contrast, in the *Setubandha* he remarks that *kula* means whomever belongs to one's own caste (*jāti*) but that if one follows a certain shared Dharma, he or she becomes the same caste, presumably brahman.[45] The shift here is subtle but of critical importance for understanding Bhāskararāya's attitudes about caste. He has not dismissed the importance of caste. Rather, he has shifted the meaning of caste from birth to a shared set of principles and behavioral patterns that create an alternative clan.

Amṛtānanda, in his *Yoginīhṛdayadīpikā*, gives "kaula" a meaning that equates it with Śrīvidyā. He says that Kaulas are those who identify five elements in their spiritual lives, the so-called *śrīpañcakam* frequently referred to by contemporary practitioners: (1) the Self (*ātman*) identified with the universal Brahman; (2) the guru; (3) the *śrīvidyā*, that is, the fifteen or sixteen syllable mantra; (4) Śrīmata or the Auspicious Mother, that is, Devī in her beneficent aspects; and (5) the *śrīcakra*.[46] Amṛtānanda's identification of the Kaula path (*mārga*) with the *śrīpañcakam* is the first historical definition of Śrīvidyā in sectarian terms. Bhāskararāya repeats Amṛtānanda's interpretation at least twice in his commentaries on *Lalitāsahasranāma* and *Vāmakeśvara Tantra*.[47]

Bhāskararāya also says that *kula* means scripture (*āgama*) because it explains and is identical to the thought of the worshiper and the object of worship. This also appears to be a definition of scripture. The goddess, he goes on to say, is the center of scripture because she is the object of *kula* knowledge.[48] But Bhāskararāya continues to distinguish meanings of *kula* since these, he observes, are preserved in a specific set of scriptures; he quotes the *Paraśurāmakalpasūtra* (6.39) to the effect that *kula* sources should be kept secret.[49]

The more esoteric meanings of *kula* occur beside those already mentioned in the commentaries on *Yoginīhṛdaya*. These begin to draw sectarian lines *within* Śrīvidyā. Amṛtānanda says that *kula* means the body, a viewed repeated by Bhāskararāya and reminiscent of Abhinavagupta. Kaulas, he goes on to say, are those who remain connected with the outer world.[50] In the *Setubandha* Bhāskararāya continues this line of thought when he says that a Kaula is one who has made the identification of knower, knowing, and object of knowledge with the conscious self, the same definition he gives for a Śrīvidyā adept.[51] He repeats this idea in the *Saubhāgyabhāskara* in slightly different terms quoting the Kashmiri source *Cidgaganacandrikā*, attributed to Kālidāsa. He says *kula* is the measurer (*pramātṛ*), the thing to be measured (*prameya*), and the measuring (*pramāṇa*).[52]

In other passage, Amṛtānanda says that since the body is the *kula*, holding the body to be superior is called the "practice of *kula*" (*kulācāra*) while revering the shoes (*pāduka*) of the teacher, that is, following the disciplines taught by the guru, is principled conduct (*samayācāra*).[53] It is not clear from this single reference if Amṛtānanda is distinguishing the Samayācāra branch of Śrīvidyā identified later with Lakṣmīdhara. Amṛtānanda does not seem to be aware of a sectarian distinction that Lakṣmīdhara formalizes, especially considering his Kaula emphasis on external forms of practice and physical disciplines.

Some two hundred years after Amṛtānanda, Lakṣmīdhara makes it clear that Samayins reject the Kaula injunctions for external worship. He instead centers on the Samayin's claim that the entire spiritual discipline, including all types of ritual, must be done only internally.[54]

Bhāskararāya, a self-proclaimed Kaula, was aware of the internal division within Śrīvidyā but preferred the esoteric, yogic meanings of *kula* and *samaya* to Lakṣmīdhara's sectarianism. Surely it would not have been in Bhāskararāya's political interests to take up the controversies of legitimate behavior in his own brahman community since his Kaula beliefs would put him in the center of the dispute over community ethics. But neither would it be incumbent upon him to comment on Lakṣmīdhara's Samaya interpretation. Though he often cites Lakṣmīdhara favorably, and sometimes uses the nickname "Lalla" to refer to him, Bhāskararāya does not always endorse his views. In his remarks on the seven names of the goddess that mention *kula* (*LSN*, n. 90–96) and the following two that mention *samaya*, Bhāskararāya eschews the opportunity to discuss sectarian divisions and instead concentrates on esoteric meanings.[55] He gives a typical "sacred etymology" to *kula* based on esoteric associations rather than strict grammatical formulas. He says *ku* means the earth and *la* absorption, that is the *mūlādhara cakra*, the lowest of the six basic yogic centers within the body; the central path paralleling the spine, the *suṣumnā*, is also called "*kula*" because it is connected with the *mūlādhara* center.[56] Quoting *Svacchanda Tantra* he says that the goddess resides in the thousand-petal red lotus, which has its pericarp at the vault of the skull and is called "*kula*"; in the petals she is embodied in the *kulaśaktis*.[57] He then quotes an unnamed Tantra as saying, "'*Kula* means Śakti, *akula*, Śiva, and union of Kula with Akula is called "Kaula'. *Kaula* means the essence common to both Śiva and Śakti, hence Devī is called 'Kaulinī'."[58] Abhinavagupta repeats the gist of this remark in the *Tantrāloka*, which is quite possibly Bhāskararāya's source.[59]

Lakṣmīdhara maintains that Samayins differ from the Kaulas by rejecting the use of convention-defying substances or practices in ritual and by the complete internalization of contemplative worship (*antaryāga*). The rejection of the *pañcamakāras*, for example, and other Kaula practices that deliberately violate conventional brahman ethics is confirmed by contemporary Samayins in Tamilnadu. His claim that the internalization of the ritual is an exclusive Samaya doctrine is debated and rejected by Kaulas. Lakṣmīdhara also splits the Kaula path in two, according to its Earlier (*pūrvakaula*) and Later (*uttara*) forms. The distinction is based on the manner of worship characteristic to them: *Pūrvakaulas* worship the *śrīcakra* inscribed in gold, silk, or some other substance while the *Uttarakaulas* perform worship to the female organ.[60] *Uttarakaula* practices are considered outside the Vedic fold since they involve left-handed practice (*vāmācāra*), defined as the use of the prohibited substances and unsanctioned behaviors. Samaya worship, in contrast, he says is performed solely within the yogic centers of the body; here the goddess resides in her subtle forms and no longer requires to be worshiped with ritual substances, gestures (*mudrās*), or verbalization including mantras. Lakṣmīdhara leaves no provision for outward expressions of piety, despite the fact that contemporary Samayins continue to perform external rituals (*bahiryāga*).[61]

Kaulas who favor external forms of ritual and sanction the use of the convention-defying behaviors also accept the superiority of ritual internalization (*antaryāga*).[62] Bhāskararāya, for example, in his Upaniṣad commentaries discusses at length the transformative qualities of external worship and the necessity of gradual internalization.[63] Contemporary practitioners explain this position by saying that external rites should continue in order to maintain discipline and as an example for those who may never reach the higher stage of internalization. The precedent for such behavior is the exoteric teaching of Kṛṣṇa in the *Bhagavadgītā* in which the yogi is enjoined to act as an example for others and to spare confusion.[64]

Lakṣmīdhara's belief that Samayins worship only internally while Kaulas employ external forms may have been based on regional traditions.[65] However, his preference for ideas and practices acceptable to high caste Hindus does not exclude non-twice-borns (*atraivarṇikas* or *advija*) from Samaya Śrīvidyā. This point should be emphasized since a misstatement of his views has been supported by a host of reputable scholars.[66] In his commentary on verse 11 of *Saundaryalaharī*, Lakṣmīdhara states plainly that even outcastes (*śūdras*) can be qualified (*adhikāra*) for contemplative worship (*upāsana*) on the *śrīcakra*. He goes on to say that in Vaidika rituals, *traivarṇika* caste persons are preferred.

Had Lakṣmīdhara restricted Śrīvidyā to only twice-born males (*dvija*) he would have formally distinguished it from all other Tantric traditions since caste is not used to exclude potential initiates. While the content of spiritual discipline (*sādhana*) can be restricted or determined by caste, access to some form of initiation (*dīkṣā*) cannot. Like all Tantrics, Lakṣmīdhara does not dismiss caste but rather distinguishes Tantric and Vedic qualifications.

Lakṣmīdhara also makes theoretical and practical distinctions between Samayins and Kaulas, some of which are upheld by later Kaula commentators, including Bhāskararāya. In one of their most distinctive interpretive shifts, the Samayins maintain that the *śrīcakra* should be envisioned opposite to that of the Kaulas. The whole configuration is turned upside down, as it were, such that the central *bindu* is no longer in the middle of the central triangle but in the space directly above it.[67] This repositioning is accompanied by a major theological reinterpretation; the resulting four downward facing major triangles are identified with Śiva while the five upward facing are Śakti. While this Samaya version of the *śrīcakra* still appears in some contemporary traditions it is not the popular figure; neither has Lakṣmīdhara's theological reinterpretation gained a following among contemporary Samayins. (See diagram A1 for the Samaya version of the *śrīcakra*.)

The repositioning of the *śrīcakra*, Lakṣmīdhara contends, parallels yet another Samaya/Kaula difference. The Kaulas, he says, conceive the *śrīcakra* only according to the method of dissolution (*samhārakrama*) while Samayācārins prefer the creation method (*sṛṣṭikrama*). The practical implications of this distinction are straightforward: the dissolution method conceptualizes or "draws" the *śrīcakra* from the outermost lines towards the central triangle while the creation method begins at the central *bindu* and expands outward. This alteration implies a major adjustment in ritual practice (*pūjā*) since the identification of deities with the *cakra* must be radically revised.

Later Śrīvidyā Kaulas do not seem to be aware of Lakṣmīdhara's strict identification of methods by schools or at least evince no interest. Bhāskararāya passes over the issue as a factional dispute and discusses both methods of conceptualizing the *śrīcakra* with equal deference.[68] Lakṣmīdhara's sectarianism is, once again, unaccounted for in other scriptural sources, suggesting that he describes practices and interpretations familiar to his region, current to his times, or peculiar to his lineage.

Contemporary Śrīvidyā does follow Lakṣmīdhara on the so-called left-handed (*vāmācāra*) and right-handed (*dakṣiṇācāra*) distinction. The left-handed path, defined by the use of "prohibited" ritual substances including sex outside marriage, is identified with the Kaulas. Right-handed worship rejects these practices and follows the "orthodox" views of *smārta* brahmanism. Only the right-handed path is deemed appropriate to the Samayins. Lakṣmīdhara is not the first to articulate the right/left distinction in these terms. He also seems to reflect the historical situation even though Kaulas do not always follow left-handed methods or take ritual injunctions literally.[69]

Bhāskararāya rejects the interpretation of left- and right-handed worship in terms of specific "antinomian" practices. Instead he offers an esoteric distinction based on the acceptance of certain gods in worship.[70] His opinion apparently is intended to counter popular understanding of the left/right distinction. For Bhāskararāya, denying the use of powerful but convention-defying substances would undermine the effectiveness of the Śrīvidyā path.[71] Without naming Lakṣmīdhara, Bhāskararāya rejects his opinions and avoids a potentially controversial subject. Bhāskararāya simply implies that Lakṣmīdhara's Samaya views are a mistaken account of an undivided tradition.

Bhāskararāya also interprets *samaya* to suggest that there have been fewer doctrinal and practical distinctions between the two schools than might be assumed from Lakṣmīdhara. On *Lalitāsahasranāma* n. 97 (*samayāntaḥsthā*) Bhāskararāya assents to the idea that *samaya* worship is internal when he says, "*Samaya* is commonly... explained as offering worship, etc. to a *cakra* in the ether of the heart...."[72] He then identifies this teaching with the yogic process of uniting spiritually with the eternal Śiva in a ritual called the "*mahāvedha*." While details of the ritual he has in mind are uncertain, his general interpretation is not: "The method of effecting this must be learned from a guru. This is what is meant here by *samayācāra*."[73] He later refers to Samaya as a tradition of teachers and scriptures, "*Samaya* also means the five books of Vaśiṣṭha, Śuka, Sanaka, Sanandana, and Sanatkumāra, because they describe this internal worship."[74] Here he echoes Lakṣmīdhara even though there are no texts bearing these names either in Bhāskararāya's own references or as independent works.[75]

As in the case of the term *kula*, the use of sacred etymology is crucial for determining the esoteric meanings of *samaya*. He says *sama* means "equality" while *ya* is the "one who attains the goal," thus the term refers to "the equality [*sama*] between the goddess and Śiva."[76] But apart from these references, Bhāskararāya makes no explicit mention of the theoretical or practical divisions in Śrīvidyā noted by Lakṣmīdhara.

The split between Kaula and Samaya is far deeper than a disagreement about terminology or theoretical points of divergence, such as the refashioning of the *śrīcakra*. The central issue revolves around the acceptance or rejection of practices at the heart of Tantric tradition, namely, the use of powerful substances and behaviors that are ordinarily prohibited or rejected according to high-caste canonical interpretations. For Bhāskararāya and the Kaulas these practices define Śrīvidyā as Tantric and distinguish it from practices enjoined in the Vedas. Though he does not insist on their literal, external practice, he views their practice as integral to Tantric discipline. Lakṣmīdhara, representing more conservative social and religious forces, is unwilling to compromise on these issues; he is at pains to emphasize that external practice of *any* rite is a "lower" form of discipline (*sādhana*) and that all rites associated with Kaulism should be abandoned by the twice-born. Thus, he makes the exclusion of external rites a significant part of Śrīvidyā's soteriology and suggests that anyone participating in Kaula rites is unfit for "higher" *sādhana*. Only the Samayins, he maintains, achieve the final state of grace and insight.[77] That the majority of Tantric sources do not support Lakṣmīdhara's interpretations cause him no concern. These sources are rejected outright or accepted only as partial truths.

Like other Śrīvidyā writers, Lakṣmīdhara resorts to a hierarchical interpretation that places his own Samayācāra at the apex of theological possibilities. However, he also suggests that the tradition rather than the guru has the ultimate authority to determine which portions of scriptures present the "correct" or "highest" forms of worship. In south Indian traditions, the controversy and confusion concerning Kaula/Samaya terminology continues though the dispute over the central issue dividing the schools, as Lakṣmīdhara posited it, remains one of the clearest and most important divisions within contemporary Śrīvidyā.

The evidence suggests that Śrīvidyā either began among high caste persons, most likely *smārta* brahmans not antagonistic to Kaula values, or that Kaula followers were the first to codify the tradition in written texts. Those who rejected Kaula values and practices may not have been involved in the composition of Tantras since they would be ill-disposed to associate Śrīvidyā with Kaulism. Other texts important in south Indian Śrīvidyā, especially the *Saundaryalaharī* attributed to Śaṅkarācārya, do not appear on the historical scene until well after the emergence of the written Kaula Tantras.[78] There is no evidence to suggest that Śrīvidyā was exclusively Kaula from its inception or that Kaula values crept into the system only gradually: both opinions held by contemporary adepts holding opposing interpretations.[79]

Before proceeding further into the history of Śrīvidyā's texts and ideologies, it is appropriate to consider first new evidence about its emergence in south India and to attempt to track Śrīvidyā's development in the context of other important movements and ideologies.

Chapter 2

Earliest Historical Evidence for Śrīvidyā in Tamil Literature

The earliest Sanskrit sources devoted specifically to Śrīvidyā—sources linking the figure of Lalitā to the *śrīcakra* and/or fifteen or sixteen syllable mantra—cannot be realistically dated before the eighth or ninth centuries. The *Devī-*, *Kālikā-*, *Liṅga-* and *Brahmāṇḍapurāṇas* frequently cited by later Śrīvidyā adepts, may well harken back to a hoary antiquity but efforts to read Śrīvidyā into these texts are impossible to verify. The situation is comparable to the prototypical images resembling Śiva found on the coins of pre-Aryan civilizations, which are often cited as "evidence" of the god's ancient worship.[1] Texts such as the *Lalitāsahasranāma* and the *Nityāṣoḍaśikārṇava*, the first part of the *Vāmākeśvaratantra*, may be much older than their written forms but neither textual nor historical evidence can verify traditionalist claims. The notion that a systematic theology erupted in a flurry of literary activity, as it has been suggested, seems unlikely considering the precedents of oral transmission elsewhere in Tantrism and the epigraphical evidence linking comparable materials before the emergence of the first written sources.[2]

Determining which texts first codified Śrīvidyā's teachings depends to a large extent on the mention of titles or fragments of text in other sources and whether these provide reliable historical evidence. A comparable example is the mention of a portion of a line that appears in a late Śaiva *Āgama* and occurs in an inscription at the Kailāsanātha temple in Kāñcipuram; the inscription is dated to the sixth-century Pallava King Rājasiṃhavarman.[3] Does this epigraphical evidence refer to the actual Āgamic source that takes a literary form centuries later? Without specific references the connection remains tenuous though it has been assumed as evidence for the early appearance of Āgamic texts. Whether this citation refers to a familiar, later *written* text has not yet be proven. However, there may have been established fixed oral texts that were later written.[4]

The presence of the *śrīcakra* and the *śrīvidyā* suggests at least prototypical forms of worship later systematized. The mere mention of the goddess Lalitā or Tripurā would not suffice in the same way. There is no *necessary* link between these names of the goddess and

Śrīvidyā forms of worship employing the mantra or yantra. Wherever the *śrīcakra* or the *śrīvidyā* mantra are present, however, there is almost certainly a connection to the beneficent supreme goddess (*parāśakti*). While the mere mention of Śrīvidyā's mantra or yantra does not indicate systematic presentation, it suggests a stage in the formation of the tradition.

Local goddesses in south India are identified with the beneficent, supreme Śakti no later than the sixth century.[5] While an autonomous Tripurā cult seems to have taken shape well before the time of the Kashmiri Śivānanda—perhaps as early as the eighth century—there is no comparable south Indian evidence in Sanskrit.[6] The first explicit evidence that demonstrates the presence of either Śrīvidyā's distinctive mantra or yantra comes from the sixth or seventh-century Tamil *siddha* Tirumūlar. While Tirumūlar's reference tells us little about the popularity or importance of the cult, it unambiguously demonstrates the presence of at least prototypical Śrīvidyā worship in Tamilnadu during this period.[7]

If Tirumūlar's *Tirumantiram* is authentic, and there is no reason to believe it is not, and dates from his lifetime or shortly afterward, then by the seventh century Śrīvidyā's key elements had evolved to warrant mention in the work of poet not directly involved in Śākta worship. Tirumūlar does not indicate the extent to which Śrīvidyā's mantra and yantra elements may have been part of a coherent pattern of ritual and theology. Since there is no comparable evidence in north Indian vernacular sources, we know nothing about Śrīvidyā's regional diffusion prior to its emergence as a fully mature, written Sanskrit tradition in about the ninth century.[8]

The *śrīvidyā*'s presence in the *Tirumantiram* indicates that at least elements associated with systematic Śrīvidyā existed before seventh century. By whom the mantra was used and how it was incorporated into a larger pattern of worship remains a mystery.

Tirumūlar's mention of the mantra further suggests that Śrīvidyā did not require a particular Śaiva context in which to flourish, despite its ideological dependence on Kashmiri sources.[9] His remarks suggest a good deal of speculation on the esoteric meaning of the Śrīvidyā mantra in the circles of yogis and *siddhas*. These speculations, concerning the identification of specific colors and sounds within the *śrīvidyā* mantra, do not appear to have carried over into Sanskritic Śrīvidyā. It may be that Tirumūlar knows of an independent strand of Śrīvidyā interpretation that does not survive or adapts his own views to Śrīvidyā.

Traditionally counted among the sixty-four Tamil Nāyanār poet/saints of the Śaivas, Tirumūlar was a *siddha* (Tamil, *cittar*), an accomplished yogi whose supranormal powers and bizarre personality are legendary.[10] When compared to the works of other Nāyanārs, especially the later Tiruñānasampantar and Appar, Tirumūlar's works appear fragmentary and unsystematic. What is lacking in thematic continuity, however, is made up by the poetry's suggestive qualities and the author's powerful command of archaic Tamil. Like other *siddhas* Tirumūlar shifts topics whimsically even within the same stream of thought. Zvelebil suggests that the continuity of the *Tirumantiram* lies in its integration of Upaniṣadic wisdom, yoga, *bhakti*, and the influences of the Tantric movement.[11]

Tirumantiram, which means *Śrīmantra* in Sanskrit, was not written merely for poetic expression or devotional purposes but as mantra.[12] Many verses are little more than obscure, mystical expressions of transcendence or recitations of mantras. These mantraṣ are rendered into a cryptic, poetical Tamil evincing strong Sanskritic influences.

Tirumantiram, 1307, the first verse of the twelfth chapter entitled *Puvanāpati cakkaram* (Sanskrit, *Bhuvanāpati cakra*), is an explicit reference to the Śrīvidyā mantra in its fifteen syllable configuration beginning with the syllable *ka*.[13] The first letter of each of the *śrīvidyā*'s three *kūṭas* (here called *vidyās*) occurs as the first Tamil letter of the first word in each of the verse's three lines. The Tamil configuration makes this evident:

kakarāti yoraintuṅ kaniya poṉmai
akarāti yorarārattamē poḻum
cakarāti yornāṉkun tāṉcutta vēnmai
kakarāti mūvittai kāmiya muttiyē[14]

Though in its Sanskrit configuration the second *kūṭa* of the *śrīvidyā* begins with the syllable *ha* rather than *a*, as the second line of Tamil verse begins, this is a result of the substitution in literary Tamil of *a* for *ha*. In the third line of the verse the Tamil *ca* is the common letter used for all three forms of the Sanskrit sibilant and should be taken as the first Sanskrit *sa*.

The semantic meaning of the verse, however, also draws an explicit reference to the *śrīvidyā*. It might be translated:

> The letter *ka* and five letters are golden colored.
> The letter *a* [i.e., *ha*] and the six are red in color.
> The four letters beginning with *ca* [i.e., *sa*] are pure white.
> The three *vidyās* [i.e., *kūṭas*] beginning with *ka* give desired liberation.

The connection between this obscure and suggestive verse and the *śrīvidyā* mantra is unambiguous. "The letter *ka* and five letters" refers to *ka, e, ī, la,* and *hrīṃ,* the first *kūṭa* of the fifteen syllable mantra; "The letter *a,*" which refers to the Sanskrit *ha,* "and the six" refers to *ha, sa, ka, ha, la, hrīṃ,* the second *kūṭa;* and "The four letters beginning with *ca,*" refers to *sa, ka, la, hrīṃ,* thus completing the mantra in its so-called *kādi*-version. Tirumūlar makes no further mention of the mantra nor does he say anything about its place in his own spirituality.

Tirumūlar's use of the *kādi-* variety of the *śrīvidyā* only reinforces the idea that other versions such as the one beginning with *ha* (i.e., the *hādi*) were either derivations of *kādi-*, as some contemporary practitioners maintain, or historical afterthoughts developed to complete a larger pattern of mantra speculation. The use of this particular mantra is not conclusive evidence that only the *kādi-* form was in vogue—Tirumūlar's failure to mention other forms of the *śrīvidyā* may not even mean this was the only form he knew. We can only conclude that Tirumūlar was familiar with the *kādi śrīvidyā* and that this mantra was known to Śaiva *siddhas* in south India during this period.

Tirumūlar's explanation of the mantra as tripartite is significant since it indicates familiarity with an important technical aspect of later Śrīvidyā—the three portions of the mantra's fifteen letters are identified with three portions of the goddess' anthropomorphic form and are each associated with different sets of spiritual accomplishments.[15]

While the reference to the mantra is unmistakable, its context does little to clarify its place in Tirumūlar's thought. The verse does not, curiously enough, appear in the section dedicated to Tripurā. Modern Śrīvidyā adepts point to the peculiar nature of the *siddha* to explain this discrepancy.[16] Literary study of *Tirumantiram* offers other examples of out of context statements and a general disregard for systematic (or sometimes coherent) presentation of ideas.

The *śrīvidyā*'s mention in *Tirumantiram* affirms that it was established as part of general and popular mantric lore and that speculations on its meanings had already begun in earnest. Interestingly, later Sanskrit writers do not mention Tirumūlar's reference nor do they place him anywhere in their preceptorial lines.

Tirumantiram [verses 1045–1074] describe the goddess Tripurā and the so-called Tripurā cakra under the heading *cattipētam tiripurai cakkaram,* the Tripurā's cakra and seat of power (or throne of the goddess).[17] The figure of Tripurā described here is the familiar aspect of the goddess emerging in full form in the *Lalitopakhyāna* and the *Lalitāsahasranāma*. Tirumūlar does not, however, make any connection between this image of Tripurā and the *śrīvidyā* mentioned in verse 1307; nor does he link Tripurā to the *śrīcakra*. Instead he describes a separate Tripurā cakra whose connection with the *śrīcakra* cannot be reasonably established. The Tripurā cakra described here is not a part of later Śrīvidyā tradition nor does it emerge again in later Tantric literature. Like many of the specifics in Tirumūlar's work, this particular Tripurā *cakra* appears to have faded into obscurity possibly because of the later (?) identity of Tripurā with the *śrīcakra*.

From the verses describing the Tripurā *cakra*, it is clear that Tripurā in her inveterate anthropomorphic form is identified with the supreme deity and that her worship is known in south India by Tirumūlar's time. It is impossible to say if Tirumūlar made any connections between Tripurā, the Tripurā cakra, and the *śrīvidyā*. The mention of Tripurā's divine superiority is itself rather remarkable considering Tirumūlar's overwhelming Śaiva orientation. Like other Nāyanārs, Tirumūlar was committed to the absolute sovereignty of Śiva in the divine pantheon, Śakti is only a secondary figure in his theology.

There is, however, suggestive evidence for the presence of the *śrīcakra* in south India in the seventh century in yet another section of *Tirumantiram*. In verses 884–913 under the section entitled *Tiruvambalam cakkaram*, Tirumūlar describes the cakra or a portion of it associated with Śiva Naṭarāja at Cidambaram. The section heading Tiruvambalam is an unambiguous reference to Cidambaram in old Tamil. In these verses, Tirumūlar discusses some seven varieties of Śiva cakras including a portion of the so-called *sammelanacakra* or combination cakra associated with Naṭarāja's secret (*rahasya*) form. The connection of the *sammelanacakra* with *śrīcakra* is matter of speculation among contemporary adepts. It appears Tirumūlar corroborates their view that the *sammelanacakra* is at least, in part, a *śrīcakra*.

If Tirumūlar's Śiva yantra and the *sammelanacakra* can be linked to the *śrīcakra* then it is possible that elements of Śrīvidyā were present in an established Śaiva temple from at least the seventh century. The evidence confirming the relationship of the *sammelanacakra* to the *śrīcakra*, however, comes only in the thirteenth-century work of Umāpatiśivācārya. Contemporary Śrīvidyā adepts claim that the part of the cakra discussed by Tirumūlar is only the "Śiva portion" of what is described as a combination of Śiva and Śakti elements.[18] In verse 930, he says that the author of the *tiruvambalam cakkaram* is Śiva himself and, in v. 938, that the totality of creation in the form of *brahmāṇḍa* is nothing other than the *tiruvambalam*. Whether the *tiruvambalam cakkaram* known to Tirumūlar includes the Śakti portion of the *sammelanacakra* is a matter for further investigation since Śrīvidyā devotees have long suspected the Śakti portion of the yantra to be a portion of the *śrīcakra*.[19]

South Indians devoted to Śiva Naṭarāja maintain that the *sammelanacakra* was part of the original portions of the Cidambaram Naṭarāja temple and therefore was known to Tirumūlar. The connections between these bits of evidence, however, are unattested. More significant than the date of the so-called Cidambaram *rahasya* within the Naṭarāja sanctum is the simple fact that it is associated with a Tantric yantra and the Śrīvidyā cult. No other cakra or configuration has been associated with Cidambaram Naṭarāja. Tirumūlar's failure to mention the Śakti portion of the *sammelanacakra* or the *śrīcakra* explicitly does not preclude the possibility that his *tiruvambalam cakkram* is, in fact, a portion of the *sammelanacakra*. Tirumūlar was preoccupied with Śiva, and the absence of a mention of Śakti does not mean she was absent from the scene. If the hypothesis that Tirumūlar describes at least a portion of the *sammelanacakra* is correct, as many contemporary Śrīvidyā practitioners maintain, then the composition of this mysterious *cidākāśarahasya* or Secret of Consciousness-Space is at least partially solved by Tirumūlar. In verse 904, he supplies a description of the Śiva aspect of the cakra.

> Draw six lines vertically and six horizontally, thus you create five squares by five and within these are written the syllables of the Śiva mantra.[20]

With other evidence pointing to the existence of Śrīvidyā's characteristic elements within a Śaiva temple no later than the thirteenth century, one can hypothesize further about the composition for Śrīkula sources. Given the extensive development of Śrīvidyā's elements by Kashmiris and the early references to the Kaula movement in north India, it is likely that the formative period of the school's theology also took place in north India.[21] By the mid-eleventh century there can be no doubt that Śrīvidyā had gained a distinctive identity in Kashmir.[22] As a mantra and perhaps as a practice involving the use of yantras, Śrīvidyā is present in south India by the time of Tirumūlar and perhaps earlier if the evidence at the Cidambaram temple is deemed trustworthy. This would lead us to believe that the development of Śrīvidyā's mantra and yantra comes before the sixth century. If Kālīkula sources are, as Teun Goudriaan says, well before the Śrīkula then these elements in prototypical or unsystematic forms must also be earlier than the sixth century.[23] While this is hardly a novel hypothesis, it is perhaps the first time it has been sustained with historical and literary evidence.

The *śrīcakra*'s presence within the Cidambaram temple, allegedly in the seventh century, would mean that elements associated with systematic Śrīvidyā were part of the approved worship of at least some Vaidikas. Śrīvidyā's original development then might well have been among Vaidikas not opposed to being associated with certain Tantric values. In his discussion of the earliest strands of Tantric literature in Sanskrit Goudriaan remarks:

> It was not based upon a popular movement, but was the outgrowth of the specialist position of an intellectual elite of religious functionaries from the upper classes, as a rule of Brahmans.[24]

Our evidence not only corroborates Goudriaan's point but suggests a developed ritual tradition accompanying the formation of such Tantric concepts as mantra and yantra worship from a period well before the emergence of written sources.

Chapter 3

Śrīvidyā Tantras and Early Sources

DETERMINING ŚRĪVIDYĀ SOURCES IN THE SOUTH INDIAN TRADITION

Madhu Khanna divides the literature of the Tripurā cult into two major categories. First, there is the body of texts that "roots itself in Vedic authority."[1] By this Khanna means the materials that likely arose in south India within the highly Vedāntic traditions of *smārtas* and Śāṅkara followers. The second category "springs from a radically different religious milieu," namely, the nondualist *Āgamas* of Kashmir. This latter category, Khanna argues, provides the earliest exegesis of Śrīvidyā from the so-called *hādimata* perspective and is distinct from the work influenced by Vedānta thinkers.[2] Writers within both categories seek to locate Śrīvidyā within Vedic traditions and none were radically anti-*smārta* or anti-brahman.

While none of Khanna's historical analysis is disputed here, and much will be adopted, our strategy for understanding Śrīvidyā's history is perhaps more ambitious. Rather than focus on the earliest sources in order to differentiate Śrīvidyā from either Vedānta or other Kashmiri sources, we shall review the written canon that shapes the agenda of contemporary south Indian practitioners. The distinction between sources that "mock *śruti* literature," that is, the Vedānta-oriented materials that are largely southern in origin, and Kashmiri materials rooted in the Śaiva *Āgamas* is retained only for analytical purposes. Most contemporary practitioners eschew such distinctions and are unconcerned with the debts, intellectual or historical, that they may owe to other traditions. Rather than argue over the origins of Śrīvidyā, I propose to distinguish its south Indian canon.

Our aim is to discuss primarily the *perception* of texts in light of their historicity. One might ask: For whom would a narrow textual or theological self-definition be necessary? Aside from the common distinction between revelation (*śruti*) and reflection (*smṛti*), most Śrīvidyā writers prefer to take up matters thematically on the basis of ideology or ritual practice. As one contemporary adept put it:

> We are aware that Śrīvidyā is a special discipline and we keep it secret to protect those not ready for its teachings. But we do not wish to draw unnecessary attention to ourselves. We do not consider Śrīvidyā a sect but the source of all teachings. So I may discuss

> Viṣṇu or Śiva or any other god and any other topic, but this does not interfere with my own tradition. We do not concern ourselves with being called Tāntrikas or Vaidikas, though I consider myself both. Since Śrīvidyā is the *vidyā* of *vidyās* it is proper to use any text that contributes to its wider interpretations.[3]

Despite these remarks one finds a startling lack of interest among contemporary adepts in lineage teachings other than their own.[4]

THE ŚRĪKULA TANTRAS AND OTHER EARLY SOURCES

The Śrīkula Tantras are traced in Kashmir to a period roughly concurrent to Tirumūlar's reference to the *śrīvidyā* mantra.[5] Only four Śrīkula Tantras commit to the position that Śrīvidyā is the preeminent form of Śākta worship. The foremost of these, the *Vāmakeśvara Tantra*, must also be considered the oldest in Sanskrit.

Vāmakeśvara Tantra (*VT*) combines the *Nityāṣoḍaśikārṇava* (*NSA*), also known as the *Catuḥśati* since it consists of four hundred verses, and the *Yoginīhṛdaya* (*YH*), called by some commentators the *Sundarīhṛdaya*.[6] The latest and most important commentator of the south Indian tradition, Bhāskararāya, treats these two works as a single text and refers to the *NSA* as the "first" (*pūrvacatuḥśati*) and the *YH* as the "latter" (*uttaracatuḥśati*) four hundred verses of the *Vāmakeśvara Tantra*. Despite his assertion that these two portions reflect respectively the exoteric and esoteric Śrīvidyā *sādhana*, they appear to have different origins representing distinct intellectual and historical traditions.[7] As Goudriaan has remarked:

> Both...[texts] testify to a complete mastery of the subject which appears as a full-grown system.... There can be no doubt that here we have two of the most accomplished products of Hindu Tantric literature. It is clear that these texts are still within the learned tradition which produced the intellectual masterpieces of Kashmir Śaivism.[8]

There can be little disputing Goudriaan's placement of the text(s) within the Kashmiri intellectual tradition.[9]

The contents of the *NSA* are ably summarized by Goudriaan.[10] The title is noteworthy, literally, "The Ocean of the sixteen *nityās*," since it refers to the sixteen "eternal" goddesses (*nityādevatā*) identified with the phases (*kalā*) of the moon.[11] The text itself has rather little to do with *nityā* worship, especially when compared to the later *Tantrarāja Tantra*.[12] The primary foci of the text are the various practices associated with the worship of Tripurā, mantras, and practices for accomplishing worldly goals, such as obtaining wealth or children.

The second portion of *Vāmakeśvara Tantra*, the *Yoginīhṛdaya* begins with the goddess asking for a further explanation of points left unclear in the *Nityāṣoḍaśikārṇava*, thus providing the basis for Bhāskararāya's claim that *NSA* deals with external worship (*bahiryāga*) and *YH* with internal worship (*antaryāga*).[13] Its three chapters on the secret meanings of the *śrīcakra*, *śrīvidyā*, and the worship (*pūjā*) of the goddess are the most detailed exposition of Śrīvidyā's inner core of teachings available in any primary Tantric source.[14]

Vāmakeśvaratantra's earliest commentaries are by Kashmiris, though the text is known in the south perhaps by the tenth century. The *Nityāṣoḍaśikārṇava* is the earlier portion of the Tantra. No named commentary on the *Yoginīhṛdaya* appears until the fourteenth century though the *Tantrarāja Tantra* (*TT*) (also known as the *Kādimata Tantra*), a source certainly not later than the twelfth century, lists it as an old text.[15]

The earliest extant commentary on *Nityāṣoḍaśikārṇava* belongs to Jayaratha, the twelfth-century Kashmiri best known as the author of the *Vivaraṇa* on Abhinavagupta's *Tantrāloka*. He calls the text *Vāmakeśvarīmata* and does not seem to be aware of the *YH*. He says that *Vāmakeśvarīmata* was commented upon earlier by Īśvaraśiva, the prominent ninth-century Kashmiri thinker who wrote a verse exposition (*vārttika*) entitled the *Rasamahodadhi*.[16] K. C. Pandey suggests that Jayaratha's reference to Īśvaraśiva as the *avatāraka* or "one who brought down" the text, indicates that Īśvaraśiva first systematized this presentation of the tradition.[17] Other than Jayaratha's reference to Īśvaraśiva there is no further data about this early commentary and its verses are not cited in later sources.[18]

If L. Silburn is correct in dating Maheśvarānanda to the twelfth century then it is entirely possible that Śivānanda's *NSA* commentary, entitled *Ṛjuvimarśinī*, must come from sometime in the eleventh century since Śivānanda is frequently referred to by Maheśvarānanda as his teacher's teacher.[19] Khanna, however, argues that Śivānanda dates to the first portion of the thirteenth century (c. 1245, *c.e.*). Maheśvara, an important Kashmiri intellectual, evinces no direct interest in Śrīvidyā though both his grand-teacher Śivānanda and his pupil Puṇyānanda compose important Śrīvidyā works.[20]

Among southern authors the distinctions between Śaiva and Śākta forms of worship are more pronounced than in Kashmir. Sectarian features are stressed precisely because there is no comparable continuity within Śaiva intellectual movements and literature. Early southern Śaiva figures, such as Tirumūlar or the Tamil poets Appar and Tiruñānasampantar, express little interest in Śākta theology and have no ties to Kula Tantrism.

Ideas common to later southern Śākta Tantrics, such as Bhāskararāya, and medieval Śaivas are not traced to a mutual interest in Kula sources but to the more tangentially related Śaiva Siddhānta sources. These Śaiva Siddhānta sources share with Kula Tantrism important theological principles, such as the thirty-six *tattvas*, and have historical links to Kashmir, but do not belong to Kula Tantrism. Umāpatiśivācārya the southern Śaiva thinker of the thirteenth century, for example, links Śrīvidyā with Śaivism in his devotional poem to Naṭarāja, the *Kuñchitāṅghristava*. He does not comment upon Kula sources but rather focuses his life's work on Śaiva Siddhānta tradition.

Vidyānandanātha's commentary on *NSA*, *Artharatnāvalī*, refers to Śivānanda and is the closest to him chronologically. He may have been south Indian or spent time in south India. His work, however, bears all the marks of a Kashmiri traditionalist. Some contemporary practitioners think him identical to Śrīnivāsa Bhaṭṭa the influential author of the ritual treatise *Saubhāgyaratnākara* who shared the same initiate name (*dīkṣānāma*).[21] However, this is not the case.

The three Kashmiri-based commentaries of Jayaratha, Śivānanda, and Vidyānanda form the basis for all subsequent interpretations of the *Nityāṣoḍaśikārṇava*. Only Jayaratha's work is well known to contemporary south Indian practitioners; the other two, though now available in print, are known primarily by Bhāskararāya's references.[22]

Amṛtānanda, the Kashmiri pupil of Puṇyānanda, who wrote the authoritative *Kāmakalāvilāsa* (*KKV*), is best known for his so-called *hādi* tradition commentary on the *Yoginīhṛdaya*.[23] Though the *hādi* tradition has no following in contemporary south India, this does not seem to have diminished the author's importance. His work is best known because Bhāskararāya cites it frequently and usually favorably.[24] Abhinavagupta (*Tantrāloka*, 28.123) refers to a *Nityā Tantra*, another name associated with the *Nityāṣoḍaśikārṇava*, but this appears to be another text altogether.[25] While a comparable title does not appear on the traditional lists of sixty-four Tantras, Bhāskararāya's claim that it is the independent sixty-fifth suggested in the *Saundaryalaharī* is widely accepted by contemporary south Indian adepts.[26] Traditional views aside, there is no evidence that written versions of the *Nityāṣoḍaśikārṇava* are earlier than the eighth century.[27]

Bhāskararāya's *Setubandha*, the only major commentary that covers the "whole" *VT*, states that *Yoginīhṛdaya* takes up matters left unclear in the *NSA*. Renown for his expertise in technical speculative and ritual matters, Bhāskararāya refers to Jayaratha, Vidyānanda, and Śivānanda by name. He also mentions traditions, opinions, and earlier *vṛttis* that do not appear in the cited Kashmiri sources. Though constrained by the commentary format, the *Setubandha* consolidates and anthologizes

Śrīvidyā's tenets, values, and practices—at least as the tradition is understood in south India during the middle eighteenth century. The *Setubandha* is to south Indian Śrīvidyā what Abhinavagupta's *Tantrāloka* is to Kashmiri Śaivism: the authoritative and encyclopedic source book for the entire tradition that follows it. In contemporary south India even those who challenge Bhāskararāya's views cannot ignore him. All existing avenues of interpretation lead eventually to the *Setubandha*.

There are three obvious and interrelated reasons why Bhāskararāya has attained such a status in contemporary south India: (1) He is the most recent textual authority in Śrīvidyā, one whose reputation for spiritual and literary achievements goes beyond the concerns of practitioners. Bhāskararāya is a saint in the sense of being one whose spiritual achievements are recognized as part of popular lore; (2) He settled in Tamilnadu in Thañjavūr district in the village of Bhāskararājapuram on property granted him by the Maratha ruler Seforji. His links to the land, though no longer maintained, have made him a son of Tamilnadu despite his having been an immigrant from the north.[28] His political patronage clearly contributed to his spiritual fame and his gifted property provided him the means to teach; and (3) His presence in the south leads many in contemporary lineages in Tamilnadu to trace their descent from Bhāskararāya and his pupils.

Bhāskararāya's encyclopedic knowledge of Śrīvidyā also grants him special status. The *Setubandha*, his independent treatise the *Varivasyārahasya*, the commentaries on *Lalitāsahasranāma*, and the *Bhāvana* and *Tripurā* Upaniṣads are the most widely read and definitively regarded sources in contemporary south Indian Śrīvidyā. Bhāskararāya has eclipsed others by responding with his own arguments. Though committed to the superiority of his own beliefs, he accommodates others without patronizing or antagonizing them. In this respect he resembles the historical Śaṅkarācārya: firm in conviction but lacking in vindictiveness. Because he travelled and lived in northern India for a portion of his life, Bhāskararāya's influence extends beyond regional boundaries.[29]

Though there is little interest in Kashmiri Śrīvidyā in contemporary south Indian Śrīvidyā, Kashmiri sources deeply influenced southern writers, such as Bhāskararāya and Śrīvidyānandanātha. The same degree of influence cannot be attributed to works originating in Bengal. This may be due to the fact that Bengali Śāktism has been dominated by Kālīkula rather than Śrīkula traditions. It is a curious footnote to these relations within Śrīvidyā between Kashmir and Tamilnadu to observe connections with other traditions, notably Śaiva Siddhānta and traditions of dance and aesthetics.[30] As one contemporary adept said:

> There is a special relationship between Śrīvidyā in Kashmir and in the south, especially here in Tamilnadu. There was much exchange between the two regions and it is our belief that Śaiva Siddhānta was deeply influenced by Kashmiri Śaivism. This is a point that Tamil purists [*sic*] will never admit. The regional distinctions in Śrīvidyā are more pronounced between the south and Bengal, and between the worship in Kerala and in the other southern states. The Kashmiri tradition is not unlike our own though I believe their interest in more philosophical matters is the reason why the ritual tradition is no longer so easily found.[31]

Another important Tantra for south Indian Śrīvidyā is the *Kādimata Tantra*, better known as the *Tantrarāja Tantra*.[32] The author's basic distinction between traditions termed *Kādimata* and those he calls *Kālīmata* is no longer maintained in contemporary southern circles. There appear to be no other historical references regarding the differences he has in mind between these ostensible preceptorial lines (*mata*).[33] The contrast is significant because it appears to be the first mention of a distinction within the Tantric schools according to *mata*, "conviction" or "practice." *Kādimata* is likely used as a synonym for Śrīkula, or even Śrīvidyā, since it appears to refer directly to the mantra; *kālīmata* appears to specify the Kālīkula.

The term "*mata*" warrants analysis since like other comparable terms for "conviction," "practice," or "preceptorial line," it appears again in later Śrīvidyā sources. *Mata* is usually associated with the different Śrīvidyā mantras, especially when compounded as *kādi-* and *hādimata*. But *mata*, according to Jayaratha (*Tantrāloka*, 1.18), is also used as a general specification for a doctrinal school.[34] The *Sammohana Tantra*, a work of special interest in Kashmiri traditions and quoted frequently in Śrīvidyā works, uses *mata* combined with the names of deities such as Kubjikā, Piṅgalā, and Nandikeśvara, suggesting worship associated with these divinities.[35] But for Amṛtānanda or Bhāskararāya the term is interchangeable with *ācāra* "practice," *mārga* "path," *sampradāya* "tradition," and *krama* "method."

The term for "doctrine" or "practice" is not as crucial in Śrīvidyā as the term with which it is compounded.[36] Lakṣmīdhara, for example, interchanges *mata*, *ācāra*, and *mārga* with *samaya*. The crucial term here is *samaya*. To Lakṣmīdhara the Samayamata or Samayācāra is "conduct according to *samaya* principles," which he differentiates from the *kulamata*, or "conduct according to *kula* tradition."[37]

Abhinavagupta says that the *Tantrarāja Tantra* presents a secret worship described in Kaula literature.[38] Bhāskararāya refrains from commenting on the text directly, preferring instead to cite it to support his interpretations of other texts. He only says that *Tantrarāja* is not a separate Tantra nor part of the "original" list of sixty-four.[39]

In addition to Bhāskararāya's citations, contemporary adepts know about *TT* primarily because Sir John Woodroffe brought it to print more than half a century ago. The *TT*'s ritual of the sixteen *nityās* is rarely practiced as presented in the text but serves as a theoretical embellishment to the expanding ritual liturgy.

The *Jñānārṇava Tantra* (*JT*) is the third major Śrīvidyā Tantra. It, too, states a preference for so-called *kādi* traditions. Frequently cited, especially by Brahmānanda and Pūrṇānanda, its *terminus ante quem* is before the sixteenth century.[40] Despite its late date it remains authoritative for contemporary practitioners, especially with regard to Śrīvidyā's symbolic triads and mantric hierarchy.[41] Several ritual handbooks (*paddhatis*) claim "to be based on the authority" of this Tantra.[42] The conspicuous absence of the five controversial substances, the *pañcamakāras*, has not escaped the attention of conservatives who oppose their use. This fact is used to support the claim that the *makāras* are not a part of Śrīvidyā's "original" teachings.

The *Śrīvidyārṇava Tantra* (*SVA*), despite its proclaimed human authorship and recent sixteenth-century date, has also enjoyed popularity among southern Śrīvidyā adepts.[43] The close connection between Śrīvidyā and the Śāṅkara tradition, which Vidyārṇava Yati the author has emphasized, is the point most frequently raised by contemporary practitioners. *Śrīvidyāṇava* is frequently quoted on other matters and its positions, including the *kādi-/kālimata* division, are assumed in entirety. Curiously, the author has no aversion to Kaula sources, which are cited as authorities, despite their being at odds with the Śāṅkara tradition's values.[44] The *SVA* has left its mark on recent south Indian traditions as a comprehensive synthesis of Śrīvidyā ritual and theology.

Of the four Tantras, the *Vāmakeśvara, Tantrarāja, Jñānārṇava,* and *Śrīvidyārṇava*, most frequently cited and commented upon sources in contemporary south Indian Śrīvidyā tradition, only the *SVA* appears to have had a limited regional appeal. Śrīkula Tantras, such as *Paramānanda Tantra* and *Ānandārṇava Tantra* have, in comparison, had only a minor impact on living tradition. The other Tantras of the Śrīkula have all but disappeared from memory of contemporary south Indian lineages. Instead, theological discussions are put in terms of ritual; the focus remains squarely on the practical ritual handbooks (*nibandhas* and *paddhati*)[45].

GAUḌAPĀDA, ŚAṄKARA, AND THE ŚĀṄKARA TRADITION

No historical figures are more frequently mentioned by contemporary Śrīvidyā practitioners in south India than the eighth-century nondualist Vedānta theologian, Śaṅkarācārya (c. 700 *c.e.*) and his teacher's teacher (*paramaguru*) Gauḍapāda. Scholarly opinion has long debated the historical Śaṅkara's affiliations.[46]

While historians may dismiss the traditional claim that Śaṅkara, author of the *Brahmasūtrabhāṣya* and *Upadeśasahaśrī*, also composed the *Prapañcasāra* (*PS*), *Lalitātriśatibhāṣya* (*LTSB*), and the *Saundaryalaharī* (*SL*), the majority of Śāktas, as well as the contemporary purveyors of Śāṅkara tradition, accept these works as authentic.[47] These four Śākta texts, together with the *Śrīvidyāratnasūtras* and *Subhagodaya* attributed to Gauḍapāda, are seminal to contemporary Śrīvidyā's self-understanding.

The *Prapañcasāra*, an eloquent exposition of mantra science (*mantraśāstra*), mentions Śrīvidyā's twelve traditional teachers and twelve forms of root-mantra (*mūlamantra*).[48] We should assume that the tradition had gone through most of its elaborate theoretical expansion by the time of its composition.[49] Of high literary quality, like all the Śākta works attributed to Śaṅkara, it should be dated no later than the eleventh century.[50] Śivānanda frequently cites it in the *Ṛjuvimarśinī*; it appears as well in the *Īśanaśivagurudevapaddhati*.[51] A *vivaraṇa* commentary, attributed to Śaṅkara's disciple Padmapāda, is complemented by a number of others, several of which are of south Indian origin; none match Padmapāda's in popularity.[52] The *vivaraṇa*'s author aligns himself with the *hādimata* though he does not illuminate differences with *kādimata*. The suggestion that the Śāṅkara tradition follows the *hādimata* because the Padmapāda *vivaraṇa* takes this position is not maintained in contemporary traditions. However, the attribution of the *vivaraṇa* to a direct disciple of Śaṅkara indicates the author's intention to view the root text as part of a continuous tradition of Śrīvidyā.

Bhāskararāya uses the *PS* to support his mantric interpretations and, like virtually all post-twelfth-century authors, he does not dispute Śaṅkara's purported authorship or that of the *vivaraṇa*.[53] He refers to Śaṅkara frequently as "Śrī Bhagavatpāda," a common epithet for all the heads of the Śāṅkara *maṭhas*, but clearly he has the "original Śaṅkara" (*ādiśaṅkara*) in mind.[54] The author of the *PS* is not likely the "original Śaṅkara," for a host of reasons including his acceptance of the theories of *śabdabrahman*, a position which Śaṅkara the *Brahmasūtrabhāṣya* author rejects.[55]

The Commentary on Lalita's Three Hundred Names (*Lalitātriśatistotra*) attributed to Śaṅkara (*LTSB*) bears directly on Śrīvidyā.[56] The primary text's myth of origins parallels that of the better known *Lalitāsahasranāma* (*LSN*). Lalitā and Śiva, in the form of Kāmeśvara, appear to Hayagrīva who relates to them the good fortune of having a disciple such as sagely Agastya. It is Agastya's devotion to the guru and to Śakti that Hayagrīva maintains is the reason for this blessed vision. Hayagrīva tells Agastya that Lalitā's three hundred names are not merely praiseworthy but are a concealed form of the fifteen syllable *śrīvidyā*.[57]

The text of the *Lalitātriśati* follows Hayagrīva's description: three hundred individual names are divided into groups of twenty, each beginning with a consecutive letter of the fifteen syllable *śrīvidyā*. While the author was aware of the *kādi/hādi* distinction—since *hādividyā* is one of the names attributed to Śakti—the text is structured to follow the fifteen syllable *kādi* mantra. This fact has not gone unnoticed by contemporary adepts favoring the *kādi* fifteen syllable (*pañcadaśī*) *śrīvidyā*:

> The *Lalitātriśati* shows that the *kādi* the superior form of *śrīvidyā* and that the *pañcadasī* is the original form of the mantra. In our opinion this must be true because there is so much dispute over the [the sixteen syllable] *ṣoḍaśī* [mantra].[58]

Internal evidence suggests that the *LTSB* must be dated well after the eighth-century Śaṅkara.[59] We should not dismiss the possibility that the Śākta texts attributed to Śaṅkara were composed by someone bearing the title of "Śaṅkara Bhagavatpāda" within the Śāṅkara *maṭhas* of south India. In fact, the texts might well be a form of apologia, written to bring the Śāṅkara tradition into a closer relationship with the Śāktism growing in popularity among south Indian *smārta* brahmans.[60] In south India the text serves as an important link between Śāṅkarites and Śrīvidyā. Contemporary adepts, who link themselves to the Śāṅkara tradition's seats (*pīṭhas*) in Śṛṅgerī or Kāñcipuram, maintain that the *LTSB* is not frequently referred to by historical commentators because it is more secret than other *stotras* including *LSN*. As one adept put it:

> The [Śrīvidyā] mantra is taught in a hierarchy. At the top is the mantra itself; next comes the teaching of it in *Lalitātriśati* where it is still in an explicit form as the first letter of the [various groups of] names. The mantra is also present at another level in the *Lalitāsahasranāma* and here it is kept out of the open so that this *stotra* can be used by any devotee. *Lalitātriśati* requires a higher form of qualification (*adhikāra*) and is not as common since it is taught more selectively. The names in the *Triśati* are less powerful, less condensed forms of the mantra. In the *sahasranāma* the mantra is fully concealed to protect the ordinary devotee. For the adept (*upāsaka*), however, even the *sahasranāma* is a source of mantric power because he knows its secrets. *Triśati* is a very popular text in the south because Śaṅkara wrote it in Kāñcipuram near the end of his days after all his philosophical work was complete.[61]

Contemporary Śrīvidyā adepts who dispute Śaṅkara's authorship of *LTSB* or do not associate him with Śrīvidyā do not necessarily reject the *LTS* itself; neither do these adepts identify themselves as part of the legacy of Kashmiri tradition. In south India any formal relationship between Śrīvidyā and Kashmiri Śaiva traditions appears to have vanished. One adept of this group explained:

> We do not believe Śaṅkara wrote this commentary on *Triśati* but the text itself is very useful. It is more of a *mantraśāstra* than a *stotra* and this is why it is not as popular as the *sahasranāma*. In general, we do not align ourselves with the Śāṅkara tradition because they are not actually Śrīvidyā *upāsaka*s but *advaita* Vedāntins.[62]

The third Śākta source attributed to Śaṅkara is popular in all Śākta traditions and across Śrīvidyā's regional distinctions. *Saundaryalaharī* (*SL*) has received attention not only from traditional Indian scholars but also westerners interested in poetic and religious values. Norman Brown's fine study and translation notwithstanding, much important scholarship concerning this text has yet to be done. While Brown correctly dismisses the attribution to Śaṅkara and observes the inadequacy of the commentarial literature for elucidating the literary meaning of the text, he does not consider the significance of Śaṅkara's purported authorship for subsequent theological traditions or indicate the important role the commentaries play in later Śaiva-Śākta traditions. While these matters are of little interest to him, they are at the center of our concerns.

Nine commentaries on *SL* are now in print and two of these stand out for their literary merit and illuminative power.[63] The most important and earliest is the sixteenth-century Lakṣmīdhara's *Lakṣmīdharī*, one of the few sources of Śrīvidyā's Samaya school.[64] Though Lakṣmīdhara is also credited with the *Śaivakalpadruma*, a ritual handbook for the worship of Śiva, the *SL* commentary makes clear the author's personal devotional to Śakti.[65] While Lakṣmīdhara stands alone on many interpretive issues without textual or historical support, his rendering of the *SL*'s esoteric meaning has become the standard for nearly all later efforts.[66]

Significantly, Lakṣmīdhara fails to mention the practical instructions involving the use of the text's verses with mantras, that is, the *prayoga*s popularly associated with the *SL*'s verses. These ritual directions, employing individual verses of the text for obtaining specific ends, are especially important in living traditions. It appears that (1) the *prayoga*s were not known to the historical commentators, or (2) did not warrant mention, and (3) are of recent origin.

Kaivalyāśrāma, whose *Saubhāgyavardhanī* is the only major commentary that does not cite Lakṣmīdhara, provides no biographical data and remains a mystery.[67] Contemporary adepts regard his opinions highly but offer no biographical or historical information.[68]

Of the other edited commentaries, three bear on the present study. Rāmakavi's *Ḍiṇḍima* is noteworthy for its effort to reconcile Tantric views of the *tattvas* with those of the Sāṅkhya school. The author identifies Śakti and Śiva with Sāṅkhya's *prakṛti* and *puruṣa* and lists the Śākta's thirty-six categories (*tattvas*) without offering an explanation of how the eleven "extra" *tattvas* in Tantric interpretations are added to Yoga's twenty-five or twelve to Sāṅkhya's twenty-four.[69] Rāmakavi also tells us that he is a native of Kāñcideśa, that is, Kāñcipuram in Tamilnadu but gives no clues concerning his date. He is, however, mentioned in the *Aruṇāmodinī* of Kāmeśvarasūri and it is certain only that he lived after Lakṣmīdhara.

The *Gopālasundarī* of Nṛsiṃhasvāmī is unique among the published commentaries inasmuch as it interprets the text from the Vaiṣṇava perspective. Śakti is called Gaurī, the goddess who emanated along with Viṣṇu from the single source called "Mahāsarasvatī." The goddess is theologically subordinate to Viṣṇu and considered his consort. This commentary is important to a very small number of contemporary practitioners born into Vaiṣṇava families who practice Śrīvidyā. One such adept said that this commentary confirmed his opinion that Śrīvidyā is not a "tradition limited to a particular point of view (*siddhānta*), but rather one that can be interpreted from either Śaiva or Vaiṣṇava perspectives."[70] While the relationship between Lalitā Tripurasundarī and Śrī/Lakṣmī does not usually suggest Vaiṣṇava theologies, Nṛsiṃhasvāmī, like some contemporary adepts, mixes images and traditions in order to establish theological compatibility.

The author of the *Sudhavidyodinī*, a commentary of unknown date and origin, is significant for his claim that the *SL* was written by his father, Pravarasena. This attribution of authorship deviates from the otherwise univocal opinion that the entire text or at least the final fifty-one verses are from the hand of Śaṅkara.

According to popular legend, Śaṅkara is responsible for gathering the *SL*'s first forty-one verses, the so-called *Ānandalaharī*, from Mount Kailāsa. In one version of the myth, he learned all one hundred from Śiva himself but, in a mishap involving Nandikeśvara, was able to retrieve only the forty-one of the *Ānandalaharī*; to these he added the rest and gave the name *Saundaryalaharī*. In another version preserved in Tamilnadu, it is said that the whole text was inscribed by Śiva on the walls of his cave on Mt. Kailāsa though his claim to authorship was disputed by Sarasvatī. In still another version, a heavenly being (in some cases a *yakṣa* named Puṣpadanta) heard them sung by Śiva and inscribed them atop Mount Meru. These were retrieved by Gauḍapāda, passed to Śaṅkara's teacher Govinda, and finally written down by Śaṅkara himself. The text of the *Ānandalaharī* portion of the text is also found as an inscription on the wall of the temple to Sugandhikuntalāmbā within the sub-temple of Matrubhūteśvara at the Rock Fort complex in Tiruchirapalli, Tamilnadu. Local tradition claims Śaṅkara himself made the inscription as he travelled through the city on the way to Rāmeśvaram; he then completed the final fifty-nine verses before the image of the goddess Akhilandeśvarī in nearby Tiruvanaikoil. This southern tradition is still maintained in the Śāṅkara *maṭha* in Kāñcipuram where Akhilandeśvarī's association with the goddess Lalitā Tripurasundarī is established by her use of the *śrīcakra* as earrings.[71] Like the other "Śaṅkara" texts, it is possible that *SL* was composed either in the Śāṅkara *maṭha* of Śṛṅgerī or Kāñcipuram.

The attribution of these four works to Śaṅkara solidifies connections between *smārta* brahmans, who identify with one of the southern Śāṅkara *pīṭhas*, and Śākta and Śrīvidyā traditionalists. Śrīvidyā appears to have undergone something of a reformation in the south in the period of the composition of these texts. Between the ninth and twelfth centuries, southerners distance themselves from Kashmiri Kaulism in order to distinguish Śrīvidyā from morally suspect Tantrism. Śākta non-dualism is broadly construed to be compatible with Śāṅkara's *advaita* Vedānta, though points of difference are rarely articulated and no serious effort is made to address them. For example, those commentators knowledgable about Vedānta and Tantra, such as Bhāskararāya, gloss over the discrepancy between the Tantric view that creation is a real transformation (*parināma*) of the Absolute and the Vedānta view of illusion (*māyā*) or cognitive error (*vivarta*). The unhappy consequences of inconsistency are ignored. Bhāskararāya seems more interested in invoking the name of Śaṅkara than in the content of his teachings. His interests appear to be political rather than philosophical.

By the tenth or eleventh century south Indian Śrīvidyā assimilates politically advantageous views and associations and leaves aside controversial topics. This method of interpretation without addressing points of dispute or inconsistency continues as part of the living tradition's hermeneutics.[72] For example, *Saundaryalaharī* appears to be a refinement of Śākta Tantrism suited to the needs of conservative brahmans. The inconsistencies between the *SL*'s theory of bodily cakras and the usual Tantric explanation reflects this effort to accommodate Tantric theories generally and dissociate from unacceptable specifics. Another explanation of *SL*'s content is given by contemporary adepts:

> *Saundaryalaharī* is a poem extolling the praises of Devī and giving some of the details of Śrīvidyā without going into the intricacies of the *pūjā* or the theory. This is why it lacks the sort of technical descriptions you see in other texts such as *Vāmakeśvara Tantra*. We must remember that this is a *stotra*, not a Tantra, it was meant to be read with secret and special teachings included *only* in the oral tradition. Lakṣmīdhara provides many of these details. Those who view the text from the purely literary point of view will not be able to appreciate these hidden and unstated matters. In fact, we can say that those who reject that these secret or implicit teachings are actually in the text have been led purposefully to this conclusion by Śaṅkara. He wished to protect the uninitiated and leave the text open to all. He accomplished this by leaving out all the technicalities and instead using the secret and suggestive method of teaching. Those who think it is just a poem praising Devī and not an exposition of Śrīvidyā have seen only the surfaces, they appreciate merely the waves of beauty (*saundaryalaharī*) but not the ocean of meaning.[73]

Lakṣmīdhara uses *SL* to define Samayācāra because it omits mention of even remotely objectionable Kaula elements, such as the five m's (*pañcamakāra*). Like all the texts attributed to Śaṅkara or Gauḍapāda, *SL* is made acceptable to even the most conservative Hindus at the expense of the distinctive Kaula Tantric marks common to most Śrīvidyā literature.

The two Śrīvidyā works attributed to Śaṅkara's *paramaguru* Gauḍapāda have a comparable stature in contemporary south India. If Gauḍapada's authorship of *Subhagodaya* and *Śrīvidyāratnasūtras* could be proven authentic, these would be the earliest independent treatises in Śākta Tantrism. Unfortunately there is no reason to believe this is the case. Adding to the difficulty is confusion regarding the *Subhagodaya*, which is sometimes attributed to Śivānanda and other times to Gauḍapāda.[74] There exist, however, at least two different texts with this title, the more common version attributed to Śivānanda (appearing in Dwiveda's edition of the *NSA*) and sometimes attributed to Gauḍapāda, and a more obscure text attributed to Gauḍapāda alone.[75] The latter text describes the goddess's ability to confer various forms of empowerment (*aiśvarya*) on those who worship her mantra and yantra and thus explains the many ways she is considered propitious (*saubhāgya*). Like other Śāṅkara tradition sources, it does not mention controversial Tantric ideas; it is used by contemporary Samayins as an example of the "original" Śrīvidyā tradition.

The *Śrīvidyāratnasūtras*, also attributed to Gauḍapāda, are better known in the contemporary tradition than the *Subhagodaya*.[76] Primarily an exposition of the two most important forms of the goddess's mantra, that is, the *kādi* and *hādi śrīvidyā*, its theological emphasis is the absolute identity of the deity, guru, and mantra. Bhāskararāya in his independent treatise on mantras, the *Varivasyārahasya*, makes a similar argument. Once again modern technology appears to have played an important role in the dissemination of tradition: the most commonly available printed edition of the *Śrīvidyāratnasūtras* is accompanied by the *Dīpikā* of Śaṅkarāraṇya. Manuscripts of the text are preserved in the Śāṅkara *maṭhas* at Kāñcipuram and Śṛṅgerī and Gauḍapāda's authorship is accepted without dispute.

Neither internal literary evidence nor historical records give an indication of the date of the *Śrīvidyāratnasūtras*. While it does not seem plausible that Gauḍapāda (c.600?) who wrote at least portions of the *Māṇḍūkhyopaniṣadkārikās* composed either of these Śrīvidyā texts, his role in southern Śrīvidyā tradition is secure. Both texts are particularly important for contemporary Samaya and Śāṅkarite Śrīvidyā. As one such adept said:

> There is nothing offensive about the Śrīvidyā works of Śaṅkara and Gauḍapāda. You will find no mention of the *makāras* and other unacceptable behavior. We accept them as fully authentic since it is our tradition that Śaṅkara was a great devotee of Devī. If he were not devoted to Śakti he could not have attained such fame.[77]

Many pious Śrīvidyā practitioners will reject any suggestion that Śaṅkarācārya or Gauḍapāda were not Śāktas. These works and ideas *should* belong to them not only because of their high literary qualities but also because of their deeper spiritual and communal values. Viewed as pillars of conservative orthodoxy, Śaṅkara and Gauḍapāda bring a legitimacy to Śrīvidyā that sublates other claims of a relationship with Kaula Tantrism. Precisely how and when the Śāṅkara traditions adopted Śāktism remains unknown, that they *did* is the crucial fact for post-eleventh-century Śāṅkarites.

RITUAL SOURCE BOOKS, TREATISES, AND LATER TRADITION

In the thirteenth and fourteenth centuries, Śrīvidyā undergoes its most prodigious growth at the hands of commentators. During this period the Kashmiris Śivānanda and Amṛtānanda flourish and Śrīnivāsa Bhaṭṭa composes his *Saubhāgyaratnākara*.[78]

Amṛtānanda's teacher Puṇyānandanātha is best known for his *Kāmakalāvilāsa* (*KKV*), a text frequently translated into European and Indian vernacular languages, including Tamil.[79] The most noteworthy of contemporary translation and commentary was composed in Madras around 1938 by one N. Subrahmanya Aiyar, also known as Cidānandanātha.[80]

The *KKV* expounds the *kāmakalā*, the "aspect of desire," as both a theory of Śākta cosmogony involving the expansion of the *śrīcakra* and a controversial form of meditation involving erotic elements. The text's main foci, however, are the relationships of the *śrīcakra*, the *śrīvidyā*, the deity, and the adept in the creative process. It adopts Śrīvidyā's standard theological position: liberation requires theoretical knowledge and the ritual expertise that create a direct experience (*anubhava*) of the One becoming Many in the form of the *śrīcakra*. The text itself contains no language or imagery objectionable to conservative Śrīvidyā adepts; its intellectual approach to the *kāmakalā* concept is particularly appealing in light of Bhāskararāya's interpretations that involve the worship of the female organ. The *Cidvallī* of Naṭanānanda is the most important of the commentaries on *KKV* and, like the root text, assumes the so-called *hādi* line of Śrīvidyā interpretation. Especially noteworthy for contemporary practitioners is Naṭanānanda's frequent use of Vedic sources in support of his interpretations.

Puṇyānanda's origins are unknown. Bharati claims he is "a renowned Bengali tantric" while contemporary adepts say he was originally a Keralite who migrated to Kashmir.[81] Puṇyānanda's conservative and intellectual approach to his work, coupled with its aesthetic appeal, make him a fine candidate for adoption as a southern native son. His *hādimata* interpretation is deemed irrelevant for contemporary *kādimata* followers as far as his cosmology is concerned.[82]

Some verses from Amṛtānanda's independent treatises, the *Saubhāgyasudhodaya* and the *Cidvilāsastava*, may in fact be Puṇyānanda's words. While Amṛtānanda acknowledges his own authorship he also praises his teacher's inspiration. Amṛtānanda's independent works are receiving increasing attention from contemporary southern adepts since they have come into print.[83] Like the *KKV* they are essentially speculative rather than ritualistic; the primary subjects are cosmology, the *śrīcakra*, and devolution of sound from its source in *śabdabrahman*. More important has been his *Dīpikā* on the *Yoginīhṛdaya*, though this, too, has gained in importance because of its publication and the subsequent recognition of its influence on Bhāskararāya. Bhāskararāya, however, does portray Amṛtānanda as an innovator but rather as a representative of tradition.

The *Subhagodaya* of Śivānanda combines both speculative and ritual elements and for this reason has gained importance among some contemporary interpreters. The text is largely a ritual handbook (*nibandha* or *paddhati*) while the extensive gloss, entitled *Subhagodayavāsanā*, provides the theoretical basis for the interpretation of *śrīcakra* deities.[84] Portions of both texts are quoted by later influential figures such as Maheśvarānanda in the *Parimala* autocommentary to his *Mahārthamañjarī* (*MAM*), Amṛtānanda in his *Dīpikā*, and Naṭanānandanātha in his *Cidvallī* gloss on the *KKV*. References in the *Ṛjuvimarśinī* confirm Śivānanda's authorship of these two works. Khanna, following the lists of preceptors in a variety of *hādimata* sources, maintains that Śivānanda is separated from Dīpakācārya, the author of the *Tripurasundarīdaṇḍaka*, by seven generations and that there are no texts ascribed to intermediary preceptors. Following Silburn's placement of Maheśvarānanda in the twelfth century, Śivānanda would naturally be considered much earlier since he is repeatedly referred to as the *paramaguru*.[85] Śivānanda's date now seems settled, however, as Dwiveda and Khanna argue convincingly for a later date for Maheśvara and thus place Śivānanda in this thirteenth- to fourteenth-century period of high literary activity.[86]

Śrīnivāsa Bhaṭṭa, better known by his initiated name Vidyānandanātha or Śrīvidyānandanātha, leaves no doubt about his commitment to Śrīvidyā despite the strong possibility of his having written the Śaiva ritual compendium entitled *Śivārcanacandrikā*.[87] His immense *Saubhāgyaratnākara* (*SRK*) is perhaps the most extensive of handbook of Śrīvidyā *yantra* worship (i.e., *śrīcakra pūjā*).[88] His teacher, Sundarācārya, a Kashmiri from Jālandhara, composed the voluminous *Lalitārcanacandrikā* (*LAC*) under the initiated name Saccidānandanātha. He did so, it is said, in order to dispel the doubts of his students.[89] The *LAC* is certainly a *paddhati* devoted to *śrīcakra* worship though it is not today influential.

Śrīnivāsa Bhaṭṭa's lineage is traced to his *paramaguru*, Svayamprakāśānandanātha who contemporary practictioners say was also an important Śrīvidyā adept. Like the Vidyānanda of the *Artharatnāvalī*, Śrīnivāsa is dated to the late twelfth century.[90] His detailed exposition of Śrīvidyā ritual, however, would seem to indicate a somewhat later date since there are no other comparable ritual elaborations available from this period. Bhāskararāya's frequent citations of Śrīnivāsa Bhaṭṭa likewise contribute to the authority of his work. Several living lineages in south India, including some that do not trace themselves to Bhāskararāya, deem Śrīnivāsa an incontrovertible authority. Unlike others, his works are influential in modern south India despite being unpublished. This would suggest that he left an imprint on oral traditions. While most contemporary practitioners do not have access to manuscripts, several stated that Śrīnivāsa was another migrant to the south from Kashmir. Being either a native son or a southern settler would suggest an enduring spiritual legacy even if his own lineage (*paramparā*) had vanished. Practitioners cite Śivānanda as an analogous example of the connections between Kashmiri and southern traditions.

The preeminent place for ritual textbooks in south Indian Śrīvidyā is reserved for the *Paraśurāmakalpasūtra* (*PKS*). The text's attribution to the divine Paraśurāma suggests to contemporary practitioners further evidence of its southern origins.[91] Teun Goudriaan's belief that the text is not much older than the sixteenth century remains unproven; several verses are quoted without recognition in the *Artharatnāvalī*.[92] The long chapters on initiation and the worship of Gaṇeśa have become standard references for contemporary practice.

Unlike other Vedānta-influenced texts of the Śaṅkara tradition, the *PKS* is undoubtedly a Kaula text heavily indebted to Pūrva-Mīmāṃsā; it includes mention of the *pañcamakāras* and elaborately describes *kāmakalā* meditation. Yet its authority is undiminished among conservative interpreters who ignore problematic issues. Though there is no internal evidence suggesting a relationship with the *Tripurā Upaniṣad*, Bhāskararāya states in his commentary on the Upaniṣad that "what is not found in one is found in the other."[93]

Rāmeśvara Sūri's nineteenth-century commentary on *PKS* entitled *Saubhāgyodaya*, which accompanies the popular printed edition, is best known for its virulent opposition to Bhāskararāya's (reputed) disciple Umānandanātha. Rāmeśvara was a south Indian Śrīvidyā initiate claiming a direct descent from Bhāskararāya through an unnamed disciple. His name curiously does not appear in any contemporary lineage lists, most of which trace themselves to Bhāskararāya through Umānandanātha. His popularity, it seems, comes from his inclusion in the available printed edition: once again, modern technology has helped shape the course of tradition.

Rāmeśvara disputes the established tradition that Bhāskararāya revised and approved Umānanda's *paddhati* stating that it is utterly inconsistent with the master's teachings. His criticism is often well-taken. Rāmeśvara offers no clues as to how Umānanda became identified as the authority on Bhāskararāya's work. Rāmeśvara depends on Bhāskararāya and his frequent identical citations indicate a special reliance on the *Setubandha*.[94]

Umānandanātha's *paddhati*, the *Nityotsava*, composed in 1775 C.E. is well-known by contemporary adepts though it is not considered as authoritative as the *PKS*. Perhaps its lack of divine authorship renders it open to criticism.[95] Several contemporary *paddhatis* claim "to base their presentation" on the *Nityotsava* but none appear to use the language of the original. Contemporary adepts claiming inheritance through Umānanda usually dismiss, ignore, or explain away Rāmeśvara's criticisms. In one instance, Umānanda's reference to the *vṛttatraya* as three circles surrounding the two sets of lotus petals of the *śrīcakra*—an interpretation Bhāskararāya does not accept—is interpreted as actually following Bhāskararāya's hidden intentions.[96]

Umānandanātha, like Bhāskararāya, was a Mahārāstran brahman. His given name was Jagannātha Pāṇḍita and while some claim he is the same person as the great logician of the same name, this cannot be the case.[97] In addition to the *NS*, he is also known for his biography of Bhāskararāya, the *Bhāskaravilāsa*.[98] The biography's exaggerated claims, including a long list of attributed but unrecovered works, unfortunately make it an unreliable historical document.[99] Umānanda's recently recovered *Hṛdayāmṛta*, however, is a poem of considerable merit though it adds little to our understanding of Śrīvidyā theology.[100] The limited circulation of the published edition of this text has not brought it the notoriety among contemporary practitioners it would otherwise doubtless achieve.

The dilemma of the attribution of sources to historical authors finds no better example than Bhāskararāya. Though unquestionably the dominant figure in contemporary Śrīvidyā tradition throughout India, the facts concerning Bhāskararāya's life are shrouded in the mythology of his spiritual accomplishments and culled almost entirely from Umānanda's pious biographical sketch.[101]

According to traditionalists, Bhāskararāya was born in the southern Vijayanagara kingdom but received the bulk of his education in Benares. His father, Gambhīrānanda, a Ṛg Vedic brahman of the Viśvamitra *gotra*, was himself a well-known scholar of the *Mahābhārata* and it was he who placed Bhāskararāya under the tuition of Narasiṃhadhvarin so that he might learn the eighteen traditional sciences.[102] During his sojourn in Benares, Bhāskararāya distinguished himself as a master of Vedic ritual and took full initiation (*pūrṇābhiṣeka*) into Śrīvidyā under the guru Śivadatta Śukla. Settling first on the banks of the Kṛṣṇa river at the request of his disciple Candrasena and later in the tiny hamlet of Tiruvalankādu in modern Tañjhavūr district, Tamilnadu, Bhāskararāya was gifted a village (or at least the *agrahara* portion) by the Maratha king Seforji sometime around 1750 C.E. The village on the opposite bank of the Kaveri river from Tiruvalankādu was named (or renamed) after him, Bhāskararājapuram.[103] Some contemporary biographers claim he was a leper cured by the power of the sun. This is mentioned to account for his name "Sun's Rays" (*bhāskara-rāya*) and his consistent use of words for the sun in the titles of his works. Bhāskararāya's tendency to use portions of his own name or synonyms for the sun in his titles seems to contemporary adepts an otherwise bizarre and egoistic flaw in his character.

Bhāskararāya's *Saubhāgyabhāskara* commentary on the *Lalitāsahasranāma* was completed in 1728 and his short, but extremely influential mantra treatise, the *Varivasyārahasya*, or "Secret of Worship," at about the same time. The *Setubanda* commentary on the *Vāmakeśvara Tantra* was completed in 1733 or 1741 C.E. and his three commentaries on the

Śākta *Bhāvana*, *Tripurā*, and *Kaula Upaniṣads* after nearly all his other work was finished.[104]

Bhāskararāya endorses Śrīvidyā according to the *vāmācāra* Kaula tradition more comprehensively than any earlier writer. Tolerant of others and self-disciplined in his approach, he focuses on issues rather than disputes. For example, rather than attack Lakṣmīdhara with whom he often disagrees he concentrates on establishing the reliability of the Kaula Tantras; he will even refer to him to support his own views. Determined to include Śaṅkara as part of Śrīvidyā, Bhāskararāya seems utterly unaffected intellectually by Śāṅkara *advaita* Vedānta.

Like other authors before him, Bhāskararāya seeks to instruct the initiated rather than apologize, defend, or promulgate his theology. Viewing themselves as mainstream Vaidikas, Śrīvidyā writers seem nonplussed by advocacy of convention defying behaviors; as Tantrics, they make no special effort to explain their tradition to "outsiders." In short, Śrīvidyā is not viewed as an alternative to some other tradition. Rather, all other forms of theology and ritual practice are viewed as subordinate to its secret practice. The absence of arguments for such claims of spiritual superiority only serve to reinforce the established view. This dual-edged strategy of maintaining popular, mainstream theological and ritual concepts and, at the same time, remaining aloof from outside criticism has not always worked as successfully for other Tantrics as it has for Śrīvidyā adepts.

While Śrīvidyā practitioners do not usually discuss their Tantric *sādhana* publicly, they have had a visible influence on Hindus who are not privy to their teachings or textually prescribed practices. Bhāskararāya is also an example of this type of figure: renowned as a Vedic scholar, a master of *mantraśāstra*, and a ritual expert, he was respected by conservatives, favored by the ruling class, and influential in popular religious activities of his day. With societal leadership came at least the appearances of the private tradition and, most evidently, the appearance of the *śrīcakra* in public forms of Śaiva-Śākta temple worship. Bhāskararāya is credited with the establishment of *śrīcakra*s as primary objects of worship within already established Śaiva-Śākta shrines throughout south India.[105] The same is true of Śaṅkarācārya.

The placement of the *śrīcakra* in public temples creates an "unsanctioned" ritual and iconographic element that supercedes established sources, such as Āgamas. As one contemporary adept noted:

> There is no scriptural source sanctioning the presence of a *śrīcakra* within a Hindu temple, or the practice of any *śrīcakra* worship. In every case what we see is that the *śrīcakra* has been put there by a saint or Śrīvidyā teacher whose own spiritual power has permitted

> him. People who know what is sanctioned in the Āgamas accept this unsanctioned form of worship. This is because there is no disputing that this is the highest form of the Devī and that some of the practice can be done openly. But what you see in temples is not the *śrīcakra* worship you see when it is done privately.[106]

REGIONAL AND VERNACULAR SOURCES OF ŚRĪVIDYĀ AND FURTHER REMARKS ON THE CONCEPT OF AUTHORITY AND SCRIPTURE

There is no better example of Śrīvidyā's influence on regional literature in south India than the *Navāvaraṇakīrthās* of Muttusvāmī Dīkṣitar. These Sanskrit songs praise various beneficent aspects of the goddess and take their name from the division of the *śrīcakra* into nine subcakras or *āvaraṇas* (literally, "obstacles"). As a theological source for Śrīvidyā they have not been particularly influential, but as part of Tamil devotionalism their importance extends far beyond initiated Śrīvidyā.

Contemporary practitioners maintain that Muttusvāmī, one of the three most famous composers of Karnatik classical music, was a Śrīvidyā adept and displayed a rather typical interest in other deities and forms of worship. One adept remarked:

> The songs are meant to praise and worship Devī in ways accessible to everyone. They are part of Śrīvidyā at the level of being available to all no matter how limited their qualifications for other forms of worship such as *śrīcakra pūjā*.[107]

While there is no historical evidence to support these claims, the songs themselves are frequently heard as devotional additions to the formal prescriptions of Śrīvidyā worship. The argument, however, is not that the songs have influenced Śrīvidyā but rather that Śrīvidyā has influenced Muttusvāmī.

The bulk of regional literature in south Indian vernacular languages consists of devotional songs, such as Muttusvāmī's, liturgies for worship, and commentaries that gloss major Sanskrit works. Since virtually all oral instruction in Śrīvidyā is given in local languages, the vernaculars are particularly important in the transmission of tradition and the study of Sanskrit sources. Without the vernacular oral tradition, the Sanskrit sources that form the core of Śrīvidyā teaching become increasingly remote and inaccessible to all but a few highly qualified initiates.[108]

While Sanskrit sources can cross regional boundaries, a given text's fate depends on the traditions of particular lineages. There are also cases of Śrīvidyā gurus having acknowledged the influence of particular works but then not including them as part of their formal instruction. Such sources necessarily do not become canonical for succeeding generations and yet remain a part of a lineage's collective consciousness. Gurus have retained the right to read all forms of scripture to suit their needs and to decide each disciple's case individually, be they Tantras claiming a divine origin or *śāstras* with known historical authors. Selective reading of sources and even more discriminating and selective transmission of materials remain key factors for determining the continuity of a particular lineage.

Some Sanskrit texts, such as the *Tripurārahasya* (*TR*), appear to have gained ground recently but were not important to historical writers.[109] Such texts appear to follow the spheres of influence established by popular gurus. There is no evidence, for example, that *TR* exercised an influence on Bhāskararāya or his eighteenth- and nineteenth-century disciples. While some works, such as the *VT* and *TT*, are important enough to transcend regional factors, others, such as *TR*, have exercised influence only in certain restricted areas—in this case the south.

Numerous examples can be given of sources reflecting predominantly northern strains of Śrīvidyā, such as the *Sammohana Tantra*.[110] This late Tantra's origins are unknown but its influence has been felt primarily in Bengal and Kashmir and one might tentatively conclude that it was composed somewhere in northern India (Bengal?).[111]

Śrīvidyā gurus frequently go beyond their own teachers both in terms of textual sources and in assimilation of other influences. In this way the tradition is not limited solely to materials individual teachers choose to pass onto students. As one adept put it:

> It is our duty to go beyond what our teachers have taught, that is, to become even greater than him. But this is not an easy task. The guru is like Śiva, whatever he says we are to do we must do. But this does not mean that we can do whatever he does without his permission. He may drink a caldron of hot iron to quench his thirst but what would happen to us if we followed him in this? If I study a work that my teacher has not taught me I must ask his spiritual permission and if he is no more [living] then I must ask my inner mind if it is part of our tradition. But I must never assume that what I think is tradition is important unless I receive some signal from some authority that it is acceptable. I may read anything but I can only adopt limited things.[112]

For a text to gain entry into a lineage's canon, a guru will usually claim that its content was either taught previously within the lineage or that it reflects lineage belief or practice. As the adept cited above points out, he is not free individually to make this decision but must respond to "tradition" and his own lineage's understanding of Śrīvidyā.

In contemporary Śrīvidyā, all sources bearing the title "Tantra" are subjected to this rather indeterminate test. Thus, a Tantra, may be deemed "scripture" inasmuch as it is agreed to be of divine origin, taught by Śiva or Śakti at a certain time to address specific needs, but it may not be deemed "authoritative" in a given lineage because it is either (1) unimportant to a given disciple's *sādhana* or (2) outside the lineage's self-understanding. Lakṣmīdhara when discussing Samayācāra, for example, never says that "objectionable" Kaula Tantras are not the words of Śiva nor does he imply that they may lack authority for non-Samayācārins; he merely maintains that they do not apply to Samayācārins.

The authority of scriptures is thus determined by appealing to criteria of qualification. Thus, when twice-born caste initiates are prohibited from performing certain activities, others (i.e., *śūdras*) are not so constrained. Lakṣmīdhara's view does not vitiate an entire catelogue of texts but rather imposes canonical standards for his tradition (*sampradāya*).

In their process of selective reading Śrīvidyā gurus seek out sources considered relevant to the qualifications of their lineage. Kaula Śrīvidyā adepts, for example, maintain that the sources espousing the use of the *pañcamakāra*s are of a higher order than others but then say only gurus may decide who is qualified to follow them. In contrast, Lakṣmīdhara rejects the *pañcamakāras* for Samayins and twice-born practitioners but does not exclude non-twice-borns from Samayācāra. One adept summarized the method of selective reading and reliance on the guru's discretion in this way:

> As a Śākta and a Tantric I accept all the Tantras as authoritative and by that I mean that all of them have come from God. But I do not necessarily follow them. This is not different than what we do with the Vedas. I am a Yajur Vedin, I follow the *Yajur Veda* on certain ritual matters and for some things the *Apastamba Dharmasūtra*. This does not mean that I reject the *Ṛg Veda* or the other Vedas or that I reject other Dharmaśāstras. It only means that I follow this one, not that others are not true. The same is true of the Tantras. We follow the teaching we are taught because it is suited to us. It may not be suited to others who have been taught something else.[113]

Śrīvidyā has avoided becoming a historical fossil primarily because it has successfully integrated theoretical and speculative elements into practice and has accommodated change by retaining powerful links to the past. This viability in the tradition is a result of its flexible but conservative structure of authority and the open but principled interpretation of scripture.

Chapter 4

The Goddess Lalitā Mahātripurasundarī:
The *Sthūla* Aspect

LALITĀ THE GREAT GODDESS

Śrīvidyā's principal deity, Lalitā Tripurasundarī, is a great goddess (*mahādevī*) conceived to subsume and surpass all others.[1] While Lalitā's origins in myth, iconography, and theology are uncertain, she is related to the "complete" pantheon of Hindu gods and goddesses. Śrīvidyā is self-consciously familiar with the characters of Vedic, Purāṇic, and Tantric literatures as well as those mentioned in local and regional traditions. All such figures are considered either Lalitā's creations or forces that she can control.

The goddess's image and myth described in Sanskrit texts is designed to advance Śrīvidyā's ultimately sectarian claim that *their* goddess is supreme. The ritual corpus is also augmented by creating liturgical as well as narrative works. This chapter describes the imagery and mythology of the goddess Lalitā Tripurasundarī and considers briefly the broader uses of texts in which she appears as a member of the pantheon of Tantric and Purāṇic deities.

The origins of the names "Lalitā" the "lovely" and "Tripurā" the "three cities," like her images and myths, are also uncertain. It is unclear whether the names "Lalitā" and "Tripurā" were originally compounded—as "Lalitā Tripurasundarī"—or if the names refer to two or more goddesses combined in a single figure. Certainly the goddess's icon and myth crystallized before corresponding mantric and yantric aspects.[2] As a proper name for the goddess, "Lalitā" appears in the early Purāṇas and in special connection with pilgrimages made to her shrine in the city of Prayāg.[3] "Lalitā" becomes a pan-Indian goddess no later than the seventh century.[4]

The two most important literary sources for Lalitā Tripurasundarī are not ancient. Both are post-ninth-century texts, of likely south Indian origin, attached to the *Brahmāṇḍa Purāṇa*. The *Lalitopākhyāna* or Tale of Lalitā contains the goddess's origin myth—to which we shall return. *Lalitopākhyāna* appears to have roots similar to the *Saundaryalaharī* attributed to Śaṅkara. It, too, was likely composed in either the Śṛṅgerī or Kāñcipuram Śāṅkara *maṭhas* in south India.[5] The Thousand Names of Lalitā (*Lalitāsahasranāma*), like other "thousand name" compilations, is a liturgical text composed in imitation of the *Viṣṇusahasranāma*.[6] It certainly predates *Lalitopākhyāna* but also assumes the interests of high-caste, Sanskrit-literate traditionalists. For Śrīvidyā practitioners Lalitā's thousand names, unlike her Tale, is a liturgical *and* theological resource for worshiping and understanding the goddess in her most accessible and physically recognizable aspect (*sthūlarūpa*).

THE MAKING OF A GREAT GODDESS

Śrīvidyā conforms to a basic theological structure common in Hindu Tantrism: the initially unified Absolute becomes a dyadic divinity composed of masculine and feminine complements; the binary godhead creates from its union a universe composed of triadic structures. Creation is understood as a process self-expansion (*prapañca*) in which the universe is considered identical to *and* different from the Absolute. Put differently, the Absolute creates a reflection (*vimarśa*) projecting its own inherent self-illumination (*prakāśa*).

The goddess encompasses both the dyadic godhead and the triadic structures that emerge as a consequence of the combination of masculine and feminine principles. Bhāskararāya makes this clear in his commentary on *Lalitāsahasranāma*:

> Thus there are three forms of Devī, which equally partake of both the illuminative (*prakāśa*) and reflective (*vimarśa*) aspects, namely the physical (*sthūla*), the subtle (*sūkṣma*), and the supreme (*parā*); the physical has hands, feet, etc.; the *subtle* consists of *mantra* and the *supreme* is the *vasanā* (though it means ideal or mental; according to Mantra-śāstra it is a technical word meaning real or own).

The *sthūla*, literally, the "physical" or "gross," image is considered the goddess's simplest form and refers essentially to her anthropomorphic icon. Śrīvidyā asserts that Śakti in her supreme aspect (*parāśakti*) manifests as benign (*saumya*) and beautiful (*saundarya*), rather than as terrifying (*ugra*) and horrifying (*ghora*). Thus, Lalitā is deliberately contrasted with such figures as Kālī and Durgā. Lalitā Tripurasundarī, however, is a totalization of great goddess conceptions.[7] In other words, Lalitā is identified with every aspect of the goddess in every possible form and mode of depiction. While primarily depicted as benign, she is also described as terrifying; similarly, she is both auspicious and inauspicious. These oppositions, as Frederique Marglin has pointed out, are not mutually exclusive but encompassing and dynamic.[8]

LALITĀ TRIPURASUNDARĪ AND HER SUBORDINATES

As a mythic character Lalitā is best compared to quasi-independent goddesses, such as Kālī and Durgā.[9] Unlike Viṣṇu's consorts Śrī or

Lakṣmī, Lalitā's auspiciousness (*śrī*) and beneficence (*saumya*) are not attributes derived primarily from her subservience to a male deity.[10] Lalitā, however, is never totally severed from her consort Śiva; instead she is identified with Pārvatī, Umā, and other consorts of the ascetic god.[11]

Śrīvidyā literature refers to the great goddess by several variants on the name Lalitā Tripurasundarī including Tripurā, Tripurasundarī, Mahātripurasundarī, and Rājarājeśvarī, "the Queen of Kings."[12] Contemporary Śrīvidyā practitioners prefer to call the goddess by the generic "Śrīdevī." While this name resolves no ambiguities of association, Śrīvidyā writers make clear that their "Śrī" is differently conceived than the Vaiṣṇava's Śrī who is ever subordinate to Viṣṇu. But like Śrī who consorts with Viṣṇu, Lalitā, too, is the ideal Hindu woman conforming to Sanskritic ideals. Being the supreme deity does not prevent her from being a dutiful and obedient wife, an "auspicious one" (*sumaṅgalī*) who fulfills both domestic roles and the social expectations of brahman tradition. She is called "*saubhāgya*," the "prosperous" or the "bountiful," because as wife and mother she confers on others the blessings of prosperity and life-giving auspiciousness (*śrī*).[13]

Lalitā is also capable of destruction and is called by the names of goddesses considered horrific (*ghora*) or especially horrific (*ghoratarā*).[14] However, in her primary mythic portrayal in which she destroys the demon Bhaṇḍa, she retains her benign appearance and so represents "the potency of the joining of both auspiciousness and inauspiciousness."[15] Her auspiciousness is made stable and consistent by her relationship with Śiva and therefore, unlike Śiva, she is utterly predictable in her anger and perfectly under control even when it is unclear if she controls herself.[16]

The physical (*sthūla*) goddess is also the primary focus for ritual acts of loving devotion (*bhakti*). Rāmeśvara in his commentary on *PKS*, 1.5. says that the goddess's physical form (*sthūlarūpa*) is known through meditational verses (*dhyānasloka*), which describe her and provide a basis for contemplation.[17] These meditational verses appear commonly in ritual manuals and mantric digests (*paddhatis* and *nibandhas*) and create a hierarchy of sub-aspects each bearing its own traits and serving different purposes in worship. Included among Lalitā's sub-aspects is Bālā, the "youthful" or "virginal," Tripurasundarī, who is described as a physical form but who is worshiped almost exclusively in the subtle form (*sūkṣmarūpa*) of a mantra. Bālā's mantra is often used in preparation for the "higher" mantras of the Auspicious Tripurasundarī (Saubhāgyatripurasundarī) or the Great Tripurasundarī (Mahātripurasundarī). Thus, in addition to the hierarchy of physical forms (*sthūlarūpa*) there is a concomitant mantric hierarchy. To worship any mantric form requires a higher level of qualification (*adhikāra*) than any physical form.

Meditational verses that describe subordinate deities either fulfill certain theological expectations or provide access to specific aspects considered appropriate to accomplish a given objective. Precisely which verse should be used and which aspect of the goddess is invoked depends on lineage custom. Some concentrate only on the goddess in her supreme (*parama*) aspect, leaving aside those considered subordinate or preliminary. Others utilize the hierarchy of goddess aspects and invoke other, lesser deities to accomplish "lesser" tasks. As one contemporary adeptly put it:

> The supreme form of *devī* can accomplish all things but should not be called upon for anything less than the highest goal of liberation. Sometimes we call upon other *devīs* and sometimes other gods, such as Gaṇeśa, depending on the circumstances. One does not call an electrical engineer to change a light bulb.[18]

Not all Śrīvidyā practitioners consider worship of a subordinate goddess, like Bālātripurasundarī, necessary before worshiping the great Tripurasundarī. Thus, the creation of a pantheon of subordinate aspects of the goddess does not mean there is a strict hierarchy of initiation and worship or that tradition demands specific normative ritual patterns. In some lineages Bālātripurasundarī worship is considered a necessary means by which to introduce Śrīvidyā to fledgling initiates. In other lineages, Bālātripurasundarī and other goddesses are not part of regular worship or patterns of initiation. Instead such deities should be seen as part of Śrīvidyā's expanding catalogue of divinity which is designed, in part, to provide for certain types of ideological and ritual elaboration.[19]

Subordinate deities and lesser aspects of Lalitā are generally not important to historical commentators of *Śrīkula* Tantras. Rather they appear in ritual digests that do not usually function as practical liturgies but as the preferred medium through which to advance theological speculation. In other words, it is more important to consider Bālātripurasundarī's place in Lalitā's hierarchy of aspects than it is to worship her formally.

Lalitā Tripurasundarī's meditational verses (*dhyānaśloka*) distill the elaborate picture drawn in other Sanskrit texts, especially the Thousand Names of Lalitā (*Lalitāsahasranāma*). Meditational verses are usually recited before and during the worship of the *sthūla* goddess:

> I contemplate the goddess who is red [in color or dress and] bears [in her four hands] the noose, the goad, the flower arrows and the

bow [of sugarcane], [She who] with [her] lustre envelops the [twelve *siddhis*] beginning with the power to be minute.[20]

In *Lalitāsahasranāma*, Lalitā is seated on the lion's throne like a great queen (n. 2–3) who emerged from the altar of the fire of consciousness (n. 4). Manifesting herself to fulfill the wishes of the gods (n. 5) and shining like a thousand suns (n. 6) she has four arms and holds in her hands the noose of desire (n. 7–8 and n. 810), the elephant goad of wrath and worldly knowledge (n. 9), the sugarcane bow of the mind (n. 10) and the arrows of the five essences (*tanmātras*) (n. 11). This description sets Lalitā apart from other goddesses and puts her in league with other great goddesses.[21]

The description continues: She bathes the universe in her rosy complexion (n. 12), she has *campaka, aśoka, puṃnāga,* and *saugandhika* flowers in her hair (n. 13), and wears crown of jewels (n. 13–14). She bears the auspicious mark of marriage [between her eyes] and appears modest in her demeanor (n. 16–25); her thin waist is burdened by heavy breasts (n. 36). The Lord of Desire or Śiva in the form of Kāmeśvara drowns in the fullness of her smile (n. 28); she is dressed in red adorned with a belt of jewelled bells and the crescent moon glimmering above her crown (n. 29–51). *Saundaryalaharī* augments Lalitā's description as the archetypal Indian beauty and dutiful wife. In addition, she is Queen Mother of the universe:

> Banded with tinkling girdle, heavy with breasts like the frontal lobes of elephants, slender of waist, with face like the full moon of autumn, bearing on the palms of her hands bow, arrows, noose, and goad, let there be seated before us the pride of him who shook the cities.[22]

Lalitopākhyāna completes the goddess's image:

> Anklets and other ornaments on her feet produce a charming tinkling sound. The sound of her bangles is likewise charming. Her lower legs have subdued the pride of the Love's arrow quiver. Her thighs bear a complexion like that of an elephant's trunk and forelobes or a plantain tree. Her loins are rapped by a thin red silk cloth, smooth to the touch.[23]

Lalitāsahasranāma's statement that the goddess wears the thread signifying marriage (n. 30) offers the best evidence that the text is south Indian in origin since this custom is non-Vedic and is not practiced by north Indians.

Her description is also theologically significant. She wears a pearl nose ring composed of the collected scriptures (n. 290); she has eyes like lotuses (n. 247) and lips that put to shame the color of fresh corals and bimba fruits. Elsewhere she has a thousand eyes (n. 282) and a thousand feet (n. 284) and is without beginning or end (n. 296). She is attended by Hari (i.e. Viṣṇu), Brahmā (i.e., Śiva), and Indra as well as by Lakṣmī and Sarasvatī who stand on her left and right and bear fans (n. 614) to honor her. She is surrounded by herds of elephants conducted by the deity Sampatkarī (n. 66) and tens of thousands of horses conducted by Aśvārūḍhā, a Tantric goddess (n. 67).[24] In one place she is seated on the lap of Śiva in the form of Kāmeśvara (n. 52), in another, it says she sits on the five corpses of Brahmā, Viṣṇu, Rudra, Īśvara, and Sadāśiva (n. 249).[25] Surely *Lalitāsahasranāma*'s author(s) understood that even the depiction of the goddess should be dynamic. Further, the text views Lalitā as the divinity behind members of the Hindu pantheon.

Three characteristics unify Lalitā's mythic and iconic symbolism: She is royal, auspicious, and subsuming. All three characteristics are manifestations of her most essential attribute: power (*śakti*).

Lalitā's royalty is related to her auspiciousness (*śrī*), which includes material prosperity, well-being, and power. She is worshiped by the king of kings (n. 305) and is called "Queen" (*rajñī*, n. 306) because she rules over the universe, including all the fourteen worlds (n. 294). Presiding over a kingdom (*iśvarī*, n. 271) as its protectress (n. 266), she acts like a loving, but firm mother (n. 1 and 823) towards her wards. She slays demonic enemies both generic (n. 318) and particular (n. 65) and removes fear (n.121) from those who worship her; she grants the wishes of all (n. 291) by dispensing justice, including good and bad results (n. 288). She is herself beyond all states and emotions (n. 263) and so is devoid of virtue and vice (n. 255) in the sense that she does not act in self interest. As divine royalty she is omnipresent (n. 256), not confined to a body (n. 147), unchanging (n. 145), tranquil (n. 141), and indestructible (n. 143).

In sum, she is the embodiment of all encompassing power (*śakti*) that manifests in two distinct ways. First, as a conscious and creative personality her power is dispositional. That is, she has the capacity to transform creation however she wishes. She limits her dispositional power herself and by submitting to her masculine counterpart Śiva. Second, her power is episodic. *Lalitāsahasranāma*, for example, notes instances in which the goddess has intervened to alter the course of events in the world. Contemporary practitioners assert that the goddess continues to act episodically in their lives and in the course of world events. The goddess's episodic power is primarily directed towards rectification; she sets aright situations by adjudicating the Law (*dharma*). But unlike sovereigns who are caught in the conundrum of authority in which they must act in ways that invariably defile the eternal law by having to assert their own political self interests, the goddess manages both realms with equal efficiency and without compromising her status.[26]

Lalitā's royalty further signifies her conservative social and religious nature. Lalitā is a deity designed to endorse and legitimize the social and historical vision of aristocratic brahmanism. She is called *varṇāśramavidhyāyinī* (n. 286), the one who establishes the four estates (*varna*) of brahman, kṣatriya, vaiṣya, and śūdra and the four stages of life (*āśrama*), student, householder, forest-recluse, and mendicant. Likewise, she is known through the four Vedas (n. 335) because she is the mother of the Vedas (n. 338) and is fond of the five sacrifices prescribed in the Vedas (n. 946).[27] Quoting the *Kurma Purāṇa*, Bhāskarārāya summarizes the goddess's convention-affirming nature:

> *Karman* is ordained by the Srutis and Smrtis according to castes and orders; always perform this *karman* associated with knowledge of the Self for the sake of liberation. Devotion arises from righteousness (*dharma*), by devotion the supreme is attained. *Dharma* means sacrifice, etc. ordained by the Srutis and Smrtis. *Dharma* is not to be otherwise known, because from Vedas alone *dharma* came into existence; hence the aspirant for liberation should depend on the Vedas which are my form, for the sake of *dharma*. By my command the divine Brahmā, for the sake of protecting the Vedas, created the Brāhmanas at the beginning and established them in their respective duties.[28]

Lalitā bestows on worldly sovereigns the right to rule (n. 692) even as she delights in dominion (n. 686) and subjugates all the worlds (n. 698). She destroys heretics, by which is meant those who espouse traditions or religions that are anti-Vedic. However, she is also the form of all the Tantras (n. 206) and embodied in certain controversial Tantric rituals, such as *kāmakalādhyāna* (n. 322). Without the slightest sense of controversy or contradiction, Lalitā is made into a Tantric image of potency and power completely in control of herself and in conformity with the values of male-dominated brahmanism. She seeks to uphold the status quo but will not be bound to it; she gives life and fortune, but reserves the right to take it away; she embodies enjoyment (n. 293), sensuality (n. 321), and playfulness (n. 340) as well as restraint (n. 900) in her role as chaste wife (n. 128) devoted to her husband (n. 320). It is in this role she most clearly displays her second characteristic: auspiciousness (*śrī* or *maṅgalā*).

Lalitā embodies auspiciousness (n. 967), which implies her life-giving roles of mother (n. 457) and wife.[29] While Lalitā's royalty indicates power over the universe, her particular auspiciousness emphasizes the transfer of power to others, especially to her husband. As the paradigm of the married female or *suvāsinī* (n. 970) who confers blessings by her fulfilling her assigned roles as loyal wife (n. 820) and mother, she is called *sumaṅgalī* (n. 967). Quoting the *Brahmāṇḍa Purāṇa*, Bhāskararāya observes that as *Satī* the goddess who is the daughter of Dakṣa (n. 598) and the wife of Śiva is "the faithful spouse...she ever dwells with Śiva and he is never deserted by her."[30] Such dutiful submission is hardly inconsistent with her role as sovereign since the sovereign rules to serve others.

By combining royalty and auspiciousness the goddess gains an edge over her male counterparts. Bhāskararāya characterizes the nature of her auspiciousness by quoting the *Devī Purāṇa* in his remarks on *Lalitāsahasranāma* n. 200, *sarvamaṅgalā*, which means literally, "all auspiciousness":

> The *Devī Pr.* says, "She gives all the good fortune [longed for] in the heart, all desired good objects, hence she is called Sarvamaṅgalā. And she removes the pain of devotees and gives to Hara all the best and choicest things, hence, Sarvamaṅgalā.[31]

Lalitā's sensuality, which flows with desire and pleasure (n. 863), is yet another facet of her auspiciousness. However, her passion arises as a legitimate human aim (*puruṣārtha*) and so is reserved for her husband (n. 796) to whom she is utterly devoted (n.320).

All of the goddess's qualities are complemented by their opposites. The goddess's sensuality is accompanied by both asceticism and independence. On at least two occasions she is called "independent" (n. 723 and n. 914) and one who exists "without support" (n. 877), features which stand in contrast to her admission of dependence and submission. The stately and aristocratic Lalitā, who is called tranquil (n. 141 and n. 963), is likewise capable of enormous power, anger, and destruction—all of which are directed at some manifestation of evil, ignorance, or inauspiciousness. Embodying opposites is critical to understanding the third thematic continuity in Lalitā's portrayal: her totalizing character.

There are two fundamental ways in which Lalitā's totalizing character is expressed. First are those names and descriptions that suggest logical ultimacy, finality, or conceptual nonduality. For example, when she is called "the eternal" (n. 136 [*nityā*] and n.951 [*sāsvatī*]), "reality itself" (n. 907), "the great" (n. 774), or beyond all gender distinctions, the idea is to reach beyond comparison and conceptualization.[32] Second are depictions that rely on either comparison or contrast, such as those in which other deities or beings are deemed inferior, dependent, or her partial manifestations. As we have already noted, contrasts are drawn with respect to her own character such that seemingly contradictory or complementary attributes are made to encompass all possibilities. Such contrasting attributes account for the majority of epithets in *Lalitāsahasranāma*.

The most important contrast in her character is her identification with the dangerous, horrific, and courageous warrioress who is the consumer of the universe (n. 890) and the slayer of a host of different demons. *Lalitāsahasranāma* identifies Lalitā as both the great Kālī (n. 751) and Durgā (n. 140). These identifications serve Lalitā's followers in at least two ways. First, she is identified as the goddess behind these popular and powerful figures; such implicit comparison among great goddesses (*mahādevī*) makes explicit the claim that Lalitā is foremost among them. Second, these identifications restate Lalitā's relationship with Śiva and imply parallel myths or comparable theological structures.[33]

Lalitā's violence, like her asceticism and eroticism, is calculated and necessary to sustain order in the universe. Were Lalitā utterly benign, the forces of evil would prevail; were she not erotic, Śiva would create an imbalance through his ascetic *tapas*; and were she not married and appear submissive to Śiva, she would not be able to project her full potential as the source of his power; were she not the source of auspiciousness and inauspiciousness, the world of complementary opposites would cease to be of interest. Lalitā not only balances and counters Śiva, but demonstrates how Śiva is ultimately dependent on her.[34]

The Tantric Vaiṣṇava Pāñcarātra creates a similar set of complementary parallels between Viṣṇu and Lakṣmī and differs significantly from descriptions of Śrī as a subservient and unequal partner, such as in Śrī Vaiṣṇava theology. Lalitā, like the Pāñcarātra conception of Lakṣmī, acts independently by taking over the cosmic functions of the male deity; yet she does not defy the god's wishes.[35] In contrast to most Vaiṣṇava conceptions of Lakṣmī, however, Lalitā destabilizes temporarily for the purpose of reasserting order.[36]

The most important mythic portrayal of Lalitā clearly places her in the pattern of Durgā as slayer of the buffalo demon (*Mahiṣāsuramardinī*). It may even be the case that the author(s) of the Lalitā myth have the *Devīmāhātyma* in mind: a seemingly invincible demon wrecks havoc on the world and the gods and must be destroyed to restore harmony to the cosmos.[37] There are six stages in the structure of the Durgā myth.[38]

1. The demon gains power usually through austerity, is rewarded with a boon, and becomes nearly invincible.
2. The demon defeats the gods and usurps their roles.
3. The gods prepare revenge by creating a special adversary who can

defeat the demon in spite of the boon or else lesser gods petition one of the great deities (Śiva, Viṣṇu, or a great goddess) for help.
4. The battle takes place, often with an army created by the hero or heroine.
5. The demon is slain or subdued.
6. The gods praise the demon slayer.

This pattern is repeated in the *Lalitopākhyāna*'s version of the slaying of Bhaṇḍāsura with a few important variations and embellishments. The myth begins with the destruction of Love by Śiva who resents the disturbance in his meditative yoga. The story continues:

> The figure of a man is fashioned out of the ashes of Love by Citrakarmā, the lord of the *gaṇas*. He then propitiates Śiva who teaches him a mantra called the *śatarūdriya* which he repeats to Śiva's great pleasure.[39] Śiva grants his eulogizer a boon which unites to his own strength half the power of his antagonist. Further, he is granted the power to rule for sixty thousand years, and Śiva praises him saying, "Bhaṇḍ! Bhaṇḍ!," from which he gains his name. However, since Bhaṇḍa was "born of the fire of anger," he becomes dreadful and through the urging of Śukra, the preceptor of the *daitya* demons, he increases his power by rebuilding the city of Soṇitapura to resemble the city of the gods, by worshiping Śiva and by performing Vedic sacrifices.[40] In the meantime, his sixty thousand year reign under the protection of Śiva lapses. Viṣṇu then creates Māyā to enchant Bhaṇḍa in order to reclaim some of the strength of Indra and the sages, who now fear for the welfare of the world. The sage Nārada implores Indra to perform penances to propitiate the supreme goddess who alone can alter Bhaṇḍa's increasing strangle hold over the world. Bhaṇḍa, on the advice of a demoness named Bhīmakarmā, attempts a preemptive strike against the city of the gods in order to check Indra's influential penance offered to the goddess. The goddess prevents the demon army from entering by creating a series of ramparts that are successively destroyed. The gods, however, are fearful of Bhaṇḍa's boon that appropriates their own strength; Indra enjoins them to sacrifice their own flesh according to Vedic rites. At the conclusion of this rite the goddess appears before them; they are cured of their fears and aliments and begin to sing her praises.
>
> The goddess is pleased and agrees to defeat Bhaṇḍa and to bless all those who eulogize her with virtue, fame, learning, long life, and progeny. In the meantime, with the celestial city under siege, the gods, sages, and demi-gods, led by Brahmā arrange for the goddess's marriage to Śiva in the form of Kāmeśvara, who then becomes her battlefield ally.[41] Lalitā honors her husband but proclaims her independence. After a number of years elapse, Lalitā marches into battle with her cavalry of *śakti*s and creates a variety of special weapons, particularly missiles and other machines (*yantra*) from the

noose and goad that she holds in two of her hands. Her accompaniment includes the female yogis (*yoginīs*) who preside over the "king of cakras" (*cakrarāja*), that is, the *śrīcakra*, all of whom are but parts of her. Bhaṇḍa, on hearing of the approaching army, boasts about his strength and dismisses the army of *śakti*s as "feeble women."[42] He is further assured upon hearing that the leader of army is named "Lalitā" who is "true to her name" and therefore "soft and delicate in features like a flower."[43]

Lalitā's army, however, proves to be more than a match; Bhaṇḍa's generals begin to fall in succession followed by his sons who are slain by Lalitā's daughter, Bālāmba. Lalitā also creates the elephant-headed Gaṇeśa—in this instance from her own laugh—in order to destroy a particularly powerful weapon and the brother of Bhaṇḍa.[44] Having accomplished this task, Gaṇeśa then issues forth from his own mouth a host of elephant-faced heroes in order to destroy an army of demon elephants. Lalitā, being pleased with her son's exploits, grants him as a boon the right of being worshiped before all other deities. The rest of Bhaṇḍa's immediate family is slain until, finally, Bhaṇḍa is forced to fight himself. He unleashes an arsenal of specialized missiles which create new hosts of demons. Lalitā is undaunted; she laughs in challenge and from this laugh emerges the goddess Durgā. Durgā ornaments herself with jewelry fashioned by the Vedic blacksmith Viśvakarman and wields weapons given to her by Śiva, Viṣṇu, Varuṇā, Indra, and the Maruts. She strikes down the demon Mahiṣa. Lalitā then creates several of the *avatāra*s of Viṣṇu, including the tortoise and boar to dispatch specific elements of Bhaṇḍa's formidable army. Bhaṇḍa then knits from his eyebrows tens of thousands of Hiraṇyakaśipus. Lalitā, in turn, creates Prahlāda who slays the Hiraṇyakaśipus and discharges the remainder of Bhaṇḍa's self-created army by fashioning more powerful adversaries from her fingernails. Bhaṇḍa counters by creating the demon Rāvana who is destroyed by Kodaṇḍarāma and Lakṣmana created from Lalitā's index fingernail. In the end, only Bhaṇḍa remains. Lalitā slays him with the missile called "the great kāmeśvara" (*mahākāmeśvara*), which has the splendor of a thousand suns. Lalitā is praised by all the gods who implore her on behalf of Love's wife Rati to revive the god of Love, out of whose ashes Bhaṇḍa was created. She complies with their request, Rati is overjoyed, the gods again eulogize Lalitā, and Love declares his unending gratitude.[45]

Lalitāsahasranāma offers only slight variations on the *Lalitopākhyāna* account and creates a list of epithets that deal specifically Bhaṇḍāsura's slaying, all of which deal with the prevailing themes of power (*śakti*) and auspiciousness (*śrī*).[46] In the myth, Lalitā's power (*śakti*) is linked to but not dependent on her ability to create confusion or deception, that is, her *māyā*. She is capable of ferocity but prefers to create ferocious images out of small portions of herself and therefore remain a predominantly benign and life-giving (or auspicious, *śrī*) goddess. Ultimately, she slays the desirous demon with desire, that is, with the missile called "lord of desire."

While the goddess is petitioned here as the most powerful of divinities her dispositional power allows her to carry out her will without involving herself in the activity. Like a royal commander, Lalitā delegates authority and enters the fray only when no other figure can match the adversary. Lalitā's benign image is initially underestimated and even mistaken by Bhaṇḍa, ostensibly by her power of deception (*māyā*). There is no mistaking Durgā who enters to slay Mahiṣa or the various *avatāras* of Viṣṇu who fulfill equally familiar Purāṇic roles. Lalitā's form may deceive but deception is only an aspect of her method and character: others, like Bhaṇḍa, deceive themselves by thinking that a life-giving, beneficent, and compassionate female is incapable of righteous anger or displays of power.

Lalitā's myth in *Lalitopākhyāna* resembles her portrayal in *Lalitāsahasranāma* in several important ways. First, Lalitā is a distinctive and identifiable goddess with her own particular associations and activities. She is capable of assuming either a feminine or masculine gender and also of transcending gender. She is the origin of deities who other Hindus treat as their supreme divinity and, in this sense, she is clearly a sectarian figure. She requires only a minimal effort to manufacture other great gods: all emerge either from her fingernails or her laughter. Lalitā not only surpasses all other powers and divinities but creates them. She is royal in the sense of being commander-in-chief and the undisputed leader of the gods, and she is auspicious, in the sense of being the ultimate life-giving force who creates and takes away life. Even in war she defines the boundaries of legitimate (i.e., dharmic) relationships.

Second, Lalitā's story conforms to a well-established structure of great goddess myths. Continuity in form with other goddess myths does not diminish Lalitā's stature nor dilute her distinctive character. Rather, by fulfilling normative expectations and offering significant elaboration, Lalitā is raised to the level of "every-*śrī*," that is, every form and every ideal associated with the notion of *śrī*: prosperity, well-being, royal power, and capability.[47] As a battling goddess her identity is rooted in Purāṇic associations and theological values; there are no Vedic goddesses involved in either blood sacrifices or battle.[48]

Third, the anthropomorphic Lalitā (*sthūlarūpa*) becomes an exoteric goddess to be propitiated and worshiped by everyone. Both *Lalitopākhyāna* and the *Lalitāsahasranāma* insist that love (*bhakti*) alone can bring the worldly enjoyments (*bhukti*) and the ultimate liberation (*mukti*). Whatever else is said in Śrīvidyā texts about levels and types of worship, here she is portrayed as a goddess for everyone.

Fourth, Lalitā's names and activities can be associated with specific regions and local deities. The *Lalitopākhyāna* names several places in particular; the *sthūlarūpa* divinity later becomes part of a method of locating and localizing Śrīvidyā in south India.

The fifth and final point is that Lalitā's physical form is used as a gateway to her more abstract mantric and yantric forms. *Lalitopākhyāna*, for example, associates her with the *cakrarāja*, which it describes in unmistakable terms as the *śrīcakra*. In this case, however, the yantra's esoteric symbolism is encoded and obscured deliberately by identifying her army leaders' names with the yantra's attendant deities. While there is no mistaking her association with the esoteric symbolism of the *śrīvidyā* mantra or the *śrīcakra* even in myth, the emphasis on the anthropomorphic form (*sthūlarūpa*) is meant to create a more intellectually accessible and ritually localized goddess.

THE ICONOGRAPHIC AND MYTHIC LALITĀ IN SOUTH INDIAN TEMPLES

Lalitā's relationship to specific local goddesses and places is confirmed by textual epithets or myths. In south India she is unambiguously identified with Kāmākṣī of Kāñcipuram whose image is nearly identical to the descriptions of *Lalitopākhyāna* and *Lalitāsahasranāma*. *Lalitāsahasranāma* calls her Kāmākṣī (n. 62) which Bhāskararāya glosses as "the special name of the presiding deity of Kāñcipura."[49] *Lalitopākhyāna* says, "She is Lalitā. She alone has manifested herself as Kāmākṣī in Kāñci. Sarasvatī, Rāma, and Gaurī worship that primordial deity alone." The Śāṅkara tradition in Kāñcipuram, which is associated with the authorship of these texts, today controls the Kāmākṣī temple and reinforces the association of the goddess with the interests of the *smārta* brahman community.

While relatively recent dates must be assigned to the Kāmākṣī temple and cult (post-tenth century, C.E.), common depictions of Lalitā put the *śrīcakra* at her feet in a fashion similar to Kāmākṣī of Kāñcipuram. Kāmākṣī's image differs from Lalitā in only two minor ways: her left leg is crossed rather than extended from her seated posture and a parrot sits atop the flowers she holds in her lower right hand. Kāmākṣī's iconography has important theological implications. Kāmākṣī's four arms (instead of two) suggest that she is more like Lalitā than other important benign (*saumya*) goddesses in south Indian temples; her status as a quasi-independent figure who can stand apart from Śiva as a *mahādevī* is assured by this iconographic feature.

Lalitāsahasranāma (n. 734) also identifies Lalitā as the dancing goddess (*naṭeśvarī*). Bhāskararāya informs us this is none other than

Śivakāmasundarī, the consort of the dancer Śiva Naṭarāja of Cidambaram. Śivakāmī is a two-armed standing figure who resembles Lalitā only inasmuch as she is a benign consort of Śiva.

In those Śrīvidyā texts associated with south Indian rather than Kashmiri tradition—that is, *Lalitāsahasranāma, Lalitopākhyāna,* and the works of Śrīvidyānanda, "Śaṅkara," "Gauḍapāda," and Bhāskararāya—there is a willingness to extend the imagery and character of Lalitā Tripurasundarī beyond the confines of her specific iconography and associations.[50] In Tamilnadu Sanskritic traditions identify most local goddesses with *mahādevī* and by implication with the texts that center on Lalitā Tripurasundarī.

In addition to Kāmākṣī and Śivakāmasundarī, two other important figures in the south Indian temple tradition are associated with Lalitā: Mīnākṣī of Madurai and Akhilandeśvarī of Tiruchirappalli. While Mīnākṣī's associations with Śrīvidyā are recondite, Akhilandeśvarī is more obviously connected since she wears the *śrīcakra* as earrings. Mīnākṣī's association with the *śrīcakra* has been a part of her cult in recent times but is largely unacknowledged by her priests. While the priests condone these associations, they do not discuss them nor do they incorporate them into their ritual.[51] For example, the image of Mīnākṣī is embossed on coins or amulets, the obverse of which bears a *śrīcakra*. These coins, along with pictures of Mīnākṣī standing above a *śrīcakra,* are popular images sold in shops inside the Madurai temple; they are ostensibly sanctioned by temple authorities.

The association of Akhilandeśvarī and Mīnākṣī with the *śrīcakra* establishes an important principle. Local goddesses need not physically resemble Lalitā nor must they be mentioned by name in Śrīvidyā texts. The local goddess retains her own particular anthropomorphic characteristics, mythology, and her own meditational verse (*dhyānaśloka*); yet each is identified with the *śrīcakra* that connects local divinities with the "greater" ideology of Lalitā Tripurasundarī. Other goddesses, such as Candrāmba of the village of Bhāskararājapuram, are similarly identified.

In his commentary on *Lalitāsahasranāma,* Bhāskararāya seems especially keen to identify Lalitā with regional goddesses both in north and south India. For example, on *Lalitāsahasranāma,* n. 936, *viśvālākṣī,* literally "large-eyed," Bhāskararāya remarks, "According to Padma Pr. she is the deity worshiped at Benares. Though the word *viśāla,* means Badrikāśrama, here it means Nepālapīṭha as both the places are in the Himalaya regions."[52]

The absence of a major temple in south India dedicated to Lalitā or Tripurasundarī does not suggest that these names are wanting in familiarity. *Lalitāsahasranāma,* for example, is extremely popular in south India at all levels of society. Śrīvidyā's conception of Lalitā's *sthūlarūpa* and her identification with local goddesses places her squarely within Hindu devotional traditions (*bhakti*) of worship (*pūjā*) based on seeing the deity (*darśan*).

Further, the physical image of the goddess becomes an important vehicle for asserting the intellectual and ritual interests of south Indian Śaiva *smārta* brahmans who identify with the Śāṅkara tradition. By commanding the literature and the interpretation of Lalitā's icon and myth, Śrīvidyā-oriented *smārtas* gain a degree of influence over both temple rites and private forms of Hindu spiritual discipline (*sādhana*)—influence that they might otherwise not be able to exercise since they are not usually temple priests or formal ascetics.[53]

The Śāṅkara *maṭhas* likewise use devotion to the goddess's *sthūlarūpā* to extend their influence. By treating orthopraxy as orthodoxy, the Śāṅkarites diminish the significant differences between Śaṅkara's non-dualistic (*advaita*) Vedānta and Śrīvidyā's Kashmiri Śaiva-based monism.[54] With serious philosophical differences reduced to mere scholasticism, the two traditions connect by sharing imagery, worship (*pūjā*), and ideas of devotion (*bhakti*). Further, the traditional Tantric disdain for renunciation, shared by most Śrīvidyā writers, is rendered moot by the Śāṅkarites' public embrace of a tradition that emphasizes both enjoyment (*bhukti*) of this world and ultimate liberation (*mukti*). Śāṅkarites need not abandon the claim that renunciation is a viable method for liberation but neither are they forced to argue (as Śaṅkara did) that one may obtain liberation only in this *āśrāma*. While later Śrīvidyā writers, such as Bhāskararāya and Rāmeśvara Sūri, endorse the historical association of the Śāṅkara tradition with Śrīvidyā, public worship of the goddess by members of the modern Śāṅkara tradition adds a social dimension to Śāṅkarite influence that would otherwise be absent.

The historical connections between Śrīvidyā communities and exoteric goddess worship deserve more detailed investigation, though several important observations can now be made. First, the textual exposition of Lalitā's iconography and mythology cannot be understood without taking into consideration the social and religious settings in which texts were composed. Both the *Lalitāsahasranāma* and *Lalitopākhyāna* appear to have been written with the deliberate intent to expand the great goddess cult beyond esoteric interests and to bring Lalitā worship into the public domain. At the same time, the parochial theological interests of the texts are declared to be in every Śākta's interest. Sometimes specific historical and theological relationships are put at stake, such as the relationship between *Saundaryalaharī* and the Śāṅkara tradition or *Lalitopākhyāna* and the Kāmākṣī cult of Kāñcipuram.[55] Second, the texts are designed as descriptions and narratives as well as for ritual use. In other words, the texts' visual images and ideological values are often described in terms of ritual acts and are designed to expand the ritual repertoire. For example, descriptions of Lalitā's *sthūlarūpa* can be used as mantras or devotional liturgies in different situations and at different levels of ritual practice. Thus, Lalitā becomes accessible *in the form* of a liturgical text that provides both the structure and content of devotion.

Śrīvidyā practitioners distinguish themselves from non-initiates who use *Lalitāsahasranāma* and other texts focused on the *sthūlarūpa* in two ways. First, the descriptions of the goddess's *sthūlarūpa* become foci for expanded commentary on the subtle (*sūkṣma*) mantra and transcendent (*parā*) yantra manifestations of the goddess. Though Hindus not initiated into Śrīvidyā may know next to nothing about the esoteric significance of the *śrīcakra*, few would fail to connect the beneficent goddess and her yantra. To Bhāskararāya, for example, *Lalitāsahasranāma* provides another context in which to discuss the meaning of Lalitā's mantra and yantra. Second, the texts become a part of the goddess's subtle manifestation (*sūkṣmarūpa*) as first-level mantras that dilute the power concentrated in the root-mantras (*mūlamantra*). Later texts, such as the Three Hundred [Names] of Lalitā or *Lalitātriśatī*, expand on this model. The *Lalitātriśatī* allegedly "condenses" the thousand names of Lalitā and so further distills her essence in both content and form. Before examining the subtle (*sūkṣma*) mantric manifestation of the goddess, the esoteric interpretation of the goddess's physical and mythic image (*sthūlarūpa*) warrants further elaboration.

THE ESOTERIC INTERPRETATION OF LALITĀ'S IMAGE AND MYTHOLOGY

Bhāskararāya offers esoteric or secret (*rahasya*) meanings to many names in the *Lalitāsahasranāma* including "Lalitā" and "Tripurā." Others names, such as "Kuṇḍalinī" (n. 110), suggest that the goddess has esoteric forms beyond her physical descriptions. Bhāskararāya often explains both the exoteric and esoteric significance. While the former require no special initiation to understand or experience, the latter assume privileged experiences and private rituals. For example, in his comment on *Lalitāsahasranāma*, n. 843, "Turning the wheel of earthly existence" (*bhavacakrapravartinī*), he gives the full range of possible interpretations:

> She turns the wheel of *samsara* like a wheel. The *Manu Smr.* (XII. 124) says, " He, pervading all the beings by the five forms and constantly making them, by means of birth, growth and decay revolves like a wheel."

> *Bhavacakra*, the Anāhatacakra, (heart) because it is the place of *Bhava* (Śiva).
>
> A *cakra* is defined in the Tantras as consisting of angles and petals...the meaning...that there are angles in the pericarp of these lotuses (Mūlādhāra, etc.) they are properly called *cakras*, like the Binducakra, Aṣṭadala, Ṣoḍasadala, Vṛttatraya and three Bhūgṛhas which are included in the Śrīcakra.
>
> Or *Bhava*, Śiva, *cakra*, mind, *pravartinī*, she guides. For the *Viṣṇu Pr.* says, *cakra* means mind, "Viṣṇu bears in his hand, mind in the form of disc [*cakra*] which is constantly in motion, swifter than wind."[56]

Some names of the goddess, such as "Her lotus face represents the divine *vāgbhava* group [of five syllables within the 15 syllable *śrīvidyā* mantra]" (n. 85) or "Severing the knot called 'Brahmagranthi' [which occurs in the yogic body in proximity to the *svadhiṣṭhāna* center]" (n. 100), are overtly esoteric. Others, such as "Lalitā" and "Tripurā," are made esoteric by being treated as secret rather than technical.

Lalitā is the less complex of the two common names that bear hidden meanings. Bhāskararāya explains at the outset of the *Lalitāsahasranāma* that this goddess should not be confused with lesser forms or other goddesses bearing the name "Lalitā." He says:

> *Lalitā*: lit. one who plays.... Above Śakti and Śiva, there exist manifestations of Paraśakti and of Sadāśiva; each has its own grades and spheres; but Mahāśakti, which is the same as Paraśiva, crossing all worlds, has her residence in that supreme sphere called Mahākailāsa, Aparājita, etc. Her body is formed of pure and concentrated *sattva* without any admixture of *rajas* and *tamas*; whereas the other *śaktis* merely have a preponderance of the *sattva* over the other two (*rajas* and *tamas*) and not pure *sattva*. Hence she is the highest, the prototype of Parabrahman. There are many secret manifestations of this Goddess, but in this work that particular manifestation termed Kāmeśvarī and known as Lalitā is referred to.[57]

In contrast, the *Tantrarāja Tantra* devotes nearly three chapters (chs.4 to 6) to the worship of Lalitā as one of the "eternal deities" or Nityās.

Other gods in their respective supreme aspects are identified with Lalitā. The fourth section or *Chinnamāstakhaṇḍa* of the *SST* identifies Kṛṣṇa with Lalitā and Rāma with Śiva. These identifications are common to contemporary southern adepts.[58] Rāmeśvara (*PKS*, 3.1), with Bhāskararāya's comment on *LSN*, n. 1000 (*Lalitāmbika*) in mind, quotes the same passage from *Padmapurāṇa* as his spiritual mentor in order to provide an esoteric etymology for the name Lalitā. He says:

> The explanation in the *Padmapurāṇa* is "transcending the worlds (*lokanatītya*) she sports (*lalate*) and therefore is called Lalitā."[59]

He continues by explaining that Bhāskararāya means "Lalitā" is the goddess imagined as the embodiment of *śṛṇgārabhava*, the sentiment of erotic love, which is the foremost of the aesthetic qualities (*rasa*) of poetic expression (*dhvani*).[60] Bhāskararāya, however, takes the explanation of Lalitā's name to be less important than how this name relates to the five preceding names which assert her ultimacy. He says:

> Thus...the goddess is indicated as the creator, preserver, and destroyer of the universe, ...she is indicated as possessing two other functions, namely annihilation and re-manifestation which belong to no other deity...the same deity who possesses these five functions is described in different ways and is indicated by the name Lalitā which is her special name and belongs to no other deity.[61]

Regarding the *Padmapurāṇa*'s etymology, Bhāskararāya glosses it by saying:

> "Worlds" means her surrounding lights or deities. "Transcending" being above their abodes in the *bindu*-place. "Sports" shines brilliantly. The wise say, "The word *lalitā* has eight meanings, namely brilliancy, manifestation, sweetness, depth, fixity, energy, grace and generosity; these are the eight human qualities." The *Kāma-śāstra* says: *Lalitā* means erotic actions and also tenderness; as she has all the above-mentioned qualities, she is called Lalitā. It is said also, "Thou art rightly called Lalitā for thou hast nine divine attendants [in the Śrīcakra] and your bow is made of sugar-cane, your arrows are flowers, and everything connected with you is lovely (*lalitā*)." The word *lalitā* according to the *Sabdārṇava* means beautiful.[62]

The esoteric meanings of "Tripurā" or Three Cities are considerably more complex, since they suggest the myriad of symbolic triads that abound in exoteric Hindu lore as well as those specific to Tantric speculation and to Śrīvidyā.

(1) *Mythological Tripurā*

The most common association with the term "Tripurā" is with the popular Purāṇic story of the fortress of demons destroyed by Śiva. Though a favorite myth among Tantrics, the tale is not related directly to the cultic worship of the goddess Tripurā.[63] When considering her name literally as "Three Cities," however, no Śrīvidyā commentator misses the opportunity to identify Tripurā with the three images (*trimūrti*) of Brahmā, Viṣṇu, and Śiva. Bhāskararāya remarks on *LSN*, n.626 (*Tripurā*), "...Devī is called Tripurā because she is older than the three persons (Brahmā, Viṣṇu and Rudra)."[64] Rāmeśvara on *PKS*, 10.83 makes a similar comment saying, "[She] is eternal, that is, ancient (*pura*), occurring before the three, creation, maintenance and dissolution."[65] Quoting the *Laghustava*, Bhāskararāya summarizes the symbolic triads identified with Tripurā:

> There are three Devas, three Vedas, three fires, three energies, three notes (*svaras*), three worlds, three abodes, (or according to another reading, three cities, three sacred lakes, three castes, namely *brāhmaṇa*, etc. Whatever in the world is threefold, such as the three objects of human desire, all these, O divine one, really belong to your name.[66]

Commenting on n. 997 (*śrīmattripurasundarī*), Bhāskararāya refers to the goddess as the consort of the male Tripurasundara, that is, Paraśiva, the Supreme Śiva. He is called "Tripura," Bhāskararāya says, "...because the three, Brahmā, Viṣṇu and Rudra are his body."[67] He goes on to quote *Kālikāpurāṇa*:

> By the will of the *pradhāna* the body of Śiva became triple. Then the upper part of Maheśvara became Brahma with five faces, four arms, and whose body had the colour of the pericarp of the lotus. His middle part became Viṣṇu of the blue colour, having one face, four arms, bearing the conch, disc, club and lotus. The lower part became Rudra having five faces, four arms and the colour of a white cloud and the moon as a crest jewel. As these three Puras are in him, he is called Tripura.[68]

(2) *Cosmological/Epistemological Tripurā*

The epistemological Tripurā is best summarized by Bhāskararāya's succinct comment on *LSN*, n. 234 (*mahātripurasundarī*). He says that she is called "Tripurā" because she is, "the measurer, the measuring and the thing measured" or more directly, the knower, knowing, and object of knowledge.[69]

Śivānanda, quoting *Prapañcasāra* 9.2, offers a corresponding cosmological Tripura. He states that she is called Tripurā not only because she has the three forms (of Brahmā, Viṣṇu, and Śiva) and is the three creations (heavens, earth, and underworlds) but because she has the nature of Śiva, Śakti, and ātman.[70] These identifications link Tripurā with all creation, in both latent and manifest forms, and establishes the nondualistic identity of the Absolute Brahman with the individual soul (*ātman*). Thus Tripurā is knowledge itself, the process of obtaining knowledge, and the situations in which knowledge is critical. She is identical to all the components of a valid cognition and hence is not different from the cognizer, the object cognized, or the act of cognizing.

The epistemological Tripurā identifies correct understanding of the goddess with the goddess herself. In other words, to know reality is to be in the process of becoming it; and in this realization there is nothing "new." As Bhāskararāya says:

> ...Devī is the means to attain one's own real nature. The meaning is that Moksa is the attainment of one's own real nature...the *jīvas* which were before Brahman, became embodied through the influence of nescience; when he has got rid of that influence, he has no longer any body and becomes one with Brahman.[71]

According to Śrīvidyā, liberation is an epistemological process of reintegration. By knowing how creation has come about materially in the form of the three *guṇas* and as being, consciousness, and bliss (cf. *Ṛjuvimarśinī*, 1.12), it is possible to reverse the process and return to the source of being through diligent spiritual discipline (*sādhana*).

Bhāskararāya brings the *śrīcakra* directly into the discussion. He identifies Tripurā with the *śrīcakra* as a triadic symbol of the cosmos. He then divides the soteriological path into triads. In his introductory remarks to the commentary on *Tripurā Upaniṣad* he condenses five levels of liberation into three paths identified with the "Three Cities." He says:

> There are five types of liberation.... Among these [five] the first and the last are one path (*mārga*) each and the middle group of three are another path....
>
> Because there are three paths the cities...are understood to be three. Because [She] pervades the three cities, fills [them] and is in the form of them, the Supreme Deity is called Tripurā.... This five-fold division [of liberation] into three [paths] explains the attainment of the Goddess.[72]

He goes on to say:

> That [initial] modification [of the One into Three] is [technically] called *śānta* [literally, peaceful] because it is the aggregate form of desire, knowledge, and action. It [insofar as She is identified with Brahman] is called transcendent (*parā*) because it is the aggregate form of the [primordial sound as it emanates, technically called] *paśyantī, madhyamā,* and *vaikharī*.... She is the aggregate form of [the three consorts of Brahmā, Viṣṇu, and Śiva and their respective powers, namely] Vāmā, Jyeṣṭhā, and Raudrī.[73]

Describing creation as an emanation from the one, represented by the *bindu* on the *śrīcakra*, which becomes more explicitly material and manifest in the form of "threes" (such as the three *guṇas*), represented by the expanding sets of triangles, Bhāskararāya summarizes the identification of Tripurā and *śrīcakra* by quoting *Kālikāpurāṇa*.

> Her *maṇḍala* consists of triangles (*trikoṇa*), the outer gates (*bhūpura*) consist of three lines; Her mantra also is said to consist of three syllables [or three groups of syllables] and similarly She has a threefold form. *Kuṇḍalinī* śakti is threefold and there are three deities in creation. Because everything [connected with her] is three, She is called Tripurā.[74]

Bhāskararāya, like other Śrīvidyā theologians, links cosmological speculation to ritual practice. By recognizing the cognitive process to be a manifestation of Tripurā, one sets out on the three-staged path to liberation and ascends by ritual identification with the cosmological form of the *śrīcakra*—itself composed of sets of triangles. Ritual identification of Tripurā with the *śrīcakra* is central to the process of reintegrating consciousness in dualistic reality (represented in by the symbolic triad of the "Three Cities") with its nondual source (represented by the *bindu* at the center of the *śrīcakra*).

(3) *Yogic*

The full implications of these cosmological patterns are evident only when Tripurā is interpreted as part of the yogic body. Bhāskararāya (*LSN*, n. 626) quoting the *Tripurārṇava Tantra* identifies Tripurā with the three basic *nāḍī*s or subtle channels that, according to the theories of *kuṇḍalinī* yoga, control the passage of the breaths.[75] The bodily cakras described in *kuṇḍalinī* yoga are systematically identified with the sub-cakras of the *śrīcakra* and so relate the microcosmic body to the macrocosmic universe.

Whatever else might be said of the goddess's physical and mythic image, Bhāskararāya appears to have had the last word about the difficulties of interpretation. In his closing remarks on the *Lalitāsahasranāma* he declares that the goddess's names are indeed a great secret and that, "...the practice of Śrīvidyā, the worship of Śrīcakra and the repetition of this holy *Sahasranāman* are not attainable by a slight penance."[76]

Chapter 5

The Śrīvidyā Mantra: *śrīvidyā*

THE SUBTLE ASPECT OF DEVĪ

> The one who repeats the fifteen-syllable mantra of Tripurā attains all desires, all enjoyments, conquers all the worlds, causes all words to emerge; achieving identity with Rudra, one breaks through the veil of Viṣṇu and obtains the supreme Brahman.[1]

Critical to Śrīvidyā's external (*bahir-*) and internal (*antaryāga*) ritual is a series of initiations (*dīkṣā*) involving a hierarchy of mantras that lead to the root mantra (*mūlamantra*) of Lalitā Tripurasundarī. Repetition (*japa*) of Lalitā's root mantra is at the heart of all Śrīvidyā practice; analysis of the mantra's use and meanings (*artha*) forms a major component in both the tradition's self-identity and its discussion of ritual and metaphysics.

The term *śrīvidyā* is a grammatical compound variously interpreted. Śrīvidyā is the *vidyā* of Śrī, that is, the wisdom or knowledge of the goddess (*Śrī*) who embodies auspiciousness (*śrī*).[2] It is both the knowledge (*vidyā*) that liberates and the wisdom that leads to material prosperity (*śrī*). Śrī is the substance of prosperity, the life-giving power (*śakti*) of auspiciousness, and the one who bestows these gifts. Thus, the *śrīvidyā* is the ontological "stuff" of the goddess in her subtle form (*sūkṣmarūpa*) and an expression of her dispositional power (*śakti*).

The *Kāmakalāvilāsa* states the traditional viewpoint about the mantra: "the privileged know that there is absolutely no difference between the *vidyā* and the true divinity."[3] The *Lalitāsahasranāma* divides the goddess's image in thirds and creates a correspondence among the three portions of the goddess's figure and the three segments (*kūṭa*) of the *śrīvidyā*. Thus, her face represents the first segment of the mantra, from throat to waist the second, and from waist to feet the third.[4]

Jan Gonda, in "The Indian Mantra," observes:

> The essence of a mantra...is the presence of the deity: only that mantra in which the *devata* has revealed his or her aspects can reveal that aspect. The deity is believed to appear from the mantra when it is correctly pronounced.[5]

Bhāskararāya repeats the traditional "esoteric" etymology when he writes, "Mantra is pure thought, because it has the quality of protecting (*tra*) the person during meditation."[6] He makes a further distinction is his opening remarks on the *LSN*. He writes:

> The difference between *Mantra* and *Vidyā* is that the former has reference to male deities and the latter to female ones. To show the identity of Śiva with Śakti, the word *vidyā* is...used along with the word *mantra*.[7]

Śrīvidyā literature refers to the *śrīvidyā* both as a *vidyā* and a mantra, the former term preferred because it means "knowledge" or "wisdom" and because it is grammatically feminine in gender. The question remains, however, what *do* Śrīvidyā Tantrics mean when they assert identity between the goddess's forms and the different manners and modes in which she is signified?

INTERPRETING THE CANON OF SIGNS

Semeiotic analysis provides one approach to understanding how Tantrics use words, sounds, images, and other *signs* to establish the divinity's relationship to its modes of representation. There are at least two different perspectives on interpreting signs: the analyst's point of view and the attempt to translate the Tantric theologian's view. Śrīvidyā begins with the theological assumption that the real presence of divinity (*devatāsadbhāva*) is present in the sign beyond the individual or collective imagination.[8]

C. S. Peirce's work on the definition and classification of signs remains the starting point for such an analysis. He writes:

> A sign, or *representamen*, is something which stands to somebody for something in some respect of capacity. It addresses somebody, that is, creates in the mind of that person an equivalent sign, or perhaps a more developed sign. The sign which it creates I call the *interpretant* of the first sign. The sign stands for something, its *object*.[9]

For the Śrīvidyā practitioner, the icon and the mantra of the goddess are signs (*representamen*) that create equivalent and more developed signs (*interpretant*). The physical (*sthūla*) and subtle (*sūkṣma*) forms (*rūpa*) of the goddess function as the *interpretants* of the icon and mantra. These respective physical and subtle forms stand for the *object*, namely, the goddess herself. The significance of the icon or mantra depends on the *interpretants* that create associations between signs.

Signs associate in different types of relationships. The most important issue involves the relationship between the *representamen* (icon and mantra) and their object (the goddess) and treats the different functions of the signs as critical to their interpretation and application. For the Śrīvidyā initiate, the icon and the mantra do not function merely as *symbolic* signs but also as *indexical* signs. E. Valentine

Daniel articulates the difference between symbolic and indexical signs:

> A symbol is not related to its object either by contiguity, by shared quality, or by resemblance. Convention alone links a symbol to its object. *Convene* and *convenant* both derive their meaning from the Latin *convenire*. In a symbol the conventional sign, object, and representamen are brought together within the sign relation by virtue of an agreement and not by virtue of any quality intrinsic to either object or representamen. Words are of the order of symbols. The object to which a word refers is of a general nature; symbols are not indicators of any particular occurrence of a thing but of a "kind of thing."[10]

In contrast,

> An indexical sign...is a sign in which resemblance or shared quality does not define the relationship between object and representamen, but, instead, contiguity or concurrence defines the significant link. Smoke and fire, red litmus and acidity, and deictics in language—all of these are examples of indexical signs. Indexical signs are what we call facts.[11]

In Śrīvidyā theology, neither the mantra nor the image are ultimately related to the goddess by contiguity, by shared quality, or by resemblance. In other words, the relationship between the mantra and the image as signs and the goddess as object does *not* depend on mere convention or agreement of the observers. Neither the mantra nor the goddess's physical image are believed to indicate a "kind of thing" but rather the particular occurrence of a thing. Thus, the relationship between the mantra, image, and the goddess is not a convention based on resemblance but a concurrence between signs and object.

Further, the mantra is *not* language, but meta-language and therefore does not function like a word. In fact, the mantra, as Jan Gonda pointed out, does not depend on its conventional meaning in Sanskrit to gain significance nor does it resemble its object symbolically. Accordingly, the mantra, like the icon, is not merely symbolic of divine reality but also functions indexically.

Śrīvidyā Tantrics acknowledge that the same sign can function both symbolically and indexically. Such functions are kept analytically distinct, suggesting a hierarchy of possible interpretations and uses. The *interpretants* in this matrix of signs—in this case, the "gross" (*sthūla*) and "subtle" (*sūkṣma*) descriptions—suggest not only different values of the respective *representamens* but different levels of interpretation.

For the Tantric the indexical function is logically superior to the symbolic in at least two ways. First, an indexical sign signifies its object without being dependent on a potentially flawed interpreter or on an *interpretant* and is therefore meta-cultural, meta-social, and meta-linguistic. The indexical sign is not of human origin (*apauruṣeya*) and is considered an unmediated manifestation of divinity. Second, an indexical sign has soteriological efficacy that is not present in a symbolic sign. For example, the *śrīvidyā*'s syllables are variously interpreted as symbols; the goddess's "diluted" mantric names in the *Lalitāsahasranāma* lend themselves to multiple symbolic associations and significations.

Yet Śrīvidyā interpreters would insist that knowledge of the symbolic meanings of mantras or icons does not alone empower the initiate. Rather, one requires access to the power (*śakti*) present in the indexical sign. Obtaining power requires divinity's grace (*prasāda*) and grace depends on obtaining an immediate experience (*anubhava*) of the relationship between oneself and the divine. Only through the proper use of an indexical sign can one dissolve the false distinctions that lead one to believe mistakenly that the divinity's signs are different from one's own intrinsic being.

To obtain an immediate experience (*anubhava*) of the divine one requires initiated knowledge by which the divinity in the form of different signs can be appropriated both symbolically and indexically. Thus, a sign may be symbolic *and* indexical and have two distinct functions within the system.

As a symbol, the sign, be it *representamen* or *interpretant*, creates or enhances the possibility of a dispositional power (*śakti*) which exists as a capacity to gain knowledge. In other words, one learns the possible symbolic meanings about the potential power that resides in the sign. For instance, one might learn the esoteric meanings of the goddess's mantric names in order to know *about* the power of the mantras. As an index, the sign creates or enhances episodic power which effects worldly enjoyment (*bhukti*) and liberation (*mukti*). Using the sign indexically, for example, would be to use a mantra ritually to create an occasion of power. Bhāskararāya implies this analytic distinction when he comments on *LSN*, n. 88, "She is the root mantra itself" (*mūlamantrātmikā*):

> *Mūla* root, this is the fifteen syllabled *mantra, Pañcadasī*, it is the root of the four objects of human desires (*puruṣārthas*): *Mantra, man* repetition; *tra* protection—it protects those who repeat it. It is declared, "*Mantra* is said to be that, with increasing repetition [*manana*] of which, with full reflection of 'I-ness,' destroys one's transmigratory life [*samsāra*], and protects [*tra*] him."

Bhāskararāya's discussion of the mantra's symbolism as an indication of the goddess's dispositional powers stands in contrast to his exhortation to "repeat it," which places emphasis on the mantra's episodic power to liberate and protect. Episodic power is not knowledge about the mantra's symbolism but rather requires using it in contemplative worship (*upāsana*). Put differently, being able to use the power of the mantra requires an appropriation of its indexical significance. Symbolic values can enhance one's knowledge about mantras or icons, but symbolic meanings are only knowledge *of* or knowledge *about* the divine power present in them.

From the analytical perspective the Tantric chooses "divine" signs in precisely the same way the canon is formulated. Just as Śrīvidyā Tantrics emphasize the "givenness" of the textual horizon and prescind from commenting on the principles of reduction at work within the tradition, so icons and mantras are treated as "given" *representamens* and the goddess as their *object*. One observes a "sacred persistence" in the use of signs comparable to that which is at work in the formulation of the canon. Similarly, Śrīvidyā's sacred signs are not a "given" but, in a positive sense, require selection from the possibilities that form the horizon of the practitioner's intellectual life as a Hindu.

What the Śrīvidyā Tantric understands as "original" or "primordial" choices made by the divinity, the historian of religion sees as part of the Tantric's endeavor to refine and interpret a relationship with the world. The signs, like the canon, suppose the presence of an interpreter whose task is to extend the domain of signs over everything that exists—without altering the signs in the process.[12] Essential to the extension process is not only the choice of signs but the attribution of different functions.

The indexical function of particular signs that follows from the assertion of the real presence of the divinity (*devatāsadbhāva*) is viewed differently by the historian of religion. Where the historian of religion observes symbols, the Tantric sees indices: the difference rests on the matter of the assumption regarding the presence of the *object*, the divinity.

More important is that Śrīvidyā Tantrics persist in using signs in the explicit absence of a written canon's closure. Signs function as an equivalent to written text, whether or not the text is present. The discourse of signs creates a totalistic system; everything can be interpreted as either a symbolic or indexical sign function.

The sign's sacrality is determined, in part, by asserting that everything in creation is essentially a devolved form of the *object* present in the divinity's indexical signs. In other words, sacrality is a function of how signs are used, just as texts become sacred or canonical when there are procedures and restrictions attached to their use.

Understanding the interpretation and function of signs not only advances our understanding of Śrīvidyā's concept of god but of tradition. By sorting out the various functions that govern the canon of signs and texts one can map more precisely the relationship between ideology and behavior. At stake is not only the interpretation of what others' say about themselves but a consideration of the interpretive choices that govern the construction of a given map of the universe. The latter task requires one to investigate both what *is* done with a given set of signs and what could *possibly be* done with these signs. Only then do others' maps of the universe provide us insight into what human beings imagine to be descriptively *and* normatively real.

HISTORICAL AND MYTHICAL DERIVATIONS OF THE *ŚRĪVIDYĀ*

Śrīvidyā's claims about the superiority of the goddess's root mantra occur at two distinct levels. At the first level are claims about the goddess as a sectarian deity (*iṣṭadevatā*).[13] At the second level are more specific claims about variations of the *śrīvidyā*. These latter claims preoccupy historical writers. Most would agree with Bhāskararāya when he writes:

> Śrīvidyā is the best of *mantras*.... He who regards as equal to the other [Vidyās] with the Vidyā of Lalitā, also this *mantra* with other *mantras*...that man is only bewildered in mind.[14]

Further, Śrīvidyā identifies itself as that tradition most qualified to interpret all aspects of mantra science (*mantraśāstra*). Contemporary Śrīvidyā adepts, like their historical predecessors, continue to achieve notoriety for their ability to use, interpret, and distribute mantras.[15] For example, contemporary south Indian Śrīvidyā adepts commonly initiate individuals who seek worldly or spiritual goals into all sorts of mantras and practices other than those distinctive to Śrīvidyā tradition. Śrīvidyā adepts have achieved a reputation for "related" skills such as astrology, clairvoyance, and even miraculous power—all of which is part of their accomplishment in the "*vidyā* of *vidyā*s, the *śrīvidyā*."[16] As one put it:

> When a person has accomplishment (*siddhi*) in Śrīvidyā, then all matters become under his control. This enables him to help others. His accomplishment (*siddhi*) in other mantras and practices is merely a by-product of his mastery of the *śrīvidyā* that comes through the grace of Devī and the guru.[17]

Lalitā Tripurasundarī's root mantra (*mūlamantra*) is known as *pañcadaśākṣarī* or *ṣoḍaśākṣarī*, respectively "fifteen-" or "sixteen syllables." The tradition debates the superiority of the sixteen syllable or *ṣoḍaśī śrīvidyā* over the fifteen syllable *pañcadaśī* as an issue separate from the variations that occur in different traditions. While the debate over the fifteen and sixteen syllable forms is shrouded in ambiguity and a subject rarely raised in texts, the *śrīvidyā*'s variations is significant and widespread from the emergence of textual traditions in the ninth century.

All major historical writers who consider the sixteen syllable mantra treat it as an elaboration of the fifteen syllable *śrīvidyā*. Thus, all the discussion of the *śrīvidyā* correctly begins with a discussion of the fifteen syllable or *pañcadaśī* mantra.

While the *Śrīvidyārṇava Tantra* describes twenty-four *śrīvidyā*s and the commentaries of the *Saundaryalaharī* list fifteen, Bhāskararāya, in accordance with the list in *Tripurātāpinī Upaniṣad,* cites twelve mantras—the number most frequently cited in contemporary south India. An account of the "original" revelation given in *Tripurātāpinī Upaniṣad* lists both the twelve versions of the mantra and the names of the sages and demigods associated with them.[18] *LSN*, n. 238 *"Manuvidyā"*, is the name of the goddess that prompts Bhāskararāya to produce the founders' list. He remarks:

> The Śrīvidyā is of twelve kinds differentiated according to the twelve devotees, "Manu, Candra, Kubera, Lopāmudrā, Manmaṭha, Agastya, Agni, Sūrya, Indra, Skanda, Śiva and Krodhabhattāraka [Durvāsa]. These are the devotees of Devī."[19]

Only two of the twelve mantra forms play important roles in Śrīvidyā's development; the other ten leave no record of their being part of the instantiated ritual tradition. The two of historical importance appear to provide the model for the others. The ten *vidyā*s without verifiable instantiation were likely created to meet ritual or speculative expectations generated from within the intellectual tradition; in this sense they are similar to some aspects of the physcial goddess which also are designed for ritual but are not often worshiped.

South Indian Śrīvidyā from at least the sixth century is dominated by the version of the *śrīvidyā* attributed to Śiva in the form of Manmaṭha, a deity more frequently referred to as Kāmeśvara or Kāmarāja *vidyā*. The other important version of the mantra is called the "Lopāmudrā *vidyā*" and is attributed to the wife of the sage Agastya who is also one of the Lords of the *vidyā* or *vidyeśvaras*. The Lopāmudrā mantra is important to Śrīvidyā texts closely aligned with Kashmiri traditions. Though Lopāmudrā is a major interlocutor in certain Śrīvidyā texts, it is unclear why her version of the mantra is singled out for special treatment.[20] Those in her lineage offer no particular reason. In south India Lopāmudrā *vidyā* traditions apparently have fallen out of use. Kashmiri writers, such as Jayaratha, state clearly that the Manmaṭha or Kāmarāja *vidyā* dominates Śrīvidyā but imply that it is not the *vidyā* of most Kashmiri adepts.[21] While such statements do little to support the contemporary south Indian claim that Śrīvidyā is of southern origin—a claim rejected implicitly by Kashmiris—it does offer evidence that south India was considered a major center for Śrīvidyā during the heyday of Kashmiri Śrīvidyā. Further, it seems clear that, at one time, there were two distinct preceptorial lines (*sampradāya*) rooted in the difference between the two *vidyās*.[22] To Śivānanda and others the term "*vidyā*" suggests not simply a variation of the *śrīvidyā* mantra but a preceptorial line. Thus "*vidyā*" can function as a synonym for the terms "*mata*," "*ācāra*," and "*sampradāya*."

The importance of the ten unattested *vidyās* is difficult to evaluate since they are discussed only theoretically and do not have companion ritual handbooks (*nibandha* or *paddhati*) specifying their use. One can assume two possible scenarios. The *vidyās* may be either theoretical constructs developed to give a role to important mythic figures, or the names of lineage founders whose lines of transmission, for one reason or another, failed to be maintained. Contemporary adepts favor the second interpretation since this would likewise account for other variants, such as those in the *Śrīvidyārṇava Tantra*.[23] The "broken lineages" explanation meets with only marginal support in historical sources. *Yoginīhṛdaya* 2.14 says that the mantra has come through an uninterrupted succession of teachers from Śiva to the present. Amṛtānanda, like other commentators, emphasizes that the mantra is efficacious only when transmitted in a traceable lineage (*paramparā*).[24] Umānandanātha in his liturgy, the *Nityotsava*, has provided a list of teachers for both popular mantras, lineages that presumably carry their transmission into his own day.[25] Other lines of tradition (*sampradāya*) associated with the Lopāmudrā *vidyā* are also attested.[26]

Whether the list of twelve "original" teachers or any lineage (*paramparā*) refers to instantiated Śrīvidyā practice is perhaps less important than that traditionalists have been preoccupied with the construction of the *guru paramparā*. These efforts contribute to legitimizing current thought and practice by creating indissoluble, sacred links with the past. All Śrīvidyā practitioners trace their immediate lineage branch (*paramparā*) to either the Kāmarāja or Lopāmudrā *vidyās*.

In the *Śrīvidyāratnasūtras* attributed to Gauḍapāda, the author offers an explanation of the emergence of the Manmaṭha/Kāmeśvara and Lopāmudrā *vidyās* without mentioning the remaining ten. He says that Devī after creating the universe and the gods took the form of the goddess to establish the Law (*dharma*). She next took the form of the sages to increase knowledge when in the middle of the ocean of jewels arose Kāmarāja and Lopāmudrā who established Śrīvidyā lineages.[27] In either case the goddess herself is identical to the *śrīvidyā*, which is the nameless consciousness (*cit*) that pervades reality.[28] The *Śrīvidyāratnasūtras* are only one example of how Śrīvidyā authors slant discussions towards the two mantra traditions that have had an historical impact.

Lineages create guru genealogies to mandate their own distinctive interpretations of theory and practice. For example, contemporary adepts who claim a lineage relationship with Bhāskararāya confer on themselves a privilege of association with this great teacher. While Śrīvidyā Tantrics reject literal consanguinity and caste considerations as prerequisites for initiation, they maintain an alternative "caste" formulation based on continuity within the family (*kula*) of gurus.

The proper "familial" connections, that is, to be within a *kula* implicitly confers a right to interpret and even alter tradition. The perception that one is a *kaulika*, a "family member," is crucial even if such connections are not historically instantiated. Without the proper pedigree, the Tantric lacks the credentials that provide an alternative or parallel to Vedic claims.

KĀMEŚVARA AND LOPĀMUDRĀ: *KĀDI* AND *HĀDI VIDYĀS*

The *śrīvidyā* in fifteen or sixteen syllables and in any of the twelve configurations of the sages is the subtle (*sūkṣma*) form of the goddess and the second corner of Śrīvidyā's triadic theology. Bhāskararāya echoes the views of earlier commentators when he says:

> Thus there are three forms of Devī, which partake of both the *prakāśa* and *vimarśa* aspects, namely the physical (*sthūla*), the subtle (*sūkṣma*), and the supreme (*parā*); the physical form has hands, feet, etc.; the *subtle* consists of *mantra* and the *supreme* is the *vāsanā*.... The subtle form again is threefold...[29]

Rāmeśvara Sūri commenting on *PKS*, 1.11 identifies the physical deity with the subtle mantra and with the guru, which he says is also not different than the subtle body (*sūkṣmaśarīra*).[30] Amṛtānanda adds that repetition of the mantra when identified with the supreme goddess defines contemplative worship (*upāsana*).[31]

The Kāmarāja *vidyā* is also called *kādividyā* because it begins with the syllable *ka*. The term *kādividyā* refers to both a mantra and to a preceptorial tradition. Lopāmudrā's *vidyā* is called *hādi*, "beginning with *ha*," and counts among its historical adherents Puṇyānanda and his disciple Amṛtānanda. The doctrinal differences between *hādi* and *kādi* as "schools" (*mata*) are more technical than substantive. Since there are only a few examples of historical liturgies and no living *hādi* traditions, the ritual differences that must have distinguished these schools are beyond our scope. If Śivānanda's work is any indication of the *hādimata*'s actual ritual, then *hādi* and *kādimatas* seem practically indistinguishable.

The fifteen-syllable *kādi* mantra is the one form of the *śrīvidyā* about which there is little controversy, the form of *hādividyā* being a less settled issue. *Kādi* conforms literally to the fifteen syllable prescription and is quite possibly the mantra from which the other eleven formulations are derived. Even the attested Lopāmudrā *hādividyā* is most frequently viewed as a derivative form of *kādi* and, with a few notable exceptions, takes second place in the majority of texts.[32]

THE *ŚRĪVIDYĀ*, ŚĀKTA SPECULATIONS, AND TRIADIC SYMBOLISM

The *kādi śrīvidyā* occurs in three separate portions described as peaks (*kūṭas*). These are the *vāgbhavakūṭa* or peak which is the nature (*bhava*) of speech (*vāk*), the *kāmarājakūṭa* or peak of Kāmarāja (literally, King of Desire) and the *śaktikūṭa* or peak of Śakti or "power." The fifteen syllable (*pañcadaśākṣarī*) *kādi śrīvidyā* is:

Vāgbhavakūṭa:	*ka e ī la hrīṃ*
Kāmarājakūṭa:	*ha sa ka ha la hrīṃ*
Śaktikūṭa:	*sa ka la hrīṃ*

The mantra is the focus of contemplative worship (*upāsana*); its repetition (*japa*), like its configuration, is triadic and hierarchical: classified as silent, self-audible, or openly verbalized.[33]

The chart below outlines the theoretical and descriptive associations of the *śrīvidyā*'s three *kūṭas*. Each set of triads corresponds to three aspects to body, speech, and mind.[34] For example, the identification of the *śrīvidyā* with *auṃ* (i.e. the *praṇava*) is located within the body, verbally articulated, and mentally contemplated as the source of creation. Bhāskararāya, in his Secret of Worship (*Varivasyārahasya*) observes that the mantra's three *kūṭas* are like the beads of a garland, one naturally flowing into the next.[35]

Mantra *kūṭas*:	Vāgbhava	Kāmarāja	Śakti	Fourth
Pranava:	*a*	*u*	*ṃ*	
Sound Stage:	Paśyantī	Madhyamā	Vaikharī	Parā
Goddesses:	Vāmā	Jyeṣṭhā	Raudrī	Ambikā
Śakti:	Icchā	Jñāna	Kriyā	Parā
Yogic Center:	Mūlādhāra	Svadhiṣṭhāna	Anāhata	Manipūra

[Or:	Anāhata	Ajñā	Lālatamādhya]	
Cosmos:	Agni	Sūrya	Soma	
Consort:	Brahmā	Viṣṇu	Śiva	Brahman
Lalitā:	Head	Body	Lower Extremities	
Consciousness:	Waking	Dreaming	Deep Sleep	Turya
Function:	Creation	Preservation	Destruction	
Yogic Body:	Iḍā	Piṅgala	Suṣumṇā	
Guṇas:	Sattva	Rajas	Tamas	

The universe of triadic signs is said to reflect the supreme deity's own intentionality. At the moment of creation the cosmos emerge from the Absolute's pure illumination (*prakāśa*) which propels (*sphurat*) itself into a state of reflective consciousness (*vimarśa*).[36] Put theologically, the illuminative (*prakāśa*) Śiva initates a reflection (*vimarśa*) of his own individuality called "Śakti." This act of reflection produces the dualistic universe which emerges from Śiva's own being.[37]

From the point of self-reflection forward, Śiva becomes a secondary figure in Śākta cosmology. Śakti is the active, manifest, and creative component of the universe and, in effect, subsumes the role of Śiva. Inasmuch as he is the purely illuminative (*prakāśa*), Śiva is the Śākta's reference for the unmoving eternal. As a reflection of eternal consciousness (*vimarśa*), the One Brahman takes the form of the Self (*ātman*) in each individual. The *ātman* is thus identified with Śakti. These cosmological events are paralleled in the human consciousness: the true identity of the inner Self (*ātman*) with Brahman occurs as a dynamic process of reflective cognition (*vimarśa*) in which there is a simultaneous recognition of the source of its being, the pure consciousness (*cit*) of the illuminative (*prakāśa*) Brahman.

For Śāktas dualistic consciousness begins when the subject's emerging self-awareness engages the objective world. By discriminating the mere accretions of self-reflection from their source in the Self (*ātman*), the adept realizes that the remainder is identical to Śakti in her pure reflective state (*vimarśa*). The adept concludes that reflection (*vimarśa*) without the dualistic misconceptions caused by ignorance (*avidyā*) is none other than the purely illuminative (*prakāśa*) Brahman.

For Śāktas the goddess is the focus of ritual worship because she is the source of the individual Self's own self-cognitive reflection as an "I." She thus provides the initial access to the source of cognitive reflection.

Śakti's first manifest reflection (*vimarśa*) is the mantra, which is nothing other than Self's incipient act of self-reflection. The stages of creative devolution are described in terms of the *śrīvidyā*. These phonic emanations of Brahman parallel the material world as it devolves from four stages of sound, beginning with the transcendent (*parā*) level. The mantra finally emerges into the physical form of ordinary speech (*vaikharī*) after having passed through the body's subtle yogic centers. Each stage of speech is associated with the goddess in a particular aspect (as shown above in the chart) and each of these corresponds to her creative forces of desire (*icchā*), knowledge (*jñāna*), and action (*kriyā*). With each of these divine aspects of the supreme Śakti is identified the corresponding male deity and their respective powers. The goddess emerges in her supreme form designated by the term "Ambikā" or mother. She is wholly identical to the eternal Śiva (Brahman or *sadāśiva*) and simultaneously in the process of transforming (*parināma*) herself into the universe.

The elegance of the Śrīvidyā system, however, is apparent only when the associations of the mantra with the *śrīcakra* are brought into picture. The fundamental macrocosmic/microcosm symbolism, which identifies the *śrīcakra* with the universe and the human body, is correlated to the mantra and cakra; thus, the three *kūṭa*s of the mantra and the *śrīcakra*'s nine sub-cakras (identified with the nine "gates" of the body) become verbally and visually identified. The mantra's three *kūṭa*s correspond to three sets of sub-cakras and to the sides of the triangle at the center of the *śrīcakra*. The three *kūṭa*'s are also identified with one of the six yogic centers in the body (to which three more are added) and these, respectively, with the sub-cakras of the *śrīcakra*.

The *śrīvidyā* is an expression of primordial sound (*vāk* or *śabda*), though it is not merely *one* of the phonic emanations that parallel the material world but *the* form from which the whole of creation has evolved.[38] At the first level of symbolic identification, the *śrīvidyā* is linked to *auṃ*, the Vedic *praṇava*, and the Ṛg Vedic *gāyatrī*. Śrīvidyā writers suggest that whatever is said about *auṃ* either as a triadic symbol or as the primordial emanation (cf. *Chāndogya Upaniṣad*, 1, 4; 9, 23,2) applies to the *śrīvidyā* by inference since the *śrīvidyā* is the *praṇava*'s hidden form.[39] The three *kūṭa*s correspond to the three constituents of *auṃ* (*a-u-ṃ*).[40]

Contemporary adepts explain the *śrīvidyā* in terms of Gauḍapāda's discussion of *auṃ* as tripartite in the *Māṇḍūkhyakārikās*.[41] The links between Śrīvidyā adepts and the Śāṅkara tradition make allusions to Gauḍapāda appear all the more germane. While the *kūṭa*'s of the *śrīvidyā* correspond directly to the triadic *praṇava*, more needs to be said about the the *śrīvidyā* and the holiest of Vedic mantras, the *gāyatrī*.

THE *ŚRĪVIDYĀ*, VEDIC *GĀYATRĪ*, AND VEDIC TRADITIONS

South Indian Śrīvidyā goes to great lengths to establish the identity of the *śrīvidyā* with the *gāyatrī* mantra of *Ṛg Veda*, 3.62.10. Commetators with allegiances to both Vedic and Tantric traditions create a hierarchy of interpretations that correspond to mantric hierarchies.

Bhāskararāya states that the *gāyatrī*, most sacred of Vedic utterances, has two forms, one explicit (*spaṣṭham*), the other deeply concealed (*gopanīyataram*).[42] By this he means that the *śrīvidyā* is the *gāyatrī*'s secret essence. Like the *praṇava*, the *gāyatrī*, too, is identical with Brahman. Further, he says, *Tripurā Upaniṣad* gives the secret meaning of the *gāyatrī* and that each of the *śrīvidyā*'s three *kūṭas* is a microcosm of the esoteric *gāyatrī*.[43]

In Sanskrit the Ṛg Vedic *gāyatrī* mantra is: *tát savitúr várenyam bhárgo devásya dhīmahī dhíyo yó naḥ pracodáyāt*. Its explicit formulation would appear to have nothing to do with the fifteen syllables of *śrīvidyā*, to say nothing of the *praṇava auṃ*. Unlike the *śrīvidyā*, which is composed entirely of seed syllables (*bījākṣara*) and has no semantic meaning, the *gāyatrī* (*Ṛg Veda* 3.62.10) has a meaning in Sanskrit: "Let us contemplate the lovely splendor of the god Savitṛ that he may inspire our minds." The distinction between a mantra with and without an "ordinary" meaning is the one key to understanding Śrīvidyā's mantric hierarchies.

In Śrīvidyā the *gāyatrī*'s semantic meaning is of minimal importance. While in the Tantras the Vedic *gāyatrī* is variously interpreted, in Śrīvidyā it acquires a very specific significance. The majority of Śrīvidyā commentators maintain the Vedic view that the *gāyatrī* is restricted to male members of the upper three estates (*traivarṇikas*).[44] However, qualification (*adhikāra*) for the esoteric *gāyatrī*, the *śrīvidyā*, is not determined by birth or gender and, in this sense, the mantra is distinctively Tantric rather than Vedic.

There is no more explicit symbol of Vedic mantra traditions than the *Ṛg Veda*'s *gāyatrī* mantra—what Basham has called "the most holy passage of that most holy scripture."[45] By identifying the *śrīvidyā* as the secret (*rahasya*) *gāyatrī*, Śrīvidyā goes beyond merely legitimizing itself as a "Vedic" tradition. Rather, it usurps the position of superior tradition within the Vedic fold.

The individual syllables of each *kūṭa* of the *kādi śrīvidyā*, Bhāskararāya points out, are actually a portion of the *gāyatrī*, as the chart below shows.

Vāgbhavakūṭa

ka	= *tát*	= *Kāmeśvara*	= *Brahman*
e	= *savitúr várenyam*	= *Kāmeśvarī*	= *(Śakti)*
i	= *bhárgo devásya dhī-*	= *Śiva*	
la	= *mahī*	= *Earth*	
hrīṃ	= *dhíyo yó naḥ pracodáyāt*	= *Māyā*	

Kāmarājakūṭa

ha	*= tát*
sa	*= savitúr (Three syllables = Three Words of the Mantra)*
ka	*= várenyam*
ha	*= bhárgo devásya dhī- (One syllable = Six Syllables)*
la	*= mahī*
hrīṃ	*= dhíyo yó naḥ pracodáyāt*

Śaktikūṭa

sa	*= tát savitúr várenyam*
ka	*= bhárgo devásya dhī-*
la	*= mahī*
hrīṃ	*= dhíyo yó naḥ pracodáyāt*

Bhāskararāya's interpretation from his *VVR* is based on *Tripurātāpinī Upaniṣad* (*TTU*).[46] Thus, *TTU*, verses 7–15 explain the *vāgbhavakūṭa* as the *gāyatrī*. The first word, *tat* (that), is identified with the eternal Brahman, who comes forth as the manifest world filled with desires and hence is called "Kāmeśvara, that is, Śiva.[47] Verse nine links *gāyatrī* not only to the *śrīvidyā* but to the *śrīcakra*. The syllable *la* is understood as the earth (*mahī*) in the form of the goddess.[48] The five syllables of the *vāgbhavakūṭa*, it is concluded, are the five elements that make up material creation.[49]

The interpretation of the *kāmarājakūṭa*, called in *TTU* the "*kāmakūṭa*" (literally, "desire's peak"), first identifies portions of the *gāyatrī* with syllables of *śrīvidyā* "located" within the bodily cakras according to the six cakra theory of *kuṇḍalinī yoga*.[50] The *kāmarājakūṭa* further suggests the secrets of the "aspect of desire meditation" or *kāmakalādhyāna* performed to the female organ. The meanings of *kāmakalā* are directly associated with the six syllables of the *kāmarājakūṭa*. The third *śaktikūṭa* is identified with *gāyatrī* by linking portions of the mantra to the individual Self (*ātman*), Śiva (found again, as in the *vāgbhavakūṭa*, in the syllable *ka*) and Śakti (especially within the seed-syllable (*bījākṣara*) *hrīṃ*).

In the *Jñānārṇava Tantra* each of the *śrīvidyā*'s three *kūṭas* are identified with the acquisition of certain levels of empowerment; the accomplishment (*siddhi*) of the *vāgbhavakūṭa* is, as the name itself suggests, a mastery of speech; the *kāmarājakūṭa* gives splendor (*tejas*) like that of Indra, and the *śaktikūṭa* attracts the three worlds such that they cooperate with the wishes of the adept.[51] It is noteworthy that this explanation does not dwell on the mantra's soteriological power, but rather on its capacity to confer various types of worldly mastery and enjoyment (*bhukti*). In contrast to other mantras, which give specific and limited accomplishments, the *śrīvidyā* is said to confer generic powers and have unlimited applications.

Bhāskararāya and other writers generally agree that the daily repetition of the *śrīvidyā* does not exempt twice-born males from Vedic obligations, including *gāyatrī* recitation at the daily junctures (*sandhyavandana*). Rāmeśvara maintains the common position that twice-born males must keep both Vedic and Tantric mantra and ritual obligations even when they are parallel or redundant. In contrast, some contemporary interpreters consider parallel or redundant Śrīvidyā practices to be optional for twice-borns performing Vedic rites.[52]

In ritual contexts, the Vedic *gāyatrī* mantra's meanings are related to its functions. For example, it can be used to purify an individual (cf. *Vaśiṣṭha Dharmasūtra*, 28.10–25) and create a safeguard to life and lineage (cf. *Gāyatrī Upaniṣad*).[53] Thus, the predilection for esoteric interpretation is seen in both Tantric and non-Tantric sources.[54] The key issue remains the power of the mantra as a prescribed and restricted utterance that can influence nature, human events, and the supernatural, including the gods.[55] Śrīvidyā claims that these dispositional and episodic powers are rooted in the mantra's ontology: esoteric or exoteric symbolic meanings are secondary to the indexical mantra that articulates the subtle form of material and spiritual reality.

The *śrīvidyā*, because it consists of "indestructible seed" syllables (*bījākṣara*) rather than words, transcends such "mundane" considerations as semantic meaning. Accordingly, a *bīja*-only mantra is not merely esoteric but inherently superior. As Frits Staal has pointed out, the use of apparently meaningless sounds is not unknown in ancient Vedic sources, especially in ritual formulations.[56] Thus Vedic *gāyatrī* is a more explicit mantric reality and hence a "lower form" of the *śrīvidyā*. According to Śrīvidyā, the *gāyatrī* gains its esoteric significance only when it is interpreted as the *śrīvidyā*. In contrast, the *śrīvidyā*, can be interpreted *only* esoterically. As one Śrīvidyā adept put it:

> Because it is purely seed-syllables [*bījākṣaras*], *śrīvidyā* is the purest form of mantra. It does not make a request or praise the god, it is God's purest expression. *Gāyatrī* is great but it cannot match *śrīvidyā* because it is still in language; it is Veda and mantra but when transformed into the *śrīvidyā* its greatness increases.[57]

Śrīvidyā also maintains that while the explicit Vedic form is an obligation (*nityakarma*) determined "merely" on the basis of birthright, the esoteric *gāyatrī*, the *śrīvidyā*, requires a "higher" spiritual disposition (*adhikāra*). The caste and gender restrictions of the explicit Vedic *gāyatrī* are not rejected but rather are deemed less consequential to the spiritually adept. "Higher" Tantric values sublate birthright qualifications but not the obligations of a birthright.[58]

Śrīvidyā adopts the Vedic pattern of obligatory rites (*nityakarma*) in the sense that those privileged to be initiated are required to perform certain daily rituals in which the mantra is the centerpiece. In most contemporary south Indian lineages, the Vedic *gāyatrī* remains an obligation for Vaidika Śrīvidyā adepts though its importance in Śrīvidyā *sādhana* engenders debate and controversy.

Śrīvidyā also interprets its mantra to be Vedic in other ways. Bhāskararāya says that because the *śrīvidyā* appears in the *Tripurā Upaniṣad*, this is proof that it is originally a part of Vedic revelation (*śruti*). Traditionalists who mention such Upaniṣads do not dispute their authenticity as ancient Vedic sources.[59] Nor is the mantra's presentation in the Upaniṣad the only esoteric formulation in the Vedic *śruti*.

Śrīvidyā maintains that its mantra is mentioned at *Ṛg Veda*, 5.47.4, in the phrase "*catvāra īṃ bibharti kṣemayantaḥ*," which literally translates: "the four [priests], desiring benefit for themselves, worship [this god]."[60] Bhāskararāya gives the verse its standard esoteric interpretation when he says it means "that which contains the four *īṃ*s confers benefit."[61] The four *īṃ*s refer to the four occurrences of the letter *ī* in the fifteen syllable *kādi* mantra (*pañcadaśākṣarī*), that is, the *ī* vowel in the first *kūṭa* and the three *ī* vowels occurring within the syllable *hrīṃ*. This interpretation indirectly asserts the "originality" of the *kādi pañcadaśākṣarī* since no other fifteen syllable mantra (including the *hādi*) contains four long *ī* vowels. According to some contemporary adepts, the *ṣoḍaśī* or sixteen syllable *kādi* mantra provides in its sixteenth syllable, the fourth *ī*.

Some say that the so-called *ṣoḍaśī* or *ṣoḍaśākṣarī* is formed by adding the seed-syllable (*bījākṣara*) *śrīṃ* to the end of the fifteen syllable *kādi pañcadaśī*. This sixteenth syllable is so secret that it is not ordinarily discussed explicitly even in the most secret (*atirahasya*) sources. Thus, the first *ī* vowel occurring in the *vāgbhavakūṭa* (that is, the *ī* not part of the *bījākṣara hrīṃ*) is not the first *ī* referred to in the Vedic verse. The three *ī*'s of *hrīṃ* are coupled with the *ī* of the seed-syllable *śrīṃ* to complete the pattern of "four *īṃ*s" (*catvāra īṃ*).[62] The effort to derive all the four *ī*'s from the *hrīṃ*s rather than accepting the *ī* of the *vāgbhavakūṭa* is due to the esoteric significance of *īṃ*, which is deemed equivalent to the secret *kāmakalā*.[63] This particular formation of the *ṣoḍaśī* mantra, however, in which *śrīṃ* is the sixteenth syllable is not without controversy. Others maintain that the addition of *śrīṃ* is not the "great *ṣoḍaśī*" (*mahāṣoḍaśī*) but merely the "abbreviated *ṣoḍaśī*" (*laghuṣoḍaśī*, literally the "light sixteen"). Accordingly, the Vedic verse refers only to the fifteen syllable mantra since the "great mantra of sixteen" (*mahāṣoḍaśī*) does not consist of sixteen syllables but rather is a collection of syllables counted as a single unit.

More needs to be said about the *śrīvidyā*'s expansion from fifteen syllables. At stake in this issue is Śrīvidyā's claim to be the most secret teaching of the Vedas.[64] Some Śrīvidyā traditionalists, however, hold that explicit forms of Vedic revelation are not particularly suitable to the expeditious and privileged path of Tantric *sādhana*. The alternative Tantric interpretation is kept a strict secret because of its inherent danger to the uninitiated. *PKS*, 1.30 delivers the final word on the explicit forms of Vedic revelation:

> Like a prostitute the mantras [or teachings, *vidyā*] of the Vedas and other [teachings] are explicit. Among all views this [Śrīvidyā] is [most] secret.[65]

Rāmeśvara further explains that Vedic teaching can be obtained for a price while Śrīvidyā can only be the gift of the guru's grace; the *vidyā* that leads to the realization of Brahman (*brahmavidyā*), he says, is not available even for gold.[66] Rāmeśvara does not, however, make these remarks at the further expense of the Vedic tradition, preferring to emphasize the role of initiation and the need for an authentic teacher. Rather than reject Vedic injunctions, Śrīvidyā prefers to subordinate them by claiming its teachings are the Veda's esoteric meaning.

In comparison to other Tantrics, Śrīvidyā traditionalists rarely lash out at Vedic orthodoxy. Contemporary adepts compare the *PKS*'s vituperation of the Vedas to Kṛṣṇa's criticism of brahmans and Vedic practices in the *Bhagavadgītā*; Kṛṣṇa, they say, does not repudiate Vedic tradition but interprets within its boundaries. Likewise, they assert, that their positions offer a secret and, hence, a more valuable interpretation of the Vedas. Contemporary south Indian Śrīvidyā, we should note, exhibits strong conservative tendencies that may not, in fact, reflect the pan-Indian historical tradition.[67]

ESOTERIC MEANINGS OF THE *ŚRĪVIDYĀ*

The seed-syllables (*bījākṣara*) of the *śrīvidyā* have not only a collective symbolism but also individual esoteric meanings. These points are elaborated in the *Yoginīhṛdaya* and in Bhāskararāya's *Varivasyārahasya*. A few examples will suffice to demonstrate the breadth of interpretation and the impact such speculation has had on mantric initiation and practice.

Each syllable of the *pañcadaśī* is associated with at least one particular deity and sometimes several. These deities are considered subordinate aspects of Lalitā and reflect certain qualities or attributes of her nature.[68] The *bījākṣara hrīṃ*, which occurs three times in the *kādi śrīvidyā*, attracts the most attention. When taken separately it represents the goddess of the earth, Bhūvaneśvarī, who is one of the ten so-called great goddesses (*daśadevatā*).[69] Within the *śrīvidyā*, *hrīṃ* is the subject of elaborate esoteric interpretation. Bhāskararāya, for example, says *hrīṃ* has twelve distinctive elements each with a significance for the interpretation of the entire *śrīvidyā*.[70] Since *hrīṃ* is composed of four constituents each of these is also liable to interpretation. The vowel *ī*, for example, has manifold symbolism; it is source of the primordial sound (*nāḍa*) that creates the first three sub-cakras of the *śrīcakra* at the moment of creation. It is responsible for and representative of a portion of the creation of the universe. It is also the cause of dreaming consciousness in which the four components making up the individual consciousness (the inner organ (*antaḥkaraṇa*) composed of the *manas, buddhi, ahaṃkāra,* and *citta*) operate.[71] The *r* of *hrīṃ* is the cause of the illuminative form (*prakāśarūpa*) characterizing the waking state of consciousness while *ṃ* is the cause of deep sleep.[72]

The esoteric explanation of the *śrīvidyā*'s syllables also links cosmological patterns of creation to yogic concepts and practices. For each sound within the mantra there is a series of identifications with different parts of the universe's subtle and parallel physical forms. Each of these correspond to aspects of human consciousness and parts of the body. The mantra's syllables are then identified with the emergence of the universe in the form of the *śrīcakra*.

The Śrīvidyā practitioner must internalize the mantra's esoteric meanings during the period leading to and following initiation. It is not as if with each recitation of the mantra the adept contemplates the meaning of the mantra's individual syllables. Rather, the meaning of the syllables contributes to the efficacy of the mantra's recitation. Out of interpretations so long studied and contemplated, the adept adds another dimension to the mantra's power. Without imbibing the mantra's meaning in all its complexity its recital is deemed useless. As Bhāskararāya says:

> The utterance of sound without a knowledge of the [true] import bears no fruit, [even as] the offering thrown over ashes in the absence of fire does not burst into flame. Those who are merely reciting the different sounds without a knowledge of their meaning are like asses carrying loads of sandalwood.[73]

Thus, the mantra's power is inherent but latent until one acquires a specific kind of knowledge. Put in terms of our earlier analysis, the mantra's indexical value must be accompanied by its symbolic values in order for it to be put to use properly in ritual. Bhāskararāya's states that the mantra simply will not do what is expected without this esoteric knowledge, just as an offering will not burn without fire. From the perspective of the Śrīvidyā adept, the theological interpretations of the mantra validate its ritual uses and provide a necessary set of qualifications to prevent the uninitiated from gaining access to the full power of latent divinity. Viewed from the standpoint of the historian of religion, the inverse would appear to be the case: the ritual use of the mantra validates and coordinates theology. In other words, because the religious virtuosi emphasize the mantra's *restricted* ritual use as a means by which to advance their privileged claims, such theological interpretations enhance the conditions under which restrictions may be legitimately imposed.

The *Yoginīhṛdaya* creates a common source for six esoteric meanings (*artha*) of the *śrīvidyā* which apply to all variations. Bhāskararāya's explanation is the one best known to contemporary south Indian adepts. The first of the six meanings he explains:

> The Supreme Goddess (Parādevata) who is the aggregate of the seven Śakti-s, Vāmā, etc. and is the embodiment of the thirty-six Tattva-s does not differ from this Mantra [even by the smallest measure].
>
> The letter *a* and the letter *ha* which are identical with Śiva and Śakti, which are devoid of form, which embrace each other and which pulsate and shine, are [no other than] the Supreme Brahman mentioned in the Upaniṣad-s.
>
> These two are manifest in the Mantra itself as the first [letter] of the last Group and the fourth [letter] of the middle Group. Hence, the identity of the Goddess, the Mantra, and the universe is established as *bhavārtha*.[74]

The *bhavārtha* or "existential meaning" refers to the ontological identity of the mantra's sounds with ultimate reality. The *bhavārtha* indicates the mantra as a single, indexical sign which corresponds to the goddess as a single object. Accordingly, the universe as a dynamic process of "becoming" does not undergo any ultimate change in its "being." *Bhavārtha* secures the ontological anchor of monism but, at the same time, asserts a plurality of being brought about by the Absolute's *real* transformation (*parināma*). The plurality of being is neither unreal nor imaginary (*vivarta*). Further, the mantra's *bhavārtha* guarantees that creation is under the purposeful guidance of a divine being.

The *sampradāyārtha* or "traditional meaning," the second of the mantra's meanings, identifies the *śrīvidyā*'s syllables collectively with the five physical elements and the thirty-six *tattvas* or categories that make up reality.[75] According to Bhāskararāya:

> As there is no difference between the cause and its effect, between the thing signified (*vācya*) and the word which signifies the thing (*vacaka*), and between the Brahman and the universe, so also the universe and this Vidyā are identical [in relation to each other]. This is the Sampradāyārtha.[76]

The meaning (*artha*) is "traditional" (*sampradāya*) in the sense that it is the customary explanation that accounts for the transformation of divinity into the manifest world. Thus, the the purview of the mantra's meaning can be extended into concepts and categories that may be explained differently elsewhere. From an analytical perspective the traditional meaning asserts that the mantra is, in fact, an index of the goddess's presence and not simply symbolic.

The third or "hidden meaning" (*nirgarbhārtha*) is explained as the identity of the individual's Self (*ātman*), the guru, and Śiva while the fourth *kaulikārtha* (the "meaning according to the Kula") sets forth the identity of Self, guru, and goddess.[77] This fourth meaning also includes the identification of the mantra with the planets, the asterisms (*nakṣatra*), the senses and their respective objects, and the material (*prakṛti*) and spiritual world (*puruṣa*).[78] The *kaulikārtha* establishes a relationship between the mantra's components and the microcosmic/macrocosmic universe. The objective of this procedure is to authorize the ritual methods that restate these relationships. Thus Bhāskararāya identifies microcosmic/macrocosmic elements with the *śrīcakra*'s sub-cakras and states that the Self, guru, and goddess are sources by which the *kaulikārtha* of these relationships are known. By identifying the mantra's meanings with parts of the *śrīcakra* and locating the "orthodoxy" of such an interpretation in the guru, Bhāskararāya accomplishes two things. First, he mandates a connection between the *śrīvidyā* and the *śrīcakra* and thereby creates a vital interpretive link between two distinctive components of the goddess and her ritual worship. That is, he makes explicit a connection between mantra and yantra that would otherwise appear to be arbitrary. Second, he establishes the guru as the source of power inherent but, as it were, locked inside the mantra. His aim is not merely to explain the guru's role in the process of obtaining the mantra's meanings (*artha*) but to suggest that without a "correct" ritual initiation and pedigree, one does not have access to the mantra's inherent power as an indexical sign. Summarizing, Bhāskararāya says:

> In this manner the identity of the Mother, the Vidyā, the Cakra, the Guru and the [pupil's own] self [is patent]. This is the *Kaulikārtha* of the Mantra.[79]

The fifth or "secret meaning" (*rahasyārtha*) identifies the mantra with the body's yogic centers and completes the pattern of microcosmic/macrocosmic symbolism by linking the human form to the universal forms set forth in the previous four *arthas*. At this level a critical connection is drawn between that which is external and internal with respect to oneself. By placing this connection at the fifth level of meaning, Śrīvidyā adepts affirm the necessity of a personal *experience* that occurs when one "awakens" the divinity within the individual. Here we observe how Śrīvidyā is unrelenting in its *description* of an experience of theistic nondualism.

Comprehending each meaning brings a new level of realization. The sixth and final level expresses the "meaning of ultimate reality" (*mahātattvārtha*). At this final level, all previous dualistic identifications between subjects and objects are transcended. The "meaning of ultimate reality" fulfills a logical requirement for Śrīvidyā's nondualistic philosophy by placing the experience of the ultimate beyond linguistic boundaries. The conclusion is ontological monism, a position that seeks to sublate but not obviate the difference between the adept's own self (*ātman*) and the godhead.

The most important facet of Śrīvidyā's *artha* theory is the cosmological link established between the goddess as mantra and as yantra. Creation is envisioned as a process involving the *śrīcakra* and corresponding mantras; the yantra and mantra thus serve both as the form creation takes and as a type of map that leads to the "original" state of dissolution. While the mantra must be ritually identified with the human body and the *śrīcakra*, the identification process, Bhāskararāya says, is completed only in the contemplative experience of the mantra's six interconnected meanings. In the final analysis he concludes:

> Unapproachable by word or mind and other senses, transcending the [thirty-six] Tattva-s, bigger than the biggest and smaller than the smallest, with a place loftier than the skies, identical with the universe, assuming the [subtle] forms of Consciousness (*cit*) and Bliss (*ānanda*): [such is Brahman] and therein should one concentrate his self with a view to attaining identity...[80]

The *śrīvidyā*'s meanings (*artha*) are interpretations of the signs that map creation: comprehending the mantra means that material reality and its subtle sound counterparts are no longer viewed as distinct or parallel entities. Rather, one obtains two perspectives on the same reality. Mantras are conferred the status of being the source of reality, physical or mental; they are not a parallel creation or simply means for achieving stated goals. In other words, Śrīvidyā's *artha* theory restates the common Tantric notion that creation *is* sound and is *created by* sound. Further, sound is treated as a "natural resource" since, when it occurs as a mantra, it is not a cultural artifact of human origin but a hierarchically superior form of the divine. However, since a guru learns the mantra's secrets, understanding the mantra's significance (as an indexical *and* symbolic sign) is understood to be cultural rather than natural. Śrīvidyā creates important cultural checks, such as the discretion of the guru, to control what is imagined to be non-cultural or natural creation process in which the goddess devolves into her specific mantric form. Without an indispensable and acknowledged human factor brought into the interpretive process, there would be no way to insure that the link between human and divine is truly indissoluble and that creation occurs as a deliberate and meaningful act on the part of both parties.

The relationship of guru to divinity creates a moral universe in which discretionary action and knowledge are intertwined. Were it not required that a guru interpret the mantra's meanings, creation's ultimate meaning would be either arbitrary or determined wholly by impersonal karmic law. By linking the mantra's perceived inherent powers to its meanings and ritual use, Śrīvidyā confers on itself the privilege of interpretation and avoids the unwanted consequences of living in a universe governed under laws that are not wholly understood or under conditions that cannot be controlled. The acquisition of esoteric knowledge, therefore, links the human acquisition of power to the goddess's power manifest in the mantra.

Each of the fifteen syllables of the *kādividyā* are given esoteric etymologies that make them derivative of particular Sanskrit verbal roots and their meanings. Bhāskararāya, like other Tantric commentators, was aware these etymologies could not be justified according to Pāṇini's grammar. In short, etymology was used as another vehicle for the acquisition of esoteric knowledge. As the chart below shows, even the syllables within the *śrīvidyā* that repeat may not be derived from the same verbal root and several syllables (or parts of the *bījākṣara hrīṃ*) are given no verbal derivative. Bhāskararāya is interested only in interpreting the *kādi śrīvidyā*:

Syllable Derivative	*Verbal Root*	*Esoteric Meaning*
Vāgbhavakūṭa		
ka	*kan*, to shine	Śiva, the Illuminator
e	*in*, to study	Instrument of learning i.e., the buddhi
[*ka* + *e* indicates the luminous intellect]		
ī	*ī*, to pervade	Pervading all reality
la + *ha* + *rī* =		Predominance
m		Cause of Predominance

Syllable Derivative	*Verbal Root*	*Esoteric Meaning*
Kāmarājakūṭa		
ha	*han*, to injure	Valor, *ha* is the cause of vanquishing the enemy
sa	*so*, to enjoy or *su*, to procreate	Wealth, an aid to enjoyment
ka	*kam*, to desire	Women, who are attracted by the mantra and who are the objects of desire
ha	*oharn*, to go	Refers to achievement of valor, wealth, desire, etc.
la + *ha* + *rī*	*ī*, to shine	Fame
ṃ		
Śaktikūṭa		
sa ka la		Are that by which the above actions are brought about
hṛ	*hṛ*, to remove	The destroyer of the universe
ī		Radiance, the cause of creation and preservation

[*hṛ* + *ī* = the Mother who shines in the heart and dispels pain, *hrī* is a dependent determinative compound (*karmadhārya*) with *ṃ*]

ṃ		Primal sound (*nāda*) or knowledge

This compounded meaning (*samastārtha*), Bhāskararāya says, is so called because it involves compounding several words, attributing to the mantra the accomplishment of all human desires, and providing an essential meaning for the *vidyā* in an abridged form.[81] The point of such an exercise appears to be that the mantra's constituent *bījas* or seeds are both ontologically "indestructible" *and* partially dissolvable inasmuch as they are derived from verbal roots esoterically interpreted. The search for meaning is, ultimately, a search for secret roots and origins.

THE *ŚRĪVIDYĀ* APPENDED TO OTHER MANTRAS

In its ritual use the *śrīvidyā* is sometimes appended to other mantras and particularly to a *gāyatrī* form devised for Tripurā. Tantric sources have created mantras styled on the Vedic *gāyatrī* by substituting terms within the basic skeletal pattern. These are especially popular in the worship of local goddesses. For example, Śivakāmasundarī, the consort of Cidambaram Naṭarāja, has a *gāyatrī* mantra that follows this pattern. Śivakāmasundarī's *gāyatrī* is: *devadaveśī vidhmahe śivakāmeśī dhīmahī tannasśiva pracodayāt.*[82] *PKS* offers a form of Tripurā *gāyatrī* mantra that is to be recited with the *śrīvidyā.*[83] Tripurā's *gāyatrī* is interspersed with the *śrīvidyā* and reads: (1) [*vāgbhavakūṭa*] *ka e ī la hrīṃ tripurasundarī vidhmahe;* (2) [*kāmarājakūṭa*] *ha sa ka ha la hrīṃ pitakāmani dhīmahī;* and, (3) [*śaktikūṭa*] *sa ka la hrīṃ tannaḥ klinna pracodayāt.* While meditating on this mantra Rāmeśvara explains that one should imagine the *śrīcakra* on the disk of the sun. This links the original relationship of Vedic *gāyatrī*'s Savitṛ with Tripurā. While several contemporary adepts knew of this mantra, none practiced it. Other mantras appended to the *śrīvidyā* do not appear to have comparable textual sources. For example, one south Indian lineage connects the worship of Cidambaram's Naṭarāja root-mantra (*mūlamantra*) to the *śrīvidyā.* Thus, mantras not only connect divinities but whole traditions, creating a series of social and historical relationships that implicate groups and ideologies that are otherwise distinct and sometimes disparate.[84]

TRIPURĀ UPANIṢAD, HĀDI, AND *KĀDI VIDYĀS*

Tripurā Upaniṣad provides Bhāskararāya an opportunity to stake out his own position on the *kādi* and *hādi śrīvidyās.* Unlike the *Tripurātāpinī Upaniṣad* which compares *śrīvidyā* to *gāyatrī* and discusses the twelve mantra configurations, the *Tripurā Upaniṣad* considers only the *kādi* and *hādi* mantras. Verses eight and nine of *Tripurā Upaniṣad* disclose each mantra's syllables in a technical, encoded vocabulary. Bhāskararāya remarks that, "Because this mantra is deeply secret it should be learned only from the guru."[85] The words used in these Upaniṣadic verses give no indication of their esoteric meanings. Bhāskararāya begins by pointing out that this particular esoteric revelation is unlike the explicit form of revelation evidenced in the Vedic *gāyatrī.* He says:

> In some places the *gāyatrī* [mantra], the Mother of the Vedas, is recited explicitly even though it is the same [from the esoteric point of view as the *śrīvidyā*].

Translated literally verse eight of the Upaniṣad reads:

> Desire, womb, lotus, wielder of the thunderbolt, cave, *ha*[-]*sa,* the wind, cloud and Indra. Again cave, *sa*[-]*ka*[-]*la* and Māyā—this is the primordial mantra [or original knowledge, *ādividyā*], Mother of the Universe, the Ancient.[86]

The only clue that the verse indicates the mantra is the ambiguous term *ādividyā* which can be taken either in the sense of "original mantra" or in the more literal sense of "original knowledge." Without the commentators, the verse is virtually nonsensical. More important, the verse offers an example of the tradition's efforts at purposeful secrecy.

The most significant aspect of *Tripurā Upaniṣad*'s treatment of the *śrīvidyā* is that *hādi vidyā* is treated as a derivative of *kādi*. Bhāskararāya notes that *Jñānārṇava Tantra* regards these two as the mantra's superior forms. He concludes by saying, "because the *kādividyā*...has been described first, its priority (*ādhikya*) is suggested."[87] Despite having had such influential adherents as Puṇyānanda and Amṛtānanda, the status of the *hādimata* is ambiguous. Bhāskararāya states in one place that *kādi* is superior while in another he remarks with characteristic tolerance that, "...since all *vidyā*s are not different, a comparison of one to another is merely for the sake of praising [one and encouraging its performance]."[88] Contemporary Śrīvidyā traditionalists maintain that the *kādi pañcadaśī* is the original mantra, the *ādividyā*.

The only controversy regarding the "priority" of *kādi* over *hādi vidyā*s in south Indian Śrīvidyā occurs in the presentation of *Saundaryalaharī*, which presents *hādi* in verse 32 and *kādi* in verse 33. Commentators favoring one view or the other use the text to assert the correctness of their own interpretation. Bhāskararāya, like most contemporary adepts, sees little point in questioning the sources or practices of mantric traditions. Since diverse mantra traditions (*mata*) are accepted, there is little at stake in the discussion other than a passing reference to the superiority of one's own practice.[89]

The configuration of the *hādi śrīvidyā* is not without controversy and some confusion.[90] The *hādi* mantra suggested in the *Tripurā Upaniṣad* is the fifteen syllable configuration. As verse nine says,

> [Replacing] the three root [syllables of each *kūṭa* of this [Kāmarāja *kādividyā* as described in the previous verse with the letters *ha*, *sa* and *ka* represented by the words] six, seven, and fire (*vahni*, also meaning Śiva) they [i.e., the devotees come to] dwell [in the Lopāmudrā *hādividyā* mantra].[91]

Thus, *hādividyā*'s configuration in fifteen syllables is:

Vāgbhavakūṭa:	*ha sa ka la hrīṃ*
Kāmarājakūṭa:	*ha sa ka ha la hrīṃ*
Śaktikūṭa:	*sa ka la hrīṃ*

In some versions, however, it is not merely the first three syllables of the first *kūṭa* that are replaced but the entire first *kūṭa*. The result is a sixteen syllable configuration in which the *vāgbhavakūṭa* is identical to the *kāmarājakūṭa*. Whether the Lopāmudrā tradition considers this sixteen syllable version its sixteen syllable mantra (*ṣoḍaśī*) is unclear.

Whether there are important doctrinal differences between *kādi* and *hādi* traditions is difficult to assess for two reasons. First is that *kādi* proponents do not mention noteworthy differences. Late texts pay little attention to the details of mantra differences. Apparently the conduct (*ācāra*) and ritual of the two *mata*s did not differ significantly, as was clearly the case between Kaulas and Samayins. Lakṣmīdhara, who offers brief comments on certain theoretical *kādi/hādi* differences, is not supported by any other historical figure.[92] Second, differences raised by *hādimata* proponents, such as Śivānanda, deal with extremely technical matters of interpretation. Contemporary adepts have little interest in such arcane disputes. On the surface, the *mata*s appear to differ only to the degree that each favors its own mantra contemplation (*bhāvanā*). However, there are no extant ritual manuals for *hādividyā* in south India. Only Śivānanda presents *hādimata* as a liturgical tradition but his remarkable efforts presage no later developments along these lines. None of the dozens of ritual *paddhati*s that I have examined in south Indian manuscript libraries and in the private hands of adepts—texts at the heart of ritual practices—employ the *hādividyā*.[93]

Contemporary traditions shed no light on this disparity between *kādi* and *hādi* texts since there are neither ritual liturgies of *hādimata* available nor living adepts to offer explanation. Curiously, neither Puṇyānanda in *KKV* nor Amṛtānanda in his *YH* commentary offer any clues as to what, if any, ritual factors change with the substitution of *hādi* for *kādi*.[94] We cannot safely conclude that the practice of the *hādividyā* was strictly a Kashmiri or north Indian phenomenon, despite the absence of a living *hādimata* tradition in the south. Bhāskararāya, for example, writes as if *hādividyā* is practiced in south India in his day. We know little more about *hādi* and *kādi* tradition differences than that they involved a transformation of the root-mantra's syllable configuration.

Qualification for each form of the *śrīvidyā* is sometimes associated with a predominance of either Śiva or Śakti in the individual personality. Contemporary oral traditions echo the views of the *Śrīvidyāratnasūtras* in which it is maintained that there are two dominant factors (*tattva*s) permeating reality, Śiva and Śakti; Śiva *tattva* is associated with Lopāmudrā (i.e., *hādividyā*) while Śakti *tattva* is associated with Kāmarāja (*kādividyā*). According to some, those more in need of (or endowed with) the Śakti element receive the *kādividyā* and, since this is the majority of persons, *kādi* is the more popular form of the mantra.[95]

All Śrīvidyā traditionalists place their teachers in a succession from the "original" *kādi* and *hādi* gurus who learned the *vidyā* from Śiva. Bhāskararāya notes that the lineages of Kāmarāja and Lopāmudrā keep distinct meanings for the mantra but that these are only learned from the tradition and through a guru and "not from anything else."[96] Without a living tradition of Lopāmudrā lineage traditionalists it is impossible to assess the importance of these distinctions.

ṢOḌAŚĀKṢARĪ: THE SIXTEEN SYLLABLE FORM OF THE *ŚRĪVIDYĀ*

The *ṣoḍaśī* is mentioned in Śrīvidyā sources but rarely discussed in any detail. Bhāskararāya explains the emergence of this form of the mantra:

> This (*ṣoḍaśī*) sprung from the Mūlādhāra of the great Mother, and proceeding through the stages of Parā, Paśyantī, etc. emerged from her mouth in the Vaikharī form; and it was transmitted from teacher to pupil.[97]

There are two other comments about *ṣoḍaśī* worth noting in the *LSN*. The first identifies *ṣoḍaśī* as the sixteen year old virginal Lalitā; the second says it is the sixteenth hidden digit (*kalā*) of the moon that adjoins the usual fifteen phases (*tithis*) identified with the fifteen eternalities (*nityā*) that preside over them.[98] The addition of a sixteenth element to an established set of fifteen is analogous to the addition of a fourth element to established triads.[99] The "sixteenth" element deliberately plays on the symbolism of "plus one," that is, a set of three or fifteen plus one more element. For example, the fifteen *nityās* are identified with the innermost *trikoṇa* of the *śrīcakra* and placed five to a side; the sixteenth, the higher and more subtle emanation, is then placed on the *bindu* in the center. Thus, the sixteenth *nityā* by its being identical to the symbol of absolute nonduality, the *bindu*, is outside the ordinary realm of the fifteen *nityās* identified with the periphery of the central triangle. Like the fourth *puruṣārtha*, *mokṣa*, or the fourth state (*turya*) in the description of waking, dreaming, and dreamless consciousness, the sixteenth element pushes beyond the realms of ordinary reality and is identified with the achievement of ultimacy or the final goal of liberation. The sixteenth element, like the fourth in a set of threes, subsumes and encompasses the others as well as completes the symbolic pattern of meanings. This interpretation, which parallels the sixteenth element of the *śrīvidyā* with the fourth element of triadic symbols, is not uncommon among contemporary Śrīvidyā votaries.

Bhāskararāya mentions the *ṣoḍaśī* when the *LSN* cues a discussion but it is clear that for him the term *mūlamantra* is reserved for the fifteen syllable *kādividyā*.[100] He expresses little interest in the explanation of the *ṣoḍaśī* and leaves it out of his most elaborate discussion of mantras, the *Varivasyārahasya*. *Ṣoḍaśī* is also not mentioned in such important ritual texts as Śrīvidyānandanātha's *Śrīvidyāratnākara*. However, contemporary adepts make the sixteen syllable mantra the centerpiece of ritual. Though few are interested in the mantra's esoteric significance the way historical commentators are, the majority assert that it is the most secret and superior form of the *śrīvidyā*.

Ṣoḍaśī's adherents consider its secrecy one of the most significant aspects of its efficacy and the primary means of preserving its status. Oral transmission remains the basic method for elucidating *ṣoḍaśī*'s structure. Its forms are mentioned only rarely in privately circulated ritual manuals without attention to its symbolic interpretation.

According to the *kādimata*, there are two forms of the *ṣoḍaśī*, the abbreviated or "light" (*laghu*) version and the "great" (*mahā*) version. The *laghuṣoḍaśī* retains the literal sixteen syllable configuration by adding the seed-syllable (*bījākṣara*) *śrīṃ*.[101] This form has lost currency in contemporary south India where the *mahāṣoḍaśī* is favored. *Mahāṣoḍaśī* does not conform literally to the sixteen syllable structure but rather adds two (or three) sets of syllables which are counted as a single unit. Instead of being divided into three *kūṭas*, the mantra is usually structured into six units:

1. *om śrīṃ hrīṃ klīm aiṃ sauḥ*
2. *om hrīṃ śrīṃ*
3. *ka e ī la hrīṃ*
4. *ha sa ka ha la hrīṃ*
5. *sa ka la hrīṃ*
6. *sauḥ aiṃ klīṃ hrīṃ śrīṃ*

The *mahāṣoḍaśī* occasionally appears without the second of the six units; the form cited above is favored by the majority of contemporary adepts. The sixth unit, which reverses the first unit's syllables, represents the most secret form of the *kāmakalā*, that is, the female organ esoterically referred to by the phrase "half the letter 'h'." To those who regard *ṣoḍaśī* as superior to the fifteen syllable mantra (*kādividyā pañcadaśī*), its ritual use is considered an extension of an earlier initiation into the *pañcadaśī*. However, not all agree that the *ṣoḍaśī* is the superior mantra. Several contemporary lineages maintain that because of the seeming confusion in the *ṣoḍaśī*'s structure, the fifteen syllable (*pañcadaśī*) is not only the original form of the mantra but also superior.

THE MEANING OF THE VIDYĀ, INITIATION, AND OTHER MANTRAS

> The devotion of the inept to the external ostentation [of the *śrīvidyā*], being without aptitude for what is necessary, is like a body in which life has perished, or a puppet from which the strings are detached.[102]

Bhāskararāya's remark is a common reminder in Śrīvidyā literature that the efficacy of the *mūlamantra* is realized only when its meaning precedes ritual practice and transmitted according to the prescriptions of initiation.[103] The aptitude for initiation and the results of its practice are succinctly stated by the *SL* commentator Kaivalyāśrama who quotes the *Rudrayāmala* to the effect that, "He who has no other birth receives the supreme *pañcadaśākṣarī.*"[104]

Śrīvidyā has always considered its initiation (*dīkṣā*) an elite form of spirituality, linked to the concept of favorable karma acquired over the course of countless previous births.[105] In this way, the subtle form (*sūkṣmarūpa*) differs significantly from the physical (*sthūlarūpa*), which is generally considered to be open to all Hindus.

Initiation requires an extended period of instruction culminating in an elaborate ritual, the focus of which is the giving of the *śrīvidyā*. Bestowal of the mantra is frequently accompanied by a gift of a physical *śrīcakra* that becomes the initiates personal object of worship. These two aspects of the goddess are considered entrusted knowledge, not to be spoken of openly in the company of non-initiates. The initiate usually continues to worship the physical icons (*sthūlarūpa*) of Lalitā though is now considered an embodiment of auspicious (*śrī*) wisdom (*vidyā*).

Ramānanda remarks that knowledge in the form of the mantra (*vidyā*) is of two kinds, higher (*parā*) and lower (*aparā*); the higher form entails knowledge of Brahman and is in the subtle form (*sūkṣma*) of the goddess (i.e., the mantra itself) while the lower form, expressed in ritual and discussed in ritual portions of the texts (*karmakhaṇḍa*), is concerned with the goddess's physical appearance (*sthūla*). He goes on to say that the *vidyā* of the supreme Brahman is *śrīvidyā*.[106]

Śivānanda makes another interpretive distinction. After remarking that the goddess is the essence of the knowledge of mantras, present in the form of the *vidyā*s, and the heart of the Vedas and Kaula tradition, he states that she is the cause of the universe in her higher aspect (*parā*) and the actual effect, that is, the material world, in her lower aspect (*aparā*). This cause and effect process is brought about by an act of the goddess's grace that occurs when she is in absolute unity with Śiva. In the undifferentiated form of Brahman as sound (*śabda*) the mantra begins at the supreme unarticulated level, that is, at the *parā* aspect. It then gradually devolves to the level of articulated speech (*vaikharī*) and in doing so becomes the manifest universe.[107]

Śrīvidyā maintains that to perform the required forms of contemplative worship (*upāsana*) under the appropriate conditions is to be guaranteed these accomplishments.[108] Contemporary adepts emphasize that all *siddhi*s other than liberation (*mokṣa*) are secondary accretions of the higher spiritual discipline; in other words, the Śrīvidyā initiate should aspire only to liberation when meditating on the mantra but, in the process of worshiping with the *śrīvidyā*, is sure to acquire all other physical and spiritual powers.[109]

PKS 1.9 states that all forms of accomplishment (*siddhi*) are obtained through mantras and Rāmeśvara clarifies the point by saying that the *śrīvidyā*, though only one of many mantras, is the only mantra capable of producing all *siddhis*.[110] *Yoginīhṛdaya*, 1.4 makes clear that only the *śrīvidyā* can bring about liberation and not any other *vidyā*.[111] The connection between the mantra's power and initiation deserves further explanation.[112]

Rāmeśvara aptly summarizes the opinions of Śrīvidyā adepts on the importance of initiation. Quoting the *Paramānanda Tantra* he says that "the first step of the palace of liberation (*mukti*) is initiation (*dīkṣā*)."[113] The disciple worthy of this initiation is a paradigm of virtue; one no longer driven by material desires but by the urge to find the liberative truth.[114]

For Bhāskararāya and the vast majority of contemporary adepts loyalty to the guru's interpretation on all matters is absolute. The truly qualified teacher cannot err since he is none other than Śiva himself.[115] In addition, Śrīvidyā, unlike some other Tantric traditions, advocates devotion to a single teacher (*ekagurūpāsti*) for all forms of Tantric instruction. Curiously, several important historical figures, including Bhāskararāya, received non-Tantric instruction from teachers other than the one who initiated them into the *śrīvidyā*.

Mantra initiation is only the beginning of the spiritual path, an indispensable requisite for the higher forms of knowledge within the tradition, including the contemplative worship of the goddess.[116] The student is guaranteed that the mantra will gain in efficacy through use, provided it descends through an attested lineage. In contemporary practice, however, little effort is spent to consider the guru's lineage. If one is considered a Śrīvidyā guru, he is accorded a respect that prevents the curious from making probing inquiries. Contemporary adepts maintain that they rely instead on clear demonstrations of the accomplishments of Śrīvidyā practice. An etiquette of tradition that surrounds the guru with an aura of indisputability generally prevents inquiries into a particular individual's qualifications despite attempts to create accountability.[117]

The process of initiation in the Śrīvidyā tradition is described elaborately. The *PKS*, for example, devotes an entire chapter to the subject.[118] Before receiving the *śrīvidyā*, the initiate goes through extensive purificatory rites and receives initiation into other prefatory mantra.[119] If the lineage includes the sixteen syllable mantra (*ṣoḍaśī*) then the *pañcadaśī* is given first and *ṣoḍaśī* may (or may not, depending upon the student's qualification as determined by the guru) be given at the same time or in the future.

All lineages include as a prerequisite to *śrīvidyā* initiation the root-mantra (*mūlamantra*) of the god Gaṇapati. Rāmeśvara remarks that while worshiping the elephant-headed Gaṇeśa is merely an accessory to the great *vidyā* (*mahāvidyā*) of Lalitā, it is nonetheless necessary because this god insures the removal of all obstacles.[120] Umānanda concurs that Gaṇapati's root-mantra (*mūlamantra*) must be given before the initiate receives the *śrīvidyā* but disagrees with Rāmeśvara's reluctance to accept the guru's instruction as absolute.[121] It is noteworthy that Bhāskararāya chose to write a commentary on the Thousand Names of Gaṇapati.[122] No commentator refers to Gaṇapati's role in Lalitā's destruction of Bhaṇḍāśura.

Some texts also prescribe initiation into the mantra of Bālātripurasundarī prior to initiation into Lalitā Mahātripurasundarī's root-mantra (*mūlamantra*).[123] Initiation into Gaṇapati precedes Bālātripurasundarī and so is hierarchically subordinate to it. But, while Gaṇapati plays an important role in all later forms of ritual and contemplative worship, Bālātripurasundarī recedes into the background.[124]

In the case of Bālātripurasundarī the pure seed-syllable configuration is maintained and the mantra itself is formed from the *bījākṣara* elements of the *mahāṣoḍaśī*. It appears in two units thus:

1. *oṃ aiṃ klīṃ sauḥ*
2. *sauḥ klīṃ aiṃ*

The repetition of syllables in reverse order draws another parallel to the construction of *mahāṣoḍaśī* though it is unclear if this mantra was created with *mahāṣoḍaśī* in mind. As far as the ritual use of Bālātripurasundarī is concerned, the meditational verse (*dhyānaśloka*) describing the physical form (*sthūlarūpa*) of Bālā, which usually precedes the mantra's repetition, is not included in any of the forms of worship associated with the fully mature Lalitā—there is, as it were, no designated place for Bālātripurasundarī in either physical or mantric forms in any Śrīvidyā worship employing the *śrīcakra* and incorporating the *śrīvidyā*.[125] Thus, for *kādimata* followers maintaining the supremacy of the *ṣoḍaśī*, Śrīvidyā's mantric hierarchy culminates with *ṣoḍaśī* and is followed by *pañcadaśī*, *bālātripurasundarī*, and the ever present *mahāgaṇapati* mantra.[126]

SECRECY AND THE ARTICULATION OF THE MANTRA

All Śrīvidyā sources maintain some type of secrecy regarding the mantra's utterance, usually involving the use of technical language.

For example, in texts such as the Upaniṣads and the *Saundaryalaharī*, one commonly finds the *vidyā* encoded in technical or mystical language. Rarely, however, does one find in Śrīvidyā sources the use of poetic or metaphoric simile such as is common in the so-called *sandhābhāṣa* or "twilight language" of Buddhist Tantra.[127]

Only in ritual manuals are the forms of the mantra written explicitly. These texts are meant to be used only by a closed circles of initiates. Many contemporary adepts object to any explicit mention of the mantra be it verbal or written, fearing misuse by the uninitiated. Adepts do not ordinarily verbalize the mantra in a manner that would allow others to hear it except during ritual or under private instructional circumstances. So long as texts circulate only among the initiated and ritual prescriptions restrict the presence of non-initiates, the mantra's secrecy is maintained. However, the astute listener often hears the "secret sounds" of the *śrīvidyā* in public and semiprivate rituals in contemporary south India.

The theological reasons for the mantra's secrecy are straightforward: it is the subtle nature of the Absolute, not merely a name or representation of it. Thus, to utter it is to enunciate the source of power that creates, maintains, and destroys the universe. Reciting the mantra aloud in the presence of the uninitiated is considered potentially dangerous because it might then be used without proper instruction. Despite the belief that the mantra becomes fully empowered only through initiation and has liberative power only when its esoteric meanings are comprehended, it is part of a meta-linguistic reality and as such contains an inherent power.[128] By its being identical with the Vedic *praṇava* and *gāyatrī*, and thus a form of the Absolute Brahman, the mantra is an expression of power that can be used or misused for any material or spiritual end.[129]

The mantra's power stems from the combination of its inherent capacity as an emanation of the goddess with the acquisition of grace and diligent self-effort. Since the mantra is a concentrated form of divine power it has the capacity to bring about events that defy all normal and conventional modes of understanding. The guru, an embodiment of both Śiva and Śakti, is the primary source for bringing out the mantra's latent power. The student not only depends on the teacher for the mantra's esoteric meaning but to empower the sounds themselves. Since the mantra is itself in a direct chain of transmission from Śiva and Śakti, the guru provides what no written source can: the living embodiment of the mantra's meaning and power.

Thus, initiation into the *śrīvidyā* is an act of the guru's grace on whom the student's continuing welfare and achievement are dependent. The necessity of acquiring the guru's grace does not mean that individual self-effort is vitiated but that without this personal instruction there can be no claim to a continuity of spiritual power that has followed the mantra from its eternal source. The goal of mantra *sādhana* finally depends upon the initiate's own contemplative efforts and response to the guru's instructions. Thus, Śrīvidyā combines three distinct but interrelated soteriological strategies: "science" (i.e., the inherent power of mantras), empowering grace, and self-effort. To understand how these strategies become ritual techniques, it is necessary to consider the third element of the goddess's theological triad, her yantra, the *śrīcakra*.

Chapter 6

Śrīcakra: The Transcendent Aspect of Devī

INTRODUCTORY REMARKS

> When She, the Supreme Śakti, out of her own will [assumes] the form of the Universe, observing her own self effusion (*sphurattama*), the [*śrī*-]cakra emerges.[1]

The *śrīcakra*, literally the "wheel of Śrī" or "prosperity," is perhaps the most famous visual image in Hindu Tantrism, yet its interpretation has remained obscure to most Tantrics and non-Tantrics alike.[2] The *śrīcakra*'s theological interpretation and ritual worship are best treated separately—an approach assumed by the *Yoginīhṛdaya* and by contemporary Śrīvidyā practitioners in south India.[3]

This chapter's discussion parallels the tradition's own interpretative strategies. The *śrīcakra* represents the process by which the originally unified, undifferentiated divinity assumes the binary character of the masculine and feminine Śiva and Śakti, and creates the universe through an on-going process of devolving particularization (*kalā*).

Śrīvidyā retains the structure of Kashmiri Śaivite theology: Śiva is unchanging consciousness (*cit*) and being (*sat*) who through a willful (*icchā*) and playful (*līlā*) act of self-recognition reflects upon himself and thus creates through his own self-delimitation (*māyāśakti*). From the Śaivite point of view, the goddess herself is the manifestation of Śiva's delimitation. It is she who manifests as power in three modes: willful self-emanation (*icchāśakti*), cognitive self-recognition (*jñānaśakti*), and the creative act (*kriyāśakti*). In essence, Śakti is the dynamic power of self-differentiation emanating from the primordial Śiva.

The *śrīcakra* not only represents the process of creative devolution but is its actual form. Put differently, the *śrīcakra* is a symbol of the universe's primordial structure and, at the same time, the index of reality that forms its structure. Put theologically, the universe is a projection or reflection (*pratibimba*) of divinity's own self-reflection. The *śrīcakra*, like the universe itself, is both identical to and different from its source. Just as a reflection creates an isomorphic image of its subject and yet is not its subject, so the *śrīcakra* is both reality's form (*rūpa*) and its most perfect reflection (*bimba*).

Śrīcakra visually mimics its symbolic and indexical functions. Śiva's unified being is represented by the central "drop" or *bindu* at the *śrīcakra*'s center; Śiva's conjunction with Śakti occurs in the form of nine intersecting triangles from which are projected the "lesser" forms represented by lotus petals and rectangles. Microcosmically, the *śrīcakra* is the human body, itself a "palace of nine gates," that is, with nine apertures.[4]

Of uncertain historical origins, the *śrīcakra* appears in established Hindu temples in south India no later than the middle tenth century.[5] Also called the "*śrīyantra*," the image is not usually referred to as a *maṇḍala* (literally, circle) as such figures are commonly referred to in Buddhist sources. Methods for its drawing and its symbolism are detailed in textual sources only from the period of the *Vāmakeśvara Tantra*, about the same time it appears in southern temples.[6] However, the *śrīcakra* must have emerged in its inveterate form much earlier than these written and historical references indicate. Historically, there is no verifiable textual or epigraphical evidence of its presence before the sixth century. Precisely when and where it first appeared and by whom it was composed is not known. Śrīvidyā tradition expresses interest only in mythological and metaphysical descriptions of it as divinity's primordial form.

Traditionalists claim the *śrīcakra*, like the *śrīvidyā*, is referred to in ancient Vedic texts. The passages they cite, however, offer no verifiable literary evidence.[7] Adepts say these references are esoteric; the Vedic seers have deliberately concealed references to the cakra to protect unqualified persons from delving into matters which may prove dangerous to them. The meanings of these esoteric passages can be brought to light only by a qualified teacher.

Like other yantras, the *śrīcakra* was conceived by specialists as part of a broader ritual and speculative system. In other words, the *śrīcakra* is part of a process of thinking by means of ritual rather than a conceptual form first conceived and afterwards attributed its ritual roles. There is no reason to think that the cakra's speculative meanings were the cause of its creation or that they were intact at its inception. Rather, ritual appears to be at the heart of its origins; the cakra's ritual uses seem far too consistent and coherent for it to have been created *without* ritual in mind.

The *śrīcakra*'s private ritual use has always overshadowed its public worship and its interpretation presupposes the oral traditions of Śrīvidyā's lineages. As a *yantra*, it conforms to Stella Kramrisch's general definition:

> A Yantra is a geometrical contrivance by which any aspect of the Supreme Principle may be bound (yantr, to bind; from the root 'yam') to any spot for the purpose of worship. It is an artifice in which the ground (bhūmi) is converted into the extent of the manifest universe.[8]

Kramrisch has in mind yantras used for temple construction, that is, as symbols of the metaphysical plan upon which temples are based. This general notion also applies to the *śrīcakra* inasmuch as it, too, has served as a model for temples and religious structures though it was not conceived for such purposes.[9] Śrīvidyā tradition, however, regards the *śrīcakra* as the source of all *yantras*: the *śrīcakra* is *the* model of the universe. Put differently, the *śrīcakra* is the technology of the Absolute skillfully fashioned in divinity's own self-image.

Theologically, the *śrīcakra* is *not* part of the natural world nor a product of human labor. Rather, it is divinity's own form (*svarūpa*) and has come about independent of its interpretation by human beings. From a critical perspective, the *śrīcakra* signifies the sacred inasmuch as its meanings and uses are implicitly restricted.[10] The *śrīcakra* is a religious object not because it signifies the exceptional and abnormal, but rather that which is deemed constant and regular, namely, the process of creation.[11] Representing "the regular march of the universe," it does not signify the unforseen but rather the sacred.[12] The *śrīcakra* is called *parā* or transcendent in the sense of being a sacred and a religious object.

According to Śrīvidyā, one must undergo a metamorphosis, an initiation, by which one leaves behind the world of natural and ordinary mental images to enter into the world of the sacred *śrīcakra*. This transformation is *not natural* nor is it a part of regular human development but rather the product of a deliberate action by which "the mind irresistibly refuses to allow the two corresponding things to be confounded."[13] Put differently, initiation makes the *śrīcakra*'s sacrality accessible. Were the *śrīcakra* sacred in the sense of having no connection with the profane, it would be useless.[14]

Adepts consider the *śrīcakra* more than a description of the "regular" process by which the divine creates. This is not to say that creation at its source is in entropy. Rather, it too is nothing but power (*śakti*). The *śrīcakra* may also serve as a map that shows the way back to creation's source. Like all maps its graphic forms must be read according to specified patterns of meaning, which in this case are so specialized as to require initiated instruction. The process in which such map-reading is elevated to art and practical procedure is ritual worship (*pūjā*).

But unlike a map which merely depicts reality, the *śrīcakra* is reality albeit esoteric reality; each part of the cakra is the manifestation of reality it represents. If the *śrīvidyā* is Brahman's sound then the *śrīcakra* is Brahman's shape, emblematic of creation's ordinarily unobserved process. One notes increasing variegation over the possibilities that divinity has chosen to assume as it devolves from its purest, undifferentiated form (*bindu*) and assumes diverse manifestations represented through the increasing number of small triangles produced from the juxtaposition of the nine large triangles. Beyond the interlocking triangles are more distant, more diverse, and mundane manifestations of the divine represented by the two sets of lotus petals, numbering eight and sixteen, and the outer three-lined rectangle. The presiding deities attributed to each level of the *śrīcakra* further indicate the descent into more "ordinary" levels and human perceptions of reality. The Śrīvidyā adept claims to have the esoteric knowledge necessary to identify *each* level of cosmic devolution and the ritual skill to trace divinity's course.

Ritual is the key to reading the *śrīcakra* as a divine map and to gaining access to the divine presence, for it is in ritual that the *śrīcakra* is elevated from being divinity's self-generated pattern for reality to divine presence (*sadbhava*). The *śrīcakra*'s form is not intended to represent all the various constituents of the visible, material world; it is, rather, the world emerging in its essential aspects (*kalās*) or manifestations (*tattvas*) that particularize from the amorphous Brahman. As Śivānanda notes, the *śrīcakra* is not merely an external form of the goddess but is identical with her. Since it is the goddess' transcendent form and substance it is also capable of yielding, like the goddess herself, all imaginable desires and powers. These achievements, however, are contingent upon the adept identifying in body and soul with the *śrīcakra* and *śrīvidyā*.[15] Puṇyānanda suggests a similar idea when he says there is no difference between the supreme deity and the *śrīcakra*; at the cakra's center, he says, is seated Śiva, the original guru, who along with the goddess creates the lineages of teachers.[16] Thus, to learn the meaning of the *śrīcakra*'s elements is to gain partial access to its creative power. The *śrīcakra*, Vidyānanda remarks, is the clear medium in which the goddess is reflected; it is Śakti's form (*rūpa*) as well as a reflection (*vimarśa*) of her. Thus, he concludes, the one who meditates on the cakra is capable of achieving any wish since it is the reflection of all material and spiritual powers.[17]

The *śrīcakra* functions on three levels for the initiated adept: (1) it is a map of creation's divine essences projected visually; (2) it is divine power which can become accessible to those who obtain initiated esoteric knowledge about its use; and (3) it is the real presence (*sadbhava*) of divinity, worthy of worship, admiration, and even fear because of its potential to transform one's relationship with the sacred.

Śrīvidyā traditionalists do not disagree about the identification of the *śrīcakra* with the beneficent goddess or about its power to confer worldly and spiritual aims. However, variations in the *śrīcakra*'s configuration are part of sectarian and theological differences. The Samaya school, for example, turns the usual form of the *śrīcakra* "upside down." Other variations, such as those having to do with the cakra's "three circles" (*vṛttatraya*) referred to by Bhāskararāya, are best appreciated in light of the configuration's catholic interpretation. Figure 1 in appendix 1 is the *śrīcakra* to which most historical and modern traditionalists commonly refer and follows the description of the meditational verse (*dhyānaśloka*) found in modern ritual handbooks:

> [The central] *bindu*, [the inner triangle called the] *trikoṇa*, [the sub-cakra of eight triangles called the] *vasukoṇa* [and the two sets of] ten [sub-triangles] conjoined [that follow the *vasukoṇa*]; *manvaśra* [the sub-cakra of fourteen triangles] is joined to the serpentine (*nāga*) [eight lotus] petals [and to these] the sixteen [lotus petals] and the three circles and the three palaces of the earth [that make up the outer gateways]: this is *śrīcakra* of the supreme deity.[18]

This *dhyānaśloka*, like the verse describing Lalitā's physical (*sthūla*) form, defines the *śrīcakra* deemed most suitable for ritual worship (*pūjā*). However, it is not usually included in the liturgies of ritual worship that assume a complete familiarity with both the cakra's arrangement and its meanings. The meditational verse is the beginning of theological interpretations since it assumes a particular order to the *śrīcakra*'s unfolding. Following the so-called *sṛṣṭikrama* or "creation method," it begins from the center with the *bindu* and proceeds outward, listing the names of the nine sub-cakras formed by the interlocking of the major triangles, the three surrounding circles, lotus petals, and outer gateways.[19]

The term "cakra," literally "wheel," can mean any identifiable pattern of figures or configurations which, when taken as a single unit, is a center of specific properties. Thus, the *śrīcakra*'s sub-cakras are traditionally called "cakras" when discussed as single entities.

Śrīvidyā tradition pays relatively little attention to the symbolism of the nine major triangles that are the *śrīcakra*'s trademark. The nine represent the union of the goddess Śakti with her consort Śiva; the five downward facing major triangles are symbolic of Śakti while the four upward facing indicate Śiva. The most common interpretation, which establishes Śakti as the five major triangles, indicates her slight advantage over Śiva. *Brahmāṇḍapurāṇa* makes clear the notion of divine embodiment and union:

> The *śrīcakra*, the body of Śiva (*śivayorvapuḥ*), is established by the nine cakras, [that is,] by the four cakras of Śiva and by the five cakras of Śakti.[20]

Śrīvidyā accepts as self-evident that Śiva and Śakti combine to form the various manifestations of the universe. It is the results of combination that are deemed most interesting.

The sub-cakras are taken as individual units, each with its own name, characteristics, presiding deity, and forms of power. From the cosmological perspective the movement from the central *bindu* towards the outer gateways (*bhūpura*, literally, the "city of Earth") symbolizes increasingly more recognizable and mundane devolutions of reality.

In the *bindu*, Śakti and Śiva are in a state of absolute unity, not merely in dichotomous union as the intersecting nine major triangles represent. There is both an explicit and esoteric sexual symbolism expressed here. The five downward facing Śakti triangles are the "aspect of desire" (*kāmakalā*) and represent the female organ. The four upward facing Śiva triangles are symbolic of the *liṅga*. The combination represents the sexual embrace formed by their joining. However unambiguously sexual this image may be, the predominate image of embodiment acknowledges Śiva and Śakti's sexual union but defies the *appearance* of explicit eroticism. The *śrīcakra* is an anerotic image whose sexual valences require an intellectual leap of imagination. It is little wonder that such an "encoded" eroticism appealed to the conservative morality of high caste brahmanism.

The five Śakti triangles are also symbolic of the five elements that make up the created world, that is, earth (*pṛthvī*), water (*ap*), air (*vāyu*), fire (*agni*), and space (*ākāśa*). The four Śiva triangles, also called "Agni triangles," symbolize the principles that give shape to the material world; their function is to provide a metaphysical basis upon which the material universe is organized. These four Agni (or Fire) principles are known by their technical names: (1) *māyā*, the power of deception that permits the one to appear as many; (2) *śuddha vidyā*, pure knowledge in the form of mantra that permeates all things as the phonic source of being; (3) *maheśvara* or the Great Lord (Śiva) who stabilizes the creative flux of Śakti; and (4) *sadāśiva*, the eternal Śiva who is the basis upon which all the rest are established.[21]

The nine intersecting triangles are at the root of two of the most basic cosmological functions, creation and dissolution. As the *Yoginīhṛdaya* states:

> The fivefold Śakti [cakras] are [identified with] creation and the fourfold Agni [i.e., Śiva cakras] are [identified with] dissolution; the [nine sub-cakras] arise from the conjunction of the five Śaktis and the four Vahnis [i.e., Śivas].[22]

The five Śakti triangles are also the source of the five material components of the human body, namely, flesh, fat, skin, blood and bone, while the four Śiva triangles are the components that give rise to marrow, semen, breath (*prāṇa*), and life (*jīva*).[23] Thus, the *śrīcakra* is both macrocosmic and microcosmic in meaning.

The focus of interpretation, however, centers not on the major triangles themselves but on their resulting intersections, that is, on the sub-cakras of minor triangles, two sets of lotus petals, and three lines forming the outer gateways. The nine sub-cakras are also identified in groups with Śakti and Śiva. The five sub-cakras of minor triangles are associated with Śakti while the two sets of lotus petals, the outer gateways (*bhūpura*) and, according to some interpretations, the three circles surrounding the sixteen lotuses are Śiva's. These two groups of Śiva and Śakti sub-cakras are then interidentified in order to emphasize their complementary relationship. The sub-cakras are diagrammed in the Appendix. The process of interidentification links the Śiva sub-cakras with the Śakti sub-cakras:

Śiva sub-cakras		*Śakti sub-cakras*
Three Circles (*traivalya* or *vṛttatraya*)	=	Innermost triangle or *Trikoṇa*
Eight Petalled Lotus (*aṣṭadalapadma*)	=	*Vasukoṇa* of 8 minor triangles
Sixteen Petalled Lotus (*ṣoḍaśadalapadma*)	=	Two sets of 10 triangles
Outermost Gateways of Three Lines (*bhūpura*)	=	*Manvaśra* of fourteen triangles

ŚRĪCAKRA: CREATION AS THE FORM OF GOD

For traditionalists, analysis of creation begins at the *śrīcakra*'s center, the *bindu*. When the cakra serves as a map showing the way back to this source, the analysis proceeds in just the opposite fashion, from the outermost sub-cakras towards the center. In other words, diagraming creation's process begins at the center and follows creation's method (*sṛṣṭikrama*); tracing the path back to the divine source begins at the outer precinct according to the method of dissolution (*samhārakrama*). The dissolution method permits through ritual reconstruction a return to original unity with the absolute by ascending the yantra through its various levels and piercing through the obstructions (*āvaraṇa*) of perception that manifest in each of the sub-cakras.

Tracing creation to its source begins in the midst of dualistic reality represented by the *śrīcakra*'s triangles, petals, and outer lines. Following the dissolution method (*samhārakrama*) one moves from the outermost sub-cakras towards the *bindu*, that is, from dualistic and discursive reality to the focal point of nondual, preverbal consciousness. Having dissolved one's misconceptions, there is nothing left but the empty (*śūnya*) center, the point at which the principles of binary differentiation that create the world-of-ordinary-experience cease.

The creation (*sṛṣṭikrama*) and dissolution (*saṃhārakrama*) methods of analyzing the *śrīcakra* serve distinct yet interrelated purposes. By analyzing creation as a cosmological event in which reality unfolds in steps (*sṛṣṭikrama*) assuming the shape of the *śrīcakra*, the adept intellectually grounds spiritual discipline (*sādhana*) in beliefs about cosmology, divinity, and human relationships. By creating a step by step method by which one can "undo" or dissolve (*saṃhārakrama*) the experience of reality as manifold, mortal, and bifurcated by the paradoxes of life and death, the adept becomes ritually empowered by obtaining the perspective of the immortal godhead. The *śrīcakra* not only explains how life was created but also it holds out the prospect that life's most insoluble dilemma, the paradox of life and death, can be comprehended in this world.

The *bindu* indicates the nondifferentiated state of being that precedes manifest creation. When the *bindu* in its pure illuminative state (*prakāśa* = Śiva) emerges as a reflection (*vimarśa* = Śakti) in the form of everyday reality, it has already assumed a "triadic" shape, that is, it has taken shape as the triangles, lotus petals, and lines of the *śrīcakra*. This "triadic" shape symbolizes the world's basic epistemological and ontological patterns; for example, reality depends on the triadic relationship of subject, object, and process of cognition.

In metaphysical terms the real nature of the *śrīcakra*, Śivānanda points out, is the undivided essence of Śiva and Śakti who are the source (*bīja*) of subject/object distinctions.[24] The unified Brahman undergoes no change to assume this binary form. It remains a single reality with two features that are distinguished only at the ordinary level of epistemological dualism. From the perspective of yogic knowledge there is no difference whatsoever between Śiva and Śakti, the One Brahman remains intact even as it self-cognizes into multiplicity; creation is thus a continuous cognitive act on the part of a divine cognizer. The person who lacks yogic knowledge fails to see the playful act of the imagination that creates the world as an ontological reality. As Bhāskararāya notes, it is the mere will of the deity that creates the universe; creation issues forth from her own being at the moment of its conception.[25] Thus, creation is a projection of consciousness (*cit*) but is not an illusion (*māyā*) or an abstraction. Rather, consciousness is real (*sat*) and engages in self-cognition for the sake of its own unqualified enjoyment (*ānanda*).

In Śrīvidyā's world view, epistemological dualism is not binary but tertiary. The cognitive process, for example, accompanies the cognizing subject and cognized object. Just as the epistemological process is considered threefold so are the material transformations of Brahman and their phonic parallels. Brahman's assumption of two theological forms does not change its unified nature. At the same time, its transformation (*parināma*) is also real and assumes a shift into triadic forms. This transformation causes a plurality of real entities, all of which emerge from a single, unchanging source.[26]

Śāktas acknowledge both efficient and material causality as properties of Śakti and Śiva. Śiva is usually inert, as Śākta literature says, like a corpse without his Śakti.[27] Hence in Śrīvidyā, as in other Śākta traditions, Śiva and Śakti may be ultimately identical but Śiva is not associated with the conventional, with creative force, or with the transformation (*parināma*) into the manifest world. Śrīvidyā traditionalists equate male and female aspects so long as the discussion focuses on their original state of identity, that is, as Brahman (Śiva) united to the Self (*ātman*, Śakti). As soon as the focus shifts to the triads of dualistic reality the basic differences between Śiva and Śakti are affirmed. Śakti is given the superior position because she encompasses both material and efficient causal powers and because she is the Self that reflects (*vimarśa*) the illuminative (*prakāśa*), eternal Brahman.

THE ŚRĪCAKRA DEITIES

As Puṇyānanda states in the *KKV*, the supreme nature of the *śrīcakra* is the *bindu*, it is the cause of the nine sub-cakras and the source of the initial phonic emanations of Brahman.[28] A contemporary adept summarized these views in response to the question,"What is the *śrīcakra*?" He said:

> The *bindu* alone is the *śrīcakra*. All the rest is just an addition. In the *bindu* everything is contained since it is the very form (*śvarūpa*) of Brahman. The *bindu* is the true form of Śiva and Śakti since it is one and naturally the whole cakra is within it.[29]

The goddess is seated on the *bindu* on and the left thigh of Kāmeśvara (Śiva). There she resembles the rising sun and her three eyes are in the form of the moon, sun, and fire.[30] It is from her union with Śiva, Amṛtānanda says, that this great *bindu* was born and from the *bindu* the whole universe spewed (*vāma*) forth.[31] The *bindu*'s form, unlike the triangles and lines of the sub-cakras that are a reflection (*vimarśa*) of it, is still in the form of illumination (*prakāśa*). In this single point is the locus of reality, the source of the emerging triadic forms, shapes, and lines.

Śrīvidyā adepts do not mean to say that the *śrīcakra* is any "drop" or point in space. Rather, inherent in the *bindu*, the commentators point out, is its threefold nature, that is, the three capacities of Śakti, desire, knowledge, and activity (*icchā-*, *jñāna-* and *kriyāśaktis*) embodied in the deities Vāmā, Jyeṣṭhā, and Raudrī. These deities are subsumed under a fourth aspect called Ambikā and technically referred to as *śānta* or "peaceful." From these come the three gradations of sound (*paśyantī, madhyamā,* and *vaikharī*) that are responsible for projecting the thirty-six categories (*tattvas*) that make up material essence of reality. As Bhāskararāya says,

> Even though the *bindu* cakra [in the center of the *śrīcakra* is only one point] because it has a threefold nature each [nature] respectively has three forms.... The three deities created [and] not different from [her] peaceful (*śānta*) [aspect] are [the three *śakti*s of creation] *icchāśakti, jñānaśakti,* and *kriyāśakti*. The female deities (*śakti*) by name Vāmā, Jyeṣṭhā, and Raudrī [which correspond to *icchā, jñāna,* and *kriyā* are complemented] by the three [corresponding male] forms Brahma, Viṣṇu, and Rudra are created as undifferentiated from [the subsuming aspect called] Ambikā. The corresponding deities of speech (*vāgdevatā*) called *paśyantī, madhyamā,* and *vaikharī* are created undifferentiated from [the subsuming aspect called] supreme (*parā*). This is the meaning [of the threefold nature of the *bindu* cakra divided in three ways].[32]

This initial projection of the *bindu* assumes the form of the central triangle (*trikoṇa*).[33]

According to Amṛtānanda, the projection from *bindu* to *trikoṇa* is a manifestation of these sets of triadic deities and powers. The projection begins with inner triangle's left line and moves clockwise. Thus, each element of the symbolic triads becomes identified with the lines of the *trikoṇa*:

trikoṇa	*Left*	*Center*	*Right*	*Bindu*
goddess:	Vāmā	Jyeṣṭhā	Raudrī	Ambikā
consort:	Brahmā	Viṣṇu	Śiva	Īśvara
function:	Creation	Maintenance	Destruction	
śakti:	*icchā*	*jñāna*	*kriyā*	
sound stage:	*paśyantī*	*madhyamā*	*vaikharī*	*parā*
consciousness:	waking	dreaming	dreamless sleep	The Fourth

These identifications are meant to parallel the identification of three *kūṭa*s of the *śrīvidyā* discussed earlier. Śrīvidyā commentators are quick to point out that the mantra and cakra are simply aspects of one another, different only in degree rather than in kind. Hence the fifteen syllables of the mantra in three *kūṭa*s are identified on the *śrīcakra*'s centermost triangle following the same clockwise pattern—

one *kūṭa* to a side and the *ṣoḍaśī*, the sixteenth syllable, identified with the *bindu*.

The logic of identification between verbal forms and the *śrīcakra*'s image is consistent though its presentation is not. The three sides of the central triangle correspond to each of the three symbolic elements in each set of attributes; the *bindu* corresponds to the fourth element, or the sixteenth of fifteen elements located five to each side of the triangle. The fourth or sixteenth element encompasses and subsumes the previous three elements. Further, the fourth element and sixteenth element stand in a direct opposition to the whole set of the three and fifteen; this opposition affirms the essential binary contrast considered inherent in the divine act of creation. The *bindu* is also identified with the sixteenth syllable of the *śrīvidyā* and the sixteenth "hidden" aspect (*kalā*) of the moon's phases; both of these "sixteenths" serve the same encompassing and subsuming function as the fourth element attached to triads.

Like most Tantric terms, *bindu* has many meanings, many of which are applied to the *śrīcakra*'s *bindu*. *Bindu*, for example, can refer to semen, it can be Śiva in the form of the *liṅga*, or it can be Śiva's phallus (*liṅga*). When the *trikoṇa* is identified with the vagina or *yoni* of Śakti the sexual symbolism becomes complete: Śiva and Śakti conjoin both as the four intersecting five triangles and within the *śrīcakra*'s *bindu*. The bliss of the divinity's sexual union is analogous to the permanent spiritual bliss (*ānanda*) attained when the adept realizes the unified *and* dynamic nature of reality. Thus, the *trikoṇa* assumes the form of the *kāmakalā* or the "aspect of desire," which is usually symbolized by the female sexual organ.

The ritual identification of the *trikoṇa* with the female organ is at the basis of *kāmakalā* meditation (*dhyāna*). As a spiritual discipline, it is both sharply criticized and enthusiastically supported. Its supporters claim it encourages yogic restraint and embodies in ritual the divine activity; detractors maintain that it creates moral suspicion and is given to misuse and misunderstanding by both insiders and outsiders.

As a phonic emanation, the *trikoṇa* is considered the resulting combination of the Śiva seed-syllable (*bījākṣara*) *a* and the Śakti seed-syllable *ī*, both residing in unity within the *bindu*. The grammatical result of the *a* plus *ī* combination, the Sanskrit *e*, is the *trikoṇa*'s seed-syllable. Bhāskararāya points out that *e* in the *devanāgarī* script resembles a triangle and thus suggests the *yoni*'s shape.[34] In other words, the *trikoṇa*'s phonic reality in the form of *e* is visually paralleled. Bhāskararāya represents a movement within Śrīvidyā that seeks to establish deliberate connections between verbal and visual metaphors and thus create relationships between two usually separate motifs of Hindu tradition, the idea of the world-as-sound (*śabdabrahman*) and the idea of divinity-as-visual embodiment (*darśana*). Viewed in another way, the *bindu* is identified with the sixteenth vowel, the *visarga*, usually represented as *aḥ*. The *visarga* encompasses all the other vowels that are also considered forms of Śakti, just as the consonants are forms of Śiva. The *trikoṇa* is then identified with the remaining fifteen vowels that are ritually lain (*nyāsa*) five to a side beginning at the base of the innermost triangle moving counterclockwise. The fifteen vowels from *a* to *aṃ* (i.e., the *anusvāra*) are also identified with the fifteen *nityā*s or *tithi*s, the deities of the moon's phases (*kalā*s). Accordingly, the *visarga* is the sixteenth *kalā* and divine eternality (*nityādevatā*), which is "hidden" from ordinary view. Thus, the *bindu* and *trikoṇa* symbolize the devolution of sound at the mundane level of speech (i.e., the *vaikharī* level,) through the identification of the vowels, considered the first sounds of Sanskrit and the first substantive phonic emanation.[35]

When the *śrīcakra* is visualized three dimensionally as a so-called *meru* cakra, the *bindu* becomes the geographical peak (*kūṭa*) of the universe. Further, the *bindu* is imagined to be the seat or throne (*pīṭha*) of the city of *Tripura* atop mythical Mount *Sumeru* at the center of the universe. Bhāskararāya quoting the *Rudrayāmala* says:

> "Outside and beyond the countless myriads of world systems, in the centre of the ocean of nectar, more than a thousand crores in extent, in the gem-island (*ratnadvīpa*), a hundred crores in area, the lamp of the world, there is the supreme city of Śrīvidyā, three lakhs of *yojanas* in height and adorned with twenty-five walls representing the twenty-five *tattvas*. "...in the *Vidyāratnabhāṣya* [it] is explained as Śrīcakra.[36]

Within the body the *bindu* is usually identified with the uppermost yogic center, the *sahasradala* or *brahmandhrapadma* at the top of the skull. The *trikoṇa* is placed at the base of the spine in the lowest of the physical bodily centers (or cakras), that is, in the *mūlādhāra*. In the course of yogic ritual, the two are reunited by methods including breath control, the interidentification of phonic essences (i.e., *bījākṣaras*) in *nyāsa*, and the use of gestures (*mudrās*). Viewed macrocosmically as the center of the universe, the *bindu* is the locus of cosmic geography, the center of the physical universe. Noteworthy in this interpretation is the notion of vertical hierarchy in macro-and microcosmic identification: one must ascend to the peak of the *śrīcakra*, just as one must ascend to the peak of skull in order to move beyond a mundane awareness of reality.

External ritual worship (*pūjā*) of the *śrīcakra* usually concludes by reestablishing the divinity that was invoked from within the adept's own body. The divinity is taken back inside the body *without* going through all the previous levels necessary to awaken her. Thus, upon completion of the *pūjā*, the worshiper rejoins the ordinary world, distinguishing it from the reality of the ritual enclosure through a process of interiorization. Divinity, it is believed, is again safely contained within the body. However, the divinity is "awakened," thus making the adept categorically different than other human beings who remain limited by their ignorance of the procedures that bring the realization and the power of divinity to life.

Among the nine sub-cakras the *bindu* is called *"sarvānandamaya,"* that is, "consisting of all bliss"; the *trikoṇa* is *"sarvasiddhipradā,"* the one "bestowing all perfection."[37] The name of the sub-cakra refers to the achievements gained by worshiping its deities and the activities associated with the manifestation of divinity *within* the mundane world. Thus, by naming and identifying oneself with the powers of the sub-cakra, one acquires the powers of the transcendent deity and understands the structures by which it is connected to the mundane world.

Each sub-cakra also bears a name for its own presiding deity and the subordinate deities (*yoginīs*, that is, the female *yogis*) identified on its parts. The presiding deity of the *bindu* is the supreme Mahātripurasundarī who presides over all other "presiding" deities of the sub-cakras. The *yoginī* of the *bindu* is referred to as the "supreme of the supreme secret" (*paraparararahasya*) and is, in fact, the same deity; the presiding deity of the *trikoṇa* is known as Tripurāmbikā or Tripurā the Mother, and the fifteen *yoginīs* are called the "very secret" (*atirahasya*).[38] These fifteen deities identified with the vowels of Sanskrit are the *nityādevatās*, the "eternal deities," presiding over the moon's phases. Bhāskararāya concurs:

> The *nityās* are the fifteen Devatās, Kāmeśvarī to Citrā, who preside over the fifteen days of the lunar months.[39]
>
> The fifteen syllables [of the *śrīvidyā*] known to all devotees are of the form of *nityās*; thus, the moon's disc, Devī and the fifteen-syllable *mantra* are one. The fifteen syllables belonging to the fifteen *kalās* also become[40]
>
> The *Tantrarāja* says, "The fifteen deities are the limbs of Lalitā who is the first [of the sixteen]; as she is endowed with these limbs she is the body, of which they are parts."[41]

The next expansion (*prapañca*) of the *śrīcakra* completes its core; the remaining portions, in a sense, are all viewed as subordinate to the emerging eight minor triangles when combined with the *trikoṇa* and the *bindu*.

When the one triangle "becomes" eight, these eight minor triangles become the *vasukoṇa* sub-cakra. Just as the *bindu* is said to encompass all the remaining parts of the *śrīcakra*, so the *vasukoṇa*, when taken with the *trikoṇa*, encompasses all the symbols, deities, and powers of the remaining sub-cakras. The *vasukoṇa*'s presiding deity is Tripurāsiddhā or Tripurā who confers perfection, and its *yoginīs* (identified one to a triangle) are called "secret" (*rahasya*). These *yoginīs* are the well-known "deities of speech," the *vāgdevatās*: Vāsinī, Kāmeśvarī, Modinī, Vimalā, Aruṇā, Jayanī, Sarveśvarī, and Kaulinī. These eight subordinate deities are the source of the *mātṛkās*, the Little Mothers, identified with all the letters and sounds of the Sanskrit alphabet. The *mātṛkās* embody the basic linguistic structure of Sanskrit and are the first phonic emanations of Brahman at the mundane level; they include not only the sixteen vowels, which come first, but the thirty-two (or thirty-five) consonants.[42] As Bhāskararāya notes:

> ...the fifty-one letters (*A* to *Kṣa*) are her form, *varṇa*, the letters, *rūpa*, indicate (her).... "Just as the supreme Śiva is twofold as Śakti and Śiva, so this Mātṛkā Devī herself shines in two. The vowels indicate one form of *śakti*, the others (consonants) indicate Śiva. Thus the [Devī] of *vidyā* under the form of letters indicates Śiva."[43]

The deities of speech or *vāgdevatās* are the collective source for the *mātṛkās* identified on the remaining sub-cakras. Thus, with each of the *vāgdevatās* is associated one of the traditional groupings of Sanskrit letters. Vāsinī is associated the sixteen vowels, Kāmeśvarī the *kavarga* (*ka, kha, ga, gha* and *ṅa*), and so forth, such that Sanskrit's forty-eight (or fifty-two) letters are accounted for as species of the eight *vāgdevatāyoginīs*. The *vāgdevatās*, by subsuming the *mātṛkās* identified with speech, subordinate the remaining portions of the sub-cakras. The sub-cakras, by being associated with a particular Sanskrit letter, are nothing other than simple *mātṛkā* aspects of the *vāgdevatās*. The sounds themselves—whether grouped together as the *vāgdevatās* or taken individually as *mātṛkās* identified with a part of each sub-cakra—are not mere sounds. They are deities in phonic aspects subordinated to the presiding deity of the sub-cakra; as substances issuing forth from the ultimate, which assume the mundane form of a sound in Sanskrit, they are aspects of consciousness, not insentient entities. Within the *śrīcakra*, these sounds and deities are viewed as part of a deliberate design by macrocosmic consciousness to bring itself forth. Creation is an immanent form of the creator such that transcendence is measured in degrees rather than in substance. In other words, the *śrīcakra*'s devolution is a process of divine sentience assuming increasingly more mundane forms; it is not a process by which the sentient becomes insentient. Not only is the world a manifestation of Śakti as power, the world is essentially animate in devolving degrees of self-consciousness.

When the *trikoṇa* is included, the eight minor triangles of the *vasukoṇa* embrace not only all the sound sources of the manifest world but all the other powers and deities associated with the *śrīcakra*'s remaining seven sub-cakras. In these nine triangles (that is, the eight of the *vasukoṇa* plus the one *trikoṇa*) are all the powers and attributes of the nine major triangles and the nine sub-cakras formed in intersection.[44]

The eight minor triangles of the *vasukoṇa* and the central *trikoṇa* are identified with the nine *Yonis* (literally, wombs) that are the aspects of Śakti responsible for acquired and latent mental impressions (*saṃskāras*) entering into the mundane, karmic world.[45] The *śrīcakra*'s deities also identify the various aspects that make up the human personality, from its source in the Self (*ātman*) to its more mundane and manifest physical, mental, and verbal forms. The *Yonis* are the source of all the remaining sub-cakras, including their presiding *yoginī* deities, the accomplishments associated with their worship, and the material and spiritual aspects of the mundane world each reflects. As Bhāskararāya says:

> The nine *Yoni* cakras...arise [from the intersection of] the two [major] Śakti triangles with one [major] Vahni [or Śiva] triangle. The three lines of each [major] triangle thus joined together are the nine lines and [produce by their intersection] the forms of angles [which number] nine only. Therefore, [it can be said that] She produces the nine *yoginī*s [identified respectively with each of the eight minor *vasukoṇa* triangles and the inner *trikoṇa*]. The sense expressed here is that in these nine [sub-] cakras [composed of the eight *vasukoṇa*s plus the one *trikoṇa*] are [subtlety present] the nine [sets of] *yoginī*s beginning with *prakaṭa* [that is, all the *yoginī*s of the sub-cakras making up the *śrīcakra*] and that these [sets of *yoginī*s] are present here in the form of angles.[46]

The *vasukoṇa*'s association with the *vāgdevatā*s and the nine *Yoni*s is deemed the point at which creation is ordinarily experienced, since human experience depends on being *named* in language. Creation is itself viewed as a product of conceptualization and diversification achieved through the acquisition of speech. Speech is a product of more subtle levels of sound. As Bhāskararāya remarks, creation is a sub-set of the activity of the deities of the *vasukoṇa* and *trikoṇa*.[47]

The *vasukoṇa* is known as the cakra which "removes all disease" (*sarvarogahara*).[48] This is explained in the words of a contemporary adept,

> This means all forms of disease but actually it refers to ignorance (*avidyā*). This is the disease that afflicts all of us and if removed we are liberated.[49]

The *vasukoṇa*'s presiding deity is Tripurāsiddhā, the aspect of Tripurā that "bestows all forms of accomplishment," an appropriate name for the deity intended to subsume those that follow.

The *vasukoṇa* and *trikoṇa*, whose minor triangles add up to nine, thus form a microcosm of the whole *śrīcakra* both as the five plus four major triangles and the nine sub-cakras. As Bhāskararāya notes, under special circumstances the worship of the whole *śrīcakra* can be taken as the worship of only these nine. He says:

> In the summarized form of the [*śrīcakra*] *pūjā*, at the time of emergency (*āpatkālika*) we understand from the Tantras an injunction [to perform the *pūjā*] merely beginning from the *vasukoṇa*...to the *bindu*.[50]

At the next stage of creation's devolution the *śrīcakra* assumes the form of ten triangles called the "[sub-] cakra" that "effects all protection" (*sarvarakṣākara*); its presiding deity is known as Tripuramālinī, the "garlanded Tripurā." This sub-cakra is known less technically as the inner ten triangles (*antardaśāra*) in order to distinguish it from the next sub-cakra of ten triangles known as the outer ten (*bahirdaśāra*).[51] The two sets of ten minor triangles are usually taken as a pair though each has its own distinctive name, presiding deity, and set of *yoginīs*. The *yoginīs* of the inner ten are called "*nigarbha*," a term with manifold esoteric meanings but essentially suggesting the "hidden" realities. *Nigarbha* is contrasted to *rahasya* or "secret," which suggests deeper secrecy. The *nigarbhayoginīs* are also described by the name *devī*, or goddess, suggesting that it is at this level that identifiable, anthropomorphic forms begin to emerge in the ordinary world. The particular power and description of the deity is also the *siddhi* or form of accomplishment that its worship confers. It should be emphasized how these characteristics portray the active and worldly nature of the deities and how this sub-cakra, like those that follow it, attempts to describe reality in increasingly physical, explicit, and intentional forms. The names of the *yoginīs* and their meanings are listed below; they are identified in worship in a counterclockwise pattern beginning at the base triangle:

Inner Ten Minor Triangles: *Sarvarakṣākaracakra*

Yoginī	*Meaning and Attribute*
1. Sarvajñā (devī)	Omniscience
2. Sarvaśakti	All powers
3. Sarvaiśvaryapradā	Conferring all [forms of] empowerment

Yoginī	*Meaning and Attribute*
4. Sarvajñānamayī	Consisting of all knowledge
5. Sarvavyādhivināsinī	Destroying all sickness
6. Sarvādhārasva[rūpā or rūpinī]	Form of all Supports (an esoteric sense referring to the bodily center according to *kuṇḍalinī* yoga)
7. Sarvapāpaharā	Remover of all sins
8. Sarvānandamayī	Consisting of all bliss
9. Sarvarakṣaśvarūpiṇī	Form of all protection
10. Sarvepistaphalapradā	Conferring all desired fruits

The relationship of the inner and outer sets of ten minor triangles with the coming forth of the mundane physical world is further established through another set of identifications. Quoting an unidentified passage from the Tantras, Bhāskararāya explains how the two sets of ten minor triangles symbolize the material essence of the physical world that is emerging from the more subtle phonic forms:

> The two sets of ten [minor] triangles [within the *śrīcakra*] have the form of effulgence (*sphuratrūpa*) which depends upon illumination (*prakāśa*) [of the] ten elements (*bhūta*) and the ten essences (*tanmātra*).[52]

This remark accounts for both sets of ten minor triangles but causes contemporary adepts some confusion since Bhāskararāya does not indicate precisely what he means by the five "subtle" elements. Amṛtānanda remarking on *YH*, 1.16 says that the elements (*bhūta*), earth, water, fire, air, and space have the nature of Śakti while their essences, the *tanmātras*, smell, taste, form, touch, and sound, have the nature of Śiva. He does not make these usual five elements and their corresponding essences into ten nor does he clearly identify them with either of the sub-cakras. It would seem he has the set of inner ten triangles in mind. The outer set, he says, has the form of effulgence (*sphurat*) while both are the forms of the senses and their respective objects, numbering ten. The second set, he says, is the form of the deity Krodhiṣa, the Lord of Anger, identified with the letter *ka* and also with the ten Sanskrit letters beginning with the consonant *ka*. This is repeated by Bhāskararāya who does not mention including the consonants following *ka*. Bhāskararāya does not clarify which set of ten minor triangles Amṛtānanda associates with the elements and their essences.[53] The meaning, Amṛtānanda says, is that the two sets of ten minor triangles are in the midst of the light of the inner three cakras and as "light" have the nature of illumination (*prakāśa*) and reflection (*vimarśa*); the inner set is like a pure light and the outer set a shadow.[54] Thus, it would appear that the two sets of ten triangles are once again representative of Śiva and Śakti's primary attributes and stand in order of their ontological priority: the inner set is *prakāśa* or illumination and therefore Śiva, while the outer set is *vimarśa* or reflection and Śakti.

The outer ten minor triangles are known as the cakra that "accomplishes all aims" (*sarvārthāsādhaka*), its presiding deity is known as Tripurāśrī or Auspicious Tripurā, and its *yoginīs* are called "*kulottīrṇa*," literally, "crossing beyond the *kula*." According to the *TT*, the ten triangles represent the ten vital breaths.[55] The *yoginīs*, like those of the inner ten triangles, are ritually placed on the *śrīcakra* counterclockwise from the base at the point of the ten triangles; their meanings reflect the emergence of increasing more worldly and mundane qualities in the universe.

Outer Ten Minor Triangles: *Sarvārthāsādhakacakra*

Yoginī	*Meaning and Attribute*
1. Sarvasiddhipradā (devī)	Conferring all powers
2. Sarvasaṃpatpradā	Conferring all profit
3. Sarvapriyaṅkarī	Making all beloved
4. Sarvamaṅgalakāriṇī	Making everything auspicious
5. Sarvakāmapradā	Conferring all desires
6. Sarvaduḥkhavimocinī	Removing all suffering
7. Sarvamṛtyupraśamanī	Mitigating all [forms of] death
8. Sarvavighnanivāriṇī	Removing all obstacles
9. Sarvāṅgasundarī	Beautiful in all limbs
10. Sarvasaubhāgyadāyinī	Imparting all prosperity

The next and last set of minor triangles number fourteen and are commonly referred to by the technical term "*manvaśra*." The subcakra "imparts all prosperity" (*sarvasaubhāgyadāyaka*), has Tripurāvāsinī for its presiding deity, and calls its *yoginīs* "traditional" (*sampradāya*). Its triangles are sometimes identified with the fourteen subtle channels (*nāḍīs*) of the yogic nervous system though the more common meaning is given by Bhāskararāya. Following his interpretation the fourteen are a reflection of the two sets of ten:

> And from these [ten essences (*tanmātra*)] arose the fourteen, namely, the five organs of action, the five organs of knowledge and the four inner organs.[56]

These "organs" are, in fact, the physical and mental capacities that make up the human personality. They include the physical limbs, their corresponding capacities, and the four aspects of the mind.[57] At the *manvaśra* sub-cakra the plane of mundane existence is reached, that is, the substantive emanations emerging from the subtle aspects of Śakti and the reflective forms of those aspects directly preceding it.

The *yoginīs* of the *manvaśra* sub-cakra are specifically referred to as powers (*śakti*), and each *yoginī*'s name specifies the accomplishment (*siddhi*) associated with its worship. The key point is the multidimensionality of the *yoginī*'s powers and their role in the spiritual discipline. From the worldly perspective this entails an extraordinary kind of power and influence over natural and social events. In this way, Śrīvidyā is quintessential Tantric. Tantrics assume that powers acquired through initiated disciplines have worldly and visible effects as well as spiritual dimensions. Tantrics, in this sense, are no different than other Hindus: as Staal has noted, Hindus resort to the unseen only under duress.[58] Such powers (*siddhi*) may be used for any purpose and, by virtue of their distance from the center of the *śrīcakra* and proximity to its outer precincts, are considered an early acquisition in the practice of Śrīvidyā discipline. But, because the power to manipulate the world is so relatively accessible, another reason for the strong emphasis on secrecy and initiation becomes evident. For example, the power to influence (*sarvavaśaṅkarī*) suggests both a physical ability and the spiritual capacity to effect change in oneself and others, while the power to confuse (*sarvamohinī*) suggests the ability to cast off hindrances, such as the ill will of others. The power (*siddhi*) itself is unregulated except by the will of the adept; the divinity simply makes itself available. Thus it can, in fact, be used for any end. One contemporary adept put it this way:

> Śrīvidyā is committed only to noble spiritual aims but like any form of power can be corrupted. As a spiritual discipline we believe it truly does give what might be called supernormal abilities. These are our responsibility and we must be committed to use them only for good. This is one reason why we are so careful in accepting people to the highest forms of our discipline. But we should keep in mind that these are *siddhis* acquired at the early stages of practice, they are placed on the outer portions of the cakra. We consider them not the most important aims but only secondary to accomplishing the spiritual goal.[59]

Contemporary adepts in south India take the acquisition of powers very seriously, though most would say that the desire for particular powers is more hindrance than help. Further, by declaring such physical and potentially miraculous powers to be mundane, Śrīvidyā Tantrics find a convenient method of dismissing their importance and reducing the possibility of being called upon to display them. This is not to say that they do not believe in such supernatural capacities.

Like all Tantrics, Śrīvidyā practitioners see no reason to separate worldly achievements from spiritual accomplishments; they insist that the conventional world is ultimately identical with divinity. To know the ultimate truth gives one supreme power over all its manifestations. But in contrast to other Tantrics, contemporary Śrīvidyā adepts underplay the importance of displaying power. Another adept stated the attitude succinctly:

> The *siddhi* is there, we may use it or not. But it is not to be gained for its own sake. It is just part of our practice. The great *siddha* is one who chooses to use it only when necessary.[60]

Significant in this adept's statement is his reluctance to use these "lower" powers. In contrast, the second chapter of the *Nityāṣoḍaśikārṇava* gives explicit instructions on the use of Śrīvidyā mantras and the *śrīcakra* for worldly and "magical" ends. One may curse an enemy or attract female companionship, though few contemporary practitioners are willing to admit an interest in acquiring such powers or performing such rituals.

The powers conferred by the *yoginīs* of the fourteen minor triangles have both positive attributes used to attract or acquire certain desirable powers and negative attributes to protect or to expel undesirable ones. The deities of the fourteen minor triangles are:

Fourteen Triangles: *Sarvasaubhāgyadāyakacakra*

Yoginī	*Meaning and Attribute*
1. Sarvasaṃkṣobhiṇī (śakti)	Power to make everything restless
2. Sarvavidrāviṇī	Power to disperse
3. Sarvākarṣiṇī	Power to attract all
4. Sarvāhlādinī	Power of conferring delight
5. Sarvamohinī	Power of confusing
6. Sarvastaṃbhinī	Power to sustain
7. Sarvajṛṇbhiṇī	Power to expand
8. Sarvavaśaṅkarī	Power to influence
9. Sarvarañjinī	Power to please
10. Sarvonmādinī	Power to intoxicate
11. Sarvārthasādhinī	Power to accomplish all aims
12. Sarvasampatpūriṇī	Power to fulfill
13. Sarvamantramayī	Power consisting of all mantras
14. Sarvadvandvakṣayankarī	Power to destroy duality

Following the fourteen triangles are the two sets of lotus petals. The inner eight are called the (sub-) cakra that "makes everything restless" (*sarvasaṃkṣobhanacakra*) and has the Lovely Tripurā (*Tripura-*

sundarī) for its presiding deity; its *yoginīs* are referred to as "more concealed" (*guptatara*). The outer sixteen lotuses make up the sub-cakra that "fulfills all hopes" (*sarvāśāparipūraka*); its presiding deity is Tripureśī or the Lordly Tripurā, and its *yoginīs* are called "concealed" (*gupta*).

The *yoginīs* of the eight lotus petals display the two-dimensional significance of the *śrīcakra*'s elements perhaps better than any other sub-cakra; they are both subordinate deities with their own qualities and powers, and attributes of the adept who worships them. The names describe the physical aspect of the female deities (here called "*devīs*") and the aesthetic qualities acquired through discipline (*sādhana*).

All eight *yoginīs* are called "*anaṅga*," literally, "limbless" and thus the goddesses are the "limbless ones" who, for example, hold "flowers" (*anaṅgakusumā*) or "take delight in love" (*anaṅgamadanāturā*). As their name indicates, they are incorporeal deities with the capacity to affect events in the material world. As descriptive attributes these names convey a sense of aesthetic beauty that is characteristically Indian; esoterically, they suggest the kinds of physical powers and abilities associated with feminine deities. For example, one power is the ability to attract women. Contemporary adepts with traditionally conservative social values express deep reservations about this "achievement" but nonetheless must recognize its repeated emphasis in important sources.[61] In explanation they say that sensual pleasure (*kāma*) is one of the legitimate human aims (*puruṣārtha*). These same adepts reject the literal practice of *kāmakalādhyāna*. Others who endorse convention-defying behaviors, including sexual intercourse outside marriage, reject the idea that sex in ritual is a form of *kāma* in the ordinary sense since it is not directed towards mere physical satisfaction.

The translation of the *yoginī*'s names given in the list below focuses on the suggestive sense of the acquired attribute rather than the more obvious sense of the *yoginī*'s description.[62]

Eight Lotus Petals: *Sarvāsankṣobhanacakra*

Yoginī	*Meaning and Attribute*
1. Anaṅgakusumā (devī)	Of Limitless Fire (or Flowers)
2. Anaṅgamekhalā	Of Limitless Girth
3. Anaṅgamadanā	Of Limitless Delight
4. Anaṅgamadanāturā	Of Limitless Love (Delight in Love)
5. Anaṅgarekhā	Of Limitless Lines (or Measure)
6. Anaṅgaveginī	Of Limitless Energy
7. Anaṅgānkuśā	Of Limitless Restraint
8. Anaṅgamālinī	Of Limitless Garlands (or Beauty)

The *yoginīs* of the sixteen lotus petals bear the epithet *ākarṣiṇī* indicating the power of attraction. These *yoginīs* are likewise embodiments of worldly powers which, according to one modern adept, "are to be used for facilitating the spiritual path."[63] Ākarṣiṇī can also refer to a magnet or any instrument that attracts; in this case the deities themselves function as instruments for attracting various powers and qualities. In addition, they convey a sharpening or heightening of existing physical or mental attributes. The *yoginīs* are also called "*nityākalādevīs*," that is, the goddesses identified with the sixteen *kalās* or phases in the monthly lunar cycle. Thus, the goddesses are conceived to identify the microcosmic level of divinity that exists as part of the human constitution with aspects of the macrocosmic universe.

There is a consistency exhibited at the mantric level as well regarding the levels of power attributed to deities placed on the *śrīcakra*. In the case of these sixteen *yoginīs*, for example, the seed-syllables (*bījākṣara*) are the sixteen Sanskrit vowels, as are the *bījas* of the *nityādevatās* placed around the central *trikoṇa* to which they correspond.[64] The *trikoṇa*'s *yoginīs* are the *nityā* deities themselves while here, farther away from the center of the *śrīcakra*, they are the *nityā*'s attributes. At the level of primary phonic emanation the deity and attribute are identical. From their positioning on the *śrīcakra* the attribute or power associated with the *yoginīs* is naturally subordinate to the deity itself. One can logically appropriate the power or the characteristic of the deities before achieving a level of complete identification. The *yoginīs* of the sixteen lotus petals provide an excellent example of the principle of power that governs the *śrīcakra*'s structure: the closer to the center, the more powerful and less material the aspect of the divinity. A contemporary adept explained a few of these "attractive powers" this way:

> *Kāmākarṣiṇī* means that whatever is desired will become available. The attractions of the senses have to do with these becoming pleasurable aspects of the adept's experience but can also mean that he has this quality. For example, the *gandhākarṣiṇī* means that the adept attracts such pleasurable fragrances, that he can smell things others cannot and that he himself always has a pleasant smell. This is not unlike some of the qualities of the Buddha whose body was attractive in all these ways.[65]

At the mantric level Amṛtānanda equates the sixteen and eight lotuses with the sixteen vowels and the consonants. These lotus petals, he says, are the incipient point of the articulation of sound, that is, they are the *vaikharī* stage of sound.[66]

The list below identifies all the *yoginīs* of the sixteen lotus petals (*ṣoḍaśadalakamala*).

Sixteen Lotus Petals: *Sarvāśāparipurakacakra*

Yoginī	*Meaning and Attribute*
1. Kāmākarṣiṇī	Attracting what is Desired
2. Buddhyākarṣiṇī	Attracting Intelligence
3. Ahaṃkārākarṣiṇī	Attraction of the Ego
4. Śabdākarṣiṇī	Attraction of Sound
5. Sparśākarṣiṇī	Attraction of Touch
6. Rūpākarṣiṇī	Attracting Form
7. Rasākarṣiṇī	Attraction of Taste
8. Gandhākarṣiṇī	Attraction of Smell
9. Cittākarṣiṇī	Attraction of Mind
10. Dharyākarṣiṇī	Attracting Stability (Courage)
11. Smṛtyākarṣiṇī	Attracting Recollection
12. Nāmākarṣiṇī	Attracting Names
13. Bījākarṣiṇī	Attracting Seed(-syllables)
14. Ātmākarṣiṇī	Attracting the Self
15. Amṛtākarṣiṇī	Attracting Immortality
16. Śarīrākarṣiṇī	Attraction of the Body

Following the sixteen lotuses the meditational verse describing the *śrīcakra* introduces the term *vṛttatraya* or "three circles." These three circles, usually surrounding the lotus petals, cause controversy and have precipitated an internal sectarian split. Śivānanda in his *Subhagodayavāsanā* likens the three circles to the goddess's three eyes that have the form of the moon (*soma*), the sun (*sūrya*), and fire (*agni*).[67] This interpretation is adopted by other authors in order to identify these three forms with the three sides of the *trikoṇa*. According to Amṛtānanda, the three circles have the form of three seeds (*bījatraya*), that is, they are the three primary reflections of the physical earth (*bhūbimba*) as it emerges from the three levels of sound, namely, *paśyantī*, *madhyamā*, and *vaikharī*.[68]

The major historical commentators do not speak of the three traditions (*sampradāyas*) that interpret the ritual significance of the circles, though several contemporary ritual manuals (*paddhatis*) formalize such distinctions and support them with oral explanations.[69] The three traditions are said to maintain distinctive views. The so-called Hayagrīva tradition, which takes its name from the *avatāra* of Viṣṇu who participates in transmitting Śrīvidyā works such as the *Lalitāsahasranāma*, maintains that the three circles surrounding the lotuses should not be present at all. The Ānandabhairava tradition, though it figures the circles into the *śrīcakra*'s construction, does not attribute to them any *yoginīs* and consequently excludes them from the ritual. The

Dakṣiṇāmūrti tradition, which is presumably connected with the "south-facing" Śiva in his aspect as guru, maintains the presence of the circles, a list of *yoginīs*, and their attributes. According to the Dakṣiṇāmūrti tradition, the outermost circle is imagined as white in color, associated with the power of deception (*māyā*), and identified with the thirty-four *yoginīs* corresponding to the complete set of consecutive consonants in Sanskrit, according to the fifty-one consonant scheme. They are placed counterclockwise in an otherwise unspecified manner on the outer circle; the middle circle is red in color, associated with the seed-syllables, and identified with the sixteen *yoginīs* corresponding to the Sanskrit vowels; the third, inner circle is black in color, associated with the material creation (*prakṛti*), and identified with the sixteen "eternal goddesses" (*nityādevatā*) and the corresponding vowels as seed-syllables. The deity Kāmeśvarī is added to the usual fifteen *nityās*. This female form of the Lord of Desire, Kāmeśvara, is the aspect usually considered the subsuming sixteenth figure in this set of fifteen elements.

All contemporary adepts can be classified according to these "traditions" (*sampradāya*), even when they were not aware of the oral lore surrounding them, since they cover every possible interpretation. To those aware of these names and their meanings, the issue is of no small significance. As one adept explains,

> Everything about the *śrīcakra* is purposeful and there is no margin for error. Nothing about its form can be accidental because it is the shape of creation itself. If the *vṛttatraya* is part of the cakra then there must be a reason. According to our [Hayagrīva] *sampradāya* the *vṛttatraya* should not be there because it has no place in the *pūjā*. We follow the interpretation of Bhāskararāya.[70]

Bhāskararāya argues in the *Tripurā Upaniṣadbhāṣya* that the mention of the three circles refers not to the usual *vṛttatraya* outside the sixteen lotuses but to the three circles that demarcate the two sets of lotuses from the other parts of the *śrīcakra*. He says:

> Thus these three *maṇḍalas* or circles (*vṛttāni*)...cause auspiciousness, that is,...they ornament (*maṇḍayanti*) the Mothers [who are identified on part of the *śrīcakra*). The meaning [of this passage] is that the *śrīcakra* that is fit for worship (*kāryākṣama*) should consist of the two sets of lotus petals between which are the three circles...[71]

The alternative, according to Bhāskararāya, is to interpret scripture as referring to the three lines that make up the outer gateways of the *śrīcakra*. This interpretation accounts for the placement of the term *vṛttatraya* in the *śrīcakra*'s meditation verse (*dhyānaśloka)*, that is, between the sixteen petals and the outer gateways. Among historical commentators, only Bhāskararāya makes mention of this controversy and offers this interpretation of the *śrīcakra*'s *vṛttatraya*. He does not explicitly identify himself as a member of the Hayagrīva tradition nor does he seem aware of this method of classification. He is aware that the *vṛttatraya* is interpreted as outer circles but rejects this view. He offers his own opinion not merely as a plausible alternative but as the correct interpretation.[72]

Curiously, not all contemporary groups claiming to be part of Bhāskararāya's spiritual legacy appear to be aware of his views since their own *śrīcakras* include the three circles placed around the sixteen lotuses. Even more baffling is the presence of the three surrounding circles on the *śrīcakra* shown to me in the village of Bhāskararājapuram, the cakra claimed by its owner to have been Bhāskararāya's personal ritual object.[73] Given Bhāskararāya's uncompromising position, the authenticity of this *śrīcakra* is suspect and can be counted among the many mysteries surrounding his biography. One adept claiming descent from Bhāskararāya stated that, while tradition rejects the *vṛttatraya* as having a ritual role, it does not necessarily reject the presence of the three circles. To support this view he cited the *Nityotsava* of Umānandanātha, which includes the three circles outside the sets of lotus petals. Rāmeśvara, however, believes that Bhāskararāya supported a five line theory, adding the two inner separating circles to the outer three circles.[74]

The majority view in south Indian Śrīvidyā supports the Ānandabhairava, tradition which includes the three surrounding circles, but prescribes no worship (*pūjā*) and offers no textual or historical interpretation of them. Only rarely is the *śrīcakra* actually seen in contemporary India without the surrounding circles.[75] The absence of a ritual context for the *vṛttatraya* has not gone unnoticed by adepts who view the *śrīcakra* as a perfectly consistent ritual construction. According to one adept:

> The circles are a boundary between the more subtle parts of the cakra and the ordinary world. This is the only purpose they serve, there is no *pūjā* for them.[76]

According to another:

> There must have once been a significance to the circles and a *pūjā* for them. I do not know of one now. And if such a tradition exists I would not follow it because it is not the tradition as taught to me by my own teacher. My teacher did not explain the circles and I am led to believe that they have their own purpose which does not concern our worship.[77]

According to others identifying themselves as Dakṣiṇāmūrti traditionalists, the three circles of the *vṛttatraya* are another secret aspect of the *śrīcakra*, so secret that the significance has been lost in most lineages. The issue of worshiping the three circles is not discussed in historical texts, these adepts claim, either because it is not known to the writers or because of its secrecy. The origins of the oral tradition interpreting the three *sampradāyas* are recondite. By its absence in the works of such comparatively late figures as Bhāskararāya and Lakṣmīdhara—who is quick to point out sectarian differences of opinion—it may be a recent explanation. This would undoubtedly be disputed by contemporary Dakṣiṇāmūrti traditionalists.

The outermost gateways of the *śrīcakra* are known by several names, none more common than *bhūpura* or *bhūgṛha*, literally the "city" or "house of the earth." Composed of three parallel lines, the major issue concerning its construction is whether its "doorways" (*dvāra*) are open or closed. Amṛtānanda maintains the gates may be either open or closed; Bhāskararāya agrees both forms are seen, but prefers the gates to be closed.[78] Rāmeśvara adds that the *bhūpura* may be drawn with or without doors which may be composed of one or three lines. Those who follow the tradition of the *PKS*, he adds, should not use a *śrīcakra* without the open gateways.[79] Rāmeśvara remarks how Umānandanātha specifies open gateways and a three line composition for the *bhūpura* but criticizes him for maintaining the *vṛttatraya* as three outer circles without an explanation. At this point Rāmeśvara makes the rather astonishing claim that Umānanda may not, in fact, be Bhāskararāya's pupil as tradition suggests because his views are so drastically inconsistent with those of his master.[80] Lakṣmīdhara, too, accepts the open gateways and maintains that *Taittirīya Āraṇyaka*, 1.31 supports this view.[81] Because there is consensus about the *yoginīs* of the *bhūpura* and little dispute over its ritual significance, its precise configuration has caused no significant controversy. More interesting are the various explanations and ideas that are aired: Rāmeśvara avails himself of an opportunity to cast further doubts on Umānanda, Bhāskararāya takes a position that distances him from those who claim his legacy, and Lakṣmīdhara utilizes a Vedic text to explain a rather arcane element of Śrīvidyā theology.

The *bhūpura* is technically called the "delusion of the three worlds cakra" (*trailokyamohanacakra*), its presiding deity is Tripurā, and its *yoginīs* are termed *prakaṭa* or explicit. Amṛtānanda links this sub-cakra with the two sets of lotus petals. The three taken together, he says, represent the threefold creation in its explicit forms; to understand their collective significance is to reach the first level of spiritual attainment, the *purvāmnāya*.[82]

Vidyānanda in the *Artharatnāvali* also associates a hierarchy of spiritual levels (*āmnāya*) with each sub-cakra.[83] He observes that in the discussion of these spiritual levels there is a distinction made between the Kāmarāja and Lopāmudrā traditions. The spiritual levels, he says, are three and mark consecutive stages of realization. For each level there is a group of three sub-cakras; realization is achieved when each group of sub-cakras is ritually worshiped and its meaning internalized. The spiritual levels, like the sub-cakras, follow the dissolution method (*samhārakrama*) of analysis since they result from ritual worship of the *śrīcakra*.[84] According to the Kāmarāja tradition, Vidyānanda says, the *bhūpura* and the two sets of lotus petals form the first group called the *purvāmnāya* or "eastern" (or "upper"); these represent the "dissolution" (*samhāra*) aspect of divinity, mark the first level of achievement, and reflect the most mundane level of reality. The next three sub-cakras, that is, the fourteen triangles and two sets of ten, form the second group and represent the second spiritual level called the "*dakṣiṇāmnāya*" or "southern" (or "right") and the "maintenance" aspect (*sthiti*) of divinity. The third spiritual level, called the "*pascyāmnāya*" or the "western" (or "left"), is achieved by taking the last three sub-cakras as a group, that is, the *vasukoṇa* of eight triangles, the *trikoṇa* and the *bindu*; these represent the "creation" aspect (*sṛṣṭi*) of divinity. There is, as one might expect, a fourth level subsuming the three that correspond to the physical *śrīcakra*; this is called the "*uttarāmnāya*" or "northern" and is presided over by Śiva and Śakti.[85] The Lopāmudrā tradition, Vidyānanda maintains, reverses the order and significance of the groupings. Since the Lopāmudrā *hādimata* followers don't take up the issue, it is impossible to know if Vidyānanda's sectarian interpretations represent historical tradition. Vidyānanda's remarks are significant because they present an instance of theoretical difference between *kādi* and *hādi*, suggesting that more than a different mantra is at stake. Contemporary south Indian practitioners are largely dismissive of these differences.

Implicit in the broader interpretation of Vidyānanda, Jayaratha, and Lakṣmīdhara is that the *bhūpura* and two sets of lotus petals are not as seminal to the *śrīcakra*'s meaning as are the sub-cakras composed of triangles.[86] This follows the common, general description of the *śrīcakra* as composed of forty-three triangles without mention of the other portions and conforms to its depiction in certain temple contexts.[87] Others, however, such as the author of the *Śrīvidyāratnasūtras*, maintain that the *śrīcakra* defines the concept of "cakra" because it is not merely triangles or petals but a combination of triangles and petals.[88]

The *yoginīs* of the outer gateways (*bhūpura*) number twenty-eight in three groups assigned to specific places on each of its three lines.[89] The first group of ten *yoginīs* comprises the ten *siddhis* or spiritual accomplishments, the so-called *animādi* group.[90] The Śāktas add to the usual

Tantric group of eight *siddhis* two more: *bhuktisiddhi*, the power of enjoyment, and *sarvakāmasiddhi*, the power over all desires.[91] A contemporary adept explained his view of these accomplishments this way:

> The *siddhis* are only the first level of achievement and are not actually important. Their importance is only in facilitating other progress. But with these *siddhis* it is easy to see why the teaching is kept so secret. If these are the first level of accomplishment then it is important to see to it that they are acquired by persons who see them in the proper perspective. Like all forms of power they can easily be misused. This is the case with all aspects of Śrīvidyā—its power is part of its very nature as a teaching and should be kept under strict control. For a person with no control over their senses or with the desire to use such *siddhis* for their own gain or others' harm, there is much potential danger. Therefore we keep the teaching secret. So great is the accomplishments at higher level that these *siddhis* are considered the lowest stage of development. The responsibility for giving the teaching only to responsible persons lies with the guru. This is why the guru is like a god. He can determine by his own powers who is truly qualified.[92]

The first set are called "explicit or *prakaṭa yoginīs*" and comprise the "perfections" (*siddhi*). All except Jayaratha find a place for them on the *bhūpura*.[93] They are:

Yoginī	*Meaning and Attribute*
1. Aṇimāsiddhi	Power to make Minute
2. Laghimāsiddhi	Power to become Light
3. Mahimāsiddhi	Power to become Great (in size)
4. Īśitvasiddhi	Power of Superiority
5. Vaśitvasiddhi	Power to Control
6. Prākāmyasiddhi	Power of Irresistible Will
7. Bhuktisiddhi	Power of Enjoyment
8. Icchāsiddhi	Power to gain one's Desires
9. Prāptisiddhi	Power to Obtain
10. Sarvakāmasiddhi	Power over all Desires

Unlike some other Tantrics, Śrīvidyā traditionalists are relatively disinterested in the role these *siddhis* play in the acquisition of bodily immortality. The extraordinary capacities that these powers suggest, however, are not dismissed. Virtually the entire second chapter of the *NSA* is devoted to *śrīcakra* rituals meant to attract women, cure illness, impose one's will on others, and even become invisible.[94] These rites involving the *śrīcakra* are associated directly with the acquisition of the ten *siddhis*. More conservative contemporary practitioners often frown at the suggestion that the *siddhis* can be used for worldly purposes. As one put it:

> The *siddhis* are acquired not to be used for any ordinary purpose. Once acquired after long practice of the complete *sādhana* they are like a bank account, if you use the power it is to some degree expended; if you simply leave it in the account it draws interest for when you may truly need it.[95]

The *siddhis* are also discussed to affirm the greatness of particular personalities and to make claims about Śrīvidyā's superiority. Stories are told about Bhāskararāya, for example, to whom is attributed all such accomplishments. On one occasion it is said that he failed to show respect to a mendicant as he passed the household. The insulted and infuriated *sannyāsi* wished to condemn Bhāskararāya's actions publicly as disrespectful of the Dharmic roles of householder and renunciate. Bhāskararāya rejoined that had he shown the traditional obeisance he would have endangered the *sannyāsi*'s life. This claim provoked the angry *sannyāsi* who then challenged Bhāskararāya to prove his power. Bhāskararāya asked the mendicant to lay before him his begging bowl and staff. As he prostrated before these objects, they broke into pieces. The *sannyāsi* was, of course, suitably humbled. The story goes on, however, to moralize that such behavior towards a mendicant would set a bad example for others and, not wishing to be the cause of a degeneration of Dharma, Bhāskararāya thereafter retired to the inside of his house whenever the mendicant approached.[96]

The story exemplifies a key issue in Śrīvidyā: power should not be used unnecessarily or for the sake of spectacle. It is not merely Bhāskararāya's humility that contemporary adepts emphasize but his attitudes about the exercise of power and authority. As one contemporary adept said:

> The *siddha* never shows what he is capable of doing unless it serves another's purpose. Unless it can be turned towards the welfare of others, he rarely will do anything to draw attention to himself. He is concerned with higher matters. Egoistic displays are not part of his spiritual make-up.[97]

The second line of the *bhūpura*'s gateways shifts emphasis away from yogic powers and is identified as an abode of the "little mothers" (*mātṛkās*) who are usually mantra-associated deities. Given the numerous and early textual references to the *mātṛkās* in Śākta speculations it is little wonder they have found a place on the *śrīcakra*.[98] In Śrīvidyā they are consistently enumerated as eight: Brāhmī, Maheśvarī, Kaumarī, Vaiṣṇavī, Vārāhī, Mahendrī (also called "Indrāṇī" in some sources), Cāmuṇḍā and Mahālakṣmī. While the first seven of the *mātṛkās* are beyond any dispute, the *Devīmāhātmya*, an important early source, lists nine by excluding Mahālakṣmī and adding Śivadutī and Kālī.[99] As minor Śākta deities they are frequently aligned with the eight aspects of Bhairava, as is the case in the *Jñānārṇava Tantra*.[100] The primary function of the *mātṛkās* is to preside over the eight groups (*varga*) of letters comprising the Sanskrit alphabet (cf., *Svacchaṇḍa Tantra*, 1.33f.). The second chapter of the *Brahmayāmala* states that they issue forth from the vowels.[101] Jayaratha, though he fails to mention the other two sets of *yoginīs* usually assigned to the *bhūpura*, does not omit the *mātṛkās*. The key issue here is that the *mātṛkās* find a place on the *śrīcakra*, providing yet another example of Śrīvidyā's commandeering of important symbols and concepts.

The ten *yoginīs* of the *bhūpura*'s innermost line are the ten *mudrās* or hand gestures. Śrīvidyā traditionalists claim that the first nine *mudrās* are common to all the Śākta schools while the tenth is special to Śrīvidyā.[102] The first nine *mudrās* are identified respectively with the nine sub-cakras (following the *samhārakrama*), the tenth is reserved for Tripurā as the supreme deity. According to contemporary ritual manuals (*paddhatis*), the nine *mudrās* are shown either following the naming of the *yoginīs* of each sub-cakra during the *pūjā* or at its conclusion.[103] Certain of the nine *mudrās*, such as *yonimudrā*, are also shown at other points in ritual to effect or "seal" results. The *mudrā* is to the body what the *mantra* is to speech: the subtle expression of transcendence made manifest. The meditative act is complete only when the *mudrā* and *mantra* are in corresponding harmony, the one often considered dependent upon the other to insure efficacy.[104]

In *śrīcakra* worship the *mudrās* are first worshiped collectively as *yoginīs*, then individually as the presiding deities of the sub-cakras, and finally as the supreme Tripurā. They are both symbolic of the powers of these presiding sub-cakra deities and an indexical sign of the deity. In some cases the gestures resemble the figures the name suggests. For example, the *mahāṅkuśa mudrā* imitates the elephant goad, symbolic of influence and control, and associated with the iconography of Lalitā, Gaṇeśa, and other deities; the *yoni mudrā* represents the female organ while the *trikhaṇḍa mudrā*, the special *mudrā* of Tripurā, is so-called because its three parts (*trikhaṇḍa*) correspond to the goddess's threefold nature as it manifests in the conventional world. It would appear that in the older Śrīvidyā sources, such as *VT*, the ten *mudrās* are not given this role as *yoginīs* of the gateways (*bhūpura*). Bhāskararāya, however, clearly says that despite their omission in *VT* they should be worshiped here. Oral traditions maintain that any discrepancy regarding the appropriateness of the placement of the *mudrās* on the *bhūpura* results from the fact that the three lines create only two spaces. The question arises as to whether the deities are placed on the lines themselves or in the intervening spaces. Those maintaining the latter view accept only two sets of *yoginīs* and omit the *mudrās*. Though the issue seems technical, it raises precisely the types of questions over which ritual specialists will argue and part company.[105] The *mudrās* are frequently described in terms of the powers they embody and confer on the adept, thus:

Yoginī	*Meaning and Attribute*
1. Sarvasaṃkṣobhiṇī (mudrā)	Power to make everything restless
2. Sarvavidrāvaṇī	Power to drive anything away
3. Sarvākarṣiṇī	Power to attract anything
4. Sarvavaśaṅkarī	Power to influence or subjugate
5. Sarvonmādinī	Power to intoxicate or make passionate
6. Sarvamahāṅkusā	Power to goad or control anything
7. Sarvakhecarī	Power to fly or bind
8. Sarvabīja	Power over all *bījas*
9. Sarvayoni	Power over the (nine) Yonis or cakras
10. Sarvatrikhaṇḍa	Power over all the various sets of three aspects of reality

With the twenty-eight *yoginīs* of the *bhūpura* named, the deities of the *śrīcakra*'s major sub-cakras are completed.[106] The *yoginīs* are also referred to as *āvaraṇadevatās*, the deities of obstructions. Just as one "pierces" the six cakras of the yogic body (and the three knots (*granthi*)), so the adept overcomes the obstructions of the mundane world by ascending each of the sub-cakras and acquiring the powers associated with each. Each group of deities and powers is considered the key to achieving the next progressive stage in ascending the *śrīcakra*. Thus, *śrīcakra pūjā* is frequently called "*navāvaraṇapūjā*" or "the worship (*pūjā*) which overcomes the nine obstacles." In this sense, the rituals of the *śrīcakra* are the medium through which speculative issues are addressed. One adept summarized this general propensity saying:

> Though we believe Śrīvidyā is the most ancient teaching of the Vedas and that the *śrīcakra* is the original *yantra* what is even more important to us is that Śrīvidyā lacks nothing. We need not borrow from others since [from our point of view] it is they who have borrowed things from us. Śrīvidyā incorporates all the essential things, we do not care if some call them Tantric or Vedic or whatever. This is the original *vidyā* [i.e., wisdom] so it is natural that whatever is found here is sometimes found elsewhere.[107]

When purely theoretical elements are introduced into the symbolic scheme, their importance is often determined with respect to their ritual application. For example, the *śrīcakra* is sometimes described according to the preservation method (*sthitikrama*) in order to complement the methods of creation (*sṛṣṭikrama*) and dissolution (*saṃhārakrama*) already mentioned. According to the *sthitikrama*, the *śrīcakra* is analyzed from the outermost gates to the eight lotus petals and then from the *bindu* to the fourteen minor triangles. This approach combines and counterbalances, as it were, the other two methods but fails to serve a ritual purpose. It is therefore not surprising to learn that many contemporary practitioners had never heard of it. In the textual tradition, however, such inclusive theological elements are used to enhance Śrīvidyā's consistency and reenforce the coherence of its theology.

The *śrīcakra* completes the goddess's triadic theology and creates the central focus for Śrīvidyā's ritual practice. When combined with the *śrīvidyā* mantra, the cakra forms a distinctive matrix of concepts and practices which the textual tradition assumes includes intellectual and ritual expertise. The textual tradition, however, is curiously silent about the display or ritual use of the *śrīcakra* outside the context of initiated worship. Clearly, traditionalists have had some hand in bringing the *yantra* into public rituals, temples, and other settings in which non-initiates might come into contact with Śrīvidyā imagery. This raises important questions about the relationship between Śrīvidyā ideology and practice and about oral and textual traditions. A more thorough description of the ritual tradition will be presented in the contexts of the study of living Śrīvidyā in south India.

Part II

TOWARD A THEORY FOR INTERPRETING HINDU TANTRIC RITUAL

INTRODUCTION: WHY THEORIZE ABOUT ŚRĪVIDYĀ RITUAL?

A systematic study of Śrīvidyā's Tantric rituals would require an exhaustive comparison of liturgical texts and an elaborate description of their contents. Liturgy is the primary format in which both speculations and prescriptions for practice take shape. An equally exhaustive anthropological study of what practitioners say, say they do, and are observed to do would be required to address the interpretation of ideas and the discrepancy between prescribed and performed ritual. Such a study deserves its own monograph.[1] The more daunting task of advancing a theory of ritual that explains the structure and ideology of Śrīvidyā as a Śākta Tantric discipline would still remain. Such a theory could be used to address important questions in Tantric studies.

How does Śrīvidyā ritual compare to other forms of Hindu ritual, especially the Vedic rituals which it so deliberately imitates? How do we explain the claim of contemporary Śrīvidyā writers that its rituals "fulfill the Vedas?" Are such claims the mere rhetoric of those who locate their interests in both traditions? How does the study of Tantric rituals, such as those prescribed in Śrīvidyā, contribute to our understanding of the structure of Hindu society?

A theory that addresses Tantric ritual in light of Vedic ritual traditions will also help explain why Śrīvidyā has continued to flourish when other equally sophisticated and intellectually powerful Tantric systems failed to sustain viable traditions.[2]

I will begin by assuming that Śrīvidyā rituals must be considered within a larger structure of Hindu beliefs and activities. As Hans Penner notes, "it is the *relation* of the elements, not the elements or symbols themselves, that is important for explaining religion."[3] Since all descriptive projects are theory-laden one cannot avoid the thorny problems involved in developing a method for explanatory reduction. My analysis will be essentially structuralist in method; my comparison of Śrīvidyā ritual treats the meaning of its terms, values, and practices as the result of the simultaneous presence of other terms within a larger *Hindu* system. I will argue that Śrīvidyā formulates its doctrine and ritual through a process of continuous engagement with the Vedic tradition, especially *smārta* brahmanism. Śrīvidyā cannot be itself without a self-conscious engagement with this particular "other," both in ideology and practice.[4] In this respect, this analysis is equally attentive to the historical developments that have shaped *smārta* and Śrīvidyā traditions.

Discussing the theoretical dimensions of Śrīvidyā, and particularly its central ritual, the *śrīcakra pūjā,* will require only a minimal description of prescriptions and behaviors. The burden of this essay is to create a model for understanding how Śrīvidyā's ritual ideology addresses a situational incongruity between expectations and occurrences. This situational incongruity is rooted in human experience. Asserting that everything in creation is a divine emanation and that, as a consequence, human beings are immortal and divine in essence, Śrīvidyā ritual presents a case to demonstrate how one can know these "facts" and why ordinary experience does nothing to make them apparent.

The Śrīvidyā rituals by which one reclaims divine experience take place in the larger framework of a Hindu system of values. I will maintain—along with Louis Dumont, J. C. Heesterman, and others—that this system of values is governed by sets of relations that structure a system of complementary oppositions.[5] This model has been criticized for privileging a brahman-dominated hierarchy and for failing to represent empirical, social realities.[6]

As I will show, Śrīvidyā assumes the structural components of the "classical system" of estate (*varṇa*) hierarchy and constructs its Tantric ideology on this basis. We need not assert that the hierarchy of estates describes social relations empirically, only that Śrīvidyā assumes the structure as its normative representation of society. The conceptual oppositions that Dumont, Heesterman, Penner and others maintain govern the relations between elements of the hierarchical structure are likewise applicable.

As Frederique Marglin, T. N. Madan, and others have shown, the oppositions that govern relations within the hierarchical structure, such as pure/impure and auspicious/inauspicious, are not exclusionary or necessarily symmetrical; neither are they static or absolute. Such distinctions are not always differences in kind but in degree and in the mode of expression; such distinctions need to be understood without assuming that the categories themselves are impervious to change, adjustment, and renegotiation.

The categories and oppositions that govern Śrīvidyā's theological opposition of dynamic Śakti/eternal Śiva are likewise fluid and sometimes asymmetrical in the sense of being matters of degree and perspective. Where one *stands* in relation to others and the divine counts for everything in Śrīvidyā. Śrīvidyā's only incontrovertible truth is that the universe is a divine self-manifestation of power in which events are different in degree *and* kind only from an ordinary (i.e., ignorant) point of view. From the privileged vantage point of the Śrīvidyā practitioner, the world is nothing but divine power or Śakti. Power, in the most generic sense, entails a privileged, that is, divine perspective as well as the ability to create, sustain, or transform reality in accordance with one's desires, behaviors, or knowledge. Things are powerful in their capacities to influence, perpetuate, or transform either themselves or other realities.

THE VAIDIKA TANTRIC: ACQUIRING POWER BY EXPLOITING INCONGRUITY

That Tantric Śrīvidyā, which uses ritual to invert the values of orthopraxy and which formulates its own, separate canon, has been dominated by *smārta* brahmans seems puzzling and oxymoronic. The *smārta* tradition imagines itself entrusted with "protection" (*rakṣa*) of Vedic speech and claims authortity and expertise over the entire domain of Vedic learning and culture.[7] *Smārtas* are usually who is meant when scholars refer to the "Vedic tradition." *Smārtas* also define themselves precisely in terms of being not-Tantric.[8] This definition is as much a statement about custom and leading a life of religious orthopraxy as it is about establishing different canons and sources of authority.

I propose to begin the account of the *smārta* brahman or Vaidika who adopts Tantric Śrīvidyā with an investigation of the role power (*śakti*) plays in formulating the superstructure of Hindu thought. This is not to dismiss Dumont's theory that centers on the ideology of pollution; one does not need to dispute the importance of the dichotomy of purity and pollution when considering power.[9] Rather, I will argue that the structure of purity and pollution is epiphenomenal inasmuch as it becomes a means by which distinctions in the mundane world can be observed or affirmed.[10] The issue for Vaidika Tantrics, however, is not merely becoming or staying pure, at least not for its own sake. Rather, in Śrīvidyā the issue is how one might harness and actualize the power perceived to be inherent in all things, including social relations. The dichotomies of impure/pure and auspicious/inauspicious are important since these distinctions are mechanisms for the expression of dispositional and episodic forms of power.

The Tantric's deliberate reversal of brāhmaṇic values through the ritual use of meat, liquor, and sex, presents an opportunity to exploit the distinction between pure and impure and to utilize this fundamental opposition by exaggerating a situational incongruity. Put differently, one acquires access to power by radicalizing distinctions and then playing on the incongruity between what is normative and what is possible. This point deserves further explanation.

In her preliminary remarks to the discussion of Tantric *pūjā*, Sanjukta Gupta notes that Tantric *sādhana* consists of two principle parts, ritual worship (*pūjā*) and meditation (*yoga*). It is by combining these two parts that Tantrics create a distinctive alternative to the Vedic tradition. Tantrics, as I will show, resolve certain critical problems that arise in the course of Vedic ritual by adding the experiential dimension of yoga to the performative requirement of ritual action. In addition, Tantrics reject the Vedic idea that performative perfection in ritual is the sole means to achieve one's stated goals. These facts, however, are not sufficient to account for the adoption of a Tantric discipline by *smārta* brahmans. One might wrongly conclude that Tantrism simply adds a new dimension to Vedism, thus reasserting the claim that Vedic tradition values "orthopraxy" over "orthodoxy." This would not explain why Śrīvidyā Tantrism imitates Vedic ritual and then subverts brahman values, or how Vaidikas and Tāntrikas formulate their thoughts, actions, and objectives.

Since both Vedic and Tantric ritual traditions are obsessed with correct performance there is little about ritual orthopraxy per se that should concerns us. More important is the Tantric's revision of ritual ideology, which reclaims power by exploiting the distinction between pure and impure and auspicious and inauspicious. Tantrics engage in revisionary ritual ideology because of the *partial* failure of Vedic rituals to produce their stated results. This view is distinctively Tantric: all classical Hindus, with the possible exception of the Ritualist Pūrva Mīmāmsakas, raise the issue of the efficacy of ritual, particularly Vedic ritual. From the period of the early Upaniṣads, the content of Vedic ritual begins a radical reinterpretation—one that eventually shifts the locus of Vedic authority from the content of its ritual prescriptions to its performative forms.[11]

While all high-caste Hindus retain some notion of Vedic authority, the actual performance of certain Vedic rituals diminishes in importance from as early as the third century, C.E. Other types of ritual, especially those rooted in the Purāṇas and Tantras, supplant Vedic rituals as the dominant interest of *smārtas*. Interest in these rituals, however, has not come at the expense of the principles of purity and pollution, which are crucial to the formation and acquisition of power. Śrīvidyā reshapes the brahmans' preoccupation with purity as a means of *distinguishing* powerful substances and determining access to powerful situations by reassessing the human situation. That which is powerful, however, is not determined by its purity. The impure, in fact, is often powerful. The issue centers on the ability to negotiate powerful things, whether they are pure or impure. According to Śrīvidyā, initiation is the means by which one gains access to the highest levels of power (*śakti*) both in terms of action in the world and in relationship with divinity. At stake in performance of ritual is the potential for acquiring power, made possible through initiation. The ideology of pollution creates the structure through which one understands how power might be acquired and controlled.

Having adopted the *smārta*'s ideology of pollution, which helps generate the dichotomy of twice-born/non-twice-born, Śrīvidyā introduces another variable into the structural hierarchy. This is the dichotomy of initiate/non-initiate or Tantric/non-Tantric—a distinction that enables Tantrics to differentiate not only twice-born Tantric initiates from other Tantric initiates but also twice-born Tantrics from twice-born non-Tantrics. It is this latter distinction that becomes crucial as we analyze the relations that make up the ritual hierarchy.[12]

Gupta outlines the preliminaries and prerequisites for Tantric worship. These need not detain us.[13] She has identified some thirty-four steps in the basic structure of Śrīvidyā's *śrīcakra* worship.[14] This structure shows that the ritual worship of the *śrīcakra* is actually a series of smaller rites that are individually distinguished and combined into a larger pattern of meaning and activity. The smaller rites may also be constituents of other rituals; one is able to identify a *śrīcakra pūjā* because it employs Śrīvidyā's canon of signs and texts. We should notice that the individual elements of the ritual do not define the ritual as Tantric or as a sectarian form of Tantrism. One cannot construct a *Tantric* ritual by adding together the elements of which it is comprised anymore than one can understand caste by focusing on one or more of its elements.[15]

The individual steps of Śrīvidyā's *śrīcakra* worship might be further condensed into categories marking the progressive stages of its Tantric ritual. The most important of these steps, purification and protection, deserves extended consideration.

THE FIVEFOLD STRUCTURE OF ŚRĪVIDYĀ RITUAL

Purification and Protection

By using water, fire, and other substances, like incense and sandlewood paste, the worshiper purifies himself and his environment in order to sustain and provide an occasion for the concentrated presence of divinity.

The difference between sacred and profane environments should not be considered a distinction in kind but in degree. Since the universe in its entirety an emanation of divine power (*śakti*), the situation calls for a special environment capable of sustaining divinity's concentrated presence. A ritual creates an appropriate setting for the concentrated presence of divinity; the sacred can be invoked, sustained, and worshiped in an environment in which rules establish a distinction between ritual and not-ritual worlds. The distinction between a sacred environment in which divinity's presence is "concentrated" and a profane environment in which divinity is present but diffuse is partially a function of the pure/impure dichotomy.

Normally impure, that is, brāhmaṇically unsanctioned substances, such as liquor or meat, are not used by Śrīvidyā ritualists to purify the environment or in preparation for worship. These elements are introduced later, *after* the conventions of purity and impurity have been marked formally by ritual actions.

Divinity is nothing other than power that can be contained, appropriated, and even controlled through the mechanisms of ritual. Since power concentrates in situations (i.e., in rituals) in which the distinction between pure and impure is noticed, one can utilize the distinction to assert one's prerogative over others for whom such distinctions must be maintained. In this way Tantrics are by no means exceptional. The not-ritual environment by definition is capable of sustaining only a diffuse and therefore less powerful presence of divinity. Tantrics assert their difference from non-Tantrics by inverting or reversing the criteria that determine the dichotomy of pure/impure within the confines of ritual. In other words, in the very setting that demands the purest of substances and actions, conventional impurities are deliberately introduced. The Tantric's objective is to assert complete control over the categories that govern ritual. That is, to claim control over the substances and categories rather than be controlled by them. In this sense, the Tantric seeks to usurp the non-Tantric brahman's claim as the most powerful of all ritual specialists.

While the distinction in Śrīvidyā's *śrīcakra* worship between the pure and impure is affirmed at the outset of the ritual, maintaining the distinction does not confer power on the ritual adept; neither does the ritual cause a once-and-for-all transformation of the rules of purity and impurity. Rather, noticing the conventional distinction between pure and impure creates a means by which one can gain initial access to episodic power, that is, power (*śakti*) displayed in particular actions. Episodic power depends on creating a situtation in which the distinction of pure/impure is first noticed and affirmed, and then deliberately transgressed to signal control over the distinction itself. In other words, gaining access to the goddess's concentrated presence depends on establishing an incongruity between normative values and perceived possibilities.

The goddess herself is called pure in essence and therefore incapable of becoming impure in any worldly sense.[16] In her ritual worship the devotee must first act to fend off encroaching impurity. This marks the transition to the ritual world. Ultimately, the ritual worshiper imitates the goddess herself by disdaining all distinctions, including the conventions of purity and impurity. This is effected by creating a ritually defined environment in which power (*śakti*) can be concentrated in substances and actions and also controlled.

The first stage in which one deals with "encroaching impurity" must be dealt with systematically and with vigilance since purity itself does not prevent or protect against impurity.[17] Purity is insured not by the inherent virtue of the ritualist or by his past actions but by immediate, preventative actions, such as bathing, and by invoking minor deities who protect the ritual environment on the condition that they, too, are properly cared for. Since even the most powerful adept cannot prevent impurity from encroaching on the ritual environment, purifying actions as well as divine intervention must be reenacted for every occasion.

The distinction between purity and impurity centers on identifying substances as out-of-place; power is defined as the ability to negotiate and control places *and* substances. Danger occurs when either substances are out-of-place or when they are imbalanced by nature.[18] Both power and purity/impurity occur in degrees of difference rather than kind. Substances are powerful when they are perceived to effect a transformation—be it physical, mental, or moral—or when they can create, maintain, or destroy other substances. Not all substances can be made powerful, though ritual is a means by which the potential or dispositional power of a given substance can be utilized or enhanced. Thus, human beings must deal with the substances that make up the world in different ways. Depending on the situation, one might seek to avoid, acquire, ignore, or utilize a given substance depending on its nature, its location, and its potential for power and/or danger.

Substances become polluting when they are either misplaced or misused; those that have the power to purify are not all equal in degree. Gold and fire, for example, are more powerful and therefore more purifying than silver and holy ash (*vibhuti*). Substances that usually pollute or have the potential to pollute, however, may also be powerful and even purifying. Wine, for example, usually pollutes because it is associated with drinking and therefore with moral lassitude. Wine in the presence of a non-Tantric *smārta* is a substance-out-of-place and is to be avoided. Blood potentially pollutes because human agency cannot always control its flow—this is the case with menstrual blood, for example. While all powerful and usually polluting substances are potentially dangerous, this is not the case with all purifying substances, some of which, like milk, are considered utterly benign by nature. Substances are sometimes deemed less capable of purifying because they are either less powerful in comparison to other substances, such as silver is to gold, or because they may either purify or pollute, such as water. While all purifying substances are, to some degree, powerful, not all powerful substances are purifying.

Those substances that are usually polluting and also have dispositional power can be controlled by ritual's episodic power to contain, manipulate, or transform. Wine, as we noted, is considered powerful, dangerous, and *always* polluting as far as in-caste non-Tantric Hindus are concerned. Kaula Śrīvidyā creates an opportunity to claim access to wine's power, control its danger, and obviate it usually polluting effects. Wine remains a polluting substance to non-initiates because they do not have the means to control its danger or gain access to its power. Initiates, too, will face danger and pollution should they drink wine outside the ritual. Thus, Śrīvidyā accords to itself power over substances that other, "lesser" traditions or persons cannot control and deems ritual the mechanism of control, containment, or transformation.

According to Śrīvidyā theology, if the goddess's nature as divine power (*śakti*) were not manifest diffusely, sentient beings would be overwhelmed and incapable of proceeding along their karmic paths, paths that eventually lead to a human birth and initiation into Śrīvidyā. While Śakti's diffusion depends in part on human perception, it is also her nature. It is by this means she allows beings to revel in their own natures; further, it permits free will since humans have before them the opportunity to act on their *karman*.

By the force of individual and collective *karman*, the divine power (*śakti*), which makes up the universe, may be misrepresented, misplaced, or misused. Negative forces, such as lawlessness (*adharma*) and ignorance (*avidyā*), are not mere human misconceptions but realities that need to be negotiated; they, too, must ultimately emanate from the divine.[19] One must learn to comprehend the divine in order to harness forces and substances powerful enough to prevent the intrusion of dislocating forces. By dealing with *all* substances as manifestations of divine power, Śrīvidyā sees ritual as a process by which one relocates or readjusts substances by the use of other substances and forces by the use of other forces.

Substances differ in degrees of power determined by proximate relationship to divine essence. Since divinity is ubiquitous but diffuse, one cannot separate the issue of degrees of power from the environments in which it is possible to concentrate power. The utilization of power in the human realm depends on situations in which potency can be maximized. Thus, the ritual creates a means by which the power (*śakti*) inherent in a given action or object can brought to its fullest potential.

When a Tantric utilizes substances or sanctions actions that defy brāhmaṇical standards of ethics or propriety, the inversion of the pure/impure dichotomy occurs within strictly controlled ritual contexts. Such ritual acts do not merely subvert conventional ideologies and norms of behavior. Rather, Tantrics retain and then subordinate conventional views of purity and pollution in an expanded system of hierarchy.

In Kaula forms of worship (*pūjā*), the five m's (*pañcamakāra*: wine (*madya*), meat (*māṃsa*), fish (*matsya*), fermented grain (*mudrā*), and sexual intercourse (*maithuna*)), which violate non-Tantric brāhmaṇical norms, assert the privilege to control and transcend the boundaries of convention. The prerogative to transgress conventional boundaries of purity and pollution is a further affirmation of the self-conferred right to transgress ordinary social boundaries of caste.

In non-Tantric Hinduism the domain beyond the dichotomy of pure/impure is that of the renouncer-ascetic who, unlike in-caste Hindus, is neither pure nor impure. Tantrics also wish to transform themselves by going beyond the ordinary boundaries of purity and impurity and beyond caste. Like the ascetic, they, too, wish to stanch the flow of *karma* and sublate its effects. The Tantric method is not renunciation of distinctions and worldly involvements but rather transgression of them. In this way, Tantrics resemble the renouncer-ascetics but do not adopt their life-style or their methods. In the Tantric case, the method is threefold. First, the conventions of purity/impurity are affirmed; second, these distinctions are transgressed in order to gain access to powerful substances which articulate the difference between Tantric/non-Tantric and inside-ritual/outside-ritual; and last, the effects or "products" of ritual are "carried over" into the not-ritual domain by a claim to sustained, incontrovertible experience.

Most forms of Tantrism, it should be recalled, are anti-ascetic; they either reject formal renunciation or rationalize it as unnecessary. This is because the Tantric believes he can have it both ways. He remains an in-caste householder who ordinarily lives within the boundaries of purity/impurity outside the ritual setting; during the ritual, he gains the privileges of the renunciate who is beyond purity or pollution. Ritual privileges are gained by supplanting renunciation of the householder stage of life (*āśrama*) with Tantric initiation.

Tantrism may reject renunciation but it does not leave in doubt that its aim to achieve the renunciate's goal of transcending karma and obviating the effects of karma.

Thus, Tantrics, like renunciates, reject caste but do not imagine themselves outside the caste structure of Hinduism. Tantrics view their own caste-defying ritualism rather than renunciation as the correct complement to the worldly life that continues to operate based partially on the opposition of pure/impure. Tantrics maintain that their transcendence of *karma* is achieved through the very ritual that renunciates are no longer interested in performing.

The goals of renunciation, Tantrics assert, can be achieved without forsaking any enjoyment of the worldly life. For the Tantric, the fundamental dichotomy that structures Hinduism is not householder/renunciate but rather non-initiate/initiate. We can describe the structure of Tantrism in terms of the structure of Hinduism. Penner has described the structure of Hinduism[20]

The Structure of Hinduism

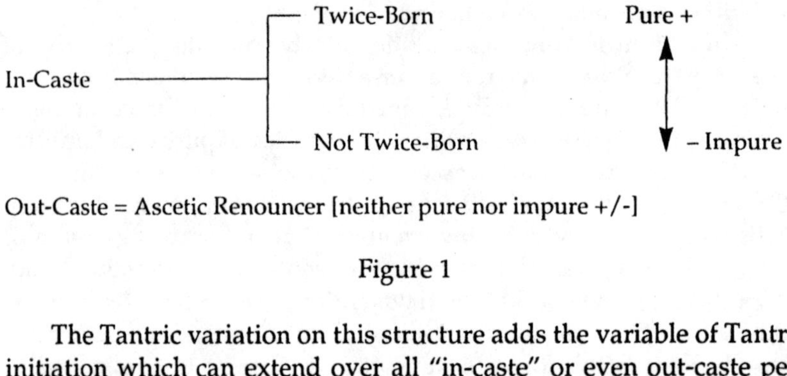

Out-Caste = Ascetic Renouncer [neither pure nor impure +/-]

Figure 1

The Tantric variation on this structure adds the variable of Tantric initiation which can extend over all "in-caste" or even out-caste persons. Śrīvidyā Tantrics prefer to ignore the out-caste renunciate and begin from within the in-caste structure of twice-born and not twice-born. Initiates can come from both twice-born and non-twice-born castes, as well as from both genders.

In Śrīvidyā some adepts, such as Bhāskararāya, who align themselves with the Śākta-oriented Śaṅkara tradition, admit tacitly that initiates can also be renouncers (*sannyāsin*). The crucial distinction, however, remains between initiates and non-initiates; renunciation, we are reminded by Bhāskararāya, has nothing to do with the acquisition of power.[21] Further, renunciation per se confers no special benefits regarding the ritual.

Śrīvidyā also rejects the criteria of pure/impure established within conventional Hinduism to determine *Tantric* qualification. This permits usually impure persons in the hierarchy of ordinary society to gain dual status. Śūdras, for example, remain impure (vis à vis brahmans) outside the ritual realm or the Tantric family (*kula*) but as Tantrics initiates are superior to all non-initiates. This does not require a rejection of the distinction between pure and impure. This is what is meant when it is said that Tantrics adopt a "dual norm." Figure 2 reveals that the Tantric's "dual norm" not only juxtaposes initiates and non-initiates but requires the distinction between being in-ritual and outside-ritual.

The Structure of Tantric Hinduism

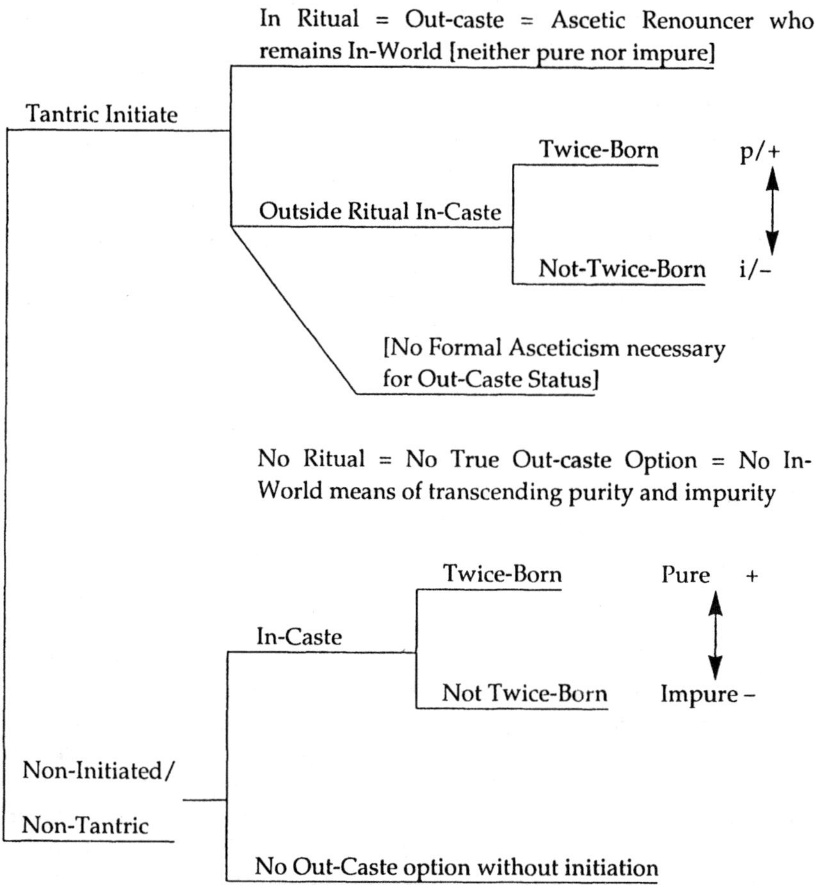

Figure 2

Gaining access to divine power includes behavior that non-Tantric Hindus consider convention-defying because such behaviors violate standards of purity and impurity. For the Tantric, ritual confers the same privilege that renunciation confers within non-Tantric Hinduism; within the ritual one can go beyond the boundaries of caste and gender by gaining complete control over the pollution that ordinarily befalls persons living in the world.[22] For example, Kaula Tantrics who argue that ritual drinking approximates the experience of unqualified bliss (*ānanda*) repeatedly condemn drinking liquor outside-ritual. While the means of ritual do not extend beyond the ritual domain, the goals of ritual clearly do.

This particular Hindu ideology of power, which utilizes the pure/impure dichotomy, is not based on abstractions or intangible realities. For non-Tantric Hindus, who are not yet ascetic-renouncers, power also involves the capacity to fend off impurity and to conduct transactions that create favorable imbalances of purity. The ability to manipulate substances by use or aversion confers the power to affect the hierarchy of relations defined primarily in terms of dichotomy of pure/impure. For the Kaula Tantric, the maximalization of power involves the ability to deal with ordinarily prohibited, that is, polluting substances and behaviors. Prohibited substances and behaviors not only allow one to overcome the conventional distinction between pure and impure but also to effect the transformation of the impure into the pure. This situation is not unique to Tantrics. For example, blood spilt, that is, flowing without containment or control is conventionally considered dangerous and usually pollution. In the *Mahābhārata*, however, blood spilt in the ritual of battle purifies by ridding the world of lawlessness (*adharma*).[23] The Tantric's ritual life functions on a similar principle: substances ordinarily restricted or prohibited can become means of purification or transcendence.

Initially, the power gained from transacting dangerous substances is confined to ritual contexts and considered to last only for the duration of the ritual. However, Tantrics make the further claim that the superhuman power, which they acquire by initiation and performance of Tantric ritual, gradually affects one's life outside ritual settings. As Bhāskararāya notes, the experience of bliss (*ānanda*) and the capacity to affect events outside ritual is comparable to "getting your sea-legs," that is, it begins in ritual and is dependent on it but then continues outside the ritual.[24] Power is, therefore, a transferable commodity provided ritual's boundaries are initially observed and, in significant ways, sustained as inviolate. Ritual, or rather the rule of ritual, is the means by which powerful substances are legitimized for those who have the exceptional capacity to deal with things usually considered impure and therefore dangerous. To become powerful is to become superhuman, that is, to be able to do things that others cannot or to come into contact with things that, for others, are routinely dangerous or polluting.

From the standpoint of the scholar, the Hindu's assertions about substances, divinity, power, and the like are relational rather than ontological terms, that is, they exist empirically inasmuch as they are oppositional categories.[25] Fundamentally, Tantrics adopt and then invert the opposition of pure/impure to establish an oppositional relationship with non-Tantrics. The Tantric's concept of transcending the purity/pollution dichotomy depends on the non-Tantric's being determined by it. For a Vaidika Tantric, the adoption of a discipline such as Śrīvidyā creates a profound and observable distinction between those who can claim control over only a portion of the world and those who can claim to command it in its entirety. Śrīvidyā's ritual ideology not only assumes but depends on a brahman-dominated view of purity and impurity even while it deliberately defies traditional brahman boundaries. The same principles may not be at work in other Tantric ideologies less self-conscious about sustaining or defining themselves in brāhmaṇical categories.

By articulating the incongruity between Tantric and non-Tantric qualifications for ritual and by upsetting conventional values involving purification and controlling dangerous substances within ritual, Śrīvidyā Tantrics seek to establish new conditions for the acquisition of power and for obtaining life's goals. Thus, expertise in ritual becomes a means by which Śrīvidyā Tantrics assert privilege over non-Tantrics, something that could occur only within a larger context in which ritual performance is itself deemed an expression of power.

Invocation/Consecration

Acts of invocation and consecration introduce into the ritual the deities who provide objectified and concentrated forms of power to be worshiped. With these deities come icons, mantras, and descriptions. After having made himself a suitable divine vessel through mantra and yogic invocation of minor deities, the worshiper performs an elaborate interidentification (*nyāsa*). Divinities are summoned from both within the adept's own body and as macrocosmic realities permeating the cosmos through such acts as displaying gestures (*mudrā*). By invocation and concentration the divine power is given *place* and *locale*. This is not to say that the deities or the rituals are bound to specific places, such as temples or the home. The place of invocation is determined not only by the Tantric's access to various liturgical formulas and his capacity to use icons, mantras, and yantras, but also by an application (and sometimes a violation) of the rules of purity and pollution.

Tantrics will often conduct their rituals in places that non-Tantrics consider most polluted, such as the cremation ground. Once again the importance of creating an inverted paradigm characterizes the Tantric's effort to define himself in opposition to non-Tantric values. Whereas non-Tantric brahman rituals are usually conducted in places that are set apart on the basis of purity, the Tantric asserts the possibility of using *any* place and particularly the most powerful *and* polluting places. It is not necessary that a ritual be conducted in a particularly powerful or polluting place; what is important is that it could be. Further, a place can become powerful by the performance of ritual. Not only can a Tantric not be bound by ordinary notions of purity and danger, he can confer power on places, persons, and things through ritual action.

Worship/Identification

Both external (*bahir-*) and internal (*antar-*) forms of contemplative worship (or sacrifice, *yāga*) are usually required in order to effect a complete relationship with the divine. In *śrīcakra* worship there are included such entities as the three groups of gurus (divine, superhuman, and human), the sixteen eternalities or *nityās*, who represent the phases of the moon, and the six portions of the deity's body.[26] The lion's share of worship is consumed by the placement and identification of the goddess's attendant deities or *yoginīs* who occupy specific places on the *śrīcakra*'s nine minor cakras.[27] Suffice it to say that the process of identification on the *śrīcakra* follows the so-called "dissolution method," or *saṃhārakrama* whereby the worshiper begins at the outer most gates of the *bhūpura* cakra and proceeds systematically towards the central bindu, stopping at designated points to identify the attendant deity. Each minor cakras' presiding deity is likewise identified and, finally, Lalitā Mahātripurasundarī is envisioned seated on the lap of Kāmeśvara on the central point (*bindu*). Worship of the supreme goddess presupposes that issues of purity, protection, invocation, and consecration have been dealt with.

The ritual process reflects the tradition's ideology of power, that is, a movement from less to more concentrated forms of divine *śakti*, from more diffuse manifestations of the goddess to her divine essence. One could also say that one ascends to the *śrīcakra*'s center and so moves into increasingly purer realms. Purity, like everything else in the universe, is a form of power (*śakti*) *and* a substance (*prakṛti*) in Śrīvidyā ideology. At the *śrīcakra*'s central *bindu*, however, all distinctions are ultimately dissolved.

Offerings/Substances

Food (*naivedya*), flowers (*puṣpa*), fire, and liquids are offered after the deities are invoked on the *śrīcakra*. One might then do the *kāmakalā* meditation and a fire sacrifice patterned after the Vedic *homa*. These additional components of the ritual are often omitted; sometimes they are separated and performed as quasi-independent rites. The actual content of the offerings is a matter for consideration in our future study of contemporary Śrīvidyā. For example, there may or may not be included in these portions of the ritual the use of convention-defying substances or behaviors (such as *pañcamakāra*) or an animal for sacrifice. There are sixty-four traditional offerings (*upacāra*) that are variously classified and arranged to be made at different intervals.

Contemplation/Praise

The yogic elements of *śrīcakra* worship are in evidence at each stage of the ritual as well as in the performance of contemplation and praising of the embodied divinity. During the internal worship, for example, the deity as *kuṇḍalinī* is identified in six or nine vital centers of the body. The *japa* or recitation of the root mantra of the goddess is a particularly significant aspect of contemplation and praise of the deity. It occurs at the most advanced stage of the ritual. One might say that everything done prior to mantra recitation is mere preparation for it: the full contingent of deities already have been invoked, the environment has been prepared and offerings have been made, and the visualizations of the divinity's threefold imagery are complete. The adept, at this point, concentrates on the correlation between external and internal esoteric realities, using the mantra and the yantra as the means to identify with the goddess and so gain access to her ultimate power.

Silent recitation of the mantra concentrating on the divinity invoked on the *śrīcakra* is followed by as series of chanted eulogies and sometimes by the worship of a woman representing the embodied goddess. The ritual may or may not culminate in sexual intercourse.

In Kulācāra traditions there is a collective worship during which ritual observer-initiates are made a part of the individual's personal *śrīcakra* worship. This is followed by leave-taking (*visarjana*) and a prayer for peace and happiness for all. After these activities, the worshiper consumes and/or distributes the offerings that have been made as the gifts (*prasāda*) of the goddess. In some traditions, there is also the worship of an unmarried girl, that is, a *kumarī pūjā* (with whom sexual intercourse is strictly forbidden). The ritual ends with another series of purificatory and protective acts that "seal" the activity and provide a formal conclusion. These final rites create a mechanism for reentry into the world outside ritual and propose a means by which the power obtained ritually can be carried into the mundane world.

Every element of the *śrīcakra* ritual can be seen as a part of this larger, five-stage structure. While the worship of the *śrīcakra* that Gupta outlines is a daily ritual that is usually considered an obligatory rite (*nitya*), such a rite is often done only occasionally. Mantra recitation and a contemplative visualization of the complete worship of the *śrīcakra* or *navāvaraṇa pūjā* frequently substitutes for the external act. In addition to the daily *pūjā*, there are other occasional (*naimittika*) and optional (*kāmya*) rites, which can be elaborated for special occasions. More important is the fact that the Tantric's obligatory rite, unlike its Vedic counterpart, is not fruitless in the sense of being an obligation with no *positive* consequences for its performance. The Tantric obligatory rite does not simply make "right" what "needs" to be accomplished nor does it rectify a temporary (and usually predictable) incongruity. Rather, it is an obligatory rite in the sense that Tantric initiation, which is always an *optional* ritual entitlement, entails certain ritual responsibilities that must be maintained. In other words, the Tantric seeks through obligatory ritual that which, in the Vedic tradition, is secured only in optional (*kāmya*) rites. This not only raises the status of the obligatory *Tantric* rite but invests in ritual a sense of power over the ordinary that is usually reserved for extraordinary and optional rites. This point will be significant for our comparison of Vedic and Tantric rites below.

TANTRIC SCHOLARSHIP AND MODES OF COMPARISON

Sanjukta Gupta's description of Tantric worship (*pūjā*) is understandably constrained by limitations of space. She has set out to make explicit her contention that "the fundamental structure of Tantric ritualism remains constant, whilst it provides scope for introducing almost infinite variations in the ritual practices."[28] She goes on to say, "A fairly regular pattern in Tantric rituals can be discerned by analyzing a simple form of daily Tantric worship of the Goddess." She then describes and lists the components of the three categories of Tantric rites, namely, the daily obligatory (*nitya*), occasional (*naimittika*), and desired (*kāmya*) in order to establish generic patterns and procedures. Explanatory reduction and theoretical issues are secondary to her descriptive agenda.[29] Gupta has succeeded in providing an outline for *śrīcakra pūjā* against which more detailed descriptions can be patterned and, in this sense, has brought the generic description of

Tantric ritual to a new level of intelligibility. Though one still requires a sophisticated appreciation of Vedic, classical Hindu, and Tantric vocabularies to follow her descriptions, the data is presented as a class of phenomena rather than as arbitrary and thoroughly idiosyncratic exempla.

It is in regard to Gupta's summarization and her attempts to generalize that Madhu Khanna distinguishes her work. Khanna writes, "whereas Gupta has given us a summary of the conventional details of the exoteric *pūjā* of *śrīcakra*, supported by tradition, we have attempted a more detailed and systematic exposition of the exoteric ritual of the *śrīcakra* along with its esoteric contemplations."[30] Khanna is concerned not only with a particular Śrīvidyā adept's work—in this case Śivānanda—she is also interested in what she calls "the *a priori* cognitive structure of the ritual dynamics" and an illustration of how the "triadic categories of the [Kashmiri Śaiva system of] Trika were assimilated in the ritual 'syntax' of the *śrīcakra*.... In this way the whole cycle of worship, we demonstrate, embodies the paradigm on which creation is conceived." In sum, Khanna is interested in detailing the internal coherence of the ritual's prescriptions and its conceptual structures in light of the theology of the Trika school of Kashmiri Śaivism. Gupta, in contrast, is interested primarily in providing generalizable patterns of *śrīcakra* worship.[31]

Both Khanna and Gupta clarify the vocabulary of the literature and provide a textual exegesis of traditions. In short, both scholars efforts are "based on tradition." In this sense, both create expository ethnographies that take seriously what Tantric texts say. However, they do not offer independent theories of translation and interpretation in which the rituals are explained in terms other than those within the tradition.[32]

My objective is neither to dispute nor to elaborate these exegetical works. I will consider *śrīcakra* ritual and the discourse surrounding it as an example of situational incongruity in the history of religions in which the events represent an effort on the part of the community of adepts to resolve certain basic religio-historical dilemmas.[33] Śrīvidyā ritual has been remarkably successful in articulating the hopes and religious values of its adepts. As I will show, it also sought to reestablish the privilege of ritual virtuosity at a time in Indian history when the ritual expert's significance had been brought into question, both from within and beyond the community of brahmans.

Śrīvidyā ritual does more than adapt and apply the principles found in Kashmiri Śaiva or other Tantric theological systems. While it is true that Tripurā worship may have originated in a religious culture steeped in Kashmiri Śaiva ideas and ritual, these particular theological structures and social influences cannot possibly account for its enduring importance and widespread popularity among high-caste Hindus. In contemporary south India, for example, where the worship of the *śrīcakra* continues to flourish, the historical origins and intellectual foundations of the ritual are entirely forgotten.[34] Very little effort is expended to comprehend or expand on the ritual theory that originates in Kashmiri sources. The ritual's historical origins and original theological paradigms have not been remembered. In fact, this gives us reason to believe that the tradition's "original" origins and paradigms are not critical to its perpetuation and interpretation as a ritually-centered discipline (*sādhana*).[35] It is not a matter of the tradition's gradual falling away from its "original" interpretations and procedure, as some have tried to argue.[36] There is no primordium to be uncovered when studying ritual, there are only various applications in history.

The more pressing question to the student of Tantrism involves Śrīvidyā's continued persistence and transformations in light of the options and the interests of its historical proponents. Put simply, why do certain individuals and groups of Hindus take interest in Śrīvidyā ritual and ideology and what problems, if any, have they imagined Śrīvidyā's ritual resolves?

To engage in Śrīvidyā involves a deliberate decision on the part of the adept; Śrīvidyā is not incumbent by birth or a traditional religious obligation that one obtains through family inheritance. Unlike the training in Vedic recitation that young brahmans receive in their youth—training that prepares them for little else than priestly ritual duties—Śrīvidyā is frequently learnt later in life and is not usually an obligation incumbent on heirs, even within families in which the head of the household is an adept.

While the classification of Śrīvidyā rituals imitates the threefold ritual pattern of obligatory, occasional, and optional rites established in the Vedic tradition, all of Śrīvidyā is in an important sense optional. There is no obligation for anyone to become an initiate. Further, Śrīvidyā is an "extra-Vedic" tradition just as other forms of sectarian devotionalism augment the Vedic ritual legacy perpetuated by high-caste Hindus. As a Tantric tradition, Śrīvidyā does not root itself in caste identity or in strict familial allegiances to a god or cult of worship. The element of voluntary choice is a significant variable when considering the role Śrīvidyā plays in the lives of adherents.

Śrīvidyā's rituals—whether they are classified traditionally as obligatory (*nitya*) or optional (*kāmya*)—are best compared to other Hindu rituals and theological traditions in which choice is a significant factor; that is, we should compare the decision to involve oneself in Śrīvidyā and the promised rewards of ritual participation to other

Hindu traditions in which there is the exercise of ritual options. I have in mind not only those traditions that augment and elaborate themselves through intellectual speculation and yogic practices, but also the Vedic traditions on which so much Tantric ritual is based.

The *śrīcakra* "worship of the nine gates" (*navāvaraṇapūjā*), though in its daily form is considered obligatory (*nitya*) for Śrīvidyā adepts, is actually better compared to the optional desired (*kāmya*) Vedic rituals, such as *agnicayana*, for two reasons. First, both become possible only when certain prior obligations are met. For Śrīvidyā, initiation and a complex ritual expertise is prerequiste; in Vedic traditions there are both complex sets of ritual prerequistes and local cultural issues. Second, both hold out the prospect for rewards that go beyond the ordinary expectations of a Hindu's life. Both Vedic and Tantric rituals promise a form of immortality and prosperity, neither of which are guaranteed to those who do not or cannot perform them. Obtaining heaven (*śvarga*) in the Vedic tradition or liberation from the cycles of death and rebirth in classical Hindu Tantra, has rarely been considered incumbent on all or necessarily possible in one's present birth. Neither set of rituals serve as domestic rites of passage nor are they required at any specific point in one's life; both sets of rituals, in fact, have exceptional restrictions that limit them to a few select members of the larger Hindu community who, for one reason or another, consider their goals important. However, the conditions under which these comparable promises and restrictions are made differ in extremely important ways.

While birth as a male in a twice-born caste is one of the many prerequisites for Vedic ritual, Tantric Śrīvidyā rejects caste and gender as predeterminative criteria. Instead Śrīvidyā privileges other criteria for qualification, particularly moral evaluations of character determined by the guru.[37] Further, the conditions for the fulfillment of ritual promises differ. While the Vedic ritualist does not expect to be transported to heaven at the conclusion of the *agnicayana*, as the texts promise he will be eventually, the Tantric *does* expect *immediate* results. In both cases we are dealing with hopes and expectations of a religious community that sees highly specialized forms of ritual as critically determinative of one's present and future condition.[38]

Leaving aside Śrīvidyā's truth claims about the efficacy of its rituals, we will focus instead on how *śrīcakra* worship forms part of "a system of ideas with which the individuals represent to themselves the society of which they are members, and the obscure but intimate relations which they have with it."[39] Rather than treat the interpretations of Śrīvidyā adepts as an explanation of the physical universe or debate the validity of their claims about eternal truth, I will simply assume that their claims *are* true, that is, that they are made in good faith. While one must eschew descriptive reduction whereby native categories are dismissed as imaginary or false, one must likewise avoid privileging native explanations.[40] The task before us is explanatory reduction: a process by which one takes seriously the reports of experience and the records of activity that are provided by participants but one that seeks to explain the data in terms that do not necessarily conform to native explanations.[41]

TANTRIC AND NON-TANTRIC WORLDS OF CONVERGENCE AND DISJUNCTURE

Śrīvidyā rituals seek to overcome disjunction, chaos, and meaninglessness but not merely by continued affirmation and repetitive practice. While Śrīvidyā asserts the interconnectedness of all things, accounts for the origins of things, and locates the adept within a coherent structure of meaning, it does so by *excluding* the uninitiated from its practice and its fruits. Śrīvidyā, like the Vedic tradition, never suggests that the uninvited will share in the benefits of its practices. Neither does Śrīvidyā ritual describe the world *outside* its ritual and ideological structure.[42]

Śrīvidyā adepts evince little interest in matters not within their immediate sphere of religious interests. Rarely are matters of any general interest mentioned in Śrīvidyā texts and there is little debate with those outside the fold of initiates on matters beyond the ritual structure. Non-Tantric issues are mentioned only when it is necessary to evoke the authority of the larger Hindu tradition in order to justify or create an analogy between Tantric and non-Tantric worlds. It is at these points of perceived convergence and intersection that we locate the interests of Śrīvidyā adepts as members of caste and familial Hindu traditions. In other words, Śrīvidyā adepts invoke the authority of the Veda or claim a relationship with ideas, texts, or practices outside their immediate sphere of Tantric interests *only in support of their Tantric arguments and to dissociate the interests of the ritual world with those of the outside world.* It is as if the world "outside" Tantric ritual did not require or warrant discussion.

Śrīvidyā creates a world *within* a world, that is, it imagines a Tantric world that it understands to exist within a non-Tantric world. The two worlds are seen as sometimes intersecting, sometimes contiguous, and, at critical junctures, separate. Śrīvidyā adepts hold together these two worlds by appealing to distinctly different social, historical, and religious forces. The process of maintaining both Tantric and non-Tantric worlds of meaning involves two different ways of mapping oneself onto the world.[43] These two maps offer contrasting strategies that, in important ways, also conflict. At points of conflict there are further strategies to overcome contradiction—not all of which, as we shall see, are successful.

Characteristic of both strategies is the desire to overcome "situational incongruity," defined as the discrepancy between what is said about the world and what actually happens. Tantrics and non-Tantrics alike are aware of situational incongruities and employ ritual to articulate and sometimes overcome them. From a critical standpoint, the issue is not whether these rituals actually resolve situational incongruities, such as the discrepancy between feeling mortal and becoming immortal. Rather, the issue is how ritual itself plays between incongruities; how ritual creates a demonstration of the difference between what is and what should be, and what should be and what could be.

The high-caste Hindus who become involved in Śrīvidyā adopt two distinct mapping strategies for making sense of the world. However, they do so for quite different reasons. By using both maps these Vaidika Tantrics secure socioreligious standing within the larger structure of Hindu society while, at the same time, fulfill the unfilled promises of the Vedic ritual. In sum, the objectives that the Vedic ritual postpones or declares to be present but "unseen" (*apūrva*), Śrīvidyā declares completely fulfilled.

CONVERGENT AND UTOPIC MAPS OF THE WORLD

The Tantric map of the world is utopic and disjunctive. That is, one seeks to flee from the unsatisfactoriness or incongruity of mundane experience by creating an alternative experience, one defined in terms of ritual experiences. The utopic map describes a world that is not identical to that which is beyond it. Outside the strict domains of the formal ritual, the utopic world persists through the creation of a specialized idiom, that is, a form of discourse that binds Śrīvidyā Tantrics together and ignores things beyond its immediate sphere of interests. For example, the eighteenth-century Bhāskararāya, who was familiar with all sorts of Sanskrit discourse and with Islam and the British, never ventures outside Śrīvidyā's idiom and canon when writing about the tradition. The key issue here is that Bhāskararāya *chooses* to define Śrīvidyā only in terms of itself and introduces non-Tantric issues only to sustain a connection between brāhmaṇic and Vedic and Tantric traditions.

Outside Śrīvidyā's idiom of esoteric and specialized discourse, which also creates a sense of autonomy and privilege, are other worlds, including non-Tantric brahmanism. These are self-consciously excluded from the world described in ritual through the use of a utopic map. The utopic map is disjunctive in the sense that it does not describe the world of ordinary activity and discourse but rather inverts or ignores the values and concepts on which the ordinary world is based. This is nowhere more clearly in evidence than in the ritual of *śrīcakra* worship. Here the main activity is to invoke the deities on the image and imprint the various identifications (*nyāsa*) with body, speech, and mind. A highly specialized, esoteric knowledge is required to use the *śrīcakra* ritually and to imagine it *as* a description of the universe. The image, the idiom, and the behaviors associated with *śrīcakra* worship are self-conscious efforts to account for every intellectual possibility but, at the same time, create a restricted sphere limited to those with the expertise to interpret it.

The Vedic ritual life of brahmans is dominated by the domestic or *gṛhya* rites which function as "'rites de passage,' life-cycle rites or sacraments, accompanying such events as birth, initiation, marriage, and death."[44] These rites are based on a different, and to some extent conflicting, map of the universe from that which is employed in Śrīvidyā to worship the *śrīcakra*. Whereas the Śrīvidyā Tantric revels in a utopic world apart sustained by its closed system of ritual and its self-absorbed reflection on that ritual, the brāhmaṇic preoccupation with domestic rites utilizes a convergent map. A convergent map is one that seeks to establish harmony with the mundane world, revels in ritual's power of repetition, and structures itself in terms of the relationships between *all* sections of Hindu society. The object of the convergent map is to overcome periods of disjunction by restating the normative values that give meaning to relationships; these rituals of convergence reestablish the primordial and dissolvable relationships that are thought to bind the universe together.

Non-Tantric brahmanism's convergent map allows for moments of disjunction, that is, for perceptions of chaos, transition, or instability. These situations are then rectified through the use of highly structured symbolic acts.[45] Thus, periods of liminality or chaos, which may or may not be predictable, such as temporary forms of pollution brought on by death, unwanted contact with things impure, or an eclipse, are resolved through ritual acts that reestablish the interconnectedness of the disparate elements that make up the universe.

The assumption of the convergent map of the world is that such moments of disjunction *can* be rectified, albeit temporarily. Domestic rites of the twice-born are examples of such attempts to overcome incongruity by fostering a sense of connection. Such rituals restore, recreate, stabilize, or seek to gain control over forces that periodically wreck havoc on the "proper" order and arrangement of the universe. These rituals bind the community and assume the logical adequacy of the symbols that are put to "work."[46] In other words, these rituals are understood as necessary and routine functions of a Hindu's social and religious life.

Rituals that follow a convergent map do not flee the mundane world but establish "proper" relations with it. This is not to say that the rituals of the utopic map necessarily express contempt for the mundane. Rather, the utopic map *recreates* the mundane in its own image and disdains the ordinary connections of the convergent map, seeing them as inadequate or simply banal. Instead of imitating the conventions and hierarchical relationships of society, the utopic map offers another set of standards and another reality. In contrast, rituals that follow the convergent map function to legitimize relations between caste groups. Thus, the brahman's purity is established with respect to the *śūdra*'s putative impurity yet the brahman is the one most vulnerable to impurity.

Domestic rituals in the Vedic tradition assert the hegemonic prerogative of the twice-born as religious virtuosi. The twice-born ritualist makes aright that which is perceived either to have fallen into disrepair or is in need of some sort of compensation. While domestic rites are individually oriented, it is also believed that the whole world becomes dysfunctional without their proper maintenance. In fact, as we have noted, the perception of individual impurity or the sense that some domestic ritual, be it obligatory (*nitya*) or occasional (*naimittika*), is necessarily a function of the larger social structure of relations that help define the boundaries of purity and pollution.

Like all rituals, Vedic domestic rites should not be seen as matters of convenience nor as necessarily fulfilling individual desires. Rather, as external *social* facts these rituals help establish collective solidarity more often by constraining than by fulfilling individual desires. Their social functions are not usually difficult to surmise even if their appearance strains the credulity of those who stand outside the community. The hallmark of such rites is that they are periodic, repetitious, and considered necessary for the regular continuance of the individual, society, and the world at large. Though these rituals likewise function to exclude from participation those not qualified because of birth, gender, or for some other reason, they are part of a highly structured scenario in which those excluded are deemed unimportant to the task of overcoming chaos and unintelligibility. Such rites employ the "proper" people who apply "correct" ritual prescriptions. As rituals that function as tools for the negotiation of everyday life, they bear few if any exotic qualities.

The domestic rites, however, are only one class of rituals perpetuated by Vedic traditions. The *śrauta* or so-called solemn rites, though partly similar in structure to the domestic rites, do not conform to the patterns of significance or the explanations that might account for the performance of domestic rites.[47] *Śrauta* rites appear to serve no *necessary* religious function in brahman society; they do not inform one's relationship to everyday affairs nor do they have as their object the maintenance of the mundane world. While they are as concerned with matters of purity and pollution as domestic rituals in terms of qualification and execution, their stated objectives do not pertain to things of this world. In short, they appear as "extras" even when they are classified as obligatory (*nitya*) rather than optional (*kāmya*). As Staal has noted, the *agniṣṭoma* ritual is obligatory for every brahman and yet is confined to those who desire heaven, which is nobody's duty.[48] Rather than resolve temporary dysfunctionality or address a concern about everyday life, these rites as liturgical events dissociate the ritual world from the ordinary.

The traditionalist's definition of ritual as that which involves the substance (*dravya*) of oblation, the deity (*devata*) to whom the oblation is offered, and a formula of renunciation (*tyāga*) of the fruits of ritual creates further situational incongruity. As part of the *śrauta* rite, the priest, on behalf of the patron, says, "this is for Agni, not for me," even though the Ritualist tradition maintains that "he who desires heaven shall sacrifice with the Agnistoma ritual."[49] The ritual's effect is renounced even as the patron performs it! This incongruity has not gone unnoticed: as an obligatory (*nitya*) rite, the *agniṣṭoma* puzzles even traditionalist interpreters who say that rites lead to happiness but *not* obligatory rites.[50]

The formula of renunciation (*tyāga*) likewise applies to those solemn rites, such as *agnicayana*, classified within Vedic tradition as optional (*kāmya*) rather than obligatory. In this case, a purely optional ritual, which is said to guarantee happiness and heaven, must fulfill its promise even as the ritual patron renounces any desire for the fruits of ritual performance. In this case, the ritualist deliberately plays on the incongruity between what is desired and what occurs, and between what is said and what is done.

While Śrīvidyā's Tantric rites include a renunciation formula, there is an important difference. Here a solution is proposed to the problem of forsaken fruits of ritual performance. In Śrīvidyā the efficacy of ritual is no longer a matter of perfect activity, for which there is no method of perfect accountability. In other words, obtaining the fruits of the ritual does not depend on its performance per se. Tantric ritual efficacy does require "correct" actions, but these include acts of yogic contemplation. Yoga provides the opportunity to have *experiences* that claim to fulfill the promises of immortality, unconditioned bliss (*ānanda*), and prosperity in *this* world. In the case of Vedic ritual, one does not necessarily know if goals are achieved since one does not experience heaven (*svarga*) in this world. Further, one has no way of knowing before death if a ritual error has vitiated the ritual's efficacy. Śrīvidyā promises a liberative experience *within* the realm of ritual actions.

Unlike other Hindu traditions, Śrīvidyā seeks to rectify the discrepancies of Vedic ritual *without* introducing a new mode of human behavior, formal renunciation or *sannyāsa*. In this respect, Śrīvidyā remains consistent to the values of householder *smārta* brahmanism. For both Śrīvidyā and Vedic tradition *sannyāsa* is an unnecessary and even foreign ideology. That Vedic and Tantric traditions disdain formal renunciation as the means by which one attains life's ultimate goals is crucial to understanding their interest in utopic maps that create an alternative to the mundane.

In this sense, Śrīvidyā looks back to Vedic ideals of ritual efficacy rather than towards classical Hindu notions of renunciation. One achieves the highest goals not by withdrawal from society but through ritual, which creates within it a setting for yogic contemplation. Thus, both external, outward forms of ritual (*bahiryāga*) and internalized sacrifice (*antaryāga*) is endorsed. In this respect Śrīvidyā imgaines itself the legacy of both Vedic ritualism and Upaniṣadic contemplative "sacrifice." Śrīvidyā affirms the brahmans' preference for householdership and worldly engagement by making ritual an alternative mode of experience.

It is possible, since most of what is said in the course of the Vedic rituals is *not* understood by the patron (and one suspects little by the priests), that the renunciatory formula is not a self-conscious act. Neither the patron (*yajamāna*) nor priest may, in fact, perform the optional Vedic ritual for its stated purpose—in this case, to obtain heaven (*svarga*) or some other fruit. However, there are compelling social reasons to perform an elaborate, expensive, and complex ritual of this sort. There are equally compelling reasons to believe that *smārta* brahmans, who were increasingly interested in Vedānta and other reinterpretations of the Vedic tradition, also viewed the Vedic ritual tradition as ideologically problematic. Even the Mīmāṃsakas, were aware of such difficulties and took them seriously. Staal explains the situation clearly:

> When a ritual performance is completed, no fruit is seen. The Yajamāna, on whose behalf the rites have been performed, does not raise up and go to heaven. Rather the opposite: he returns home and is, as the texts put it, the same as he was before. In particular, he must continue to perform the morning and evening fire rites (*agniho-*

> *tra*) for the rest of his life. The Mīmāṃsā concluded, quite logically, that the fruit of the ritual activity is—temporarily—unseen. It will become apparent only later, e.g., after death. An elaborate theory was devised to show that this is in accordance with the mechanism of *karman*, according to which every cause has an effect.... The followers of Mīmāṃsā were criticized by others (e.g., the philosophers of the Advaita Vedānta) for postulating such unseen effects. For whatever our contemporary fads may suggest—in India, the unseen is resorted to only under duress. What Mīmāṃsā in fact ended up teaching is that the rituals have to be performed for their own sake.[51]

One need not accept Staal's solution to the conundrum of ritual to appreciate his analysis of the problem.[52] For those who question the unseen (*apūrva*) consequences of ritual and the seemingly contradictory aims of Vedic ritual, the Mīmāṃsā solution proves desperately inadequate. We need only point out that the community most interested in sustaining Vedic ritual traditions, *smārta* brahmans, became deeply interested in other types of religious practice and alternative theologies.

Certainly, Vedic rituals—regardless of their classification as obligatory or optional—can be seen as socially binding for participants and critical to the formulation of a collective representation that creates, maintains, and perpetuates itself through the performance and repetition of the ritual. While this may explain, in part, how the optional (*kāmya*) *śrauta* rites were preserved, it does not address the more interesting problem of their *partial* repudiation. Brahmans who reject Pūrva Mīmāṃsā explanations have either developed alternative interpretations of the Vedic rituals' purposes and consequences, or have rejected ritual altogether as a means to the highest human aims. The latter course, for example, was adopted by the Śaṅkarites. Under no circumstances would any Hindu repudiate the authority of the Vedas per se, lest he risk both his religious and social standing in the community.[53] The issue of Vedic authority has never been content-centered. Rather, it involves their form and performance.[54]

Brahmans have not, however, questioned the efficacy or importance of domestic rites. While all the twice-born have remained committed to the regular performance of the domestic rites, the solemn (*śrauta*) Vedic rites have declined in importance. Only the Ritualist Pūrva Mīmāṃasaka can sustain the incongruities of what is said and done, and what actually occurs.

Classical Hinduism is, in part, characterized by beliefs and actions that supplant the religious objectives articulated in solemn (*śrauta*) Vedic rites, objectives that stand apart from those addressed in domestic rituals. The Vedic *śrauta* rites are precisely those Kṛṣṇa criticizes in the *Bhagavadgītā* as inappropriate and lacking in efficacy.[55] Even for those few brahmans who meet the stringent requirements for the *śrauta* rites and are sympathetic to their performance, such rituals are treated as truly optional (*kāmya*) and only occasionally performed.

While the goal of immortality is not urgent for classical Hindus, it remains an ideal that no Hindu is willing to concede. Both the gnostic reorientation represented by the Upaniṣads—evidenced in the schools of Vedānta—and populist devotionalism (*bhakti*) offer important intellectual and practical responses to the partial repudiation of Ritualist Vedism. For certain Hindu intellectuals, Śrīvidyā Tantrism provides an important alternative to Śāṅkarite gnosticism and the emotional outpourings of *bhakti*. Whereas *bhakti* frequently bypasses the ritualist and can be disdainful of specialized knowledge, Śrīvidyā reappropriates an ideology of ritual that centers on acquiring a gnostic expertise without sacrificing either theism or devotion. Śrīvidyā creates an alternative to anti-ritualist devotionalism and to the Vedānta that rejects ritual efficacy in favor of a pure gnosticism; it preserves the prerogatives of the ritualist, and claims to fulfill the Vedas by combining external and internal sacrifices.

The solemn Vedic rituals and the explanations of the Mīmāṃsakas failed to deliver in measurable ways. There is, I think, more than a logical relationship between the partial failure of Vedic ritual and the emergent interest in Tantric ritual present among brahmans from the sixth century forward. Tantric ritual becomes important among brahmans precisely at that point in the history of Hinduism when *śrauta* rites and Mīmāṃsā explanations are subjected to their most severe criticism. Śrīvidyā rites can be seen in part as rectifying the incongruities posed by Vedic *śrauta* rites. Such a rectification could not occur without the acceptance of significant new variables in the Hindu situation. Yet it is these same variables, I will argue, that are partially responsible for the perception of incongruity in Vedic ritual.

Tantrics dismiss the unseen (*apūrva*) or delayed results of the Vedic Ritualists by appealing to a common and pervasive notion that one's own experience is irrefragable. Ritual, however, remains the key to achieving such experiences. A comparison of *śrauta* and Śrīvidyā rites, particularly *śrīcakra pūjā*, will be especially important and deserves more serious consideration. First, however, we must explain more fully the strategies and objectives of Śrīvidyā's Tantric-oriented rites.

RITUAL STRATEGIES AND OBJECTIVES

Virtually all of Śrīvidyā's Tantric rites, including such acts as initiation and other occasional events, are patterned after Vedic rites. The important manuals of Śrīvidyā practice, such as the *Paraśurā-*

makalpasūtra and the *Saubhāgyaratnākara*, imitate their Vedic counterparts with respect to obligatory (*nitya*) and occasional (*naimittika*) rituals to such an extent that complete sets of parallel rites are created. Since Śrīvidyā's Tantrics do not distinguish between domestic (*gṛhya*) and solemn (*śrauta*) rituals, one must consider similarity in function and the occasions for performance in order to compare traditions. Those rites that provide regular maintenance and sustenance to the Tantric *kula* or "family" are those that most closely resemble the domestic rituals of the Vedic tradition. When complete sets of parallel rites appear to fulfill the "same" function, questions arise about their purpose and necessity.

Vaidika Tantrics, such as Rāmeśvara Sūri who comments on the *PKS*, are compelled to explain the repetition and the usefulness of "redundant" rites. Since Tantrics do not accept all the qualifications for ritual set forth by Vaidikas and vice-versa, those who stand outside one set of criteria or the other can be easily accounted for. Thus, when a non-twice-born person gains Tantric initiation, the obligation to perform certain rituals becomes part of the individual's role as a member of a Tantric tradition. The obligation is to the tradition (*sampradāya*) and to the family (*kula*). In this sense, Śrīvidyā Tāntrikas appeal to the same values that perpetuate *smārta* traditions.

The obligatory ritual of the Vedic tradition in the case of a Śrīvidyā Tantric, who is not a twice-born person, can be discounted because it does not apply; the Tantric rite is clearly not redundant. When, however, the person is a twice-born who is also a Śrīvidyā Tantric, the issue of redundancy becomes important.

Not only do Hindus eschew unseen results, but also they value economy of speech and action. It is said by the grammarians, for example, that saving but a fraction of a syllable is as auspicious as the birth of a son.[56] Given their disdain for redundancy, one may ask: Why have Vaidika Tantrics argued for the perpetuation and maintenance of redundant rites?

Like their Vedic counterparts, the Śrīvidyā rites that imitate obligatory Vedic rituals, especially domestic rituals, are based on assumptions about the adequacy of the ritual act to accomplish what is demanded under specified and often predictable circumstances. Those Śrīvidyā rites that most closely resemble Vedic domestic rites appear to favor the congruent map of the world: the fundamental issue is interconnection and the overcoming of incongruity through repetition and rectification.[57] The dichotomy that establishes the structural relationship on which the rites are based is that of initiate and non-initiate. In other words, these rites establish and set out the distinction between those who are considered initiated Tantrics and those who are not.

Examples of such rituals are initiation (*dīkṣā*), pacification (*śanti*), and expiations (*prayāścitta*). Whether or not the ritual actually "works" in a given instance, that is, whether it fulfills its goal is not as significant as the fact that such rituals assume the adequacy of symbolism to meet the exigencies of specified situations. Moreover, these rituals explicitly address the Tantric's relationship with the non-Tantric world and attempt to objectify the distinction between the two.

There is little about the Śrīvidyā Tantric versions of rites that resemble Vedic domestic rites that would cause non-Tantrics Vaidikas to object. While the traditionalist asserts that there is nothing to be "gained" from an obligatory (*nitya*) rite, both Vaidikas and Tantrics usually disqualify those who have not performed the obligatory rites from the optional (*kāmya*) rites. Thus, the necessity of the so-called redundant rite is explained as a presupposition—a price of admission, as it were, for optional (*kāmya*) rituals—in both the Vedic *and* Tantric traditions. In other words, if one is a twice-born Tantric one must fulfill the obligations of *both* Vedic and Tantric traditions before one can consider other optional (*kāmya*) rites. A failure to do what is "necessary" obviates the possibility of doing what is optional. In the Tantric case, the absence of necessary prerequisites vitiates the possibility of promised, "extraordinary" results, such as worldly enjoyment (*bhukti*) and liberation (*mukti*). No Tāntrika would dispute the fact that initiation (*dīkṣā*) is a necessary prerequisite to ritual and the highest forms of yogic contemplation.

Śrīvidyā Tantrics have chosen to imitate not only the methods and structures of Vedic domestic rituals but also have assumed that certain rituals *must* be performed for the sake of the individual as a member of the community. That is, Śrīvidyā Tantrics like Vaidikas insist that certain rituals are definitional to one's full participation in the community and essential to the continued maintenance of the cosmos. The Vedic tradition provides a preexisting model upon which many Tantrics have structured their rites. More important, however, is the fact that the Śrīvidyā Tantric is able to press the argument that Tantric rites *fulfill* the Vedic legacy because they are essentially similar in form. Tantric ingenuity does not require something "new" to be brought into the ritual structure even though Tantrics alter the ideological variables. The Tantric's genius appears in the form of an overcoming of limitation by an exercise of ingenuity over that which *already* has been admitted as significant.[58]

There is a reluctance on the part of the Śrīvidyā Tantric to alter the boundaries of ritual structure, formula, and stated purpose when it comes to matters best served by adopting a congruent map of the cosmos. Further, Śrīvidyā Tantrics accomplish these goals without proposing an alteration in social structure, that is, they reject renunciation and thus seek to identify themselves with the values that sustain the Vedic tradition.

Śrīvidyā's Tantric rites were formalized, at least in textual forms, either by brahmans or by those who assumed the normative structures of brahmanism: materials appear in Sanskrit and presume knowledge of Vedic precedents, models, and values. While the issue of the origin of Śrīvidyā's Tantric rituals remains unresolved, there is little reason to think that they are anti-brahman or anti-Vedic by definition. Tantric rites frequently absolve the Vaidika from the responsibility of fulfilling every ritual promise. In this way, the Tantric does not appear to usurp the Vedic rite but rather honor it by imitation. Such a strategy is characteristic of Vaidika Tantrics whose objective it is to avoid conflict or intrusiveness when Vedic and Tantric rites compete. However, the ways in which Tantric rites *deliberately* violate Vedic social norms warrant further discussion.

Tantric rites appear to come in conflict with Vedic traditions when more is at stake than repetition or the preservation of the status quo. Curiously, it is at this juncture that certain Tantric rites more closely resemble certain optional and obligatory solemn (*śrauta*) rites of the Veda. In both cases the rituals are "extra," even if they are classified as obligatory, such as *agniṣṭoma* or certain forms of the *śrīcakra pūjā*. Neither of these "extra" Vedic nor Tantric rites address daily concerns nor do they inform practitioners in their liturgies about the mundane world outside ritual.

Tantric rites, such as the *śrīcakra pūjā,* and *śrauta* Vedic rites do not follow congruent maps of the cosmos. Rather, both traditions find it necessary to shift strategies and assume the bias of utopic maps. That is, both sets of rites create worlds within the larger world; in both cases they are disinterested in and immune to mundane concerns. Such Tantric rites, like their Vedic counterparts, do not intend to address the world beyond the community of adepts either socially or religiously. Tantric rituals, such as *śrīcakra pūjā,* provide the Vaidika with a familiar and somewhat reassuring scenario: a context in which the privileged few revel in the things of their own creation.

Some Tantric rites, such as *śrīcakra pūjā,* intend to reverse the ethical values of the domestic Vedic rites—especially by the use of ritual substances (*dravya*) as the *pañcamakāra*s that violate classical *smārta* brahman ethical values. This type of Tantric rite throws into question the normative structures of congruence that are perceived as ultimately confining and delimiting. The mundane world is not made aright through these exceptional or solemn Tantric rituals but discarded in favor of a new mode of creation.[59]

In Śrīvidyā's deliberate inversion of Vedic values, it adopts the Tantric method of overcoming the limitations of finite existence by reversing "ordinary" relationships. The alternative relationship is established through an insular set of correspondences and explanations. The governing principle of such rituals is that the world "out there" must be stood on its head if one is to overcome its limitations. But that which is inverted or overcome by Tantrics is defined *in terms of Vaidika values*, without which the Tantric's values would become ineffectual.

Śrīvidyā's "true" explanation of the world is not offered in terms intelligible to anyone outside the circle of initiates. The *śrīcakra*, for example, as a cosmological map is a complete abstraction of the universe it represents. The ritual connections between the yantra and the cosmos are arbitrary not only to the outsider but also to the fledgling initiate. The *śrīcakra* acquires its stature and importance not because it explains the profane world or because it reproduces the cosmos in a way that anyone can appreciate. Rather, the *śrīcakra* creates the "real" world on which the ordinary is based, one in which the categories, images, and values are *not* those used to explain everyday existence. Connections, correspondences, and meanings must be *learned* by insiders who are prepared to routinize them as part of an esoteric utopic vision that effectively severs contact with those who remain outside the boundaries of the initiate community. This view of ritual explains Śrīvidyā disinterest in polemics and its *selective* use of "outside" ideas to support its positions. The system's internal coherence sustains it, its complexity preoccupies adherents, and its promises fulfill expectations left unsatisfied or unarticulated by alternatives.

Initiates, who participate in the utopic world created in ritual, may remain unaffected or disinterested in things outside its boundaries. It is, as it were, a family (*kula*) affair just as *smārta* tradition is clannish, restricted, and self-perpetuating. Thus, Tantric's closed system and elitism can be considered extensions, or rather elaborations, of the principles of Vedic elitism. Though Tantrics alter the rules for entry into the circle of initiates—principally by rejecting caste and gender as determinative criteria—they do so not to be inclusive but rather to reverse the perceived inadequacy of Vedic ritualism. Tantrism's ultimate claims are validated in yogic experiences produced first within the ritual setting and then extended beyond it.

By introducing elements into *śrīcakra* worship that deliberately violate the moral expectations of *smārta* brahmanism, Śrīvidyā seeks truth through exaggeration, the violation of expectations, and the pursuit of unconventionality. The extent to which one is willing to violate Vaidika norms and practice the "unconventional" is critical to testing the limits of Tantric legitimacy. Bhāskararāya and the Kaula segments of Śrīvidyā *demand* inversion of *smārta* ethical and ritual standards. Their claim is that such behavior does not undermine the Vedic tradition but fulfills it. The normative is precisely that which constrains and prevents one from obtaining extra-mundane goals.

In the view of Kaula Śrīvidyā the ritual boundaries of Tantrism privilege those who are qualified to engage in such activities and protect those who are not. Tantrics do not consider their practice a solution for everyone but rather a privileged option for those who have reached an advanced stage in the cycles of death and rebirth. These same Kaula Tantrics attempt to preserve their caste stature and remain legitimate members of a community of non-Tantrics. The deliberate inversions of value that Tantric ritual requires in order to transcend the mundane world, they assert, must remain completely secret to non-initiates. A similar ideology, though one that proposes different qualifications, activities, and goals, governs Vedic ritualism.

Critical to Kaula Śrīvidyā's effort to address the unfulfilled promises of *śrauta* Vedic ritual is the notion that the rules which govern ritual can control and account for discrepancies and incongruities that arise in Vedic ritual. While the substances (*dravya*) employed in the Kaula Tantric's ritual are controversial for those who see no need to subvert conventional *smārta* ethics, Kaula advocates argue that they say and do nothing that deserves the opprobrium of "outsiders." The discussion among Kaula Śrīvidyā adepts centers not on the merits of using ordinarily prohibited substances (i.e., the *pañcamakāras*), but rather on the rules that govern their use. Ritual, understood to be a distinct form of rule-governed activity set apart from ordinary activity, creates an alternative social context, one in which there is a tacit justification for deliberate acts of ethical and religious inversion. The ritual world is *not supposed to be* the ordinary world; to carry one set of behaviors into the other is strictly prohibited. The Kaula Śrīvidyā adept's treatment of ordinarily "prohibited substances" in ritual as a matter governed by rule-making procedures presents no new strategy or method. Rather, Kaula Śrīvidyā merely adopts the Vedic assumption that ritual, which is strictly controlled by rules, can produce efficacious results that are not possible without or outside of ritual. Bhāskararāya, like all Kaula Tantrics, is at pains to clarify the boundaries of "appropriate" reversals and the limits of the unconventional to overcome the banality of death and rebirth.

Kaula Śrīvidyā considers ritual efficacy to be dependent on a reversal of conventional values, even if this is limited to the recitation of mantras that endorse or only *imagine* the use of convention-defying elements. The incongruity of Vedic ritual—that is, its unfulfilled promise to bring about tangible and accountable results in this world and the next—is addressed not by overcoming incongruity but by countering it. In other words, the Kaula's strategy to deal with the discrepancy between what should occur and what does occur is to use things incongruous in the conventional sphere of existence; the Kaula fights fire with fire. The Tantric does not seek to fulfill Vedic ritual by conforming to expectations, but rather deliberately questions the values and principles that have failed to produce the desired results. For example, passion is overcome by practicing erotic rituals, such as *kāmakalādhyāna*, and knowledge is acquired by rejecting the basis of mundane knowledge, namely, the process of noticing differences.

One important reason Tantric Śrīvidyā has flourished in *smārta* communities, especially in south India, is because it has coupled the brahman community's traditional notion of privacy with Tantric secrecy. The contemporary *smārta* community in Tamilnadu provides an excellent example of this ethos of privacy, one that explains, in part, how Śrīvidyā textual commentators manage to overlook discrepancies between word and deed, and read selectively to suit themselves. The tendency of contemporary *smārtas* is not to interfere or to enquire about potential indiscretions of others. All but the most private discussions of sex—let alone sex outside of marriage, which is endorsed in Kaula rituals—are considered bad manners. Custom usually prohibits impugning the integrity of other *smārtas* or raising delicate social issues. This is, perhaps, in part attributable to their minority status as a community in Tamilnadu. To suggest that someone is eating meat, drinking liquor, or having sex outside of marriage can cause as much "damage" to the accuser as it does to the accused. While *smārtas* are not exempt from gossiping about someone's family or raising questions about their morality, when it comes to the advocacy of "immoral" ritual acts, especially when such "immorality" is confined to mantras recited in ritual, there is a clearly a difference between "saying" and "doing."

Deliberate efforts to undermine normative conventional behaviors and ideologies are a part of the utopic map's ability to create a world apart, a world not to be governed by or to be confused with the mundane world. The utopic world of ritual is, however, partially defined in terms of non-utopic and outside-ritual worlds. The restricted sphere of Kaula ritual insulates the Vaidika Tantric from "confusing" or "mixing" values and explains the double norm whereby both Vedic and Tantric worlds can be sustained. The Tantric does not deny that the mundane world goes on or even that it is somehow necessary. Rather, the Tantric finds a way to create an alternative to the mundane; he affirms the material or the sensual aspects of an everyday existence that is permanently changed through experiences acquired in and legitimated by ritual. Thus, Kaula Śrīvidyā offers an alternative ritualism, one that asserts that the promise of the *śrauta* rites remains unfulfilled and affirms that the incongruity which underlies them is empirically real. Tantric Śrīvidyā claims that ritual overcomes the discrepancy between expectations and occurrences by producing the immediate results of yogic experience.

The conflict between conventional *smārta* tradition and Tantrism is not easily resolved. Kaula Śrīvidyā adepts who are Vaidikas must contend with those who reject a reversal of values as an appropriate method of addressing incongruities and unfulfilled promises. For the conservative Samaya Śrīvidyā adept, the Kaula threatens to corrupt not only the ordinary world but the sacred world created by ritual. Samayins see the introduction of prohibited or impure substances, values, and behaviors as a direct violation of the sacred world that rituals, such as *śrīcakra pūjā*, are able to create. In other words, the Samayin attempts to meet the unfulfilled promise and the incongruity of Vedic ritual not by exceeding or reversing normative expectations but by meeting them.

Samaya Śrīvidyā retreats from the use of a utopic map of the cosmos only insofar as it rejects the necessity for reversing the patterns of mundane existence. Instead, Samaya maintains that one can attain life's most cherished goals without the unwanted social and moral consequences of reversing values and upsetting the status quo. Samaya Śrīvidyā retains the critical substantive elements of Tantric theology that set apart those who "know" from those who merely "watch." The ritual use of the *śrīcakra* and *śrīvidyā* alone is deemed sufficiently remedial and revisionary without engaging in controversial social and ethical practices.

For Samayins the double norm that permits both Vedic and Tantric worlds to remain intact does not entail keeping them separate but rather affirming their reciprocity. In contrast, the Kaula's double norm is based on the principle that a reversal of values is critical to the fulfillment of ritual promises. Thus, Kaulas make explicit that it is *through the use of ritual* that Vedic and Tantric values must be separated for the good of all. In contrast, Samayins contend that ritual binds rather than separates Vedic and Tantric worlds.

Some contemporary Śrīvidyā Kaulas who advocate and endorse convention-defying behaviors in mantras, but do not enact them literally, are not aware of what they are actually saying. The situation is comparable to Vedic rites in which it is not the *content* but the *form* of action that is important and socially binding. In contrast, Samayins exhibit a certain preoccupation with the content of the ritual that others disdain in favor of its performance. It is clear, at least in contemporary ritual practice, that mantras used in rituals have a status different from other types of language and that the issue of "legitimate practice" centers on performance rather than content. The same can be said of Vedic ritual and the claims made for Vedic authority.[60]

Śrīvidyā practitioners, especially if they are brahmans, use *both* utopic and congruent maps to interpret the world. Even Kaula Śrīvidyā admits the value of congruent maps when it comes to matters that resemble obligatory domestic Vedic rituals, such as initiation (*dīkṣā*) or periodic expiations (*prayāscitta*). Kaulism admits the need to perpetuate the mundane order so that others might eventually have the opportunity to overcome it by experiencing the divine *in this world*. The religion of the Vaidika Tantric involves a constant effort of adjustment; one must avoid unnecessary conflicts and yet establish principles of ideological superiority that make potential initiates want to take the risks involved in Tantric ritual and yoga.

There are no simple solutions to the dilemmas that arise when Tantrism and the traditions of brāhmaṇical *smārtas* co-habit the hearts and minds of members of the same community. The two traditions exist like near-neighbors who go to great lengths disavow mutual influences. Yet each tradition frequently invokes the other as part of their self-definition; for example, *smārta* rites are those which are precisely *not*-Tantric. Similarly, Tantric rituals not only imitate Vedic rituals in structure and, to a lesser extent, in content but deliberately invert *smārta* principles, which may or may not be part of the original Vedic rite.

The Tantric effort to replace non-Tantric traditions is not absolute, anymore than their utopic map of the universe is an escape from or disavowal of the "real" world. Rather, Tantrics wish to articulate what is real about the world even if this means generating a hierarchy of religious privilege within a single social and cultural community. Put differently, Śrīvidyā ritual, like other rituals "*represents the creation of a controlled environment* where the variables (i.e., the accidents) of ordinary life may be displaced *precisely* because they are felt to be so overwhelmingly present and powerful."[61] While this fact about Śrīvidyā ritual is not unique to it—especially in light of what may be said about Vedic ritual—it is significant if we are to explain the discrepancies between what Tantrics say and what they say they do.

The orientation of the solemn Vedic rituals persists and is perfected in Śrīvidyā ritual without expense to the notion of ritual itself. In this way, Śrīvidyā distinguishes itself from Śaṅkara's Vedānta and from other systems that make a commitment to articulating the failures of Vedic ritualism and the inadequacies of ritual per se. Instead, Śrīvidyā assumes without engaging in argument that rituals like the *śrauta* rituals of the Veda can be useful means to the ultimate. Brahman Kaula Śrīvidyā adepts, like Bhāskararāya, rejected the rigorous gnostic effort of the Śāṅkarites and others to disavow ritual as important to obtaining the fruits of knowledge. Instead, Tantrics assume a doctrine of combination (*samuccayavāda*) that emphasizes the importance of both action (*karma*), including ritual, and knowledge (*jñāna*).

While other brahman dominated traditions, such as the Bhedābheda of Bhāskara the Vedāntin, employ the notion of combination doctrine to maintain their relationship with ritual, Śrīvidyā claims expediency in obtaining one's goals. Not only does the tradition claim that one can obtain the four human objectives of righteousness (*dharma*), prosperity (*artha*), pleasure (*kāma*), and liberation (*mokṣa*) in this life if one practices Śrīvidyā discipline, but also claims its methods superior on the basis of their being the most *expedient*.

Further, Śrīvidyā, in part, assumes the conservative agenda of brahmanism. That is, the tradition assumes the importance of ritual virtuosity, specialized knowledge and types of activity, and the privilege of ritual expert to interpret for himself and for others. In contrast to important strands of devotionalism (*bhakti*), Śrīvidyā, like other Tantric disciplines, does not advance an egalitarian agenda open to one and all. Tantrism thus becomes a vehicle for the reestablishment of privilege in the spheres of ritual and theological discourse. Those possessed traditionally of such privileges, namely, brahmans, become deeply interested in Tantrism as an alternative to other ideologies and practices that demand either a diminution of the role of specialized knowledge (i.e., *bhakti*) or the leap into asceticism (i.e, Śāṅkara Vedānta).

Like other Tantric rituals, Śrīvidyā asserts the right of the guru to determine what is "proper" and thereby sustains the prerogative of the religious virtuosi to arbitrate that which is true and efficacious. While *bhakti* often bypasses the priest as the necessary arbiter between supplicant and divinity, Tantric Śrīvidyā reaffirms the necessity of specialized knowledge and complex ritual behavior in the person of the religious virtuosi. This latter point is not insignificant since those with the most to gain (and to lose) participate in *both* Vedic and Tantric ritual traditions.

Vaidikas would be motivated to adopt and promulgate a form of Tantric ritual for at least two reasons. First, it conforms to their religious expectations about the value and importance of ritual activity as critical for obtaining the four human aims (*puruṣārtha*). Ritual *performance* and control over the language that forms the ritual idiom are crucial factors in *smārta* community identity. Second, Tantra is a vehicle for the reaffirmation of the brahmans' role as religious virtuosi. From the socioreligious standpoint, Tantric ritual is performed for similar reasons Vedic ritual was once performed: the demonstration of the brahmans' privilege to define and create rituals which influence individuals, society, and nature. The ascetic alternative, which eliminates formal ritual and participation in worldly affairs, can be condoned in most brāhmaṇical traditions, but seems extreme in the face of Tantrism's dual norm alternative.

Tantrism in the hands of brahmans can be seen as both an anti-*bhakti* and anti-ascetic movement. This is not to say that Tantrics reject the importance of devotion to god or the value of a disciplined life. Rather, Tantrics imagine their tradition to be a reaffirmation of the religious rights of the few over the many and the importance of ritual for living a truly meaningful life without renouncing the mundane. Tantra assumes that privilege and hierarchy is part of the divine plan and sees itself as the best solution to the most difficult and incongruous human dilemmas: death and rebirth are transcended without complete dissociation from society or life's material pleasures.

A theoretical model for the interpretation of Tantric ritual requires an interpretation of what adepts believe to be at stake when they involve themselves in Tantric practice. Śrīvidyā Tantrics have never been separated socially from their non-Tantric peers nor are they disdainful of the caste values and gender distinctions they inherit as in-caste Hindus. Rather, they continue to do their work in the world without removing or isolating themselves from their customary roles within their social communities. The extent to which a Vaidika Tantric keeps his Tantric practice private or secret depends on individuals and lineage traditions.[62] Contemporary Śrīvidyā in south India offers very few examples of adepts who abandon or violate in public the customary rules that govern their immediate social community's behaviors. Śrīvidyā is, in fact, seen as the most quintessential *smārta* brahman tradition since it is associated with the Śāṅkara traditions and is considered the esoteric fulfillment of goddess worship within (and beyond) the temple.

From within the expository, liturgical, and performative domains of the Tantric idiom, Śrīvidyā creates its own rules and expectations. These rules govern the practitioner's life in ways that augment but do not intend to conflict with those that inform self-understanding as a member of a non-Tantric Hindu community. The rules of ritual distinguish Vedic and Tantric roles and enable the Kaula adept to maintain two standards of *ritual* behavior that separate the ordinary world from the sacred worlds created in ritual.

BEYOND TANTRIC AND VEDIC RITUAL IDEOLOGIES: THE RELIGIOUS VIRTUOSI

William Scott Green's work on ancient rabbinism refines the discussion about intellectual and ritual virtuosi who employ utopic maps of the world. His remarks are important enough to cite at length. He writes:

> Rabbinic documents do not introduce or explain themselves to their readers, and they provide no easy access for tyros and non-initiates. The literature as a whole...presupposes not only considerable information but also codes for interpretation. Its terse and formulaic syntactic constructions and its lean and disciplined vocabulary constitute a scholastic shorthand. Even the most elementary...statement presumes a tacit dimension of rabbinic knowledge, attitudes, behaviors, and motivations. Rabbinic literature virtually ignores the world beyond its own preoccupations. Its documents obscure their origins by neglecting the events that led to their formulation, and they report remarkably little about ordinary Jews or non-Jews. This insularity is reinforced by the nearly total absence of external witness to rabbinic religion, culture, and society. The documents present the restricted discourse of a small number of men who appear primarily engaged in observing, discussing, and analyzing ideas, opinions, and behaviors, sometimes those recounted in Scripture, but most often those of one another. Rabbinic writing addresses rabbinic specialists; it is a parochial literature wholly obsessed with itself.[63]

Green's insights about rabbinic writing and behavior can be seen as applicable to either Tantric *or* Vedic situations.

The similarity in *structure* between Tantric and Vedic worlds results from several factors. First, as we have noted, the parallels between Śrīvidyā rituals and Vedic rites are not accidental. When one considers the fact that brahmans have dominated the textual and ritual life of both the Sanskrit Tantra and Veda, the situation seems not the least bit puzzling. Not only is the structure of obligatory (*nitya*), occasional (*naimittika*), and optional (*kāmya*) rituals retained but the forms of rituals are likewise imitated. Vaidika Tantrics adopt familiar and well-tested formula thus legitimizing Tantric forms by claiming a fulfillment of the Veda both in terms of ritual structure and theological objectives. Second, both Vedic and Tantric virtuosi seek to create "worlds apart," that is, highly efficient and self-contained modes of discourse and activity that evince little or no interest in "outside" matters. While the goals of ritual and the discourse of interpretation may influence one's life in the world-beyond-ritual, the ritual world itself can and *must be* set apart in order to achieve the desired effects. If the boundaries of the ritual world are violated, both traditions maintain that the efficacy of ritual is vitiated or muted. The *rules* of ritual, which creates world-boundaries, are of utmost importance in both Vedic and Tantric traditions.

Ritual per se is deemed the appropriate mechanism by which to negotiate the incongruity of being-in-the-world and the aspiration to achieve an extra-mundane goal. No matter what the Śrīvidyā adept personally experiences, the mundane world of karmic actions persists; adepts, in fact, never argue that their own liberative or yogic experiences obviate the objective reality of the mundane world or the suffering that occurs within it.

Vedic ritual articulates the incongruity of being-in-the-world and achieving other-worldly goals most profoundly in the combination of the *tyāga* or renunciatory formula ("this [sacrifice] is for Agni...) and the Ritualist explanation for performance ("...sacrifice is for...heaven). Śrīvidyā adepts claim that the ritual *experience* is itself the realization of bliss (*ānanda*): one does not have to wait for unseen (*apūrva*) results nor does one go home, fire pots in hand, without *knowing* that one's goals are accomplished. By introducing the element of direct experience (*anubhava*), the Tantric offers a resolution to the inadequate notion of ritual as an activity causally efficacious in its own terms. Tantric ritual addresses the question: How could one actually know if one's deepest desires can be fulfilled in *this* world? The Tantric response is that ritual is a manifestation of knowledge that creates an experience which can be extended beyond the formal confines of ritual. Śrīvidyā Tantrics do not consider knowledge an abstraction of the intellect but a performative experience achieved *in the course of* ritual. Rather than adopting the more radical view of Śaṅkara's nondualism in which ritual is deemed useless, Tantric Śrīvidyā takes the more *moderate* course of adopting familiar Vedic structures and modes of articulating incongruity. Knowledge is not identical to ritual activity but rather a product of it. Therefore, the Tantric can argue that the effects of ritual persist and carry into the ordinary world even if the ritual, and the rules by which it is governed, does not.

The resolution of Vedic incongruities, however, is achieved by putting *other* incongruities in place. Kaula or left-current (*vāmācāra*) rituals, which create *deliberate* violations of Vedic ethical norms, eschew categories of holism, congruity, and static perfection. In short, neither Vedic nor Tantric ritual dispenses with incongruity as a meaningful category for understanding the human dilemma. Śrīvidyā, however, attempts to solve the problem of Vedic life—specifically, the unseen (*apūrva*) or unknown promises of heaven, immortality, and prosperity—by asserting that these goals can be achieved through ritual that itself fulfills these goals. The point is that "ordinary" life is now pervaded by, or rather interpreted in terms of the categories of experience that define Tantric ritual. The Tantric bases these claims on the analogies of proximate and residual experiences. Thus, by using wine or any of the *pañcamakāras* in the ritual one creates a proximate form of ultimate bliss (*ānanda*) which has residual effects. Eventually, the proximate experience gives way to a direct experience (*anubhava*) that is no longer temporary but permanent: the extraordinary objectives of ritual become ordinary, just as one transcends the mundane through a self-conscious process of dissolving differences.

Śrīvidyā practitioners maintain that they live in a world in which others invariably fail to obtain life's most cherished goals. Ritual creates knowledge that is otherwise inaccessible; it does so not by resolving the differences between ordinary experience and ritual experience but rather by exaggerating them. To overcome the conflict between these two radically different ways of being in the world one must know that they are not the same. Heesterman has made clear that conflict is a permanent feature of Hindu tradition. He writes:

> Tradition is determined by the particular form in which it expresses the conflict between its immanence in society and its transcendent aspiration to solve the fundamental problem of human existence. Although this view of tradition as a paradox does not look very promising, it may offer us a vantage-point for our understanding of social and cultural phenomena and processes. Instead of having to explain away the obvious rifts and fissures so as to arrive at a harmonious and coherent pattern, we may exploit the essentially fractured picture for a dynamic view of society and culture as organized around an inner conflict.[64]

Śrīvidyā's Tantric solution to the Vedic disjunction between the mundane and transcendent is to locate the transcendent ultimately within immanent. This solution does not, however, dispense with incongruity. First, the cost of admission to such privileged experience involves the creation of a ritual world and canonical discourse that closes off the "outside" world. One must participate in a ritual world in which the "real" explanations for things are inaccessible to non-initiates. Second, the Tantric solution exaggerates the discrepancy between those who ascent to its methods and values and those who don't. For the Śrīvidyā Tantric, incongruity is not a problem to be explained away, but rather the key to understanding life's most difficult problems. By taking up the Tantric life, one learns to use, and indeed to revel in, the incongruity between esoteric and exoteric realities as part of the divine's playful and deliberate plan for creation.

Heesterman has also observed how the Vedic ritual world likewise takes no interest in matters outside itself; it, too, does not inform its adherence about the world outside of the ritual.[65] One needs to spend only a brief time studying a Śrīvidyā text, such as the *Vāmakeśvara Tantra*, in order to complete the picture of the self-enclosed world of religious virtuosi. We have shown how, at the first level of comparison, Tantrism and Vedism share in this fundamental orientation. This situation is not unfamiliar in the history of religions. One might extend this interpretation to other religious settings, such as rabbinical Judaism.

For the Vaidika Tantric, the Vedic and Tantric worlds relate to one another like the two hands of a single person: they are complementary inversions of one another, bound by structural similarities and purposes and yet separate in both substance and function. A closer look at the social and historical factors involved in Vedic and Tantric traditions enable us to explain why these two very similar, sometimes coinciding traditions became important to members of the brahman community. Their sometimes puzzling relationship is an expression of certain ongoing and irreconcilable conflicts in the Hindu religious tradition, conflicts from which there is no flight and for which there are no easy solutions.

In both cases, I believe, we have evidence of what Heesterman has called the "inner conflict" of Indian tradition.[66] While Śrīvidyā's Tantric ritual is, to some extent, an attempt to resolve the incongruities of Vedic ideology, it is likewise an articulation of this inner conflict. The incongruities that Vedic rituals attempt to overcome are not the source of contention between Vaidikas and Tantrics. Both would agree that the mundane world has been split asunder and needs to be dealt with as a world in which there is a persistent tension between what is and what should be. Differences between the two traditions arise at the next level of interpretation.

The Vedic prescription usually involves reassembling parts of the world in order to make whole again that which has been disassembled. The Vedic myth of the cosmic *Puruṣa* provides the standard example of this understanding of the human dilemma. The Śrīvidyā Tantric might use similar techniques of correspondence and affirmation in his ritual and thereby imitate, or rather adopt, another important feature of the Vedic ritual ideology. However, the Tantric rectifies "what is" by rejecting as mundane that which the Vaidika asserts as "what should be." Tantric ritual celebrates a new mode of creation, unavailable to those without instruction, and beyond the strictures that govern ordinary (i.e., non-Tantric) persons; it is a world governed by rules and principles that putatively affect everyone, whether or not they are aware of them. These rules and principles, however, do not apply to everyone in the same way. Thus, much is demanded of the Tantric who participates in this esoteric world—and much less of the non-Tantric—but much is promised that is left unavailable to the outsider.

If one relies on textual and historical evidence, it would appear that Tantric Śrīvidyā not only reinforces the structures that support the Vedic hierarchy of privilege based on religious virtuosity but also reorders them to suit the changing situation that we call "classical Hinduism." As I will show in a future study, Tantric ritual and ideology continues to provide a means by which brahman society perpetuates the perception of itself as religiously privileged in the midst of radical social and economic changes that do not always privilege brahmans.

APPENDIX OF DIAGRAMS

Diagram A
The śrīcakra according to Bhāskararāya's description
in Tripurā Upaniṣadbhaṣya

Diagram A1
Śrīcakra: In the "inverted" Samaya form proposed by Lakṣmīdhara

Diagram B
Periphery: *Trailokyamohana Cakra*

Diagram C
Sixteen-petalled Lotus: *Sarvāśāparipuraka Cakra*

Diagram D
Eight-petalled Lotus: *Sarvasankṣobhaṇa Cakra*

Diagram E
Fourteen Triangles: *Sarvasaubhāgyadāyaka Cakra*

Diagram F
Ten Triangles: *Sarvārthasādhaka Cakra*

Diagram G
Ten Triangles: *Sarvarakṣākara Cakra*

Diagram H
Eight Triangles: *Sarvarogahara Cakra*

Diagram I
Triangle Inverted: *Sarvasiddhiprada Cakra*

Diagram J
Point: *Sarvānandamaya Cakra*

NOTES

NOTES TO THE PREFACE

1. My hope is that one example, well-understood, will create the possibility for generalization. Though flawed in many ways, Emile Durkheim's pioneering theories of sociological analysis were rooted in the same fundamental principle: generalization cannot come from the study of things-in-general and requires at least one thoroughly considered example.

2. Chapter 2 makes this historical point clearly.

3. Quoted from Jacob Neusner, "The Study of Religion and the Study of Tradition: Judaism," in *History of Religions*, 14 (1985): 195ff.

4. Ibid., p. 197.

5. It is also a foundational taxonomic concept within post-eighteenth century Hindu culture. As William Scott Green has shown in his examination of "religion" as a category for Americans: when terms are used as self-evident and definitional categories they become more than theoretical entities. Such categories are reified and carry claims of concretion and inherent signification. See William Scott Green, "Something Strange, Yet Nothing New: Religion in the Secular Curriculum," *Liberal Education* 73, (1989): 21–25. I am indebted to William Scott Green who uses the notion of native category in order to explain the use and misuse of the term "religion" in America and in the American Academy. What Green says about religion can be applied with equal facility and accuracy to the terms "Hinduism" and "Tantrism." His insight is so vital to the theoretical interests of this present work that it must be quoted here at length. He writes: "As the demarcation of a distinct domain of behavior, thought, and experience—and hence as a subject of study—religion is a coinage of the seventeenth and eighteenth centuries, a devising indigenous to the modern West. In America especially (though not exclusively), religion is a native category. It is a foundational taxonomic concept, a basic classification, that our culture routinely uses to sunder, sort out, and organize the complexity of human existence. The Constitution assumes religion as a given and makes the ability to identify it an elementary skill of citizenship. Because religion is a native category, we use it both as a theoretical entity and as a reification. As an abstraction—much like the category "language"—religion constitutes a conceptual paradigm that provides a comprehensive intelligibility to discrete particulars of our own or other cultures. But,

like all native categories, religion also carries a claim to concretion, self-evidence, and inherent significance. Consequently, it is evocative but inarticulate." See pp. 22–23.

6. Scholarship similarly includes those who prefer to ignore the role of Tantra in Hinduism, labeling it incomprehensibly esoteric, unimportant, or aberrant. Many with whom I have discussed the subject simply point to the dearth of available materials and the absence of interpretive models for locating Tantrism in the history of religions. On this and other matters regarding the history of scholarship see Sanjukta Gupta, Dirk Jan Hoens, and Teun Goudriaan, *Hindu Tantrism* (Leiden-Koln: E. J. Brill, 1979), p. 5f. Also Douglas Renfrew Brooks, *The Secret of the Three Cities: An Introduction to Hindu Śākta Tantrism* (Chicago: The University of Chicago Press, 1990). Here I outline the methods of definition and classification employed in this study. I also review briefly other recent and especially useful works on the subject of Hindu Tantrism, many of which appear in this series; all are listed in the bibliography.

7. See the works of Brooks, Padoux, Goudriaan, Gupta, and Bharati in the bibliography and cited above.

8. For more on the identity of the *smārtas* see part 2.

9. See also, Teun Goudriaan and Sanjukta Gupta, *Hindu Tantric and Śākta Literature* (Wiesbaden: Otto Harrossowitz, 1981), p. 1ff.

10. For example, the goddess-centered Krama schools of Kashmiri origins have texts but no widespread tradition of living proponents. In contrast, many in India who claim Tantric affiliations make no reference to any written canon, be it in Sanskrit or a vernacular language. See Rastogi's work as listed in the Bibliography.

11. There is certainly evidence of Śrīvidyā on the plains of North India and particularly in Benares. These groups, however, are neither as visible nor do they form as significantly large a community within the local culture. These matters will be discussed at length in a second volume. On the development of Śrīvidyā in Kashmir see Madhu Khanna, "The Concept and Liturgy of the Śrīcakra based on Śivānanda's Trilogy," Ph.d. dissertation (Woolfson College, Oxford University, 1986).

12. A more complete biography of his life is forthcoming.

13. This concept has been developed in detail by Jonathan Z. Smith. See Jonathan Z. Smith, "What a Difference a Difference Makes" in *'To See Ourselves as Others See Us' Christians, Jews, "Others" in Late Antiquity*, ed. Jacob Neusner and Ernest S. Frerichs (Chico, Calif.: Scholars Press, 1985), pp. 3–48.

14. Cf. *HTSL*, pp. 11–12. Here Goudriaan makes a similar remark. See also *The Secret of the Three Cities*, p. 7f.

15. The theoretical project, like the question, is derived directly from Jonathan Z. Smith whose work, along with that of William Scott Green and

Jacob Neusner, provides the foundational theoretical paradigms for this study. In particular see Jonathan Z. Smith, *Imagining Religion: From Babylon to Jonestown* (Chicago: University of Chicago Press, 1982), p. xi and p. 35 for specific references. My agenda is not simply to adopt Smith's project but to test his basic hypotheses in light of evidence with which he has had only a passing interest. It is my contention that Smith's work not only offers a fresh and fruitful methodological approach to the study of Hinduism, and Hindu Tantrism in particular, but that such an approach creates potential for conversation and comparison both in terms of theory and exempla in the study of religion.

16. Cf. *The Secret of the Three Cities* for a complete discussion of the location of Śrīvidyā with respect to Vedic and Tantric traditions and for a thorough review of the descriptive criteria that make up the polythetic classification "Hindu Tantrism." Throughout this book I have abstained from making any detailed comparisons of Śrīvidyā with other forms of Śākta Tantrism or with other types of Śiva- or Viṣṇu-centered Tantrism, such as the Śaiva Āgama or Vaiṣṇava Pāñcarātra. Only the traditions of Kashmiri Śaivism are introduced to explain Śrīvidyā's ideological origins.

17. *Imagining Religion*, p. 52.

18. Cf. Jonathan Z. Smith, *To Take Place: Toward Theory in Ritual* (Chicago: University of Chicago Press, 1987), p. 106.

19. Cf. Sir John Woodroffe, *Shakti and Shakta* (Madras: Ganesh & Co., reprint ed., 1975), p. 158f.

20. *To Take Place*, p. 104.

21. The practical application of these texts and signs in ritual is a primary consideration of the anthropological study of Śrīvidyā to be presented in volume two.

22. *To Take Place*, pp. 110–111.

23. J. C. Heesterman, *The Inner Conflict of Traditions: Essays in Indian Ritual, Kingship and Society* (Chicago: The University of Chicago Press, 1985), p. 3 (Hereafter, *Inner Conflict*); Cf. *To Take Place*, p. 110.

NOTES TO THE INTRODUCTION

1 *Tantrāloka*, 4.77. *yataḥ śāstrakramattajjñagurupta-jñānusilanāt/ ātmapratyayitaṃ jñānaṃ pūrṇatvād bhairavayat*. See *The Tantrāloka of Abhinavagupta with the Commentary of Jayaratha*, edited N. R. C. Dwivedi and N. Rastogi (Delhi: Motilal Banarsidass, reprint of the original Kashmiri Series of Texts and Studies edition by M. K. Shastri, 1987).

2. Further, in contrast to nature's rivers whose flow and currents create the environment, Śākta Tantrism is a river whose environment is made out solely of human activity. Cf. *To Take Place*, p. 11.

3. This notion of "variety" is contrasted to diversity which "...distinctively stresses the marked difference or divergence of the individuals, parts, or elements, and seldom suggests even a class or categorical likeness." Hence, there are a variety of Śrīvidyās but there may not be diverse Śrīvidyās. Both concepts are defined in *Webster's New Dictionary of Synonyms: a dictionary of discriminated synonyms with antonyms and analogies and contrasted words* (Springfield, MA.: Merriam Webster, (1984). I am indebted to William Scott Green for pointing out this distinction.

4. Cf. Jonathan Z. Smith, *Map is Not Territory, Studies in the Histories of Religions* (Leiden-Koln: E. J. Brill, 1978), p. 291f.

5. Cf. William Scott Green, "Romancing the Tome: Rabbinic Hermeneutics and the Theory of Literature" *Semeia* 40 (1987):151–168.

6. Ibid., p. 154.

7. In Śrīvidyā, ritual forms the core of a comprehensive and integrated system of theology and social behavior. The tradition seeks to enforce repetition in practice and strict obedience to the authority of the guru as the means to final liberation (*mukti*) and worldly enjoyment (*bhukti*). Śrīvidyā never claims to be different in *kind* from other schools of Tantra or other forms of Hinduism, only different in degree; their objective is to fulfill the fourfold human aims (*puruṣārtha*) of law (*dharma*), acquisition (*artha*), sensuality (*kāma*), and liberation (*mokṣa*), just like any other Hindu. That these four common aims will be achieved in one's present birth is likewise an undistinguishing criteria of difference. Historically, as we shall see, Śrīvidyā has never dissociated itself from the religious and social conventions of the Sanskrit-literate Hindu society in which it has flourished.

8. "Romancing the Tome," p. 154.

9. I have drawn this conclusion by utilizing some of the observations of Frits Staal on grammar and Vedic *śrauta* rites. See Frits Staal, *The Science of Ritual* (Poona: The Bhandharkar Oriental Research Institute, 1982), pp. 31–32.

10. Ibid., p. 32.

11. Ibid., p. 31.

12. Ibid., p. 35.

13. "Romancing the Tome," p. 158.

14. Ibid., p. 158.

15. Ibid., p. 160.

16. Cf. Thomas J. Hopkins, *The Hindu Religious Tradition* (Encino and Belmont, Calif.: Dickensen Publishing Co., 1971).

17. In fact, as I will show in volume two, Śrīvidyā initiation is treated as a *de facto* birthright among many contemporary practitioners.

18. This remark is based on a careful survey of manuscript catalogues and the holdings of the Government Oriental Manuscript Library in Madras. There are simply dozens of *paddhatis* and *nibandhas* for every commentary or speculative text written. This assessment depends, of course, on whether the number of texts and the genre criterion is, in fact, a measure of traditional interests. I suggest that we have every reason to believe this is the case since the behavior of contemporary adepts corroborates this interpretation.

19. Śrīvidyā texts have for their main interest the procedures of *nyāsa*, literally, "laying down." *Nyāsa* is the process by which a micro- and macrocosmic relationship between the body and the universe and the divinity's expanding triadic forms is created through the invocation of mantric names. The rites of *nyāsa* suggest rites of invocation (*pratiṣṭha*), purification (*śuddhi*), and the other procedures which define Śrīvidyā's worship of the goddess. Ritual, in this sense, imitates the divine act of creation through naming and projecting itself by its own inherent power (*śakti*).

20. Cf. "Romancing the Tome," p. 158.

21. These are William Scott Green's remarks on sanctity of scripture in rabbinic Judaism. See "Romancing the Tome," p. 160.

22. "Romancing the Tome," p. 160.

23. Cf. "Romancing the Tome," p. 164–165.

24. William Scott Green, "Storytelling and Holy Man, The Case of Ancient Judaism," in: *Take Judaism, For Example: Studies Towards the Comparison of Religions*, Ed. Jacob Neusner (Chicago: University of Chicago Press, 1983), p. 31. (Hereafter, "Storytelling.")

25. "Storytelling," p. 30.

26. "Storytelling," p. 31.

27. "Storytelling," p. 31.

28. Cf. "Storytelling," p. 31–32.

29. "Storytelling," p. 32.

30. "Storytelling," p. 31.

Notes to Chapter 1

1. Cf. *YH*, 2.1 and *KT*, 2.1ff.

2. *Imagining Religion*, pp.39–40.

3. Ibid., p. 46.

4. Ibid., p. 48.

5. Ibid., p. 49.

6. Just as nonliterate societies create the functional equivalent to a canon by a process of arbitrary limitation and the overcoming of limitation through ingenuity exercised over selected signs and icons, so Śrīvidyā Tantrics create their lexicon of signs and icons. Ibid., pp. 49–50.

7. Recent work on the relationship between written and oral cultures has been done by Jack Goody (as listed in the bibliography). Much of what is said here is in consideration of Goody's work.

8. See Jack Goody, *The Interface Between the Written and the Oral. Studies in Literacy, Family, Culture and the State* (Cambridge: Cambridge University Press, 1987), p. 114.

9. Ibid., p. 116.

10. Tantrics responded in what might be termed a characteristically religious way to the gradual sectarianism that took root across traditions: each group naturally viewed its own interpretations and practices as superior. Like other Hindus, Śākta Tantrics usually maintain the superiority of their own views without entirely discrediting others, that is to say, other interpretations are ranked loosely below the particular approved stance. Śrīvidyā is not exempt from this general pattern but there is surprisingly little discussion of other sects or philosophical positions. The focus is almost entirely internal. Śrīvidyā commentators delineate their own positions *within* the boundaries of the tradition's theological definition. This disinterest in "outside" matters reflects the self-contained nature of the tradition but fails to capture the general openness with which other's opinions are greeted. Śrīvidyā's self concern can easily be mistaken: views held in common with others or borrowed are not always acknowledged. This process of assimilation without engaging in formal dialogue—even in the usual philosophical manner of characterizing views in order to reject them—is discussed below.

11. An obvious example is the mantra-wise distinction of the so-called *kādi-* and *hādimatas* which is sometimes posed as a distinction based on two separate traditions of ritual and practice. The dearth of historical evidence supporting the view that each *mata* represents distinctive strands of Śrīvidyā leads to some confusion when reading traditional texts. Commentators often write *as if* they were, in fact, distinct sub-traditions when evidence seems to point primarily to differences in the construction of the Śrīvidyā mantra. See the section on the Śrīvidyā mantra in part 1 for further details.

12. In the case of the *Saubhāgyaratnākara*, for example, we observe a degree of ritual elaboration that could not have possibly been intended for actual practice. The text and the prescriptions are simply too lengthy to be performed as set forth. We might ask why such elaborations were created at all given the "practical orientation" of the contemporary ritual tradition. The answer seems to be that such texts were created in order to perfect and elaborate patterns of imagery and ritual, that is, for the sake of symmetry, numerology or to create correlations with mythical beliefs, philosophical systems, or symbols.

13. This is especially obvious when Śrīvidyā adepts with an affinity to the traditions of Śaṅkara claim their positions to be identical to the Śaṅkara who wrote the *Brahmasūtrabhāṣya*. According to Śaṅkara, for example, no ritual action can bring about a realization of the non-duality of the Self and Brahman. Śrīvidyā, like other Śāktas, maintains a "combination" of ritual and action viewpoint (*sammucayavāda*) rather than this strict adherence to an "only knowledge" position. Likewise, Śrīvidyā as a Śākta Tantric sect also accepts a classic difference-in-identity (*bhedābheda*) view of the nature of reality and does not accept either the doctrine of no-origin (*ajātivāda*) of Gauḍapāda or the absolute nondualism (*kevelādvaita*) of Śaṅkara.

14. That is, the views of the fourth century Bhartṛhari in his *Vākyapadīya*.

15. Put differently, the *śrīcakra* is considered both a synchronic and a diachronic reality. As a synchronic reality the yantra does not rely on human beings either for its creation or its significance. However, as a diachronic reality the *śrīcakra* must be made part of the tradition's self-reflection. The tradition maintains a creative tension between these two perspectives on the status of the yantra.

16. *HTSL*, p. 9f.

17. *HTSL*, p. 9f.

18. *HTSL*, p. 92ff.

19. *HTSL*, p. 92ff.

20. One need only look to Bhāskararāya's *Tripurā Upaniṣadbhāṣya* to see the variety of sources not strictly within the confines of Śākta Tantrism that he quotes; cf. his reference to the *Sūtasaṃhitā* on *Tripurā Upaniṣad*, v. 1.

21. One such example is the *Tripurārahasya*, the popularity of which has been historically confined almost exclusively to south India. Curiously this text also demonstrates how works fade in and out of prominence. Having been a favorite work of the noted Tamil saint Rāmanamahārishi of Tiruvanamalai, *Tripurārahasya* enjoyed a brief period of attention which now seems to have faded entirely.

22. The *PKS* makes mention of the prowess of Śrīvidyā adepts in traditional astrology (see *PKS, dīkṣākaṇḍa*) while Bhāskararāya in the *Tripurā Upaniṣadbhāṣya* demonstrates that his reputation for Vedic ritual is not unfounded. See also part 2 for instances of contemporary adepts noted for ritual and astrological feats.

23. See K. C. Pandey, *Abhinavagupta, An Historical and Philosophical Study* (Varanasi: Chaukhamba Publications, reprint of the second edition, 1963), p.546f.

24. Lakṣmīdhara, for example, has little regard for what he terms Kaula systems and practices. Bhāskararāya, on the contrary, like other Kaula theolo-

gians seems to permit nearly every possible interpretation and many that do not follow his own. For details on these divisions and differences of opinion see below.

25. The center of the dispute is Rāmesvara Sūri's claim that Umānandanātha is not a direct or even a genuine disciple of Bhāskararāya. See the section on the historical development of Śrīvidyā for details of this dispute.

26. Agehananda Bharati, private correspondence. *Kula,* Professor Bharati says, "is a synonym of kuṭuṃba."

27. For a more detailed investigation of the meaning of *kula* and related terms in Kashmiri Śaivism see Paul Eduardo Müller-Ortega, *The Triadic Heart of Śiva, Kaula Tantricism of Abhinavagupta in the Nondual Shaivism of Kashmir* (Albany: State University Press of New York, 1989).

28. *HTSL,* p. 18. Goudriaan summarizes the views of prominent scholars such as Kaviraj and Dwiveda on the historical development of Kaulism. The use of *kula* in Buddhist Tantric literature may also contribute to an understanding of its origins given its prominence in the early *Guhyasamāja Tantra.* Robert A.F. Thurman's forthcoming study of this Buddhist work may begin to shed more light on the origins and use of the term *kula.*

29. Quoted from Müller-Ortega, p. 55. For a more detailed discussion of the significance of the term Kaula in Kashmiri Śaivism, I refer the reader to Müller-Ortega insightful remarks in this work; cf. pp. 55–63 and 200–201.

30. Pandey, p. 547f.

31. On the independence of the *krama* system devoted to Śākta forms of worship see Pandey, p.461ff., and Rastogi, cited in the bibliography.

32. For an overview see *HT,* pp. 47–67.

33. For further discussions of *kula* and Kaulism see Pandey, p. 542ff; *HT,* p. 32f., and p. 47f. These works also offer an overview of the concepts of the *pañcamakāras* and the practice of *kāmakalādhyāna.*

34. *HTSL,* p. 49.

35. This is based on Jayaratha's remark that a commentary by the ninth-century Kashmiri Īsanaśiva precedes his own, see *HTSL,* p. 60 and also Pandey, pp. 566–571.

36. Müller-Ortega, p. 59–60.

37. Müller-Ortega, p. 60.

38. Pandey lists eight texts: 1. *Siddhayogeśvarimata Tantra,* which is summarized as the *Mālinīvijaya* and *Mālinīviyottara Tantras* and is quoted by Śrīvidyā writers (including Bhāskararāya in his commentary on *Tripurā Upaniṣad* and copiously in his *Saubhāgyabhāskara* on *Lalitāsahasranāma*); 2.

Rudrayāmala, again frequently quoted by Bhāskararāya, among others, but apparently lost since none of these citations appear in either extant manuscripts bearing this title or in the *Paratriṃśikā*, its only extant portion; 3. *Kulārṇava Tantra*, about which much is said below; 4. *Jñānārṇava Tantra*, likewise discussed below; 5. *Nityāṣoḍaśikārṇava*, but apparently not the *Yoginīhṛdaya* that combines to form the *Vāmakeśvara Tantra*, according to Bhāskararāya and others, but not according to Śivānanda and the *hādi* Śrīvidyites; 6. *Svacchanda Tantra*, a favorite of Bhāskararāya's; 7. *Netra Tantra*, less frequently quoted in the *kādimata* of Śrīvidyā than in the *hādimata*; and *Kālīkula*, which I do not believe appears in the work of Śrīvidyā authors. Silburn cites other texts which she says Maheśvarānanda frequently quotes as Kaula, including the important *Ṛjuvimarśinī* commentary on *Nityāṣoḍaśikārṇava* by Śivānanda, a key proponent of *hādi* Śrīvidyā.

For a further elaboration on this list see Müller-Ortega as cited above (p. 58). For an in-depth look at the work and thought of Śivānanda see Khanna.

39. There are two fine studies of the *Kulārṇava Tantra* available but both are in Swedish. See G. Carlstedt, *Studier i Kulārṇava-Tantra* (Uppsala: Skrifer Utgivna au Religionshistorika Insitutionen i Uppsala, 1974); and by the same author, *Till Kulas Lov, Kulamahātmyakathana ur Kulārṇava* (Uppsala: Skrifer Utgivna au Religionshistorika Insitutionen i Uppsala, 1974). For a list of the printed editions of this text see the Bibliography.

40. Bhāskararāya, for example, refers to it in the *Tripurā Upaniṣadbhāṣya*, see his remarks on verse fifteen for one such instance. Contemporary adepts also frequently cite this work despite the reservations many hold concerning its advocating the *pañcamakāras*.

41. Pandey, p. 543.

42. Khanna's assertion that the cult of the goddess Tripurā is not originally associated with the goddess Śrī may be true with respect to Śivānanda's interpretation of Śrīvidyā sectarianism. However, there is no reason to believe that simply because Śivānanda offers us an early explanation of his own views and represents an important faction of the so-called *hādimata* that he represents all others. Clearly, later commentators, whom Khanna dismisses as confusing the tradition, do not share Śivānanda's views. On what grounds are we compelled to accept Śivānanda's interpretations as the primary source for the understanding of early Śrīvidyā?

43. See Bhāskararāya on *LSN*, n. 144. *svasvavamsaparamparāprāpto' mārgaḥ kulasaṃbandhitvāt kaulaḥ*.

44. Sastry, p. 88.

45. *Setubandha* on *YH*, 2.51cd–52ab.

46. *YH*, 2.51cd–52ab; Note that *Setubandha* also identifies Śrīvidyā through these five elements.

47. Cf. *LSN, Saubhāgyabhāskara* on n. 42.

48. *LSN*, n. 93.

49. *LSN*, n. 91.

50. *YH*, 2.146–152.

51. *YH*, 2.146–152.

52. *LSN*, n. 90, see Sastry, p. 87.

53. YH, 2.76–80.

54. See Lakṣmīdhara on *SL*, v.11ff; and the section below on the *śrīcakra*.

55. See Sastry, pp. 87–92; and *LSN*, n. 90–99.

56. *LSN*, n. 90.

57. *LSN*, n. 94.

58. Sastry, p. 89; see also *LSN*, n. 94.

59. Pandey, p. 595. See also Müller-Ortega, p. 59 and note #161 in which he cites the relevant passage of Abhinavagupta, namely, *Parātriṃśikā-vivaraṇa*, p. 138, cited in Gnoli, *LDSS*, pp. 863–866.

60. See his remarks on *SL*, v. 41.

61. See his comments on *SL*, v. 32.

62. See Bhāskararāya, for example, on *Tripurā Upaniṣadbhāṣya*, v. 12.

63. Cf. *Tripurā Upaniṣadbhāṣya*, v. 7.

64. The most oft-cited verse is *Bhagavadgītā*, 3.21 and 3.26; cf. Bhāskararāya's opening remarks on *Tripurā Upaniṣad*; the translation is contained in *The Secret of the Three Cities*.

65. Lakṣmīdhara on *SL*, v. 8.

66. This position is maintained by W. Norman Brown and reiterated by Goudriaan in *HT*, p. 33 but a careful reading of Lakṣmīdhara on *SL*, v. 31f. clearly shows that his intent was to restrict twice-born persons to Samayācāra and not to restrict it to only the twice-born. Twice-borns may *not* follow any other form of Śrīvidyā practice, according to Lakṣmīdhara, while others may practice according to Kaula methods. Non-twice-borns are not precluded from Samayācāra. This issue is taken up again in the discussion of the history of Śrīvidyā literature.

67. See Appendix 1. diagram A1, for the Samaya version of the *śrīcakra*.

68. *Tripurā Upaniṣadbhāṣya*, v. 2.

69. Cf. Umānandanātha, *NS* and the criticism he draws from Rāmeśvara in *PKS*, 3.31ff.

70. *LSN*, n. 220.

71. See *Tripurā Upaniṣadbhāṣya*, v. 12.

72. Sastry, pp. 90–91.

73. *LSN*, v. 98; Sastry, p. 91.

74. *LSN*, n. 97; Sastry, p. 90.

75. The reference to the *Sanatkumāra* cannot be the *Sanatkumāra Saṃhitā*, a Pāñcarātra work, or the *Sanatkumāratantra*. See *HTSL*, p. 73.

76. *LSN*, n. 97.

77. *SL*, v. 31.

78. On the date of the *SL* see Brown's Introduction, p. 29. Rāmānanda, whose commentaries on the *Tripurā* and *Tripurātāpinī Upaniṣads* post-date Lakṣmīdhara, is the only other representative of the Samaya school as Lakṣmīdhara defines it and he does little to support the view that Lakṣmīdhara's Samayācāra represents a pan-Indian situation in the sixteenth century.

79. The Kaula/Samaya confusion within Śrīvidyā is comparable to the regional divisions posited in the *Śaktisamgama Tantra*: the Tantra's views appear to reflect a particular regional situation within a given historical setting. One cannot extrapolate on the basis of this text that its division of Śrīvidyā represents the pan-Indian situation or a widely accepted interpretation. See *HT*, p. 43.

NOTES TO CHAPTER 2

1. See Jan Gonda, *Change and Continuity in Indian Religion* (New Delhi: Munshiram Manoharlal Publishers, reprint, 1985), p. 25f. Here Gonda argues convincingly that the images of Śiva-like gods such as the those on the seals of Harrappan civilization while bearing a *resemblance* to later images of Śiva are not evidence that the Indus Valley culture was already worshipping a proto-Śiva image. In the same way, while there is circumstantial evidence for the worship of the goddess Lalitā in ancient times as recorded in the *purāṇas* there is no method for asserting an historical link between names and places and the actual worship of the deity.

2. See Mircea Eliade, *Yoga, Immortality and Freedom* (Princeton: University Press, 1958), p. 200. Here the author argues, seemingly without historical evidence, that Tantrism arose suddenly in its literary forms. Literary evidence, however, suggests that the oral tradition's transition to written forms was more gradual and served to systematize an already mature ritual and

speculative tradition. In support of this theory is internal literary evidence in the Tantras such as the repetition of whole passages in a number of different texts and the fact that certain passages seem to find their way into sources based on regional factors and the gradual diffusion of ideas. When Śrīvidyā does emerge textually it is in such a state of sophistication that it seems implausible that its oral traditions were not, at least partially, in a comparable state of "completeness." In other words, the transition to written forms follows only after the oral traditions have at least marginally solidified sources.

3. See Ch. Chakravarti, *The Tantras. Studies on their Religion and Literature* (Calcutta: University Press, 1963), p. 20; see also J. N. Farquhar, *An Outline of the Religious Literature of India* (London: Oxford University Press, 1920), p. 193.

4. In Tantric literature the case of the often quoted *Rudrayāmala* provides another example of verses (or a text) originally transmitted orally and apparently passed through Tantric lineages but now "lost." Texts bearing this title in manuscript do not contain the many verses attributed to the *Rudrayāmala* by Tantric authors. See *HTSL*, p. 47f. An example of this is also seen in the relatively recent Bhāskararāya. See his *Tripurā Upaniṣadbhāṣya*, v. 7. Here he quotes *RY* and yet the quotation does not occur in mss. or printed editions of the text.

5. It may, in fact, be much earlier given theories of goddess worship in Dravidian culture, see Eliade, *Yoga*, pp. 200–210 for a discussion of this suggestion.

6. This point is established by Khanna.

7. On Tirumūlar and other Tamil poets see K. V. Zvelebil, *Tamil Literature* (Wiesbaden: Otto Harrossowitz, 1974) and also by the same author, *Tamil Literature* (Leiden-Koln: E. J. Brill, 1975).

8. On the dating of early Tantric literature see *HTSL*, p. 21ff.

9. For a detailed study of Śrīvidyā in the *Tirumantiram* and a study of Tirumūlar's Tantrism see my forthcoming article in *The Roots of Tantra*, edited by Katherine Harper.

10. On Tirumūlar's life and personality see Zvelebil, *Tamil Literature*, (Handbuch), p. 68.

11. See Zvelebil, *Tamil Literature*, (History of Indian Lit.), p. 55.

12. Tirumūlar defines a mantra as the "perfect concentration of the mind of anything." See Zvelebil, *Tamil Literature*, (History of Indian Lit.), p. 55.

13. See *Thiru Manthiram of Tirumūlanāyanār*, Vol. 1, in Tamil, ed. Thiru P. Ramanatha Pillai (Tiruneveli, Tamil Nadu, India: The South Indian Śaiva Siddhanta Works Publishing Society, second revised edition, 1957). Pages are not numbered, see v. 1307, the first verse of chapter twelve.

14. Ibid., v. 1307, chapter 12.

15. See the section below on the anthropomorphic aspect of Lalitā.

16. One adept explained that the discrepancy is simply part of the unpredictable nature of the *siddha*. Another, more plausible explanation is that the compilers of the *Tirumantiram* (since Tirumūlar composed it only in an oral form) did not always understand the meaning of verses and that the compilation itself depends on their untrustworthy memories. Consequently, verses can be scattered or confused and there is no clear method for discerning which verses belong to which chapter.

17. *Tirumantiram* as cited above.

18. See *Tirumantiram*, v. 904. On the *śrīcakra* as a combination of Śiva and Śakti cakras see K. R. Venkataraman, "Śakti Cult in South India," *A Cultural History of India*, ed. Haridas Bhattacharyya (Calcutta: Ramakrishna Mission, second edition, 1956), vol. IV, p. 256.

19. Ibid., p. 256; this opinion is commonly held by members of the Guru Mandali in south India and is also maintained by various other individual adepts from a broad range of lineages.

20. See *Tirumantiram*, v. 904, the text reads: *tiruvampalamākac cīrccak karattait/ tiruvampalamāka īrāṟu kīṟit/ tiruvampalamāka irupattaiñ cākkit/ tiruvampalamākac ceppikkinṟa vāṟe//*

21. See V. V. Dwiveda, *Upodghāta* (Introduction) to the edition of the *Nityāṣoḍaśikārṇava* (In Sanskrit) for a discussion of the origins of Tantric literature in North India and its relation to Matsyendranāth. Also V. V. Dwiveda, "tripurādarśanasyaparicita ācāryaḥ kṛtayaśca," *Tantrayātra, essays on Tantra-Āgama Thoughts and Philosophy, Literature, Culture and Travel* (Varanasi: Ratna Publications, 1982), pp. 64–78.

22. See Khanna.

23. *HTSL*, pp. 9–10.

24. *HTSL*, p. 9.

NOTES TO CHAPTER 3

1. Khanna, Introduction, p. 4.

2. Ibid., p. 5.

3. Agastya of Gāyatrī Mandali, Madras, February, 1985.

4. Despite the fact that many contemporary adepts are known to one another by name or in reputation very few make any effort to meet or engage in dialogue. Contemporary lineages are self-contained entities with little interest in the affairs or interpretations of others. Many adepts expressed interest in why I would have such an interest. Many thought it a mere intellectual exercise that served no practical aim. The reasons for this become clear

if one reflects on the history of Tantrism and its transmission in tightly controlled lineages. Allegiance to the tradition is interpreted almost exclusively as allegiance to a particular guru and his teachings. That these teachings have common sources and a continuous history of development is only of minimal interest to adepts. As privately oriented Tantric traditions, Śrīvidyā lineages stay "within themselves" and rarely seek advice or even evince curiosity in like-minded individuals or groups.

5. See Pandey, p. 543ff. and *HTSL*, p. 59ff.

6. The most reliable editions of the *Vāmakeśvara Tantra* divide the work into its two parts. See *Nityāṣoḍaśikārṇava (tantra), with two* (Sanskrit) *Commentaries, Ṛjuvimarśinī by Śivānanda and Artharatnāvalī by Vidyānanda*, ed. V. V. Dwiveda (Varanasi: Sampurnanand Sanskrit Vishvavidyālaya, 1968) [Yogatantragranthamala, 1]; also *Vāmakeśvaratantra with the commentary entitled Setubandha by Bhāskararāya*, ed. K. V. Abhyankar (Poona: Ānandasrama, 1908) [AnSS, 56]. In addition, the *NSA* with Jayaratha's commentary is available as: *Vamakeśvarimatam with the commentary of Rājanaka Jayaratha*, ed. M. K. Sastri (Śrinagar: Government Press, 1945) [KSTS, LXVI]. The *Yoginīhṛdaya* is available as: *Yoginīhṛdaya with the commentaries Dīpika of Amṛtānanda and Setubandha of Bhāskararāya*, ed. Gopinath Kaviraj (Varanasi: Sampurnanand Sanskrit Visvavidyālaya, second edition, 1981, third edition, n.d.) [Sarasvatibhavanagranthamala, 7]. For a thorough discussion of the history of the text and a review of its contents see *HTSL*, p. 59ff. including references to the *NSA* as the *Catuḥśati* and the *YH* as *Sundarīhṛdaya*. Bhāskararāya in his *Tripurā Upaniṣadbhāṣya* also refers to *YH* as *Nityāhṛdaya*, see his remarks on v. 1. *NSA* hereafter refers to the Dwiveda edition and *YH* to the Kaviraj, third edition unless otherwise specified (sometimes specified as "Dwiveda" or "Kaviraj"; all references to Jayaratha refer to the Sastri edition.

7. Cf. *HTSL*, pp. 60–64.

8. *HTSL*, p. 64.

9. See André Padoux, *Recherches sur la symbolique et l'energie de al parole dans certains textes tantriques* (Paris: Institut de Civilisation Indienne, 1976). Here the author offers a thorough discussion of the principles of Kashmiri Śaivism and their relationship to other sources and traditions. This work has been revised and translated into English. See André Padoux, *Vāc, The Concept of the Word In Selected Hindu Tantras*, trans. Jacques Gontier (Albany: State University of New York Press, 1990).

Particularly evident is the much elaborated notion of creation through sound in three distinct stages, that is, *paśyantī*, *madhyamā*, and *vaikharī*. It is this creation theory that the *VT* parallels to the formation of the *śrīcakra*.

10. *HTSL*, p. 60f.

11. Note that to the ordinary fifteen visible phases of the moon is added one more, the "unseen" phase that is said to conceal Śiva's true nature. On the sixteen *nityās*, *tithis* or *kalās*, as they are called, see *HT*, p. 57 and p. 60.

12. See *HT*, p. 57. During *śrīcakra pūjā* the sixteen *nityās* are worshiped before the beginning of *āvaraṇa* worship. They are place on the central *trikoṇa* five to a side with the sixteenth identified on the *bindu*. For details see the section on the *śrīcakra*. In contrast to other Śākta traditions, Śrīvidyā specifically develops the ritual worship of the sixteen *nityās* in relation to the *śrīcakra*. A further identity is also established between the *nityās* and a sixteen syllable version of the *śrīvidyā* mantra.

13. *YH*, 1.1.

14. *YH*, 1.2.

15. See *Tantrarāja Tantra*, ed. Laksmana Sastri with an Introduction by Arthur Avalon, aka Sir John Woodroffe (New Delhi: Motilal Banarsidass, reprint edition, 1981); cf. Chapter 36 and the remarks made by Avalon on p. 2 and p. 71.

16. Jayaratha on *NSA* 1.47; see also *HTSL*, p. 60; Pandey, p. 578; and Khanna, p. 69.

17. Pandey, p. 578.

18. Since Jayaratha's commentary concludes after verse 33 of the fifth chapter, while later commentators extend the text eleven more verses, the possibility remains that the text either continued to expand or that different regional recensions existed. The two other Kashmiri commentaries, *Artharatnāvalī* and *Ṛjuvimarśinī* both end at 5.33 and only Bhāskararāya who composed the *Setubandha* after having reached the south goes on to verse 44. Another early commentary attributed to Śaṅkararaśi, a contemporary of Īśvaraśiva, is also discussed by Kashmiris but this, too, has unfortunately not survived. See Pandey, pp. 580–581. Further, Jayaratha states that there are other commentaries on *NSA*, the first being that of Dipakanātha, and others by one Allaṭa (for which he has little use), and Kalyānavarmā. See Jayaratha, pp. 54ff; see also Khanna's remarks on *NSA* and *YH*, pp. 69ff.

19. Maheśvarānanda is author of the *Mahārthamañjarī*; see *La Mahārthamañjarī de Maheśvarānanda avec des extraits du Parimala*, traduction et introduction L. Silburn (Paris: Institut de Civilisation Indienne, 1968), p. 9ff. For another opinion see the *Mahārthamañjarī of Maheśvarānanda with the autocommentary Parimala*, edited with an Introduction in Sanskrit (*upodghata*) V. V. Dwiveda (Varanasi: Varanaseya Sanskrit Vishvavidyālaya, 1972), p. *ka*ff.

20. For more on Maheśvarānanda's role in Kashmiri tradition see Silburn as cited above. Pegarding the historical diffusion of Śrīvidyā sources, Goudriaan apparently disagrees with Silburn and maintains that the Kashmiri Śivānanda was originally a Keralite who migrated to the north and flourished in the latter part of the thirteenth century. This opinion, it seems, is based on Dwiveda's conclusions. See Dwiveda's Introduction to *Mahārthamañjarī*, p. 5f.

21. Note that Dwiveda in his Introduction to *NSA*, p. 21, maintains that the author of the *Artharatnāvalī* is identical to the author of the *Saubhāgyaratnākāra*. This is not possible. Internal evidence to the contrary abounds in the *Saubhāgyaratnākāra* clearly demonstrating that the lineages of the two "Vidyānandas" are different. Unfortunately there is at present no available edition of the *Saubhāgyaratnākāra* in print though a recension from the Sarasvati Mahal Sanskrit Library in Thanjavur edited by Dr. G. Sundaramoorthy is forthcoming.

22. None of the seven Kashmiri commentaries mentioned by Jayaratha none appear to have survived. See M. K. Sastri's Introduction to *Vāmakeśvarīmatam*. Khanna notes that there are five unpublished commentaries on *NSA*, namely, one by an unknown author dated 1354 C.E. in Nepal; another called "*Candrasaṅketa*" by one Amṛtānanda in Bikaner; a third listed entitled "Vāmakeśvaratantradarpana"; a fourth by Mukuṇḍalāla of Benares; and last, one by Sadānanda. See Khanna, p. 69 for details. None of these commentaries appears to have had any impact on contemporary Śrīvidyā in south India and none were known to my informants.

23. Though it is treated as a separate sub-school, the *hādimata* appears to be little more than a variant mantric interpretation rather than a fully elaborated theology. For more on this see the detailed discussion in the section on the *śrīvidyā*.

24. Amṛtānanda exhibits a depth of interpretation characteristic of Kashmiri Kula Tantra intellectuals. He often clarifies the text's dense and technical material and, unlike Bhāskararāya, he is more straightforward and less technical. Amṛtānanda is also especially well-versed in the Kashmiri Śaiva Pratyabhijñā, which he views as foundational for *YH*'s explanations of Śrīvidyā. Cf. Khanna, p. 71.

25. *NSA*, 1.123. The *NSA* postdates itself to the *Rudrayāmala* since it explicitly states that it deals with matters left out in the latter. Pandey believes it is posterior to *Jñānārṇava Tantra*, another Śrīkula Tantra. See Pandey, p. 553.

26. See Avalon's Introduction to *TT*, pp. 35–36.

27. This is evident in Kashmiri Śaiva tradition especially. See *HTSL*, p. 60ff.

28. On Bhāskararāya's biography in history and legend see the Introduction in: *Varivasyārahasya and its commentary Prakāśa by Śrī Bhāskararāya Makhin*, ed. and trans. S. Subrahmanya Sastri (Adyar, Madras: Adyar Library and Research Centre, fourth edition, 1976).

29. These works of Amṛtānanda are contained in the Dwiveda edition of *NSA*.

30. According to some legends, for example, Tirumūlar was originally a Kashmiri who came to Tamilnadu and brought with him Kashmiri influenced

Śaivism. Contemporary Śrīvidyā adepts also note that traditions of classical dance (*bhāratanātyam*) written about by Kashmiri authors such as Abhinavagupta have flourished in south India. While seemingly coincidental these instances would suggest that perhaps an historical connection does exist linking Kashmiri and Tamil traditions. Certainly it is a subject worthy of more serious study.

31. Naṭarāja of Guru Mandali, Madurai, April, 1985.

32. See *HTSL*, p. 64f. for an outline of text. Note that Goudriaan's remark concerning the name of the text as "really" being the *Kādimatatantra* is perhaps an overstatement. Bhāskararāya, for example, frequently refers to the text as the *Tantrarāja*. The Tantra in its written form is certainly no later than the ninth century.

33. See *TT*, 1.5. and also *HTSL*, p. 64.

34. Cf. *HTSL*, p. 18.

35. See *HT*, p. 40.

36. Goudriaan seems to have placed to great an emphasis on the emergence of the term *mata* when instead he would better interpret the differences between groups by focusing on the "other" term in the compound. Cf, *HTSL*, p. 65, ftn. 24.

37. The text of the *Tantrarāja Tantra* is divided into thirty-six chapters (probably intended to parallel creation in the thirty-six *tattvas*) and is important in both Kashmiri and south Indian Śrīvidyā traditions. Its foremost commentary, entitled the "*Manoramā*," was written between 1603 and 1604 by the Kashmiri Subhagānandanātha, though he apparently did not live to see its completion, the task having been taken up by his disciple Prakāśānandanātha. See *HTSL*, p. 65.

38. Pandey, p. 575.

39. The text's list of sixty-four Tantras, he says, is obviously defective since it lists *VT* as a separate work from the *Sundarīhṛdaya*, which is but another name for the *Yoginīhṛdaya*. *NSA*, 1.7; See also Pandey, p. 574.

40. *HTSL*, p. 67.

41. Cf. *HTSL*, p. 68. Concerning the hierarchy of mantras, stated or implied, within Śrīvidyā tradition see the chapter on the *śrīvidyā*.

42. Since these *paddhati*s circulate privately in handwritten forms among adepts it is impossible to provide a proper citation. It is the usual situation, however, that the *paddhati* states at its outset that it claims its authority through a specific line of teachers and sometimes through a specific text. I have seen at least three different *paddhati*s of distinct lineages that claim to be based on the *Jñānārṇava Tantra* and several based on the *Paraśurāmakalpasūtra*, which includes, of course, the *Nityotsava* of Umānanda.

43. Cf. *HTSL*, p. 71f.

44. See *HTSL*, pp. 71–72. Goudriaan notes also the author's citing of the *KT* and *RY* but curiously does not point out the inconsistency between the positions taken in these works and the author's allegiances to Sāṅkara tradition.

45. Śaktisaṃgama Tantra (SST), which dates no earlier than the sixteenth century, is noteworthy because its Sundarīkhaṇḍa offers detailed examination of *śrīcakra* worship and details the magical results of other rituals. See HTSL, p. 70; also see HT, p. 43; also HTSL, p. 71. The *kādi/hādi* distinction is taken up under the Śrīvidyā mantra. The Tantra's late date may account in part for the extraordinary variety of subjects it undertakes to explain; its author also codifies mantric practices by region and sub-tradition. Tripurā is merely one of the goddesses whose worship is described in the Tantra. SST's regional distinctions do not appear to reflect the contemporary situation though neither is it groundless. It may, in fact, reflect the situation known to its compilers though its scheme is complex and not altogether consistent.

By introducing the *kādi/hādi* distinction the author implies that each mata focused on a different aspect of Śakti, a fact unsupported in other sources. The basic regional distinction, however, is the one most commonly referred to in contemporary circles. It follows what SST calls "Kashmira, Gauḍa (i.e., Bengal), and Kerala lines of tradition." Some contemporary southern adepts point out that Śrīvidyā is not associated with the Kālī traditions of Kerala. According to SST, the divisions follow region and the *kādi/hādimata* distinction:

	Kerala	Gauḍa	Kashmir
Hādimata	Kālikā	Tārā	Tripurā
Kādimata	Tripurā	Kālī	Tāranī

This scheme agrees with the situation in modern Kerala insofar as Tripurā and Kālī forms of worship are historically important. But it does not seem to follow the *mata* distinction since there is no living *hādi*-based tradition.

46. Hacker and other scholars have shown that the historical Śaṅkara was likely to have been a Vaiṣṇava. See Paul Hacker, "Eigentümlichkeiten der Lehre und Terminologie Śaṅkaras: Avidyā, Nāmarūpa, Māyā, Īśvara," *ZDMG* (1950): 246–286; Paul Hacker, "Die Lehre von den Realitatsgraden im Advaita Vedānta," *ZDMG* (1952): 277ff.; Paul Hacker, "Śaṅkara der Yogin und Śaṅkara der Advaitin," *WZKSO*, (1968/1969):119ff.; Paul Hacker, "Śaṅkarācārya and Śaṅkarabhagavatpāda," *New Indian Antiquary* (April–June 1947); K. Kunjunniraja, "The Date of Samkarācārya and Allied Problems," *Brahma Vidyā* (=*Adyar Library Bulletin*) 24 (1960):125–148; S. Mayeda, "The Authenticity of the Upadeśa Sahaśrī," *JAOS* (1965) 2:178–196; S. Mayeda, "On the Authenticity of the Māṇḍūkya and the Gauḍapādīya Bhāsya," *Brahma Vidyā* (=*Adyar Library Bulletin*) (1967–1968):74ff.; S. Mayeda, "The Authenticity of the Bhagavadgītābhāsya Ascribed to Śaṅkara," *WZKSO* IX (1965): 155–197; T. Vetter, "Zur Bedeutung des Illusionismus bei Śaṅkara," *WZKSO* (1968–1969):407–423.

47. The *Saundaryalaharī*, which has attracted at least thirty-four known commentaries, is clearly the most important. (See Brown, cited in full below, p. 26.) Śaṅkara is attributed at least of the latter portion of the *Saundaryalaharī*, which is distinguished from the first forty-one verses, the *Ānandalaharī*, usually attributed to Śiva. This matter is taken up below. On his authorship of *SL* and matters concerning the text's composition see Brown's critical edition and translation, pp. 25–30: *The Saundaryalaharī or Flood of Beauty, Traditionally ascribed to Śaṅkarācārya*, ed. and trans. W. Norman Brown (Cambridge, MA.: Harvard University Press, 1977) [Vol.43 in The Harvard Oriental Series, ed. Daniel H. H. Ingalls]. On the issue of the authenticity of the works attributed to Śaṅkara and Gauḍapāda see endnote 1 above.

48. The text has been edited in several editions. See *HTSL*, p. 131, ftn. 3 for a list of published editions and comments on the composition and content of the *PS*. All references are to the reprinted text cited as *PS*: *Prapañcasāra Tantra of Śaṅkarācārya with the Commentary Vivaraṇa by Padmapadācārya and Prayogakramadīpikā—a Vṛtti on the Vivaraṇa*, revised and documented with exhaustive introduction by Arthur Avalon (Sir John Woodroffe), ed. Atalānanda Sarasvatī, Parts I, II in One Vol., Calcutta, 1914 (as Tantrik Text Series Vol. XIX, (Delhi: Motilal Banarsidass, reprint, 1981).

49. *PS*, pp. 129ff.

50. *HTSL*, p. 29f. and p. 131f. The oral traditions surrounding this text may date from before the eleventh century if Śivānanda, author of the *Ṛjuvimarśinī*, is placed in this period. He makes mention of the *PS* frequently in his commentary on *NSA*. See *NSA*, p. 349f.

51. See *HTSL*, p. 131ff.; for references to the citations made by Śivānanda see Dwiveda, *NSA*, *vyākhyādvayoddhṛtaślokārdhanukrāmani*, pp. 349–360.

52. See *HTSL*, p. 132 for a discussion of the commentarial literature on *PS* and also the above cited *PS* edition.

53. See Brown, p. 27.

54. Cf. his *Tripurā Upaniṣadbhāṣya*, v. 9. On the distinction between Śaṅkara and Śaṅkara Bhagavatpāda see the article by Paul Hacker cited in endnote 1.

55. See Karl Potter's Introduction in: *An Encyclopedia of Indian Philosophy, Vol.3, Advaita Vedānta up to Śaṅkara and his Pupils*, ed. and intro. Karl Potter (Delhi: Motilal Banarsidass, reprint, 1981). Also Brown, p. 28.In a way comparable to the later *Sāradatilaka (ST)*, which is also cited by Amṛtānanda and Bhāskararāya as authoritative on *mantraśāstra*, the *Prapañcasāra*'s foremost concerns are the power of mantras to influence and effect change in the natural and social universe and to describe the mantric worship of deities. (For references to editions and remarks on the *Sāradatilaka* see *HTSL*, p. 134f.) Only in this limited sense is the *PS* part of Śrīvidyā's canon. Because Śrīvidyā adepts have traditionally gained a reputation for general mantric knowledge,

sources such as the *PS*, *ST*, and *Mantramahodadhi* play an important role in the development of the broader spiritual discipline rather than as sources of Śrīvidyā doctrine or ritual.

56. The "Hymn of the Three Hundred [Names] of Lalitā" is part of the *Lalitopākhyana* within the *Brahmāndapūraṇa*. *Śrī Lalitā Triśati Bhāṣya of Śrī Śaṃkara Bhagavatpāda*, trans. Dr. Chaganti Suryanarayana Murthy (Bombay: Bharatiya Vidyā Bhavan, 1975). On the transmission of the text see the introduction, p. xiv.

57. *LTSB*, introduction, pp. xiv–xv.

58. This mantra-based structure of the text also leads to long discussions of the *bījākṣara hrīṃ* since it occurs sixty times as the first component of three groups of twenty names. The quotation cited here is by Naṭarāja of Guru Mandali, Madurai, January, 1985.

59. An important indication is the emphasis the text lays on the *ānanda* or blissful aspect of Brahman identified with the realization of the goddess's ultimate nature.

LTSB, n.99, reads *paramānandarūpa muktiḥ*. While Śaṅkara interprets the Upaniṣadic attribution of *ānanda* to Brahman as a matter of course, he tends to eschew this characteristic in favor of others. In his nondualistic system the question as to *whose* is such a bliss causes serious conceptual problems. If it is the Self (*ātman*) then does it experience *ānanda* as an object? This would undermine the Self's ultimacy by positing an "experiencer." If the *ānanda* is attributed to the conceptual self (*jīva*) then how can it be a characteristic of the supreme Brahman? Hence, Śaṅkara avoids the discussion whenever possible. Śāktas, however, like all Tantrics, lay a heavy emphasis on the *ānanda* aspect of Brahman since they wish to assert its resemblance in kind to worldly forms of happiness and stress it as a primary motivating force for practicing a spiritual discipline. Under *LTS* n.240, for example, the author of the commentary asserts that the goddess grants all gradations of bliss from human forms (*manusānanda*) to the bliss of Brahman (*brahmānanda*). See also Hacker as cited above for a discussion of the role of the term *ānanda* in Śaṅkara's works. This point, equally stressed in the commentary, is inconsistent with the views of the author of the *Brahmasūtrabhāṣya*. But more substantial contravening evidence is the explicit mention of certain types of *lakṣaṇā* or metaphor used to interpret the Vedic utterances. Hacker and others, show that this style of hermeneutics is in conflict with the interpretations offered in the *Brahmasūtrabhāṣya*.

60. *LTSB*, as well as the *Lalitopākhyāna*, were likely composed in one of the Sānkara *maṭhas* sometime between the eighth and eleventh centuries. The *LTS* itself has not enjoyed the same degree of popularity as the *Lalitāsahasranāma*. It has been completely passed over by the Kashmiri commentators who are apparently not influenced by the growing contingent of Sāṅkara *advaitins* interested in Śrīvidyā. Given the usefulness of the *Lalitātriśati* and its commentary for elucidating Śrīvidyā's general theology and especially the

mantra, this omission from the works of Amṛtānanda and Śivānanda suggests that it was either unknown to them, not a part of their regional literature, or beyond the scope of their understanding of Śrīvidyā tradition.

61. A senior member of the Ānanda Mandalī, Madras, February, 1985.

62. A senior member of Gāyatrī Mandalī, Madras, February, 1985.

63. The nine commentaries are printed in a single edition that is privately published and not easily available: *Saundaryalaharī of Śrī Śaṅkara Bhagavatpadācārya with the commentaries (in Sanskrit) Lakṣmīdharā [sic], Saubhāgyavardhanī, Arnāmodinī, Ānandagirīya, Tātparyadīpinī, Padārthacandrikā, Ḍiṇḍima Bhāṣya, Gopālasundarī and Ānandalaharī Ṭīkā*, ed. A. Kuppusvami (Tiruchirapalli, India, 1976). All references to commentaries on *SL* are drawn from this edition unless otherwise specified. Another edition has drawn more scholarly reference but has been superceded by Brown. See *Saundaryalaharī of Śrī Śaṅkarācārya, with Lakṣmīdhara's Commentary, Bhāvanopaniṣat...and Devī Pañcastavi*, ed. N. N. Svami Ghanapati (Mysore: Mysore Government Press, University of Mysore, Oriental Library Publications, Sanskrit Series no.11/85, 1945; third edition, revised for reprint by Pandit S. Narayanasvami Sastry, No. 11/85/91, 1953).

Concerning the unpublished manuscripts see Brown. A review of manuscripts in the Government Oriental Manuscripts Library in Madras and at the Sarasvatī Mahal in Thanjavur revealed that one of the commentaries, the so-called *Candrikā* attributed to the famous Appaya Dīkṣita is not a gloss on *SL* at all but a work of Vedānta. It is not likely to be an authentic work of this Advaita philosopher.

64. The author was apparently patronized in the court of the Orissan King Pratāparudra Gajapati (1497–1539). On Lakṣmīdhara's life, date and work see *HTSL*, p. 147f.; also Brown, p. 26, ftn. 10.

Notwithstanding the work of one Rāmānanda who composed commentaries on both the *Tripurā* and *Tripurātāpinī Upaniṣads*. Rāmānanda follows Lakṣmīdhara's views to the letter, as it were, and frequently cites him as his source. He does not, however, contribute anything new to the Samaya view and has had no discernable influence on subsequent Śrīvidyā tradition. There is no indication of his date or reference to his work in other sources. He also appears to be almost completely unknown to contemporary adepts. Only his *Tripurā Upaniṣadbhāṣya* is available in print and at least one copy of the *Tripurātāpinī Upaniṣadbhāṣya* in manuscript form in the Adyar, Library, Madras.

65. *HTSL*, p. 147. Lakṣmīdhara's sectarianism has not precluded his becoming an authoritative source even for those who do not share his views.

66. Another important point concerning this author's work is that his commentary on the *Aruṇā Upaniṣad* is actually not an independent work but is incorporated, verses and all, into the *SL* commentary. This has escaped the notice of the several editors that include the *Lakṣmīdharī* in their editions of *SL*

as well as the editors of the Upaniṣad itself, cf., the Avalon edition of the *Kaula and other Śākta Upaniṣads*, ed. L. Sastri with an introduction by Arthur Avalon (Calcutta: University Press, 1921) [Tantrik Texts Series, Vol. X.]

67. It is held by some contemporary adepts that Kaivalyāśrāma does, in fact, predate Lakṣmīdhara by a century or two. This opinion is grounded, however, on unsubstantiated literary evidence and the absence of Kaivalya's mention of Lakṣmīdhara—neither of which authenticates the theory.

68. His popularity is restricted it would appear to southern India and manuscripts of the *Saubhāgyavardhanī* are limited to southern libraries. But these facts alone do not lead to the conclusion that Kaivalyāśrāma was necessarily a southerner. At best there is evidence of his limited regional popularity and the possibility that he is from southern India.

69. For a discussion of the thirty-six *tattvas* or categories of reality that make up reality as it emanates from Brahman see *HT*, p. 52f. It should be noted that contemporary adepts cite the *PKS* (cf. 1.4) and *VVR* (cf.,1.36) as the sources for generating lists of the *tattvas*. Discrepancies between various lists were not considered an important issue. This underlines the fact that strictly metaphysical matters are not given particular emphasis or laden with importance unless they bear on Śrīvidyā's spiritual discipline—a general propensity shared across Tantrism. More important to contemporary adepts was the identification of the thirty-six *tattvas* with the *śrīcakra* as the form of emanation. The *tattvas* themselves are important inasmuch as they are incorporated into the larger ritual picture rather than as a matter of pure metaphysical speculation.

70. A senior member of Gayatri Mandali, Madras, December, 1984.

71. The historical account of the *SL*'s authorship, like all literary issues, is handled deftly by Brown. There is no doubt, however, that the living traditions within the Sāṅkara *maṭhas* and most Śrīvidyā lineages maintain at least the core of the oral mythology: the *Ānandalaharī* was transmitted through Śaṅkara who received it from Śiva (or Śakti) while only the final fifty-nine verses are Śaṅkara's creation. South Indian traditions differ regarding the location of the text's composition but only those Śrīvidyā lineages deliberately severing themselves from the Śāṅkara tradition dispute its authorship.

72. From the textual point of view, however, the inconsistencies between the *SL* and other Tantric sources, are more difficult to explain. The cautious scholar is inclined to agree with Brown who believes that the absence of specific Tantric vocabulary within the poem points to no approximate correspondence between the *SL* and other Tantric sources.

73. A senior member of Guru Mandali, Madurai, June, 1985.

74. *HTSL*, p. 168.

75. Given Goudriaan's references to early authorities it seems likely that he has not himself investigated this situation. It is at least superficially appar-

ent that the confusion has existed because the two texts bear the same title. The *Subhagodaya* is not widely read and it is altogether possible that there are, in fact, two sources with two different authors.

These sources are in the Government Oriental Manuscripts Library, Madras and in the Adyar Library, both lacking proper identification numbers.

The appearance of two different *Subhagodayas* apparently resolves the dilemma of authorship since none of the manuscripts of the text attributed to Śivānanda that I reviewed were attributed to Gauḍapāda; I was, however, unable to find any copies of the Gauḍapāda *Subhagodaya* other than the manuscript versions available in Madras.

Khanna has translated Śivānanda's *Subhagodaya* as well as his *Subhagodayavāsanā* and *Saubhāgyahṛdayastotra*—all three central to understanding the early exposition of Śrīvidyā.

76. For editions and further information on the printed edition of the text see *The Śrīvidyāratnasūtras of Gauḍapadācārya with the Dīpikā of Śaṅkarāraṇya*, edited by Gopinath Kaviraj. Varanasi, 1926.

77. A senior member of Siddha Mandalī, Madras, December, 1984.

78. On the dates of Amṛtānanda see V. V. Dwiveda, Sanskrit preface (*Anupratāvikam*) to Kaviraj's edition of the *YH*, p. 5; also *HTSL*, p. 152.

79. For editions of the *KKV* see *HTSL*, p. 168. References made here refer to the Madras 1971 reprint edition: *Tantrarāja Tantra and Kāmakalāvilāsa together with a translation of parts of the commentary (Cidvallī) by Naṭananandanātha*, ed. John Woodroffe and trans. R. Krishnasvami Aiyar (Madras: Ganesh and Co., fourth reprint ed., 1971). Goudriaan also lists several other editions that include reference to vernacular commentaries.

80. See *Kāmakalāvilāsa*, trans. and intro. N. Subrahmanya Aiyar (Madras: Guhānanda Mandalī Trust, 1956). *Kāmakalāvilāsa* stands with Śivānanda's trilogy—*Subhagodaya*, *Subhagodayavāsanā*, and *Saubhāgyahṛdayastotra*—and Bhāskararāya's *Varivasyārahasya* as the most important independent treatises on Śrīvidyā.

81. See *HTSL*, p. 168–169 and ftn. 2, p. 169. For Bharati's remark see: Agehananda Bharati, *The Tantric Tradition* (New York: Samuel Weiser, Inc., revised American paperback ed., 1975), p. 75.

82. Puṇyānanda appears to have had religious interests other than Śrīvidyā; his expertise extended beyond the narrow scope of the rather technical interests expressed in *KKV*. Like others within the *hādi* lineages, he exhibits a complete familiarity with Kashmiri Śaivism evidenced by his facility with its technical terminology. While the *hādimata/kādimata* distinction as far as contemporary practitioners are concerned is simply a mantra variation, for Kashmiri influenced sources, such as Puṇyānanda and Śivānanda, *hādi* and *kādi* represent two distinct preceptorial lines. Later writers, including Bhāskararāya, see no serious conflict between them.

83. They are included in Dwiveda's edition of the *NSA*, pp. 306–328.

84. The work of Śivānanda has been recently studied in depth by Madhu Khanna, as cited above.

85. See Silburn, *op. cit.*, p. 9f.

86. See Dwiveda's Sanskrit Introduction (*Upodghāta*) to the *NSA*, p. 28 and Khanna, as cited above.

While Maheśvara's *MAM* is not, strictly speaking, a Śrīvidyā work it has been profoundly influential on Śrīvidyā thinkers. It's most frequent citation is among contemporary practitioners who link Śrīvidyā to Kashmiri Śaiva views concerning the devolution of sound and the relationship of Śiva and Śakti as the creators of the universe. Potentially more important would be Maheśvara's commentary on the *Paramānanda Tantra* entitled *Saubhāgyānandasamdoha*, which has not been recovered and is known among contemporary southern practitioners only by name. From the title of this work, its connection to a Śrīkula Tantra, and because of Maheśvara's relationship to Śivānanda it is possible that the author was initiated into Śrīvidyā. As it is the case with many of the Kashmiris, including Jayaratha, Maheśvara was not preoccupied with Śrīvidyā in his writings. His own commitment to the tradition, however, if measured solely against his attention to other subjects may be misleading. If contemporary tradition reflects the historical situation then it is possible the author wrote on many subjects and may not have chosen to write on the subject of his personal commitment. One contemporary practitioner, for example, is a Śrīvidyā guru and yet has spent his entire career writing on other subjects, especially on Śaiva Siddhānta theology. It seems likely with Maheśvara, as with Jayaratha, that Śrīvidyā played a central but not an exclusive role in their religious lives. As Śaivas their acceptance and interpretation of Śrīvidyā principles affirms its significance in the broader spectrum of Kaula theology encompassing Śaiva and Śākta Tantric traditions.

87. *HTSL*, p. 148.

88. The text is presently being edited for publication by Dr. G. Sundaramoorthy of Madurai-Kamaraj University. For details concerning its contents as well as selections from the text in translation see *HTSL*, p. 152f.

We should reiterate, however, that Śrīnivāsa Bhaṭṭa is not the Vidyānanda who wrote the *Artharatnāvalī* on *NSA* nor is it clear that he is the author of the *Jñānadīpavimarśinī* simply because he bears the same initiated name as that text's author. Regarding the latter text a further study of the available manuscripts must be performed before reaching any conclusion.

89. *HTSL*, p. 151. If this is the case then it is very curious that his disciple took upon himself the task of composing another, more elaborate *paddhati* covering much the same material.

90. *HTSL*, p. 148 and p. 148, ftn.41. This date seems to be based on the assumption that the author of the *SRK* is identical to the author of the *Jñā-*

nadīpavimarśinī, which is quoted by Amṛtānanda in his *YHDīpikā*. Dr. Sundaramoorthy, who is presently editing the *SRK*, has not reached a satisfactory conclusion regarding Śrīnivāsa Bhaṭṭa's date.

91. Paraśurāma is mythologically connected to Kerala. See *Bhāgavatapurāṇa*, 9.15.16ff.

92. *HTSL*, p. 150; also see *NSA* edition, pp. 349–360.

93. *Tripurā Upaniṣadbhāṣya*, v. 15.

94. Both, for example, make use of a text known only by name, the so-called *Saṅketapaddhati*. It just so happens, however, that all of Rāmeśvara's citations appear in Bhāskararāya's works even when the latter does not acknowledge this work as the source.

95. *Nityotsava* by Umānandanātha, ed. A. M. Sastri (Baroda: M. S. University of Baroda Press, 1923, revised edition by Svami Trivikrama Tirtha, 1948). [Gaekwad's Oriental Series, no. 23]

96. This interpretation making Umānanda consistent with Bhāskararāya is plausible but not likely. How then do we explain this discrepancy considering the strong stand Bhāskararāya took on the issue? One possibility is that Bhāskararāya actually taught this tradition to Umānanda for the sake of continuity with the majority view. According to contemporary adepts, Bhāskararāya actually belonged to the so-called Ānandabhairava *sampradāya* which admits the *vṛttatraya* as the three outer circles but prescribes no *pūjā* for them. This seems contrary to Bhāskararāya's stated position (see *Tripurā Upaniṣadbhāṣya*, v. 4), which would suggest that he follows the Hayagrīva *sampradāya* and does not accept the presence of the outside three circles. Another possibility is that Rāmeśvara is actually correct, that is, that Bhāskararāya did not revise the *Nityotsava*. That Umānanda was not his disciple, however, goes against all traditions but is not out of the realm of possibilities. Further investigations into the situation with Bhāskararāya's familial descendants suggest that Umānanda was his actual disciple but that he may or may not have taught this concept to his trusted disciple.

97. Neither is he to be confused with the Jagannātha who composed religious poetry in Hindi though this is not an identification made in Śrīvidyā literature.

98. Printed in the edition: *Lalitāsahasranāmastrotra with the Saubhāgyabhāskara of Bhāskararāya*, ed. M. K. Sastri (Bombay: Nirnaya Sagara Press, 1921).

99. The *Bhāskaravilāsa* cites, for example, a commentary on the *PKS* attributed to Bhāskararāya entitled the *Ratnāloka*. It seems unlikely that this text ever existed except in name since it has gone completely unnoticed by Rāmeśvara (whose commentary on *PKS* is quite complete in respect to references), and is not known at all in contemporary traditions. Cf. S. Subrahmanya Sastri in his introduction to the *VVR*, pp. xxx–xxxiv.

100. *The Hṛdayāmṛta of Umānandanātha*, ed. A. Sastri (Hyderabad, A. P., India: Ānanda Trust, 1981).

101. Like Śivānanda and other major historical figures in Śrīvidyā, the details of Bhāskararāya's life are murky and deserve a more careful study. I am presently preparing a biography of Bhāskararāya.

102. See the introduction to the *VVR*, p. xxii.

103. The fate of this gifted property and the results of his long years of teaching will be the subject of a future study.

104. For a list editions of the *VVR* see *HTSL*, p. 170, ftn. 28. All references here refer to: *Varivasyārahasya and its commentary Prakāśa by Śrī Bhāskararāya Makhin*, ed. and trans. Pandit S. Subrahmanya Sastri (Adyar: The Adyar Library and Research Centre, first edition, 1934, fourth edition, 1976). All references are to the fourth edition.

105. In one case mentioned in the *Bhāskaravilāsa* it is noted that Bhāskararāya had a temple to his family deity, the goddess Candralāmbā, constructed in the form of a *śrīcakra*. In his renovation of the temple of Bhāskareśvara in Bhāskararājapuram, according to contemporary authorities, he established a *śrīcakra*. Śaṅkarācārya is credited with establishing a number of *śrīcakras* both for the first time and within already established temples such as famous shrine of Kāmākṣī in Kāñcipuram. While there may be some truth to the claims surrounding Bhāskararāya, if there was a Śaṅkarācārya involved in the latter cases we can be certain that it was not the so-called *ādiśaṅkara* of the eighth century. The possibility that it was *a* Śaṅkarācārya still exists since all the heads of the *maṭhas* of the Śāṅkara tradition bear this name as a title. The same can be said of the written sources attributed to Śaṅkara on Śrīvidyā and Śākta topics. How an ascetic has been credited with this involvement of establishing an icon within a temple is yet another issue.

106. A senior member of Guru Mandali, Madurai, April, 1985.

107. A senior female member of Gayatri Mandali, Madurai, November, 1984.

108. This is, in fact, the case. Within the living lineages of adepts in south India one finds only one or two individuals with enough training in Sanskrit to read original sources. The situation is further complicated by the inaccessibility of printed editions and the breakdown of the traditional system of passing manuscripts on within lineages.

109. For the details concerning the *Tripurārahasya* see *HTSL*, p. 166f. The well-known sage of Tiruvanamalai, the late Rāmana Mahārsi, for example, was so influenced by the *TR* that the authorities of his *Āśrāma* trust have seen fit to publish an English translation of the work. Rāmana, they maintain, was a Śrīvidyā worshiper (though there is no direct evidence in his sayings to confirm this) and following his personal instructions a *śrīcakra* was installed within the shrine dedicated to Devī on the *āśrāma* grounds.

110. This text is later incorporated into the *SST* as its fourth *khaṇḍa*, see *HTSL*, p. 68f.

111. Cf., *HTSL*, p. 23; *HT*, p. 43. Bharati has contended that *SST* has had a significant impact throughout India though he presents no evidence to support this claim; see Bharati, p. 75.

112. Naṭarāja of Guru Mandali, Madurai, April, 1985.

113. A senior member of the Guru Mandali, Madurai, March, 1985.

NOTES TO CHAPTER 4

1. Cf. *LSN*, n. 209. Here Lalitā receives the name *"mahādevī."*

2. Textual references to the names Lalitā and Tripurā first occur in the Purāṇas and may harken back to an ancient tradition. There is, however, no substantive historical evidence to support these traditional claims. The name "Tripura" as the city destroyed by śiva appears to be distinct from the goddess in her threefold aspects; connections between the two seem coincidental. It also appears clear that while Śrīvidyā adepts may not have created the concepts and values surrounding these images, they have significantly contributed to their popular imagery and understanding. There is no suggestion in any Śrīvidyā text that other images or aspects of the goddess provided a more central focus or fertile ground for theological speculation.

3. See D. C. Sircar, *The Śākta Pīṭhas* (New Delhi: Motilal Banarsidass, reprint, second edition), 1973, p. 13. References also occur in Śrīvidyā commentaries, cf., Bhāskararāya's remarks on *Tripurā Upaniṣad*, verse 6, (the unidentified quotation of *Padmapurāṇa*) with reference to the pilgrimage center of Prayāg as associated with Lalitā.

4. The reference to Lalitā in Tirumūlar's *Tirumantiram* confirms this view. See the previous section for details.

5. Other texts, such as the *Kāmakalāvilāsa* and the works of Śivananda and Vidyānanda, only serve to embellish these earlier sources which form the *locus classicus* for all subsequent descriptions and characterizations.

6. See Jan Gonda, *Medieval Religious Literature* (*A History of Indian Literature*, vol. II, fasc.1, ed. Jan Gonda, Wiesbaden: Otto Harrossowitz, 1975).

7. Cf. *LSN*, n. 910 is "Saumya," that is, "benign."

8. See Frederique Apffel Marglin, "Types of Oppositions in Hindu Culture," *Purity and Auspiciousness in Indian Society*, ed. John B. Carman and Frederique A. Marglin (Leiden-Koln: E. J. Brill, 1985), pp. 65–83. In particular see pp. 79–80. See also T. N. Madan, "Concerning the Categories *Śubha and Śuddha* in Hindu Culture, An Exploratory Essay," *Purity and Auspiciousness in Indian Society*, pp. 11–29. See p. 24.

Lalitā's auspiciousness is described as beginningless (*anādi*) and also as flowing (*pravāha*) from her inherent nature. Auspiciousness thus arises as part of the flux of events which form the goddess's manifestation as materiality (*prakṛti*) and creative power (*śakti*).

9. Note that *LSN* n. 190 is "Durgā."

10. Cf. *LSN*, n. 210. Here Lalitā is called "*Mahālakṣmī*."

11. Cf. *LSN*, n. 246, "Pārvatī."

12. Cf. Thomas B. Coburn's "Consort of None, *Śakti* of All: The Vision of the *Devī-māhātmya*," *The Divine Consort: Radha and the Goddesses of India*, ed. John Stratton Hawley and Donna B. Wulff (Berkeley: Berkeley Religious Studies Series, 3, 1982).

13. Cf. *LSN*, n. 761.

14. Lalitā appears in *LSN* as n. 1000 and "Mahātripurasundarī" as n. 234. See also n. 978, "Tripurāśrīvasamkari," or "The ruler of Tripurā"; and n. 997, "Śrīmadtripurasundarī," or "The auspicious Tripurasundarī."

15. Ibid., p. 81.

16. Ibid., p. 81.

17. *PKS*, 1.5, p. 26.

18. Nataraja of Guru Mandali, 1985.

19. Cf. *LSN*, n. 74. Here Lalitā is distinguished from Bālā since she "rejoices in the valor of Bālā, who was ready to slay the sons of Bhaṇḍa," *bhaṇḍaputravadhodyuktabālāvikramanandità*, whereas n. 965 calls her "Bālā," or "girl."

20. *arunāṃ karuṇātarangitakṣīṃ dhṛtapaśānkuśapuṣpabanacāpāṃ/ aṇimādhibhirāvṛtaṃ mayukhairahamityeva vibhāvaye bhāvānīṃ//* This verse appears in a number of oral sources but is also preserved in nearly every ritual handbook within Śrīvidyā, see "Aṇṇa's" *Mantravidānam* for one such reference.

See *LSN*, n. 1–52. This work's impact on both historical and contemporary Śrīvidyā traditions cannot be underestimated. It is the most widely read and easily available Śrīvidyā source in modern south India. Taken apart from Bhāskararāya's commentary, the *Saubhāgyabhāskara*, the *LSN* presents a wholly coherent picture of the beneficent goddess and her multifarious qualities and attributes. With Bhāskararāya's interpretation, it takes on new dimensions, interpreted with his characteristic depth and attention to esoteric detail. The anthropomorphic figure emerging from the description in names one to fifty-two in the *Lalitāsahasranāma* is the most familiar and complete image of Lalitā's *saubhāgya* aspect.

21. One might compare this description to Durgā's in the *Devī-Mahātmya*. See Thomas B. Coburn, *Encountering the Goddess A Translation of the Devī-Māhātmya and a Study of Its Interpretation* (Albany: State University of New York Press, 1991), p. 41f.

22. See Brown, cited above, p. 50, verse 7. Note also that *LSN*, n. 847 calls her, "talodarī," that is, "slender waisted."

23. Cf. *Brahmāṇḍa Purāṇa*, Part V, p. 1286.

24. Note that the goddess is identified with Sarasvatī at *LSN*, n. 704.

25. Cf. *LSN*, n. 947, *pañcapretamañcādhiśāyinī*, that is, "reclining on a couch formed of five corpses."

26. On the conundrum of the sovereign's authority see J. C. Heesterman, *The Inner Conflict of Tradition: Essays in Indian Ritual, Kingship, and, Society* (Chicago: The University of Chicago Press, 1985).

27. Bhāskararāya glosses this name by creating various lists of five sacrifices. He says, "According to the Śruti the five sacrifices are: Agnihotra, Darśapūrnamāsa, Cāturmāsya, Paśu and Soma. According to the Smrtis they are: Deva, Pitr, Brahman, Bhūta and Manusya *yajñas* [*sic*]. The Pāñcarātragamas give the five branches of worship, namely, Abhigamana (approaching the God), Upādāna (collecting materials for God's worship), Ijyā (worship), Svādhyāyā (repetition of the Veda, etc.) and Yoga (meditation). The Kaulāgama enumerates the five kind of worship: Kevala, Yamala, Misra, Carkrayuk, and Vīrasamgraha. The *Nitya Tr.* gives out five kinds of worship which accomplish all kinds of desires, namely, Madya, etc." See Sastry, pp. 360–61.

28. *LSN*, Sastry, p. 153.

29. On the concept of auspiciousness see Marglin, cited above. Note also that *LSN*, n. 911 calls the goddess "*sadāśivakutumbini*," that is, "the wife of Sadāśiva," which Bhāskararāya glosses as the deities Syāmalā, Śuddhavidyā, Aśvārūḍhā, etc. See Sastry, p. 345.

30. *LSN*, n. 820; see Sastry, p. 316.

31. Sastry, p. 118.

32. Cf. *Devībhāgavata* 7.33.21–41 and Kinsley, p. 135.

33. Though she is called "Viṣṇu's spouse" (n. 210) (and his sister, n. 280), Lalitā is ultimately called the source from which arose the ten forms of Viṣṇu (n. 80). Like Śiva, Lalitā is at once erotic and ascetic and capable of gentility and ferocity; defining the boundaries of the natural and social order, she is herself beyond all boundaries or restrictions.

34. In fact, it she who, according to Bhāskararāya, controls Śiva. On *LSN*, n. 120 he cites an unnamed Purāṇic (?) source that says, "O Śiva, though independent, you have become subservient [to the goddess] by devotion." *LSN* (skt.), p. 161. *svatantrāpi śivabhakti pāratantryatvamasnus iti vacanāt*. Cf. Sastry, p. 102.

35. See Kinsley, pp. 29–30 for a discussion of Lakṣmī in the Pāñcarātra.

36. Unlike Kālī, Lalitā need not be tamed after entering an ecstatic frenzy

of killing. She is a goddess always in control of herself and others; one who never needs to be controlled. It is this latter characteristic that is most indicative of her benign (*saumya*) nature.

37. For a detailed account of Durgā and the Devīmāhātmya see Coburn cited above.

38. Kinsley, pp. 101–102; Kinsley cites the original source for this observation as Pearl Ostroff, "The Demon-slaying Devī: A Study of Her Purāṇic Myths," M.A. thesis (McMaster University, 1978), pp. 56–57.

39. This entire account is drawn from the *Brahmāṇḍa Purāṇa*, Part IV, 11.15–30.107, pp. 1076–1223.

40. Cf. Ibid., p. 1077, footnote 2, which says, "Although Assamese claim Tejpur as ancient Śoṇītapura, the claim of Śoṇitapura on the bank of Kedār-Ganga or Mandākini about six miles from Usāmath in Kumaun appears more acceptable [*sic*]—De, p. 189."

41. By "demi-gods" is meant the celestial musicians, the *gandharvas*, and the *yakṣas*.

42. Ibid., p. 1127; see 21.35–37.

43. Ibid., p. 1130.

44. On the variety of myths on Gaṇeśa's origins see Courtright.

45. The account given here concludes at *Lalitopākhyāna* 30.56. On the creation of Gaṇeśa see Paul B. Courtright, *Gaṇeśa Lord of Obstacles, Lord of Beginnings* (New York and London: Oxford University Press, 1985).

46. See *LSN*, n. 64–82. It is said, for example, at *LSN*, n. 77 that "Śrī Gaṇeśvara was formed by her glances at Kāmeśvara," *kāmeśvaramukhalokakalpitaśrīgaṇeśvara*. Bhāskararāya quotes the correlative passage from *Lalitopākhyāna* but does not offer the further detail that Lalitā laughs as she glances and that Gaṇeśa emerges from her laugh. Bhāskararāya then offers an esoteric interpretation of this name by breaking apart the compound and dissociating its elements from the myth. See Sastry, p. 78 for details.

47. Kinsley, p. 19f.

48. Kinsley, p. 18.

49. Sastry, p. 63.

50. In contrast to *Nityāṣoḍaśkārṇava*, *Yoginīhṛdaya*, and the works of Śivānanda, Jayaratha, and the Kashmiri-influenced *hādimata*.

51. The most complete studies of this temple's priests have been done by C. J. Fuller. Consult the bibliography for extended references.

52. Sastry, p. 358.

53. Śrīvidyā adepts claim to be the only religious virtuosi who understand the relationship between the goddess's *sthūlarūpa* and the *śrīcakra*. The expanding textual corpus on Lalitā's *sthūlarūpa* gains importance not only because of its theological content but also for the perpetuation of social and religious prerogatives that are attached to those who control public goddess worship. Śrīvidyā texts thus become yet another mechanism by which predominantly high-caste community makes itself the arbiter of public and private theology and practice.

54. For a more detailed elaboration of these philosophical differences see also Mark S. G. Dyczkowski, *The Doctrine of Vibration: An Analysis of the Doctrines and Practices of Kashmir Śaivism* (Albany: State University of New York Press, 1987), pp. 45ff.

55. Generally speaking, Śrīvidyā followers treat Lalitā either as a *kula* or family *devata* or as an *iṣṭadevata* or individually chosen deity. Within a given family of initiates another deity serve as the *kuladevata* but in terms of Śrīvidyā the *kula* deity is Lalitā Tripurasundarī. In addition, while a practitioner may have a localized Śakti, such as Kāmākṣī, as his or her *iṣṭadevata*, this deity is identified with Lalitā Tripurasundarī usually as the focus of ritual offerings or by association with the *śrīcakra*.

56. Sastry, pp. 324–325.

57. *LSN*, I. 1, *Saubhāgyabhāskara*. Sastry, pp. 7–8.

58. *Śaktisamgamatantra*, 4.9.1ff.

59. *PKS*, 3.1, p. 87.

60. *PKS*, 3.1., p. 87.

61. *LSN*, n. 1000; Sastry, p. 373.

62. *LSN*, n. 1000; Sastry, pp. 373–374.

63. See *HT*, p. 66.

64. Sastry, p. 254.

65. *PKS*, 10.83, p. 306.

66. *LSN*, n. 626; Sastry, p. 254.

67. Sastry, p. 372.

68. Sastry, p. 372.

69. *LSN*, n. 234. Sastry, p. 129.

70. *NSA*, 1.12., p. 33; cf. *PS*, 9.2., p. 128, Avalon edition.

71. *LSN*, n. 84; Sastry, pp. 84–85.

72. See *Tripurā Upaniṣadbhāṣya*, v. 1.

73. *Tripurā Upaniṣadbhāṣya*, v. 1.

74. *Tripurā Upaniṣadbhāṣya*, v. 1.

75. Saṣtry, p. 254.

76. Sastry, p. 399 and p. 400.

Notes to Chapter 5

1. *Tripurātāpinī Upaniṣad*, v. 26, cf. Warrier translation, p. 8.

2. That is, when interpreted as a genitive *tatpuruṣa* compound. See *LSN*, n. 1 and Sastry, p. 39 for a discussion of the meanings of Śrī according to Bhāskararāya.

3. Cf. *KKV*, 19, *vidyāvedyātmakayoratyantābhedaṃ āmanty āryāḥ*; cf. Khanna, II.1, note #20.

4. Ibid., II.1; cf. *LSN*, n. 85–89; Sastry, pp. 86–87.

5. Originally appearing in *Oriens* 16 (1963):244–297, reprinted in J. Gonda, *Selected Studies*, Vol. IV (Leiden-Koln: E. J. Brill, 1975), pp. 248–301. Citation is of Woodroffe's remark on p. 252.

6. *LSN*, n. 786, cf. Sastry, p. 302. The source of this etymology may well be *Kulārṇava Tantra*, 17.14. See for an elaborate discussion of this etymology, Gonda, "The Indian Mantra," p. 252. I refer to this as a sacred or esoteric etymology because scholars such as Bhāsakararāya are fully aware that there are no grammatical grounds on which to base these derivations. Instead, they offer an esoteric interpretation of the verbal root and a meaning for the term that corresponds to their ideology.

7. Sastry, p. 16.

8. Bhāskararāya makes this point clear in his opening remarks on *Tripurā Upaniṣad* where he says, "But despite the real presence of the deities, believers wavering in faith due to the karma of previous births are qualified only for the rituals described in the initial section [of the Veda] and are not [qualified] for [contemplative] worship of the deities."

9. E. Valentine Daniel, *Fluid Signs, Being a Person the Tamil Way* (Berkeley: University of California Press, 1984), p. 11.

10. Ibid., p. 32.

11. Ibid., p. 31.

12. See Chapter 1, endnote 4.

13. See Gonda, "The Indian Mantra," p. 283.

14. See Bhāskararāya on *LSN*, n. 227–228, Sastry, p. 127.

15. Bhāskararāya's legendary biography in oral traditions relates many instances of his mastery of *mantraśāstra* and the establishment of his reputation through this type of knowledge.

16. Cf. Bhāskararāya on *LSN*, n. 228.

17. Agastya of Gāyatrī Mandali, Madras, January, 1985.

18. *Tripurātāpinī Upaniṣad* is included in A. G. Krishna Warrier's translation of Śākta Upaniṣads; see *The Śākta Upaniṣads*, trans. A. G. Krishna Warrier (Adyar, Madras: Adyar Library, 1967). The popular edition of the text is in: *The Śākta Upaniṣads*, ed. A. Mahadeva Sastri (Adyar, Madras: Adyar Library), 1950. A version including a previously unaccounted for commentary by Ramānanda the Samayin was discovered in the Adyar Library Mss. Collection. This, too, has been consulted. Regarding the twelve sages of Śrīvidyā, different texts provide different lists. Cf. the minor variations from the *LSN* version (in Bhāskararāya's commentary on n. 238) with that of *Jñānārṇava Tantra*.

19. Sastry, pp. 130–131.

20. Cf. *LSN*.

21. Cf. Jayaratha's remarks in Chapter 13 of his commentary on *Vāmakeśvarimata*.

22. See Khanna, p. 51 for a discussion of the Kashmiri evidence and support for Śivānanda's view that the Tripurā cult is of Kashmiri origin. The texts cited in this case, however, do not take into account the Tamil sources cited in Chapter 2.

23. An opinion expressed by Agastya of Gayatri Mandali among others.

24. See *YH*, 2.14, p. 95, Kaviraj, second edition.

25. *NS*, pp. 46–49.

26. Cf. Khanna, pp. 45–50. Khanna provides complete documentation of the Lopāmudrā *sampradāya* as it appears in a number of sources though she does not discuss the plausibility of the lists nor does she consider why such lists were created in the first place. The significant differences that appear in the lists suggest that they were created to meet an ideological expectation, namely, that one *should* be able to create an identifiable *paramparā* that traces one's tradition to its founder. This preoccupation of Tantrics is discussed further below.

27. *Śrīvidyāratnasūtra*, Introduction and verse 1.

28. *Śrīvidyāratnasūtra*, v. 4.

29. *LSN*, n. 6, Sastry p. 47.

30. *PKS*, p. 29 in the 1979 reprint edition.

31. *Yoginīhṛdayadīpikā*, 2.18.

32. Discussed below with reference to the presentation of the mantra in *Tripurā Upaniṣad*.

33. The tripartite mantra is another example of Śrīvidyā's penchant for triadic signs. Following the general Hindu pattern, to the three components is frequently added a fourth, comparable to the addition of *mokṣa* to the *puruṣārthas* or "the fourth" (*turīya*) to the waking, dreaming, and sleeping states. Each *kūṭa* of the mantra is associated with a corresponding element in these triads. Identical associations apply to the *hādividyā*'s configuration in three *kūṭas*.

See Rāmeśvara on *PKS*, *dvitīyapariśiṣṭha*, 4.; *Kulārṇava Tantra* also discusses the three kinds of *japa*, see *KT*, 15.54.

34. See *YH*, 1.36ff.

35. *VVR*, 1.20–21.

36. *YH*, 1.12.

37. *VVR*, 1.4., p. 6.

38. See *HT*, p. 93f.

39. *VVR*, 1.7. Here the reference is actually to the Vedic *gāyatrī*, which is implied to be the same as the *praṇava*. See Bhāskararāya's remarks to that effect cited below.

40. See Gonda, "The Indian Mantra," pp. 277–278.

41. Cf. *Māṇḍūkyopaniṣadkārikā*, 1.1ff.

42. *VVR*, 1.7, p. 7.

43. *VVR*, 2.60–61, pp. 37–39.

44. See Rāmeśvara on *PKS*, 1.31 and Lakṣmīdhara on *SL*, v. 32f.

45. A. L. Basham, *The Wonder That Was India* (New York: Grove Press, 1959), p. 162.

46. Bhāskararāya says as much in his commentary on *Tripurā Upaniṣad*, v. 8 where he says, "In the *Tripurātāpinī* [*Upaniṣad*] it has been clearly stated that the Gāyatrī [mantra] designates the original knowledge [or mantra, *ādividyā*]..."

47. *Tripurātāpinī Upaniṣad*, v. 7; see Warrier edition, p. 3.

48. *TTU*, v. 13, see Warrier edition, p. 4.

49. *TTU*, v. 15, see Warrier edition, p. 5.

50. For a concise and accurate explanation of the basic principles of *kuṇḍalinī yoga* see *HT*, pp. 163–180.

51. See *JT*, chapters 11 and 12.

52. In most contemporary lineages rituals repeated as obligations are not usually duplicated when both Vedic and Tantric versions exist. In the case of *dvija* caste initiates the Vedic version is retained and the Tantric parallel foregone since it is believed that the Vedic rite subsumes the Tantric. I have never encountered a situation in which the Tantric rite is retained and the Vedic version made optional. This is usually explained as the fulfillment of a *nityakarma* in which the Vedic rite or mantra has precedence due to its antiquity. The Tantric version is *nitya* only on non-*dvija* caste initiates.

53. See Gonda, "The Indian Mantra," the first example is cited on p. 263, the second on pp. 292–293.

54. Cf. examples cited in Gonda, "The Indian Mantra," p. 279, ftn. 3, especially his remarks regarding Kanada who gives a systematic exposition of Vaiśeṣika interpretations and says that muttering mantras is necessary for gaining the objects of desire.

55. Gonda, "The Indian Mantra," p. 279.

56. See Staal's remarks in *Understanding Mantras*, ed. Harvey P. Alper (Albany: State University of New York Press, 1989).

57. Adept of the Guru Mandali, Madurai, April, 1985.

58. See *PKS*, *dīkṣāvidhi*, for details.

59. See *The Secret of the Three Cities* for the details of this argument.

60. Bhāskararāya refers to this verse at many points in his works, cf. *VVR*, 1.7; see also K. R. Venkataraman's remarks in "Śakti Cult in South India," The Cultural History of India, Vol. IV, ed. by a board of editors of the Ramakrishna Institute (Calcutta: Ramakrishna Mission, reprint, 1983), pp. 252–259.

61. *VVR*, 1.7.

62. Cf. Venkataraman, cited above, p. 257, ftn. 7.

63. Cf. Naṭānandanātha's *Cidvallī* on *KKV* cited in Venkataraman, p. 257, ftn. 7. On *kāmakalā* see *HT*, p. 145f.

64. Both *hādi* and *kādimatas* agree that the *śrīvidyā* is secretly present in *Ṛg Veda* 5.47.4 and that it is the esoteric manifestation of *Ṛg Veda* 3.62.10, that is, the *gāyatrī* mantra.

65. *PKS*, 1.30, p. 42.

66. *PKS*, 1.30, p. 42.

67. This matter will receive extensive treatment in volume two of the present work in the discussion of the mantra's use and interpretation among contemporary adepts.

Southern culture and the predominant brahman influence on Śrīvidyā suggest that the tradition's regional character has been shaped in ways that more readily conform to the expectations of upper and middle class, conservative brahmanism. Thus, there is a tendency in south India to deemphasize those comparisons that cast the Vedic tradition in a negative or inferior light. Rather, the tendency is to see *śrīvidyā* as the fulfillment of Vedic expectations. In certain striking instances, however, important southern figures, such as Bhāskararāya, deviate from these conservative patterns and still retain their popularity among contemporary conservative interpreters.

68. According to this symbolic pattern, *k* = *krodhiṣa* = *śiva* = *śrīkantha* = *a*, the first letter of Sanskrit and, *ī* = *lakṣmī*, etc., see *VVR*, 1.9–11 for one full set of these identifications.

69. See *HT*, p. 65 for a list of the *daśamahāvidyās*.

70. *VVR*, 1.12–13.

71. See *VVR*, 1.36 for the first example and 1.38 for the second.

72. *VVR*, 1.37 for the first example and 1.39 for the second.

73. *VVR*, 2.54–55.

74. *VVR*, 2.67–68, 2.73, pp. 55–56. This explanation in *VVR* follows the outline of the six *artha*s given in *YH*, 2.24ff.

75. *VVR*, 2.74–80, pp. 60–64.

76. *VVR*, 2.81.

77. *VVR*, 2.82–83.

78. *VVR*, 2.85, p. 77.

79. *VVR*, 2.102, p. 90.

80. *VVR*, 2.109.

81. Cf. *VVR*, 2.133; the chart is based on *VVR*, 2.121–126 and 2.128–130.

82. For other examples of these types of gāyatrīs and a brief explanation of them see HT, p. 123f.

83. See *PKS*, 3.5 and Rāmeśvara's remarks.

84. Such extensions or emendations of the *śrīvidyā* in contemporary tradition will be studied at length in volume two.

85. See Bhāskararāya on *Tripurā Upaniṣad*, verse 8.

86. *Tripurā Upaniṣad*, v. 8f; see the full translation below.

87. Bhāskararāya on *Tripurā Upaniṣad*, v. 9.

88. Bhāskararāya on *Tripurā Upaniṣad*, v. 9. For the remark on the superiority of *kādi* see the *Setubandha*, 1.8. Here Bhāskararāya says that of mantras *śrīvidyā* is supreme and among the versions of the *śrīvidyā*, the *kādi* is supreme. Thus, *hādi* is rejected as equal in the explanation offered in *NSA*, a *kādimata* text as Bhāskararāya asserts.

89. Only in Kashmiri sources committed to *hādimata*, and especially in Śivānanda's work, are the disagreements based on perceived differences between the *matas* deemed significant. This is perhaps the consequence of a more clearly articulated sense of location within Kashmiri Śaiva and Śākta Tantrism and the presence of other traditions in Kashmir that are strikingly similar to and different from Śrīvidyā on key issues. It may also be partly attributed to the *kādi* followers well-understood sense of being in the minority within Śrīvidyā. In any case, later south Indian writers such as Bhāskararāya and Rāmeśvara Sūri rarely point to differences between mantras or *matas* as significant matters of dispute or discussion.

90. This would appear to offer further support for the belief that *kādi* was the first form of the mantra and that *hādi*, though it is historically attested and attracted several influential interpreters, is a derivative.

91. Bhāskararāya explains the act of substitution in his commentary, that is, the way the words six, seven and *vahni* are interpreted to mean the syllables *ha*, *sa*, and *ka*.

92. See *SL*, v. 12ff.

93. In fact, there is no indication in any of the historical *kādimata paddhatis* that Śrīvidyā rituals could be performed by merely substituting of *hādi* for *kādi* each time the mantra is named. The *paddhatis* do not seem to make room for such an interpretation and the only place where *hādi* appears to be used in place of *kādi* is in the *japa*.

94. Puṇyānanda does explicitly make clear his commitment to the use of *hādi* in *KKV*, v. 18.

95. This remark initially made by Agastya of the Gāyatrī Mandali was later independently confirmed by at least four other adepts. How they make this determination is not clear.

96. See *Setubandha* on *YH*, 2.14.

97. *Saubhāgyabhāskara* on *LSN*, n. 25, Sastry, p. 51.

98. Cf. *LSN*, n. 391, n. 587.

99. The *nityas* are identified with the moon's phases and are placed on the innermost *trikoṇa* of the *śrīcakra* during ritual worship.

100. Bhāskararāya on *LSN*, n. 88 says (under *mūlamantrātmika*), "*Mūla*, root, this is the fifteen syllable mantra, *pañcadaśī....*" See Sastry, p. 86.

101. Bhāskararāya notes on *LSN*, n. 3 that in some cases the addition of *śrīṃ* comprises the sixteenth letter of the *ṣoḍaśī* and that the *śrīvidyā* has both fifteen and sixteen syllable configurations (see *LSN*, n. 7).

102. *VVR*, 2.163.

103. A very similar sentiment is expressed, for example, in *PKS* 1.30, (pp. 42–43) in which the importance of giving *dīkṣā* to only intelligent disciples is emphasized.

104. Kaivalyāśrama quoting the *RY* on *SL*, v. 8., p. 94.

105. Cf. *PKS*, *prathama khaṇḍa*, which, along with Rāmeśvara's commentary, explains in detail the requirements for guru and disciple.

106. See Ramānanda on *Tripurā Upaniṣad*, introduction, p. 4f.

107. *Ṛjuvimarśinī* on *NSA*, 1.8.

108. In this sense the notion of the efficacy of the ritual and the use of the mantra is not unlike the general concept of Vedic tradition in the period of the *Brāhmaṇas*. Tantrism seems to be harkening back, as it were, to a time when ritual and mantric powers were in a direct causal relationship to effects in the natural and social worlds. According to this world view, doing the correct ritual and following the prescriptions to the letter provided a guaranteed outcome. Dissatisfaction with this rather mechanical correspondence of natural and social forces with supernatural and ritual counterparts is, at least to some measure, responsible for the emergence of the later speculative views recorded in the early Upaniṣads and by other non-Vedic oriented traditions.

109. On the acquisition of mundane and supernormal abilities see *PKS*, 1.13 that mentions the *siddhi* of *anja*, that is, to bless and punish others, and Rāmeśvara on *PKS*, 1.9 (p. 28) where he says that all *siddhi*s come as the result of this mantra, and that even though there is only one cause, the mantra, it is capable of producing many effects.

110. It should be noted that the *siddhi*s beginning with *aṇima*, the power to become infinitesimally small, are the first the *upāsaka* gains. The design of the *śrīcakra* supports this idea by identifying these *siddhi*s on it outermost gates, another indication of their relative inferiority in the ritual process. The accomplishment of these spiritual and material powers has always been a subject of great debate within Śrīvidyā tradition. While their literal acquisition is not questioned, their importance in accomplishing the "higher" aim of liberation is continuously debated. Many adepts maintain that there should be no overt use of any acquired power since this distracts the adept and "drains" his spiritual "account"; others argue that the use of *siddhi* is a natural extension of *sādhana* and convinces the skeptical of the power of the *vidyā*.

111. See p. 200 of Kaviraj's second edition.

112. All *paramparās* list their own gurus in succession and attempt to trace themselves back to one of Śrīvidyā's twelve sages, particularly Kāmeśvara and Lopāmudrā. Curiously, some while practicing only the Kāmeśvara lineage form of the mantra, still maintain that their lineage descends from one of the other gurus. Rāmeśvara commenting on *PKS*, 1.9 defines *sampradāya* (see p. 27) and says that one gains all *siddhis* only through tradition and confidence (or faith, *viśvāsa*) in contemplative practice. He also notes that the mantra is capable of influencing any natural phenomena or social situation; in essence, he maintains that an initiate experienced in the use of the *śrīvidyā* can do anything.

113. See Rāmeśvara on *PKS*, 1.1., p. 14.

114. See also Rāmeśvara on *PKS*, 1.15–19, pp. 30–33. One observes here a remarkable similarity to the so-called *catuṣṭhaya sādhana* of Śaṅkara, a point that is not lost on contemporary adepts with links to the Śāṅkara tradition. For a discussion of *dīkṣā* see *HT*, pp.71–89.

115. See Rāmeśvara's remarks on *PKS*, 1.20 (p. 35) where he disagrees with this policy and suggests that when a teacher deviates from tradition it is the student's responsibility to tell the guru. The disciple must continuously question a guru's adherence to tradition and with the permission of the teacher the student can even correct and revise the guru's instruction. This notion is actually foreign to the majority of traditionalists who, by revering their teachers as Śiva, cannot imagine that this incarnate deity could err.

116. Rāmeśvara on PKS, 2.1. says that without *dīkṣā* one is not entitled to do *śrīvidyā upāsana*. The great mantra or *mahāvidyā*, he says, is either the *pañcadaśī* or *ṣoḍaśī* and Rāmeśvara appears to express no preference. *PKS* discusses the mantra only in terms of *kādi* and *hādi* and not as *pañcadaśī* or *ṣoḍaśī*—the *pañcadaśī* is obviously the form assumed for ritual prescriptions. Rāmeśvara also offers the meaning of *mahāvidyā* as Lalitā, but either interpretation secures it the preeminent place, in his view, in the mantric hierarchy.

117. The accomplishment of measurable power is considered a result of grace, a gift of the guru and goddess that takes place when the student fulfills his or her vows with sincerity. Thus, the tests by which one acknowledges a "proper" initiation or considers an adept's accomplishments are designed to prevent the merely curious or the overly attentive seeker. In another volume, I will investigate specific cases of initiation addressing the general notion of qualification (*adhikāra*) and more especially how Śrīvidyā interprets Tantric values that allow non-twice born persons of both genders to participate in the sect.

118. See the *dīkṣāvidhi* of the *PKS* for details.

119. For an elaboration on these purificatory rites see the Van Hoens section in *HT* as well as Gupta on *pūjā*.

120. See Rāmeśvara on *PKS*, 2.1. where he says here that Ganapati fulfills this common role of remover of obstacles. The mantra of Gaṇapati, unlike the *śrīvidyā*, has a semantic meaning. It reads: *oṃ śrīṃ hrīṃ glīṃ glauṃ gaṃ gaṇapataye varavarada sarvajannan me vasamānaya svāhā.*

121. See the *NS*, p. 10.

122. The so-called *Khadyota*, long out of print, was first published in 1889 by Nirnaya Sagar Press, Bombay.

123. Cf. *PKS*.

124. It should be noted that living traditions in south India have almost entirely forsaken initiation into the Bālātripurasundarī mantra. The use of the Bālātripurasundarī mantra receives only a cursory mention in most ritual handbooks and has drawn little attention from adepts either with respect to its esoteric meaning or its role in Śrīvidyā's spiritual discipline. In fact the Bālā mantra is mentioned only in *PKS* and *NS* while other earlier handbooks, including the *Saubhāgyaratnākara*, omit it completely. It is possible that the mantra is a late historical development, part of a larger effort to elaborate and complete the theoretical aspects of Śrīvidyā *sādhana*.

125. The usual *dhyānaśloka* of Bālātripurasundarī reads: *aruṇakirana-jālairancitāsābakāśa vidhṛta japapatīka-pustakābhītahastā/ itarakaravarādhyā phuh-lakahlarasansthā nivasatu hṛdi bālā nityakalyānasīlā//* It translates: "Let the Youthful One dwell in the heart, She whose virtue is always true, who is established in the sounds of expansion, who bears in her hands the fearless scripture, and recites [the mantra of the goddess]; she who maintains the appearance of a fawn, who is arrayed in a net of red beaming splendor."

126. Gaṇapati's subordinate but necessary role is seen in the construction of the mantra itself: as a request for certain spiritual empowerment combined with seed-syllables (*bījākṣaras*) it has a definite "ordinary language" element that the *śrīvidyā* has transcended by favoring only seed-syllables. Gaṇapati's mantra is recited before any other form of contemplative worship commences. Though of minor importance in the interpretation of Śrīvidyā tradition as a whole, Gaṇapati has the same distinctive role in Śrīvidyā ritual that he has in other Hindu ritual contexts. As Lord of Beginnings and the Remover of Obstacles, Gaṇapati is a significant ritual figure in all types and at all levels of Śrīvidyā worship.

Yet another fifteen syllable mantra is associated with Lalitā Mahātripurasundarī though it is not a part of the twelve *vidyās* and Śrīvidyā teachers. The so-called *vidyā* of prosperity or *saubhāgyavidyā* is not frequently found in current handbooks (*paddhati*) but is noteworthy for the term *saubhāgya*, "prosperous," the attribute most commonly associated with Lalitā. Śrīvidyā is sometimes referred to as the tradition (*sampradāya*) of prosperity (*saubhāgya*) but more properly, the tradition which focuses on the *saubhāgya* goddess. The structure of the *saubhāgyavidyā* is in four units (*kūṭas*) and includes the seven seed-syllables appended to the *kādividyā* in ritual formulations of *śrīcakra pūjā*:

1. *oṃ aiṃ hrīṃ śrīṃ*
2. *aiṃ ka e ī la hrīṃ*
3. *klīṃ ha sa ka ha la hrīṃ*
4. *sauḥ sa ka la hrīṃ*

(See the handbook bearing the title *Mantravidānam*, ed. Aṇṇā (Madras: Ramakrishna Matha, 1981, p. 83) In Sanskrit and Tamil. The mantra and *dhyānaśloka* appear here in a slightly different form than those private manuscripts I have seen in Madras.)

The seven additional seed-syllables or, more frequently, the four of the first *kūta* are themselves appended as a single unit to numerous ritual mantras and invocations as introductory elements. Thus, in the *śrīcakra pūjā* during the identification of sounds with parts of body (i.e., *nyāsa*) either the complete set of seven or the abbreviated four syllables are repeated before each line. It is common in ritual handbooks to see the number seven written before *nyāsa* mantras. This indicates that the seven *bījākṣaras* should be recited before the mantra. For example, in the case of the "identification of the mothers" or *matṛkanyāsa* the handbooks print: 7 *aṃ kaṃ khaṃ gaṃ ghaṃ nan aṃ anguṣṭhāyāṃ namaḥ*; or, the four as in the "identification for the purification of the hands" or *karaśuddhinyāsa*: 4 *aṃ namaḥ*. (See "Aṇṇā's" *paddhati*, p. 18 for the details of *matrkanyāsa* and p. 22 for the *karaśuddhinyāsa*. Both rituals are portions of the *śrīcakra pūjā* in which parts of the body are identified with letters of the Sanskrit alphabet which are, in turn, identified with parts of the *śrīcakra*.) These sets of *bījākṣaras*, while not associated with a form of the *śrīvidyā mūlamantra*, are essential elements of the esoteric mantra system incorporated into the larger ritual tradition. The seven seed-syllables are associated with conferring prosperity and with making auspicious other sets of mantras. This would explain why they are appended to the *pañcadaśākṣarī* in ritual contexts but omitted during *japa* and how this unusual variation on the fifteen syllable mantra is generated. Contemporary lineages differ on the question of the appropriateness of these appendages to the *nyāsa* mantras.

Another form of the *śrīvidyā* that appears to be a later development is the so-called *sādi* form. In this configuration the mantra begins with the syllable *sa*, that is, the *śaktikūṭa* replaces the *vāgbhavakūṭa*. Since it is mentioned in the *TT* the *sādi* was known from a relatively early period but does not appear as one of the forms in the tradition of twelve sages. While the *Bahvṛcha Upaniṣad* also mentions this form there is no historical evidence that the *sādividyā* was anything more than a theoretical formulation designed to complement the *kādi* and *hādi* schemes. Without ritual handbooks devoted to its description or practice, or historical figures claiming allegiance to it, there is no indication that *sādi* was made part of any instantiated tradition.

127. Cf. *HT*, p. 104.

128. Unlike conventional speech which falls into the *vaikharī*, or mundane category, Śāktas consider mantras an articulation at the *madhyamā* level.

129. This point is made by Rāmeśvara on *PKS*, 1.9, p. 28. He here notes again the efficacy of the mantra to produce tangible results.

Notes to Chapter 6

1. *YH*, 1.9cd–10ab.

2. *HTSL*, p. 58.

3. *YH*, 1.6 says, "The symbolism of the cakra, similarly the symbolism of the mantra and the *pūjā*, are the threefold symbols of the divine Tripurā." *cakrasaṅketako mantrapūjāsaṅketakau tathā/ trividhastripurādevyāḥ sanketaḥ parāmeśvarī//*. See Kaviraj, *YH*, third edition, p. 12.

4. The nine gates are the mouth, nostrils, ears, eyes, sexual, and evacuative organs. See *Bhāvana Upaniṣad* for details.

5. See the brief remarks of T. A. Gopinath Rao on the date of the *śrīcakra* as an image in: T. A. Gopinath Rao, *Element of Hindu Iconography* (Madras: Govt. Press, 1914, reprinted, Delhi: Motilal Banarsidass, 1985), in two volumes, p. 22f. See my "Auspicious Fragments and Uncertain Wisdom: The Origins of Śrīvidyā Śākta Tantrism in south India" in *The Roots of Tantra*, ed. Katherine Harper, et al.

6. It should be noted that the actual drawing of the *śrīcakra* or its being made into two or three dimensional physical objects is considered a rather mechanical process. This is not to suggest that its construction is not considered an art or that the artisans are not highly skilled. One contemporary adept even maintained that its drawing should be left to those belonging to the *viśvakarman* caste of carpenters and artisans. But like the actual casting of bronze in the West, the casting or drawing of the *śrīcakra* is not on a par with its original composition. In this case, the *śrīcakra* is not mere art but the original configuration of the universe, that is, the deity's actual shape as it becomes manifest from its original amorphous being. The numerous descriptions of drawing the *śrīcakra* following either the *sṛṣṭikrama* or the *samhārakrama*, that is, from inside out and vice versa, are primarily for its temporary ritual use. When an adept does not keep a permanent image in which the deity's presence is invoked (either permanently or temporarily) then it is necessary to draw the *śrīcakra* before its ritual worship. In some of the Samaya schools the actual, physical cakra is altogether dispensed with but this is strictly a minority position. For those drawing the *śrīcakra* anew each time for ritual purposes there are prescriptions for insuring its purity and other conditions for ritual appropriateness in addition to the actual prescriptions for its composition. There is, as it were, a separate ritual formula for the drawing of the cakra. But this is merely directed towards the worship that is to follow: to draw the *śrīcakra* is held to be a skill rather than a ritual act, strictly speaking. The cakra's sacredness lies in its ritual interidentification with the universe and the body.

7. Cf. Lakṣmīdhara on *Saundaryalaharī*, 11 where he quotes *Taittirīya Āraṇyaka*, 1.31 as referring to the four outer gateways of the *bhūpura* cakra.

8. Stella Kramrisch, *The Hindu Temple* (Calcutta: University Press, 1946;

reprinted in two volumes, Delhi: Motilal Banarsidass, 1981) See Vol.I, p. 11 of the reprint edition.

9. For example, the *maṭha* of the Śāṅkara tradition in Śṛṅgeri is said to be based on the *śrīcakra*.

10. The distinction of sacred and profane here is determined not on the basis of ontology but on a purely sociological analysis. Durkheim is the source of this distinction, see Emile Durkheim, *The Elementary Forms of the Religious Life*, trans. Joseph Ward Swain (New York: The Free Press, paperback edition, 1965), 52f.

11. Durkheim, p. 53.

12. Durkheim, p. 43.

13. Durkheim, p. 55.

14. Durkheim also enables us to consider the *śrīcakra* as a sacred object that exists within a religious system of beliefs and rites:

> But the real characteristic of religious phenomena is that they always suppose a bipartite division of the whole universe, known and knowable, into two classes which embrace all that exists, but which radically exclude each other. Sacred things are those which the interdictions protect and isolate; profane things, those to which these interdictions are applied and which must remain at a distance from the first. Religious beliefs are the representations which they sustain, either with each other or with profane things. Finally, rites are the rules of conduct which prescribe how a man should comport himself in the presence of these sacred objects. See Durkheim, p. 56.

I realize that Durkheim's analysis can prove problematic in the case of Hinduism, especially because of his qualitative distinction between sacred and profane. I think if we keep in mind that this distinction is applied to types of behavior, his analysis becomes germane.

15. See Śivānanda in his *Ṛjuvimarśinī* on *NSA*, 1.43.

16. *KKV*, v. 21.

17. *Artharatnāvali* on *NS*, 1.43.

18. Citation from the *Śrīcakraraṇādīpikā*, *Śrīvidyāsāparyapaddhat*, (Madras: Śrī Chidānanda Mandali, 1984), Frontispiece. The text reads: *bindutrikoṇavasukoṇadaśārayugma manvaśranāgadalasanyutaṣoḍaśāram/ vṛttatrayam ca dhāranisadānatrayaṃ ca śrīcakraṃ etaduditam parādevatāyaḥ//*

19. Though these sets of minor triangles are traditionally also called cakras, in the present context these sets of minor triangles are called "subcakras" since they function as minor units of the *śrīcakra*.

20. See S. Shankaranarayanan, *Śrīcakra* (Madras: Dipti Publications, 1970, third edition, 1981), p. 44 for this quotation of the text. Printed editions do not seem to include the verse.

21. Cf. *Śrīcakra, op. cit.*, p. 44.

22. *YH*, 1.7.

23. See *Śrīcakra*, p. 45, ftn.2, no citation is given as to the original source. The text reads: *tvagśṛṅmamsamedo'sthidhatavaḥ śaktimūlakaḥ / majjaśukla-prāṇajīvadhavaḥ śivamūlakaḥ //*

24. *Subhagodayavāsanā*, v. 9.

25. *Setubandha*, on *YH*, 1.10.

26. Śāktas accept *pariṇāmavāda*, according to Bhāskararāya, the doctrine that creation is a process of genuine transformation. They do not hold that the universe only appears to change but remains uncreated (*ajātivāda*) or that the transformation is mere illusion based on false perception (*vivartavāda*). In this way they differ significantly in their nondualistic (*advaita*) philosophy from Śaṅkara and the Śāṅkara schools which maintain various forms of *ajāti-* and *vivartavādas*.

The image of the spider and its web is commonly used in Śākta theology as an example drawn from the Upaniṣadic explanation. Cf. *Chandogya Upaniṣad*.

27. Cf. *SL*, v. 1.

28. *KKV*, v. 22.

29. Agastya of Ānanda Mandali, January, 1985.

30. *KKV*, vs. 37–38.

31. *YHdīpikā*, 1.10 and 1.14.

32. *Tripurā Upaniṣadbhāṣya*, v. 2.

33. Cf. *Setubandha* on *YH*, 1.10 where Bhāskararāya remarks that the *bindu* is Brahman which manifests as the central *trikoṇa*. This, he says, is not merely his own opinion but is upheld by earlier commentators.

34. Bhāskararāya says in the *Setubandha*, on *YH* 1.14: *akāra paramaśivaḥ tasya śrī ī puṇyogalakṣane nip tayoḥ samyogene ekāranispattih//*

35. Bhāskararāya glosses the term *vaikharī* as, *vi* meaning much and *khara*, hard, that is, speech in its physical form. Cf. *Saubhāgyabhāskara* on *LSN*, n. 371. Sastry, p. 190.

36. *Saubhāgyabhāskara* on *LSN*, n. 56. Sastry, p. 60. Bhāskararāya passes over the mention of only twenty-five *tattvas* or categories of reality (the number in the Yoga system) as mentioned in the quotation here from *Rudrayāmala*

(?). Sāktism accepts thirty-six *tattvas*, a point that is without controversy along sectarian lines. In the *Tripurā Upaniṣadbhāṣya*, v.1, Bhāskararāya clearly states, "...the *mātṛkā* letters...number only forty-eight."

37. Cf. *YH*, 1.79–85 which lists all the names for the nine sub-cakras.

38. *YH*, 1. 79–85ff.

39. *Saubhāgyabhāskara* on *LSN*, n. 73. Sastry, p. 76.

40. *Saubhāgyabhāskara* on *LSN*, n. 256. Sastry, p. 138.

41. *Saubhāgyabhāskara* on *LSN*, n. 391 which reads *nityāṣoḍaśīkarūpa*, that is, in "the form of the sixteen *nityās*." Cf. Sastry, p. 195. The sixteen *nityās* are the main subject of speculation and worship in the *Tantrarāja Tantra* and continue to play a prominent role in Śrīvidyā worship. Their names, here taken as deities of the *śrīcakra*, are well-known to all Śāktas: Kāmeśvarī, Bhagamālinī, Nityāklinnā, Bherundā, Vahnivāsinī, Mahāvajreśvarī, Śivadūtī, Tvaritā, Kulasundarī, Nityā, Nilapātakinī, Vijayā, Sarvamangalā, Jvalamālinī, Citrā and (Mahā) Tripurasundarī.

42. There is some dispute among Śrīvidyā adepts as the to actual number of consonants in the Sanskrit alphabet. Bhāskararāya outlines the problem in the *Tripurā Upaniṣadbhāṣya* where he takes the less popular view that the consonants number only forty-eight rather than fifty-two. See his remarks on v. 1.

43. *Saubhāgyabhāskara* on *LSN*, n. 577 which reads *mātṛkāvarnarūpiṇī*, that is, "of the form of the *mātṛkā* letters." Cf. Sastry, pp. 239–240. Bhāskararāya seems untroubled by his own inconsistency as to precisely how many *mātṛkās* make up the Sanskrit alphabet. Here in his early work he appears to accept fifty-one while in the later *Tripurā Upaniṣadbhāṣya* he argues for forty-eight by excluding *kṣa* and *jñā* as compounds and the Vedic retroflex *ḷ* as identical to *l*.

44. Cf. Bhāskararāya's comments on *Tripurā Upaniṣad*.

45. As noted by Bhāskararāya in the *Tripurā Upaniṣadbhāṣya*, v. 2 where he says, "...the nine *Yoni*s whose nature are the latent mental impressions (*samskarātmana*); some of these [latent impressions] already exist, others are still potential. These are called [in v. 2] the nine cakras (*navacakrāni*) or the agents [of creation]..."

46. *Tripurā Upaniṣadbhāṣya*, v. 2.

47. *Tripurā Upaniṣadbhāṣya*, v. 1.

48. Note here that Dirk Jan Hoens remark that the third sub-cakra is the *sarvarakṣākara* is incorrect. He has interchanged the name of this sub-cakra with the following sub-cakra of ten triangles. See *HT*, pp. 114–115.

49. A member of Gayatri Mandali, Madurai, December, 1984.

50. *Tripurā Upaniṣadbhāṣya*, v. 2.

51. *YH,* 1.79–85.

52. *Tripurā Upaniṣadbhāṣya,* v. 3. The quotation resembles *Yoginīhṛdaya,* 1.16 but is not identical.

53. This series of identifications of *yoginīs* and Sanskrit sounds does not correspond to the identification made in the Śrīvidyā ritual manuals at the point of this sub-cakra in the *śrīcakra pūjā*. In the ritual handbooks the outer set of ten triangles begins at the retroflex *ṇa* and finishes at the aspirated *bha;* the inner set begins at the next consonant in the usual order, that is, *ma* and finishes at *kṣa* which follows the ordinarily last letter of Sanskrit, *ha.*

54. *YHdīpikā* on 1.73–78.

55. See *HT,* p. 115.

56. *Tripurā Upaniṣadbhāṣya,* v. 3.

57. The senses of action, the *karmendriyas,* are the physical organs; the senses of knowledge, *jñānendriyas,* are the corresponding faculties. The four aspects of the mind are subsumed under the general term, *antaḥkaraṇa,* and refer to it plus the distinctive qualities of the *manas* or mind, the *buddhi* or capacity of judgment and the *citta* or intellectual ability.

58. Frits Staal, "The Meaninglessness of Ritual," in *Numen,* Vol. XXVI, fasc.1, pp. 2–22.

59. A member of Gayatri Mandali, Madras, January, 1985.

60. A member of the Gayatri Mandali, Madurai, January, 1985.

61. Cf. *NSA,* chapter 2 which describes the supernatural powers associated with the worship of the *śrīcakra.*

62. The translation of the *yoginī*'s names follows the oral interpretation of their meanings by contemporary south Indian Śrīvidyā adepts. It is, as it were, a composite of these interpretations which concentrated on the acquisition of such abilities.

63. Nārada of Ananda Mandali, Madras, January, 1985.

. In addition to the *pūjāpaddhatis* this is affirmed in the *KKV,* v. 33. Textual references to the *nityādevatās* abound in Śākta Tantric literature, cf. *Śaktisaṃgama Tantra,* 3.12.36ff; *NSA,* 1.25ff; and, of course, the most extensive treatment in *Tantrarāja Tantra,* Chapter 3ff.

65. Naṭarāja of Guru Mandali, Madurai, November, 1984.

66. *Saubhāgyasudhodaya,* 3.8.

67. *Subhāgodayavāsanā,* v. 11.

68. *Saubhāgyasudhodaya,* 3.9.

69. One such published *paddhati*, now long out of print, attests to this oral tradition. Cf. *Śrīviydaratnākāraḥ of Swamishriharihara̅nandaśāraswati (Shrikarapatraswami) Maharaj*, ed. Shrisitaramkaviraj (Bhaktisudha Sahitya Parishad: Calcutta, 1951).

70. Purohita of Siddha Mandali, Madras, December, 1984.

71. *Tripurā Upaniṣadbhāṣya*, v. 4.

72. Bhāskararāya argues this point not only in the *Tripurā Upaniṣadbhāṣya* but in the *Setubandha* on *YH*, 1.52–56.

73. The *śrīcakra* to which I refer was shown to me by the now late Ramacandra Dīkṣītar who claimed to possess Bhāskararāya's *śrīcakra*, a *sphaṭaka* or crystalline *kalilāsa prastāra* cakra.

74. Rāmeśvara on *PKS*, 3.9.

75. One such *śrīcakra* is seen inscribed on the wall beside the sub-shrine dedicated to Śaṅkara inside the Naṭarāja temple complex at Cidambaram.

76. Jyotiṣa of Samaya Mandali, Madras, January, 1985.

77. Naṭarāja of Guru Mandali, Madurai, November, 1984.

78. *YH*, 1.24.

79. Rāmeśvara on *PKS*, 3.9.

80. See Rāmeśvara on *PKS*, 3.9f.

81. On *SL*, v. 11ff.

82. *Saubhāgyasudhodaya*, 3.10.

83. *Artharatnāvali* on the *Nityāṣoḍaśikārṇava*, 1.32ff.

84. Ritual worship proceeds, as we have noted, according to the *samhārakrama* from the outermost sub-cakras towards the center thus the lowest level of spiritual achievement corresponds to the outermost portions of the *śrīcakra*.

85. The *āmnāyas* names are technical though their literal sense as directions can be taken to reflect their placement on the central *trikoṇa*. The fourth level, Amṛtānanda says in *Saubhāgyasudhodaya*, 3.13, encompasses the whole *śrīcakra* and its branches, which he calls here the "great cakra" (*mahācakra*).

86. See *NSA*, 1.46–58 with the respective commentaries of Vidyānanda and Jayaratha and Lakṣmīdhara on *SL*, v. 11ff.

87. The general description of the *śrīcakra* as composed of forty-three triangles is maintained in the *Tripurā Upaniṣad*, v. 4; cf. Ramānanda's remarks are v. 3. Note also that at the Cidambaram Naṭarāja temple in south India the *śrīcakra* cut in relief on a wall nearby the sub-shrine of the goddess Śivakāma-

sundari appears only as the sets of interlacing triangles, omitting the other portions. This relief is recent but is apparently based on an old painting.

88. *Śrīvidyāratnasūtra*, v. 4f.

89. For the placement of the *prakaṭa yoginīs* see the diagram in, *Śrīcakrārcanadīpikā with shadāmnāyam* (Śri Chidananda Mandali: Madras, 1984), p. 104. The presentation in this *paddhati* is consistent with other texts on the placement of *yoginīs* on the *śrīcakra*.

90. The placement of the *yoginīs* is taken up in *NSA*, 1.153f. Most *paddhatis* diagram the placements; cf. Khanna. This level of ritual detail need not detain us here.

91. Cf. the list given under *anima* in V. S. Apte, *The Practical Sanskrit-English Dictionary* (Poona: Prasad Prakashan, 1957; reprinted, Kyoto: Rinsen Book Company, 1978), p. 37.

92. Naṭarāja of Guru Mandali, Madurai, October, 1984.

93. Discussion of the *siddhis* and their placement on the *śrīcakra* is seen at *NSA*, 1.153cd. Jayaratha fails to mention the *siddhis* and, in fact, only finds a place for the eight *mātṛkās*.

94. Cf. *NSA*, 2.8ff, and 2.32.

95. Naṭarāja of Guru Mandali, Madurai, December, 1984. Several other adepts from other Mandalis made nearly identical comments.

96. This story is repeated time and again among living adepts. Its textual source I only later discovered was the introduction to the *VVR* by Pandit S. Subrahmanya Sastri.

97. Agastya of Gayatri Mandali, Madras, January, 1985.

98. For the placement of the *mātṛkās* and the other *bhūpura yoginīs* see the diagrams.

99. Cf. *HT*, p. 65.

100. *HT*, p. 65. The eight Bhairavas are: Asitanga, Ruru, Canda, Krodha, Unmatta, Kapālin, Bhisana, and Samharin. The *bījākṣaras* of the two sets correspond indicating their close relationship at the subtle mantric level. These *bījas* are the long vowels, the diphthongs and the *visarga*.

101. *HT*, p. 65f; also *HTSL*, p. 42.

102. On the interpretation and meaning of *mudrās* see Jan Gonda, "Mudrā," *Ex orbe religionum* (Studia G. Widengren, II) (Leiden-Koln: E. J. Brill, 1972). Also *HT*, p. 115f.

103. The tradition of showing the *mudrās* at the conclusion of the *pūjā* is maintained in a few ritual texts belonging to distinct *parmaparās* though

among those that use sources prescribing the showing of the *mudrās* after each set of *yoginīs* some allowances are made. In one case, for example, showing the *mudrās* is held back despite the textual prescription mandating their being shown after each sub-cakra. In this case the adept explained, "The *mudrās* belong to each of the [sub-] cakras but can shown at the end of the *pūjā*. This is alteration can be prescribed at the discretion of the guru. The point is not to lose concentration in the course of the ritual. When the *pūjā* is completely internalized we make no movements or utter mantras or sounds aloud. Everything is turned over to the internal meditation thus only after emerging from meditation do we complete the ritual necessities such as showing the *mudrās*." (Naṭarāja of Guru Mandali, Madurai, December, 1984.)

104. *HT*, p. 116.

105. The first nine *mudrās* are identified with the nine sub-cakras according to the dissolution method from the *bhūpura* towards the *bindu* while as ten *yoginīs* they are placed in precisely the same manner as the ten *siddhis*.

106. There are, in fact, other deities placed on the *śrīcakra* during its ritual worship such as on the so-called *gurumaṇḍala* and in the *āyudhapūjā* or worship of the goddess's weapons.

107. Agastya of Gāyatrī Mandali, Madras, January, 1985.

NOTES TO PART 2

1. Historical factors might likewise be considered significant for understanding the involvement of brahmans in Tantrism. To distinguish Vedic ritual ideology and practice from its Tantric counterparts and to see the brāhmaṇical interpretations of Vedism and Tantrism within a historical framework does not necessarily require one to reduce Hinduism to a mere collection of arbitrary, disconnected episodes. Our interest in Vedic ritual is not for the sake of establishing mere historical antecedents.

While a historical comparison of antecedents might serve some purpose, such a project would not necessarily help us to explain the structure of Tantric ritual. The same can be said of language or virtually any other historical phenomenon: its history is not its meaning. See Hans H. Penner, *Impasse and Resolution, A Critique of the Study of Religion* (Toronto Studies in Religion) (Toronto: Peter Lang, 1989), pp. 191–192.

The significance of history for the comparative study of Vedic and Tantric ritual ideologies begins at the point of their respective canonical closures. One need only assume that the descriptions of rituals as well as the assumptions on which they are based and the objectives they set forth provide opportunities for reflection and interpretation within a coherent system of terms and values. To fix canonical closure one must identify a group by its preoccupation with a fixed body of signs, values, and prescriptions that are no longer subject to change. While the interpretations of the elements within the canon may change, the elements themselves do not.

It will not be necessary to describe in detail the procedures of the *śrīcakra pūjā* in order to analyze its ideology and structural components. The object of Śrīvidyā's concern, that is, its canon of signs and values has been discussed in detail in part 1. Sanjukta Gupta and Madhu Khanna have offered more than adequate descriptions of *śrīcakra pūjā*. My own discussion of the ritual as it is formulated by Bhāskararāya, his disciple Umānandanātha, and their ideological adversary Lakṣmīdhara, as well as a detailed ethnography of the contemporary practice of *śrīcakra pūjā* in south India will appear in a second volume. For the purposes of the present discussion it is necessary to review only the basic structure of the *pūjā* and take notice of its critical elements and procedures.

2. With the data base now sufficient to consider theoretical issues, I will not here add to the thick description of Śrīvidyā ritual.

3. See Penner, p. 189. Yet scholars often do not explain their theoretical approaches or admit that their interpretations require acts of reduction. Instead, what is offered is assumed to be a "neutral" account that eschews attempts to reduce in terms other than those offered from inside the theological tradition. Such phenomenologies fail to notice that "this understanding of genuine neutrality, of objectivity, and 'systematics,' presupposes a norm, The Sacred." Religion is assumed to be *sui generis*; it therefore requires its own special method for the interpretation of the Sacred, which is its object. See Penner, p. 33 and p. 15. The premise of "neutral" study is that one can describe religion and the Sacred without becoming involved in either reduction or truth claims. I will not argue here for the inadequacy of such positions; Penner, Neusner, J. Z. Smith, and others have made this case forcefully elsewhere.

4. The task of explanation, as I see it, is deliberately reductionist inasmuch as the primary subjects of inquiry, religion and ritual, are theoretical and therefore require the use of terms that do not simply restate those of theologians. The point of reduction is to expand our capacity to explain Hindu religion and ritual. One need only assume that the terms and explanations offered within theological traditions are not the only ones possible and that scholarly explanations do not necessarily have to be agreeable to Hindu theologians.

5. See Penner, Dumont, and Heesterman as cited in the bibliography.

6. See Berreman, cited in the bibliography.

7. See David Carpenter, "Language, Ritual, and Society: Reflections of the Authority of the Veda in India," *The Journal of the American Academy of Religion*, (1991), forthcoming, mss. p. 3.

8. On the customs of *smārtas* see Milton Singer, *When a Great Tradition Modernizes* (Chicago: University of Chicago Press, 1980). On the definition of *smārta* traditionalism see Carpenter, cited above.

9. I will assume for the purposes of this argument an understanding of Dumont's analysis of India's religious system. For an excellent and succinct summary of the basic elements of Dumont's analysis see Penner, p. 192f.

10. Penner, p. 192. See also, Dumont.

11. See the works of J. C. Heesterman, Brian K. Smith, and David Carpenter for a discussion of this process.

12. Cf. Penner, p. 193.

13. The reader is directed to Gupta's discussion, the details of which are assumed here.

14. *HT*, pp. 139–141.

15. The elements of Śrīvidyā that make it Tantric have been discussed elsewhere. See *The Secret of the Three Cities*, *HTSL*, and *HT*. In short, a group, text, or individual should be classified "Tantric" by its possession of a host of family resemblences.

16. See Chapter 4 for details.

17. Cf. Madan, cited above.

18. This is usually determined by their classification in terms of *guṇas*.

19. This concept is detailed in the *Kaulopaniṣadbhāṣya* of Bhāskararāya, a translation of which is forthcoming.

20. Penner, p. 195.

21. Cf. *Tripura Upaniṣadbhāṣya*, remarks prefacing verse one.

22. Cf. *KT*.

23. Cf. Alf Hiltebeitel, *The Ritual of Battle, Krishna in the Mahābhārata* (Albany: State University of New York Press, 1990).

24. Similarly, one could argue that the consequences of the ritual of battle in the *Mahābhārta* transform the ritual participants (and the world) well after the ritual has concluded.

25. Penner, p. 194.

26. Cf. *HT*, pp. 139–141,

27. While their positioning on the *śrīcakra* is critical to the adept engaged in the rite, it is unimportant for the purposes of this discussion. The names of these deities and their relationship to the nine minor cakras that make up the *śrīcakra* have been given in chapter 6 (on the *śrīcakra*) of part 1.

28. *HT*, p. 122.

29. Gupta's comments about ritual per se are not of much interest to the

historian of religion; little effort is made to place the ritual in any theoretical framework.

30. Khanna, p. 18.

31. In both cases there is no explicit attempt to explain the rituals in terms other than those offered from within the theological structures of Tantrism.

32. While I sympathize with Gupta's efforts at summary and generalization because of her suggestive morphology of Tantric ritual, her attempts to establish a morphological method await a more self-conscious effort. Khanna's work, though exquisitely detailed and philologically sound, chooses to embrace Śrīvidyā's theological structures rather than explain them. Her efforts to describe the ritual's syntax reproduce Śivānanda's description of *śrīcakra pūjā* without creating or utilizing a theory of ritual syntax, such as Staal has employed to describe Vedic ritual.See Frits Staal, "Ritual Syntax," *Sanskrit and Indian Studies. Essays in Honor of Daniel H. H. Ingalls*, eds. M. Nagatomi, et. al. (Leiden-Koln: E. J. Brill, 1983); also "Ritual Structure," *Agni, The Vedic Ritual of Fire Altar* (New Delhi: Motilal Banarsidass, 1978). As a consequence, she concentrates on establishing the thematic continuity of the Śrīvidyā system as it is represented by the ritual and describes the discourse of the ritual as a symbolic, multivalent speech preoccupied with confirming (or repeating) the structures of Kashmiri Trika theology. Implicit in this exegesis is the supposition that Śrīvidyā ritual creates, as the traditionalists say it does, a process of reintegration by which the adept reestablishes his "original" relationship with the divine. Thus, the ritual functions as a reenactment of the primordial identity between the Tantric adept and the godhead, a relationship which has been severed by the misconceptions ignorant individuals impose on reality.

33. Cf. *Imagining Religion*, p. 90ff.

34. The only exceptions to this statement may be those one or two who work within the structure of the modern University who see themselves as both scholars and participants. Outside these very limited confines it is safe to say that there is no *interest* in the historical origins or the theological influences that have informed the development of Śrīvidyā.

35. Khanna, for example, implies that Śivānanda represents Śrīvidyā before its degeneration in the hands of the tradition's later representatives, such as Bhāskararāya. In contrast, I maintain that there is *no primordium* to Śrīvidyā, there are only its historical applications. I would likewise take issue with the notion of a "*a priori* cognitive structure" as being present in Śrīvidyā. I am simply at a loss to know what this sentence means. If by this Khanna means a preinterpretive agenda based on earlier historical precedents then I see my own efforts in support of this view.

36. Cf. Khanna, p. 7. Here Khanna says, "We maintain that they [i.e., the

hādimata authors] contain an original Śākta kernel expressed in liturgical categories such as *mantras*..." Her language suggests that there actually exists an "original" Śākta orientation over which is superimposed a Kashmiri Śaivite interpretive agenda. On what basis can one assert that there exists such a primordium? The study of religion should involve the study of applications, and to this extent Khanna has made a major contribution to the description of Śrīvidyā. The search for "originals," however, is a project best left to theologians.

37. Cf. *PKS*.

38. Another important point of intersection between these two ritual traditions is that Śrīvidyā has been historically dominated by the very same persons who express interest in all forms of Vedic ritual life. The decision to participate in Śrīvidyā and the benefit of such commitment needs to be seen in the context of Śrīvidyā's social and religious history as a Tantric movement predominated by brahmans. The social and religious communities that undertake Vedic ritual and Tantric Śrīvidyā are not mutually exclusive. On the contrary, Śrīvidyā both historically and in contemporary traditions has been perpetuated by persons committed to the dual norm of Vedic *and* Tantric ritual life.

It is not the objective of the historian of religion to participate in the truth claims proposed in given religious systems. Rather, the historian of religion, like the sociologist, begins with the notion that religious beliefs and practices are rooted in a given group's self representation, a process by which the universe is made intelligible and meaningful. As Durkheim noted:

> In fact...a human institution cannot rest upon an error and a lie, without which it could not exist. If it were not founded in the nature of things, it would have encountered in the facts a resistance over which it could never have triumphed... there are no religions which are false. All are true in their own fashion: all answer, though in different ways, to the given condition of human existence. (See Durkheim, pp. 14–15.)

The present essay will refrain from discussing at length the goals of Śrīvidyā ritual as they are articulated from within the theological tradition. As part 1 demonstrates and other scholars confirm, Śrīvidyā presents a highly complex and coherent theology that represents itself through a canon of objects that presuppose systematic ritual use. Śrīvidyā, in its own fashion, answers "to the given condition of human existence" as it has been imagined by Hindus.

39. Durkheim, p. 257.

40. On descriptive reduction and its many problems see Wayne Proudfoot, *Religious Experience* (Berkeley: University of California Press, 1988).

41. Ibid., p. 178.

42. *Map is Not Territory*, pp. 308–309.

43. *Map is Not Territory*, p. 289ff.

44. Staal, *Meaninglessness of Ritual*, p. 5.

45. *Map is not Territory*, pp. 308–309.

46. *Map is not Territory*, p. 309.

47. Staal, p. 5.

48. Staal, p. 6.

49. Staal, p. 6.

50. Staal, p. 6.

51. Staal, pp. 6–7.

52. Staal, p. 8f. This is not the appropriate forum in which to discuss Staal's theory of meaninglessness. Suffice it to say, that I would disagree with his assumption that religion deals with extraordinary or the ineffable. I would agree that "a transition from the domain of men to that of the gods is effected *within* the ritual." (p. 8) I would contend that ritual serves as a mechanism by which one explains the ordinary world and everyday experience. This idea is elaborated below.

53. For an alternative view of Vedic ritual see Brian K. Smith, *Reflections on Resemblance, Ritual, and Religion* (New York: Oxford University Press, 1989).

54. This point has been made eloquently by Brian K. Smith, David Carpenter, and others. See the bibliography for details.

55. My reference here is, of course, to Kṛṣṇa's blistering attack on the Pūrva Mīmāṃsā in chapter two.

56. See Malcolm David Eckel, *Jñānagarbha's Commentary on the Distinction Between the Two Truths* (Albany: State University Press of New York, 1987), p. 7.

57. Cf. *Imagining Religion*, pp. 94–95.

58. *Imagining Religion*, p. 39.

59. *Map is not Territory*, p. 309.

60. See Carpenter cited above.

61. *Imagining Religion*, p. 63.

62. I will show in volume 2 of this work the extent to which Śrīvidyā has become a form of public Tantrism and offer a number of case studies of adepts who differ on the questions of privacy and secrecy.

63. Green, "Storytelling," p. 30.

64. *Inner Conflict*, p. 12.

65. *Inner Conflict*, p. 68.

66. *Inner Conflict*, pp. 8–9.

SELECTED BIBLIOGRAPHY

SANSKRIT TITLES

Ānandalaharī. Ed. and trans. A. Avalon. Madras: Ganesh and Co., 1961. See *Saundaryalaharī*.

Bhāvanopaniṣad. Ed. Sitarama Shastri. In *Kaula and Other Upaniṣads*, ed. Sitarama Sastri with an Introduction by Arthur Avalon. Calcutta: University Press 1922 (Tantrik Texts, XI), pp. 37–65.

Catuḥśatīsaṃhitā. Unedited, also known as the Ānandārnavatantra, Ms. 6017 RASB. Occurs in 480 ślokas.

Chinnamastākhanda. Ed. V. V. Dwiveda as GOS, 166. 1979. This is the fourth khanḍa of the *Śaktisaṃgamatantra*.

Cidgaganacandrikā, with the commentary by Raghunātha Miśra entitled Kramaprakāśika. Ed. Raghunātha Miśra. Varanāsī: Sampurānand Sanskrit Vishvavidyālaya, 1980 (Sarasvatibhavana Granthamala, vol. 115). Attributed to Kālidāsa but according to Rastogi actually authored by Śrīvatsa as a commentary on a Krama stotra. (See Rastogi, N. *Krama Tantricism of Kashmir*. Historical and General Sources, vol. 1. Delhi: Motilal Banarsidass, 1981, p. 180f.;p. 195f.;p. 257; also Edited by Trivikrama Tirtha, Calcutta: University Press, 1936 (Tantrik Texts, XX).

Dakṣiṇāmūrtisaṃhitā. Edited at Benares, 1937, as No. 61 of the PWSBT Texts. The NCC, VIII, p. 297f., records about 50 Mss. Cf. also the CSC Cat., p. 34f.

Devībhāgavatapurāṇa. Ed. B. M. Pandey. Varanāsī, 1963.

Devīmāhātmya. Actually a portion of the *Markendyapurāṇa*, also known as the *Durgāsaptaśatī*. Trans. by Swami Jagadiswarānanda. Madras: Ramakrishna Mission, 1977, fifth impression, ed. F. E. Pargiter, in Markendeyapurāṇa, Calcutta, 1904. See *Durgāsaptaśatī* and the bibliography in Thomas B. *Coburn, Devī-Māhātmya: The Crystallization of The Goddess Tradition*. Delhi: Motial Banarsidass, 1984. For a retranslation by the same author see Thomas B. Coburn, *Encountering the Goddess, A Translation of the Devī-Māhātmya and a Study of Its Interpretation*. Albany: State University of New York Press, 1991.

Devī-upaniṣad. Ed. A. Mahādeva Sastri. In *The Śākta Upaniṣads*. Adyar, Madras: Adyar Library, 1950 (ALS, 10), pp. 53–60. Trans. A. Danielou,

ALB, vol. 19, 1955, pp. 77–84; trans. by A. G. Krishna Warrier in *The Śākta Upaniṣads*. Adyar, Madras: Adyar Library, 1967 (ALS, 89). Also appearing in *Śrīvidyā*. Ed. by "Aṇṇā" (in Tamil and Sanskrit). Madras: Ramakrishna Matham, 1982, third impression, pp. 213–218.

Devīyāmala. Apparently no extant manuscripts. References, however are copious and warrant mention. See Tantrāloka, 22,31;3,70;15,335;31,85f.;also Jayaratha's *Vivaraṇa* on *Tantrāloka* 28,390f. *Devīyāmala*is not quoted in the chapter on *kula* worship (*Tantrāloka*, 29). Significantly Rāmeśvara, also known as Aparājitānandanātha, the nineteenth-century author of the *Saubhāgyodaya* on the *Paraśurāma Kalpasūtra* quotes this text but it is unclear whether he does so from memory or from a manuscript. See *Paraśurāma Kalpasūtra* (*PKS*).

Durgāsaptaśatī. Ed. Vyankatarāmātmaja Harikrsnaśarma. Delhi: Butala and Co., 1984. Includes seven commentaries in Sanskrit, namely, *Durgāpradīpa, Guptavatī, Caturdharī, Śāntanavi, Nāgojibhaṭṭī, Jagaccandracandrikā* and *Daṃśoddhāra*. Most significant of these is Bhāskararāya's *Guptavatī*. For a study of the *Guptavatī* and complete list of related sources see Coburn's *Encountering the Goddess*, cited above.

Gāyatrītantra. Ed. Tārākanātha Bhattācārya. Varanāsī 1946 (Kāśī Skt. Series, 143).

Īśānaśivagurudevapaddhati by Īśānaśiva. Ed. T. Ganapati Sastri, in 4 vols. Trivandrum: Trivandrum University Press, 1922–25 (Triv. Skt. Series, 69,72,77,83). Reissued in two volumes, Delhi: Bharatiya Vishvavidalaya, 1988.

Iśvarapratyabhijñākārikā of Utpāladeva with his vṛtti. Ed. M. K. Shastri. Srinagar: Govt. Press, 1921 (KSTS, 34).

Iśvarapratyabhijñā Vivṛtti Vimarśinī of Abhinavagupta with the Bhāskarī. Ed. M. K. Shastri. Srinagar: Govt. Press, 1938–1943 (KSTS, 60, 62,65).

Jñānadīpavimarśinī. By Vidyānandanātha also known as Śrīnivāsabhaṭṭa but not the same author as of the *Ṛjuvimarśinī* on the *Nityāṣoḍaśikārṇava*, (See Vāmakeśvaratantra), incomplete in manuscript, Nepal Cat., II, p. 15; Trivandrum Cat., No. 912B. Text is quoted by Amṛtānanda in his *Dīpikā* on the *Yoginīhṛdaya* (second part of the Vāmakeśvaratantra), p. 16, (See *Yoginīhṛdaya*).

Jñānārṇavatantra. Ed. G. S. Gokhale. Poona: Ānandāśrama, 1952 (AnSS, 69); also ed. P. Ch. Bagchi in *Kaulajñānanirnaya and some minor texts of the school of Matsyendranātha*. Calcutta, 1934 (Calcutta Sanskrit Series, 3).

Kādimata(tantra). See Tantrarājatantra. Referred to under this title in several works over the centuries, cf. Amṛtānanda's *Dīpikā* on *Yoginīhṛdaya*, p. 8. (See *Yoginīhṛdaya*).

Kādambarī by Bāna. Ed. and trans. M. R. Kale. Bombay: Nirnaya Sagar Press, 1968, fourth edition, trans. C. M. Ridding. London 1896, reprinted 1974.

Kālikāpurāṇa. Ed. Biswanarayanan Sastri. Varanāsī 1972; see also K. R. van Kooy, *Worship of the Goddess According to the Kālikāpurāṇa. Part I: A Translation With an Introduction and Notes of Chapters 54–69*. Leiden: E. J. Brill, 1972.

Kālīvilāsatantra. Ed. Ch. Tarkatirtha. Calcutta: University Press, 1917 (Tantrik Texts, VI).

Kāmakalāvilāsa by Puṇyānanda. Ed. and trans. A. Avalon. Madras: Ganesh and Co., 1953, second edition; originally by the same author under his proper name, ed. and trans. J. Woodroffe. Calcutta: University Press, 1921 (Tantrik Texts X). Reprinted Madras: Ganesh and Co., 1971 in J. Woodroffe. *Tantrarāja Tantra and Kāmakalāvilāsa*, see pp. 129–245, including the commentary of Naṭānandanātha entitled *Cidvallī* (on this commentator see R. Krishnaswami Aiyar in the fourth edition of *Kāmakalāvilāsa*, p. 132). This edition is extremely faulty in notes and printing errors, as Goudriaan attests. (See *HTSL*, p. 168, ftn. 20; here he also lists other editions.). Numerous other editions not listed are available in India including the recent one by Śrī Pitāmbarapīta Sanskrta Parisad, Nagpur 1979, which also includes the *Cidvallī* of Naṭānanda with some variations from the Woodroffe edition.

Kaulavjñānanirnaya. Ed. P. Ch. Bagchi. In *Kaulajñānanirnaya and Some Minor Texts of the Schools of Matsyendranātha*. Calcutta: University Press, 1934.

Kulārṇavatantra. Also known in quotations as the *Ūrdhvāmnayatantra* (See Kṣemarāja on *Netra Tantra* 16, 34 and 18, 119) but not to be mistaken under this secondary title with other works of the same name, edited by T. Vidyāratna, Calcutta: University Press, 1917 (Tantrik Texts, V); second edition, Madras: Ganesh and Co., 1956. Cf. G. Carlstedt, *Till Kulas Lov. Kulamāhātmyakathana ur Kulārṇavatantra*. Uppsala, 1974; also by the same author, *Studier i Kulārṇava-Tantra*. Uppsala, 1974. This contains a critical edition of chapters 1 and 2. For other particulars see NCC, IV, p. 244f. Chakravarti's reference to a *Kulārṇavatantra* or *Kulācārarahasya* occurring in 12 chapters is undoubtedly a different work. See *ABORI* 13, pp. 208f. Ch. Chakravarti, "Kulārṇava Tantra: Its Extent and Contents," *ABORI* 13, 1931–32, p. 206–211.

Lakṣmīdharī. The commentary of Lakṣmīdhara on the *Saundaryalaharī*. See *Saundaryalaharī (SL)*.

Lalitārcanacandrikā. By Sundarācārya also known as Saccidānandanātha the guru of Śrīnivāsa Bhaṭṭa (aka Vidyānandanātha or Śrīvidyānandanātha). MSS. obtained from the University of Madras, Dept. of Sanskrit. See G. Kaviraj, *Tāntrika Sāhitya* (in Hindi); for details of MSS. p. 572.

Lalitāsahasranāma(stotra) with the Saubhāgyabhāskarabhāṣya of Bhāskararāya. Ed. Śrī Pithāmbarapītha [*sic*] Sanskrta Parisad. Nagpur: Śrī Pitāmbarapītha Sanskrta Parisad, 1982; also ed. M. K. Shastri. Bombay: Nirnaya Sagar Press, 1935 (including the *Bhāskaravilāsa*, trans. by R. Ananthakrishna Sastry. Adyar, Madras: Adyar Library, 1976, fifth reprint). Ananthakrishna Sastry's translation is incomplete and omits much of the Sanskrit original.

Mahānirvanatantra. Ed. and trans. A. Avalon as *The Great Liberation*. Calcutta: University Press, 1913 (Tantrik Texts, XIII), fifth edition 1952, reprinted Madras: Ganesh and Co., 1963.

Mahārthamañjarī. By Maheśvarānanda, edited M. K. Sastri. Srinagar: Govt. Press, 1918 (KSTS 11); translated into French by L. Silburn. Paris: Institut de Civilisation Indienne, 1968.

Mālinīvijayatantra. Ed. M. K. Sastri. Srinagar: Govt. Press, 1922 (KSTS, 37).

Mantramahodadhi. By Mahīdhara, ed. K. Śrīkrsnadās. Bombay: Śrī Sat Guru Publications, 1962; Reedited and translated in two separate volumes by "a panel of scholars." Delhi: Śrī Sat Guru Publications, 1984.

Mṛgendratantra (Vidyāpāda and Yogapāda). Ed. M. K. Sastri. Srinagar: Govt. Press, 1930 (KSTS 50).

Navāvāraṇakirtanas. By Muttusamidīksitar, ed. University of Madras. Madras: University of Madras Publications, 1977. See K. V. Zvelebil, *Tamil Literature*. Wiesbaden: Otto Harrossowitz, 1973.

Netratantra with the Uddyota of Kṣemarāja. Ed. M. K. Sastri. 2 vols. Bombay: Nirnaya Sagar Press, 1926–1939 (KSTS 46 and 61). See Brunner, *Netra Tantra*.

Nityāṣoḍaśikārṇava(tantra). Ed. V. V. Dwiveda. Varanāsī: Sampurāṇand Sanskrit Visvavidyālaya, 1968 (with two Sanskrit commentaries, *Ṛjuvimarśinī* of Sivānanda and *Artharatnāvali* by Vidyānanda who is not identical with the author of the *Saubhāgyaratnākara* who bears the same name); ed. in Poona: Ānandāśrama, 1908 (AnSS, 56) with the Sanskrit commentary *Setubandha* of Bhāskararāya.

Nityotsava. By Umānandanātha. Also known as Jagannāthapandita (but not the famous logician of the same name or the Hindi poet). Ed. A. M. Sastri. Baroda: Oriental Institute, 1923 (GOS, 23). Revised edition by Swami Trivikrama Tirtha. Baroda: Oriental Institute, 1948.

Padārthadarśa. By Raghavabhatta. See *Śāradatilaka*.

Paramārthasāra. By Abhinavagupta, Ed. with a French trans. L. Silburn. Paris: Institut de Civilisation Indienne, 1957.

Paraśurāmakalpasūtra with the commentary by Rāmeśvara Sūri entitled Saubhāgyodaya. Ed. A. M. Sastri and S. Y. Dave. Baroda: Oriental Institute, 1950, second edition (GOS 22).

Parimala. By Maheśvarānanda. The auto-commentary on the *Mahārthamañjarī*. See above.

Paratriṃśikā with the Vivaraṇa of Abhinavagupta. Edited M. K. Sastri. Bombay: Nirnaya Sagar Press, 1918 (KSTS 18).

Prapañcasārasārasamgraha. Ed. at Varanāsī, V. S. 1935=C. E. 1878 (IOL–SB, III, p. 1946); also recently as part of the Tanjore Sanskrit Library Series in two volumes, 1983.

Prapañcasāratantra attributed to Śaṅkarācārya. Ed. T. Vidyāratna. Calcutta: University Press, 1914 (Tantrik Texts, III); with the Sanskrit commentary *Vivaraṇa* attributed to Padmapāda edited in Calcutta: University Press, 1935 (Tantrik Texts, XVIII–XIX).

Pratyabhijñāhṛdaya of Kṣemarāja. Translated under the title *The Secret of Recognition.* With notes by E. Baer and Kurt F. Leidecker. Adyar, Madras: Adyar Library, 1938. Hindi translation by Jaideva Singh. Delhi: Motilal Banarsidass, 1973. English translation by Jaideva Singh. Delhi: Motilal Banarsidass, 1963. English translation and commentary named *The Secret of Realization.* By I. K. Taimni. Adyar, Madras, 1974.

Śaktisaṃgamatantra. Ed. (in four volumes) by Bhattacharyya. Baroda: Oriental Institute, 1932–1947 (vols. 1–3) (GOS 61, 91, 104). Vol. 1: Kālihanda; Vol. 2: Tārākhanda; Vol. 3: Sundarīkhanda; Vol. IV: *Chinnamastākhaṇḍa,* Ed. V. V. Dwiveda. Baroda: Oriental Institute, 1979 (GOS 166).

Śaktisūtras. Ed. M. D. Sastri. Varanāsī 1938, in SBG 10, pp. 182–187; Ed. K. V. Abhyankar, as Appendix II to Hayagrīva's *Śāktadarśana.* Poona: Ānandāśrama, 1966. This text seems to structure itself on the *Śivasūtras* but has had none of the same influence as the latter on the development of Śākta thought.

Śāradatilaka. By Lakṣmanadeśika, ed. M. J. Bakshi, with the Sanskrit commentary *Padārthadarśa* by Rāghavabhatta. Varanāsī, 1963 (Kāśī Skt. Series, 107).

Saṭcakranirūpana. By Purnānanda (= the sixth chapter of the author's *Tattvacintāmani*). Ed. T. Vidyaratna. Calcutta: University Press, 1913 (Tantrik Texts, II); trans. A. Avalon, *The Serpent Power.* Madras: Ganesh and Co., 1958, sixth edition (new edition New York: Samuel Weiser, 1974).

Saubhāgyabhāskara of Bhāskararāya. Commentary on the *Lalitāsahasranāma.* See *Lalitāsahasranāma.*

Saubhāgyakalpadruma. Attributed to one Mādhavānandanātha. Better known through its summary by the author's pupil Kṣemānandanātha called "*Saubhāgyakalpalatīkā.*" For manuscript references see RASB No. 6338, 6339 and G. Kaviraj, *Tāntrika Sāhitya,* pp. 712f. According to Kaviraj MSS. are incomplete. Private copies consulted during research were also incomplete.

Saubhāgyaratnākara. By Śrīnivāsabhaṭṭa (aka Śrīvidyānandanātha), presently being edited by Dr. G. Sundaramoorthy of Madurai, Tamil Nādu. For manuscripts see Nepal Cat., I, p. LXXVI, 269; Bikaner Cat., p. 610; also Kaviraj, *Tāntrika Sāhitya*, pp. 714f.

Saubhāgyasubhagodaya. Undoubtedly by Amṛtānanda despite colophons attiributing it to Vidyānandanātha (See Amṛtānanda on *Yoginīhṛdaya* 2. 17). Many verses may, in fact, be quotations of Puṇyānanda, Amṛtānanda's guru. Ed. V. V. Dwiveda in his edition of *Nityāṣoḍaśikārṇava*, pp. 306–321. Also known under the title *Saubhāgyasudhodaya*.

Saubhāgyodaya. By Rāmeśvara. A commentary on *Paraśurāmakalpasūtra*. See *Paraśurāmakalpasūtra*.

Saundaryalaharī. Attributed to Śaṅkarācārya, ed. and trans. W. Norman Brown. Cambridge, Mass. : Harvard University Press, 1958 (Harvard Oriental Series, 43); ed. Vidvan N. S. Venkatanāthacharya. Mysore: Oriental Research Institute, 1969 (Mysore Oriental Research Institute Series, 114) including the Lakṣmīdharī of Lakṣmīdhara; ed. A. Kuppuswami. Mylapore, Madras: A. Kuppuswami, 1976 (with nine Sanskrit commentaries, Hindi and Tamil renderings of verses, translation and notes in English, Tamil, prayogas, yantras, etc); ed. and trans. with commentary, diagrams and an appendix on prayoga by Pt. S. Subrahmanya Sastri and T. R. Śrīnivāsa Ayyangar. Adyar, Madras: Guhānanda Mandali, 1977.

Setubandha. By Bhāskararāya. The commentary on the *Vāmakeśvaratantra*, including both *Nityāṣoḍaśikārṇava* and *Yoginīhṛdaya*. See *Nityāṣoḍaśikārṇava*.

Śrīkuñcitānghristava. By Umāpatiśivācārya, ed. into a Tamil-Sanskrit edition by Brahmaśrī Ka. Mi. Rājakaneca Tīksitar. Citamparam, Tamil Nādu, India: Śrī Naṭarāja Trust, 1958.

Śrīvidyā. (A *paddhati* of Śrīvidyā tradition), ed. "Aṇṇā." Madras: Ramakrishna Mission, 1981.

Śrīvidyāmantrabhāṣyam. Edited with the commentary (*vyākhyā*) entitled *Trikaṇḍasārārthabodhinyākhyā* by Ke. Vīrarāghavaśāstri. Madras: Sri Rama Press, 1960.

Śrīvidyāratnākaraḥ with shrisaparyamantrabhāsya-wanchhankalpatalaksharchana and allied subjects. By Swami-Shrihariharānandasaraswati (Shrikarapatraswami) Mahāraj, ed. Shrisitaramkaviraj "Shrividyābhāskar" (Dattāreyānandnāth). Calcutta: Bhaktisudha Sahitya Parishad, c. 1958(?).

Subhagodaya. By Sivānanda. Ed. by V. V. Dwiveda in his edition of *Nityāṣoḍaśikārṇava*, pp. 284–296. This work was translated by Khanna.

Subhagodya. Attributed to Gauḍapāda. Ed. Delhi, 1983. A vastly different work than the one authored by Sivānanda. Text consulted had no proper references.

Sundarīmahodaya. Attributed to Śaṅkarānandanātha (aka Śambhubhaṭṭa), supposedly based on the *Jñānārṇavatantra* and composed as a *nibandha*. See IOL Cat., IV, p. 899f; RASB Cat., p. 520f.

Svacchandatantra with the Uddyota of Kṣemarāja. Ed. M. K. Sastri, 7 vols. Srinagar: Govt. Press, 1921–1935 (KSTS 31, 38, 44, 48, 51, 53, 56).

Tantrāloka by Abhinavagupta with the Vivaraṇa of Jayaratha. Ed. M. K. Sastri. Srinagar: Govt. Press 1921–1938 (KSTS, vols. 27–39); reprinted by R. C. Dwidvedi and N. Rastogi, Delhi: Motilal Banarsidass, 1985; trans. (into Italian) by R. Gnoli as *La Luce delle Sacre Scritture*. Turin: Classsici Utet, Boringheri, 1972. Note that this Italian translation depends heavily on Jayaratha's interpretation.

Tantrarājatantra. Part I (chs. 1–18). Ed. Lakṣmana Sastri. Calcutta: University Press, 1918 (Tantrik Texts, VIII); Part II (chaps. 19–36) ed. Sadashiva Miśra, Calcutta: University Press, 1926 (Tantrik Texts, XII); reprinted Delhi: Motilal Banarsidass, 1981 in one volume.

Tantrasāra. By Abhinavagupta. Ed. M. R. Sastri. Srinagar: Govt. Press, 1918 (KSTS 17); trans. (into Italian) by R. Gnoli *Essenza dei Tantra*. Torino: Boringheri, 1960.

Tripurārahasya. Ed. Mukunda Lala Sastri, Varanāsī, 1932 (KSS, vol. 92). Private MSS. consulted.

Tripurātāpinī-upaniṣad. Ed. A. Mahadeva Sastri. In *The Śākta Upaniṣads*. Adyar, Madras: Adyar Library, 1950 (ALS, 10), pp. 11–52; trans. A. G. Krishna Warrier in *The Śākta Upaniṣad-s*. Adyar, Madras: Adyar Library, 1967 (ALS, 89).

Tripurā-upaniṣad. Ed. A. Mahadeva Sastri. In *The Śākta Upaniṣads*. Adyar, Madras: Adyar Library, 1950 (ALS, 10), pp. 1–10; also with the commentary of Bhāskararāya in *Kaula and Other Upaniṣads*. Ed. Sitarama Shastri. Calcutta: University Press, 1922 (Tantrik Texts, XI). For a complete translation of the text with the commentary of Bhāskararāya see Douglas Renfrew Brooks, *The Secret of the Three Cities: An Introduction to Hindu Śākta Tantrism*. Chicago: University of Chicago Press, 1990. See Part 2. Also translated without commentary by A. G. Krishna Warrier in *The Śākta Upaniṣad-s*. Adyar, Madras: Adyar Library, 1967 (ALS, 89).

Vāmakeśvaratantra. The name attributed to the *Nityāṣoḍaśikārṇava* and the *Yoginīhṛdaya* when grouped as a single text. See each.

Varivasyārahasya by Bhāskararāya with his auto-commentary entitled Prakāśa. Ed. and trans. S. Subrahmanya Sastri. Adyar, Madras: Adyar Library, 1968, third edition, (ALS, 28).

Vijñānabhairavatantra. Ed. and trans. (in French) by L. Silburn. Paris: Institut de Civilisation Indienne, 1961. *Yoginīhṛdaya(tantra)*. Ed. G. Kaviraj. Varanāsī: Sampurāṇand Sanskrit Viśvavidyālaya, 1963, second edition, (Sarasvati Bhavana Granthamala, 7) with the Sanskrit commentaries

Dīpikā by Amṛtānanda and *Setubandha* by Bhāskararāya. Presently being critically edited by A. Padoux and V. V. Dwiveda and translated into French with the commentary of Amṛtānanda.

BOOKS, ARTICLES AND DISSERATIONS

Agrawala, V. S. "The Glorification of the Goddess," In *Purāṇa* V, 1. January, 1963.

Aiyangar, S. Krishnaswami, "Madurai-Talavaralaru (An account of the temple of Madura)." In *Indian Historical Records Commission, Proceedings of the Meetings* 6, 104–16.

Aiyar, R. Sathyanātha. *History of the Nayaks of Madura*. Ed. S. Krishnaswami Aiyangar. Madras: Oxford University Press, 1924.

Alston, A. J. *Śaṃkara on the Absolute*. London: Shanti Sadan, 1980.

———. *Śaṃkara on the Creation*. London: Shanti Sadan, 1980.

———. *Śaṃkara on the Soul*. London: Shanti Sadan, 1980.

Altekar, A. S. *The Position of Women in Hindu Civilisation from Prehistoric Times to the Present Day*. Benares: Motilal Banarsidass, reprint edition, 1956.

"Āmnāya," An Anonymous survey of the Āmnāyas. In *Candi*, vol. 35, 5–6, Prayag, 1976.

Appadurai, Arjun. *Worship and Conflict Under Colonial Rule: a South Indian Case*. Cambridge: University Press, 1981.

———, and Carol A. Breckenridge, "The south Indian temple: authority, honour and redistribution." In *Contributions to Indian Sociology* (NS) 10, 187–211.

Avalon, A. (see also Woodroffe, Sir John). *The Garland of Letters (Varṇamāla)*. Madras: Ganesh and Co., sixth edition, 1974.

———. *Principles of Tantra*. The Tantratattva of Śrīyukta Śiva Candra Vidyārṇava Bhattacharya. Madras: Ganesh and Co., third edition, 1960.

———. *The Serpent Power, Being the Ṣaṭcakranirūpaṇa and the Padukapanchaka*. Calcutta-London 1913 (Tantrik Texts II); Madras: Ganesh and Co., tenth edition, 1974.

———, and E. Avalon. *Hymns to the Goddess*. Madras: Ganesh and Co., 1952, reprinted 1973.

Awasthi, S. S. Shastri. *Mantra aur Mātrkāon kā Rahasya*. Varanāsī: Chaukhamba, 1966 ("The Secrets of Mantras and Mātṛkās," in Hindi).

Bagchi, P. Ch. "Evolution of the Tantras." In *CHI*, Vol. IV: *The Religions*, Calcutta: Ramakrishna Mission Publications, second Edition 1956, pp.

211–226.

———. *Studies in the Tantras*. Vol. 1. Calcutta: University Press, 1939.

Baliga, B. S. *Madras District Gazetteers: Madurai*. Madras: Govt. Press., Not dated.

Banerjea, Jitendra Nath. *The Development of Hindu Iconography*. Calcutta: University Press, 1956.

———. *Pauraṇic and Tantric Religion*. Calcutta: University Press, 1966.

———. "Some Aspects of Śakti Worship in Ancient India." In *Prabuddha Bharata* 59, March, 1954, pp. 227–232.

Banerji, S. C. *Tantra in Bengal. A Study in Its Origin, Development and Influence*. Calcutta: University Press, 1978.

Barthes, Roland. *Mythologies*. New York: Hill and Wang, 1972.

Basham, A. L. *The Wonder That Was India*. New York: Grove Press, 1977.

Beane, W. C. *Myth, Cult and Symbols in Śākta Hinduism: A Study of the Indian Mother Goddess*. Leiden: E. J. Brill, 1977.

Beck, Brenda E. F. "The goddess and the demon: a local south Indian festival and its wider context." In *Puruṣārtha* 5, pp. 83–136.

Betelille, Andre. *Caste, Class and Power: Changing Patterns of Sratification in a Tanjore Village*. Berkeley: University of California Press, 1965.

Bharati, A. "The Hindu Renaissance and Its Apologetic Patterns." In *Journal of Asian Studies* 29 (February 1970):267–288.

———. *The Tantric Tradition*. London: Rider and Co., 1965; revised American Paperback Edition, New York: Samuel Weiser, 1975.

Bhati, Desrajsimha. *Vidyāpati ki Kāvya-sādhana*. Delhi: Motilal Banarsidass, 1962 (in Hindi).

Bhattacharya, H., "Tantrik Religion." In *The Imperial Age of Kanauj* (HCIP, IV). Bombay 1965, pp. 314–326.

Bhattacharyya, N. N. *History of the Śākta Religion*. Delhi: Munshiram Monoharlal, 1974.

———. *Indian Mother Goddess*. Calcutta: Indian Studies, Past and Present, 1971.

Bohtlingk, Otto von und Roth, Rudolph. *Sanskrit-worterbuch*, 7 Vols. St. Petersburg: Buchdr. der K. Akademie der Wissenschaften, 1855–1875.

Bose, M. M. *The Post-Caitanya Sahajiyā Cult of Bengal*. Calcutta: University Press, 1930.

Bose, D. and H. Haldar. *Tantras, their Philosophy and Occult Secrets*. Calcutta: University Press, third edition, 1956.

Breckenridge, Carol A. "Madurai sthanikars: mediators of royal culture." In A. V. Jeyechandrun, ed., *The Madurai Temple Complex*. Madurai: Arulmighu Meenaksi Sundareśvarar Tirukkoil, 1974.

Briggs, G. W. *Gorakhnāth and the Kānphaṭa Yogis*. Calcutta 1938; Delhi: Motilal Banarsidass, reprint 1982.

Brooks, Douglas Renfrew. "Auspicious Fragments and Uncertain Wisdom: The Roots of Śrīvidyā Śākta Tantrism in South India." In *The Roots of Tantra*, ed. Katherine Harper, et al., forthcoming.

———. *The Secret of the Three Cities: An Introduction to Hindu Śākta Tantrism*. Chicago: The University of Chicago Press, 1990.

———. "The Śrīvidyā School of Śākta Tantrism: A Study of the Texts and Contexts of the Living Traditions in South India." Ph. D. dissertation, Harvard University, 1987.

Brown, Cheever Mackenzie. *God as Mother: A Feminine Theology in India*. Forward by Daniel H. H. Ingalls. Harford, Vt. : Claude Stark and Co., 1974.

———. "Purāṇa as Scripture: From Sound to Image of the Holy Word in the Hindu Tradition." In *History of Religions* 26 (1986):68–86.

———. *The Triumph of the Goddess, The Canonical Models and Theological Visions of the Devī-Bhāgavata Purāṇa*. Albany: State University of New York Press, 1990.

Brunner, Helene, "Importance de la littérture Āgamique pour l'étude des religions vivantes de l'Inde." In *Indologica Taurinensia* 3–4, Torino 1977, pp. 107–24.

———, "Le sādhaka, personnage oublie du Śivaisme du sud." In *Journal Asiatique* 263, pp. 411–443.

———, "Un Tantra du Nord: Le Netra Tantra." In *BEFEO*, vol. 61, 1974, pp. 125–197.

Brunner-Lachaux, Helene, trans. and ed. *Somaśambhupaddhati. Le rituel quotidien dans la tradition śivaite de l'Inde du Sud selon Somaśambhu*. 3 Volumes. Pondicherry: Institut Francais d'Indologie, 1963, 1968, 1977.

Buchanan, Francis. *A Journey from Madras Through the Countries of Mysore, Canara, and Malabar*. Vol. 1. London: Cadell & Davies-Black, Parry & Kingsbury, 1807.

Buck, Harry M. and Yocum, Glenn E., eds. *Structural Approaches to South India Studies*. Chambersburg, Pa. : Wilson Books, 1974.

Burgess, James "The ritual of the temple of Rāmeśvaram." In *Indian Antiquary* 12, pp. 315–326.

Carlstedt, G. *Studier i Kulārṇava-Tantra*. Uppsala: Skrifer Utgivna av Religionshistoriska Institutionen i Uppsala, 1974.

———. *Till Kulas Lov, Kulamāhātmyakathana ur Kulārṇava*. Uppsala: Skrifer Utgivna av Religionshistoriska Institutionen i Uppsala, 1974.

Carter, Anthony T. "Hierarchy and the Concept of the Person in Western India." In *Concepts of Person, Kinship, Caste, and Marriage in India*, ed. Akos Ostor, Lina Fruzztti, and Steven A. Barnett. Cambridge: Harvard University Press, 1982.

Cenkner, William "The Śaṅkarācāryas and Hindu orthodoxy in comtemporary perspective." In *Proceedings of the First International Symposium on Asian Studies* 4, pp. 785–796.

Chakravarti, Ch. *The Tantras. Studies on their Religion and Literature*. Calcutta: Punthi Pustak, 1972.

———. "Antiquity of Tantrism." In *IHQ*, vol. 6, 1930, pp. 114–126.

———. "Controversy regarding the authority of the Tantras." In *Commemorative Essays presented to K. B. Pathak*. Poona: Ānandāśrama, 1934, pp. 210–220 (no editor listed).

Clooney, Francis X. "Why the Veda Has No Author: Language as Ritual in Early Mīmāṃsā and Post-Modern Theology." In *Journal of the American Academy of Religion* 55, 1987, pp. 659–684.

Clothey, Fred W. *The Many Faces of Murukan: The History of a South Indian God*. The Hague: Mouton, 1978.

Coburn, Thomas B. *Devī Māhātmya: The Crystallization of the Goddess Tradition*. Delhi: Motilal Banarsidass, 1984.

———. *Encountering the Goddess, A Translation of the Devī-Māhātmya and a Study of Its Interpretation*. Albany: State University of New York Press, 1990.

———. "The Study of the Purāṇas and the Study of Religion." In *Religious Studies* 16, 1980, pp. 341–352.

———. "'Scripture' in India: Towards a Typology of the Word in Hindu Life." In *Journal of the American Academy of Religion* 52, 1984, pp. 435–459.

Cole, H. H. *Great Temple to Śiva and His Consort at Madura (Preservation of national monuments, India)*. 1884.

Daniel, E. Valentine. *Fluid Signs. Being a Person the Tamil Way*. Berkeley: University of California Press, 1984.

Das, S. K. *Śakti or Divine Power*. Calcutta: University Press, 1934.

Das, U. K. *Bhartīya Śaktisādhana*. Vol. II. Santiniketan: University Press, 1966.

Das, Veena. *Structure and Cognition: Aspects of Hindu Caste and Ritual*. Delhi: Oxford University Press, 1977.

Das Gupta, S. B. *Bhārater Śaktisādhana o Śākta Sāhitya*. Calcutta: University Press, Second edition, 1966.

Dasgupta, S. B. *Obscure Religious Cults as Background of Bengali Literature*. Calcutta: University Press, 1962, second edition.

———. *An Introduction to Tantric Buddhism*. Calcutta, 1950.

Dasgupta, S. N. *A History of Indian Philosophy*. 5 vols. Cambridge: University Press, 1922–1955.

Denny, Fredrick M., and Taylor, Rodney L., eds. *The Holy Book in Comparative Perspective*. Columbia: University of South Carolina Press, 1985.

Derrida, Jacques. *Writing and Difference*. Translated with and Introduction and Additional Notes by Alan Bass. Chicago: University of Chicago Press, 1978.

Desai, Devangana. *Erotic Sculpture of India: A Socio-Cultural Study*. New Delhi, 1975.

Detweiler, Robert. "What is a Sacred Text?." In *Semeia* 31, 1984, pp. 213–230.

Devakunjari, D. *Madurai Through the Ages: From the Earliest Times to 1801 A. D.* Madras: Society for Archaelogical, Historical and Epigraphical Research, no date.

Diehl, Carl Gustav. *Instrument and Purpose: Studies on Rites and Rituals in South India*. Lund: Gleerup, 1956.

Dimmitt, Cornelia and van Buitenen, J. A. B. eds. and translators. *Classical Hindu Mythology: A Reader in the Sanskrit Purāṇas*. Philadelphia: Temple University Press, 1978.

Dimock, E. C. *The Place of the Hidden Moon. Erotic Mysticism in the Vaiṣṇava Sahajiyā Cult of Bengal*. Chicago: University of Chicago Press, 1966.

D'Sa, Francis X. "Christian Scriptures and Other Scriptures: Thesis towards a Study of the Significance of Scripture." In Indian Journal of Theology 31, 1982, pp. 236–242.

Dumont, Louis. *Une sous-case de l'Inde du sud: orginisation sociale et religion des Pramalai Kallar*. Paris: Mouton, 1957.

———. *Homo Hierarchicus: the Caste System and its Implications*. London: Wiedenfeld & Nicolson, 1970; originally in French as *Homo Hierarchicus, essai sur le systeme des castes*. Paris 1966.

Dumont, Louis and David Pocock. "Pure and Impure." In *Contributions to Indian Sociology* 3:9–39.

Dwiveda, V. V. "Alamkārasamgrahakāra Amṛtānanda Kī Yoginīhṛdaya-dīpikākāra Se Abhinnatā." In *Rtandharā*, January–March 1972, pp. 55–62.

———. *Tantra-Yatra, Essays on Tantra-Āgama Thoughts and Philosophy, Literature, Culture and Travel*. Varanāsī: Ratna Publications, 1982 (in Sanskrit).

———. "Tripurādarśanasya paricitā ācāryaḥ kṛtayaś ca." In *Sarasvatī Susamā* (Journal of the Sanskrit Visvavidyālaya). Varanāsī, Samvat 2022 (=1971, C. E.), pp. 13–26.

———. *Upodghāta*. Introduction to the edition of the *Nityāṣoḍaśikārṇava* (in Sanskrit). See *Nityāṣoḍaśikārṇava* in this Bibliography under Sanskrit Titles.

Dyczkowski, Mark S. G. *The Doctrine of Vibration. An Analysis of the Doctrines and Practices of Kashmir Śaivism*. Albany: State University of New York Press, 1987.

———. *The Canon of the Śaivāgama and the Kubjika Tantras of the Western Kaula Tradition*. Albany: SUNY Press, 1988.

Eckel, Macolm David. *Jñānagarbha's Commentary on the Distinction Between the Two Truths. An Eighth Century Handbook of Madhayamaka Philosophy*. Albany: SUNY Press, 1987.

———. "Bhāvaviveka's Vision of Reality: Structure and Metaphor in a Buddhist Philosophical System." In *Journal of the American Academy of Religion* 55, Spring 1987, pp. 39–54.

Eliade, M. *Le Yoga, immortalité et liberté*. Paris: Librairie Payot, 1954; translated into English by William K. Trask as *Yoga, Immortality and Freedom*. Princeton: University Press, 1958, (Bollingen Series 56).

Evola, J. *Le Yoga tantrique. Sa métaphysique, ses pratiques*. Translated from Italian by M. Robinet, Paris, 1971.

Farquhar, J. N. *An Outline of the Religious Literature of India*. Reprint edition. Delhi: Motilal Banarsidass, 1968.

Filliozat, Pierre-Sylvain. "Le droit d'entrer dans les temples de Śiva au XI siecle." In *Journal Asiatique* 263, pp. 103–17.

Fitzgerald, John J. *Pierce's Theory of Signs as Foundation for Pragmatism*. The Hague: Mouton, 1966.

Frauwallner, E. *Geschichte de indischen Philosophie*. 2 Vols. Salsburg, 1953–1956.

Fuller, C. J. "Gods, priests and purity: on the relation between Hinduism and the caste system." In *Man* (NS) 14, pp. 459–476.

———. "The divine couple's relationship in a south Indian temple: Mīnākṣī and Sundareśvara at Madurai." In *History of Religions* 19, pp. 321–348.

———. *Servants of the Goddess. The Priests of a South Indian Temple.* Cambridge: University Press, 1984.

Ghosh, A. Bh. "The Spirit and Culture of the Tantras." In *CHI*, vol. IV, 1956, second edition, pp. 241–251.

Girard, René. *Violence and the Sacred.* Trans. by P. Gregory. Baltimore: Johns Hopkins University Press, 1977.

van Glassenapp, H. "Tantrismus und Śaktismus." In *Ostasiatische Zeitschrift.* Neue Folge, b. XII, 1936, pp. 120–133.

Gnoli, R. "Gli Āgama scivaiti nell'India settentrionale." In *Indologica Taurinensia*, I, Turin: Unione Tipografico-Editrice Torinese, 1973, pp. 61–69.

———. *Luce delle Sacre Scritture.* (An Italian translation of Abhinavagupta's *Tantrāloka*). Turin: Unione Tipografico-Editrice Torinese, 1972.

Gode, P. K. *Studies in Indian Literary History.* 3 vols. Bombay: Nirnaya Sagar Press, 1953–1956.

Gonda, Jan. *Change and Continuity in Indian Religion.* The Hague: Mouton, 1965.

———. *Die Religionen Indiens.* 2 vols. Stuttgart: Kohlhammer Verlag, 1960–1963.

———. "The Indian Mantra." In *Oriens* 16, 1963, pp. 244–297. Reprinted in J. Gonda, *Selected Studies IV.* Leiden: E. J. Brill, 1975, p. 248f.

———. *Medieval Religious Literature.* (A History of Indian Literature, Vol. II, fasc. 1, ed. J. Gonda). Wiesbaden: Otto Harrossowitz, 1975.

———. *Vedic Ritual: The Non-Solemn Rites.* Leiden, 1980.

Goody, Jack. *The Domestication of the Savage Mind.* Cambridge: Cambridge University Press, 1977.

———, ed. *Literacy in Traditional Societies.* Cambridge: Cambridge University Press, 1968.

Goody, Jack, and Watt, Ian. "The Consequences of Literacy." In *Literacy in Traditional Societies*, ed. Jack Goody, pp. 27–68. Cambridge: Cambridge University Press, 1968.

Goswami, B. B. and S. G. Morab. *Chamundeśvarī temple in Mysore.* Calcutta: Anthropological Survey of India (Memoir no. 35). No date.

Goudriaan, Teun. *Māyā Divine and Human. A Study of Magic and its Religious Foundations in Sanskrit Texts.* Delhi: Motilal Banarsidass, 1978.

———, ed. and trans. *The Vināśikhatantra. A Śaiva Tantra of the Left Current.* Delhi: Motilal Banarsidass, 1985.

———. "Vaikhānasa Daily Worship." In *Indo-Iranian Journal* 12 (1970):161–215.

Goudriaan, T., and Sanjukta Gupta. *Hindu Tantric and Śākta Literature.* (A History of Indian Literature, edited by Jan Gonda, Vol. II, fasc. 2). Wiesbaden: Otto Harrossowitz, 1981.

Gough, Kathleen, "Brahman kinship in a Tamil village." In *American Anthropologist* 58, pp. 826–853.

Graham, William A. *Beyond the Written Word.* Cambridge: Cambridge University Press, 1987.

———. "Qur'an as Spoken Word: An Islamic Contribution to Scripture." In *Islam and the History of Religions,* ed. Richard C. Martin. Tuscon: University of Arizona Press.

Green, William Scott. "Something Strange, Yet Nothing New: Religion in the Secular Curriculum." In *Liberal Education* 73, Nov/Dec 1987, pp. 21–25.

———. "Romancing the Tome: Rabbinic Hermeneutics and the Theory of Literature." In *Semeia* 40, 1987, pp. 151–168.

———. "Storytelling and Holy Man: The Case of Ancient Judaism." In *Take Judaism, for Example.* Ed. Jacob Neusner. Chicago: University of Chicago Press, 1983.

———. "'Otherness' Within: Towards a Theory of Difference in Rabbinic Judaism." In *"To See Ourselves as Other See Us" Christians, Jews, "Others" in Late Antiquity,* eds. Jacob Neusner and Ernest S. Frerichs. Chico, Calif. : Scholars Press, 1985.

Gupta, Sanjukta. "Viśvaksena The Divine Protector." In *WZKSO,* Vol. XX 1976, pp. 75–89.

Gupta, Sanjukta, Dirk Jan Hoens, and Teun Goudriaan. *Hindu Tantrism.* (*Handbuch der Orientalistik,* 2. Abt. : Indien, 4. Band, 2. Abschnitt). Leiden-Koln: E. J. Brill, 1979.

Hacker, Paul. "Eigentümlichkeiten der Lehre und Terminologie Śaṅkaras: Avidyā, Nāmarūpa, Māyā, Īśvara." In *ZDMG* C, pp. 246–286.

———. *Untersuchungen über Texte des fruhen Advaitavāda.* I. Die Schüler Śaṅkaras. Wiesbaden: Franz Steiner Verlag, 1951. Akademie der Wissenschaften und der Literatur in Mainz, Abhandlungen der Geistes- und Sozialwissenschaftlichen Klasse, Jahrgang 1950, Nr. 26.

———. "Die Lehre von den Realitätsgraden im Advaita-Vedānta." In ZMR. 1952, pp. 277ff.

———. "Śaṅkara der Yogin und Śaṅkara der Advaitin." In *WZKSO*, 1968–1969, p. 119ff.

———. "Śaṅkarācārya and Śaṅkarabhagavatpāda." In *New Indian Antiquary*. April–June, 1947.

Hart, George L. "Women and the sacred in ancient Tamilnad." In *Journal of Asian Studies* 32, pp. 233–250.

Hartmann, C. G. *Aspects de la déesse Kālī dans son culte et dans la litterature indienne*. Helsinki, 1969.

Hawley, John Stratton, and Wulff, Donna B., edd. *The Divine Consort: Radha and the Goddesses of India*. Berkeley: Berkeley Religious Studies Series 3, 1982.

Heestermann, J. C. "Householder and Wanderer." In *Way of Life: King, Householder, Renouncer. Essays in Honor of Louis Dumont*, ed. T. N. Madan. New Delhi: Vikas, 1981, pp. 251–271.

———. *The Inner Conflict of Tradition: Essays in Indian Ritual, Kingship, and Society*. Chicago: The University of Chicago Press, 1985.

———. "Power and Authority in Indian Tradition." In *Tradition and Politics in South Asia*, ed. R. J. Moore. New Delhi: Vikas, 1979, pp. 60–85.

———. "Reflections on the Significance of the *Dakṣinā*." In *IIJ* 3, pp. 241–258.

———. "The Ritualist's Problem." In *Amṛtadhārā. Professor R. N. Dandekar Felicitation Volume*, ed. S. D. Joshi. Delhi: Ajanta Books, 1984, pp. 436–47.

———. "Brahman, Ritual and Renouncer." In *WZKSO* 8, pp. 1–31.

———. "India and the Inner Conflict of Tradition." In *Daedalus* 102, 1, pp. 97–113.

Hopkins, Thomas J. *The Hindu Religious Tradition*. Encino and Belmont, Calif. :Dickenson Publishing Co., 1971.

———. "The Social Teachings of the Bhāgavata Purāṇa." In *Krishna: Myths, Rites, and Attitudes*, ed. Milton Singer. Chicago: University of Chicago Press, 1966, pp. 3–22.

Horton, Robin. "Levi-Bruhl, Durkheim, and the Scientific Revolution." In *Modes of Thought*, edited by Horton, Robin and Ruth Finnegan. London: Faber, 1973.

———. "Tradition and Modernity Revisited." In *Rationality and Relativism*, eds. Martin Hollis and Steven Lukes. Cambridge, Mass. : The MIT Press.

Horton, Robin, and Ruth Finnegan, eds. *Modes of Thought: Essays on Thinking in Western and Non-Western Societies*. London: Faber and Faber, 1973.

Hubert, Henri, and Marcel Mauss. *Sacrifice: Its Nature and Function.* Chicago: The University of Chicago Press, 1964, trans. W. D. Halls from the French "Essai sure la fonction du sacrifice," *Année sociologique,* 1898.

Hudson, Dennis. "Śiva, Mīnākṣī, Viṣṇu—Reflections on a Popular Myth in Madurai." In *Indian Economic and Social History Review* 14, pp. 107–118.

Hume, Robert Earnest. *The Thirteen Pricipal Upanishads.* London: Oxford University Press, 1958. Reprint of the revised second edition of 1931.

Inden, Ronald B. *Marriage and Rank in Bengali Culture: A History of Caste and Clan in Middle Period Bengal.* New Delhi: Vikas Publishing House, 1976.

Inden, Ronald B., and Ralph Nichols. *Kinship in Bengali Culture.* Chicago: University of Chicago Press, 1977.

Ingalls, Daniel H. H. "Śaṃkara on the Question 'Whose is Avidyā'?" In *Philsophy East and West,* 1953, pp. 68ff.

———. "Śaṃkara's Arguments against the Buddhists." In *Philosophy East and West,* 1954, pp. 291–316.

———. "The Brahman Tradition." In *Traditional India: Structure and Change,* ed. Milton Singer. Philadelphia: American Folklore Society, 1959.

Jacob, Col. G. A. *A Concordance to the Principal Upanishads and Bhagavad Gītā.* Reprint edition, Delhi: Motital Banarsidass, 1963.

Kakati, B. K. *The Mother Goddess Kāmākhyā.* Gauhati: University Press, 1948, second edition 1961.

Kane, P. V. *History of the Dharmaśāstra.* 5 Vols., Poona: Bhandarkar Oriental Research Institute 1930–1962, reprinted 1968–1977.

Kaviraj, Gopinath. *Tantra o Āgama-Śāstrer Digdarśan.* Calcutta: 1963 (Calcutta Skt. College Research Series, No. XXV; Studies, no. 12; in Bengali).

———. *Tantrik Vānmaya me Śaktidṛṣṭi.* Patna: Bihar Rastrabhasa Parisad, 1963 (in Hindi).

———. *Tāntrika Sādhana aur Siddhānta.* Patna: Bihar Rastrabhasa Parisad, 1979 (in Hindi).

———. *Tāntrika Sāhitya.* Lucknow: Rajarsi Purusottam Das Dandan Hindi Bhavan, 1972 (in Hindi).

Keith, A. B. *The Religion and Philosophy of the Veda.* 2 Vols. Cambridge, Mass. : Harvard University Press, 1925 (Harvard Oriental Series, 31 and 32).

———, trans. *The Veda of the Black Yajus School entitled Taittirīya Samhitā.* Vol. 2. Cambridge, Mass. : Harvard University Press, 1914.

Khanna, Madhu. *"The Concept and Liturgy of the Śrīcakra based on Śivānanda's Trilogy."* Ph.D. diss., Oxford University, 1986.

Kinsley, David. *Hindu Goddesses: Visions of the Divine Feminine in Hindu Religious Tradition.* Berkeley: University of California Press, 1986.

Kramrisch, Stella. *The Hindu Temple.* Calcutta: University Press, 1946.

———. "The Indian Great Goddess." In *History of Religions* May 1975, vol. 14, no. 4, pp. 235–265.

———. *Manifestations of Shiva.* Philadelphia: Philadelphia Museum of Art, 1981.

———. *The Presence of Śiva.* Princeton: Princeton University Press, 1981.

Laine, J. "The Notion of Scripture in Modern Indian Thought." In *ABORI,* Spring, 1984.

Levi-Strauss, Claude. *Structural Anthropology, Vol. I.* New York: Basic Books, 1963.

———. *Structural Anthropology, Vol. II.* New York: Basic Books, 1976.

———. *The View from Afar,* trans. Joachim Neugroschel and Phoebe Hoss. New York: Basic Books, 1985.

Logan, Penelope. "Domestic worship and the festival cycle in the south India city of Madurai." Ph. D. diss., University of Manchester.

Lord, Albert B. *The Singer of Tales.* Cambridge, Mass. : Harvard University Press, 1960.

Lorenzen, D. N. *The Kāpālikas and Kālāmukhas, Two Lost Śaivite Sects.* Reprint edition, New Delhi: Motilal Banarsidass, 1972.

Luders, H. "Die Ṣoḍaśakalāvidyā." In *Philologica Indica,* pp. 509ff.

Malamoud, Charles. *Le Svādhyāya: Recitation personnelle du Veda.* Paris: Institut de Civilisation Indienne, 1977.

———. "Terminer le sacrifice: Remarques sureles honoraires rituals dans le brahmanisme." In *Le Sacrifice dans l'Inde ancienne,* eds. Madeleine Biardeau and Charles Malamoud. Paris: Presses universitaires de France, 1976, pp. 155–204.

———. "La Théologie de la dette dans le brāhmanisme." In *Puruṣārtha* 4 (1980):39–62.

Marriott, McKim. "Hindu Transactions: Diversity without Dualism." In *Transaction and Meaning: Directions in the Anthropology of Exchange and Symbolic Behavior,* ed. Bruce Kapferer. Philadelphia: Institute for the Study of Human Issues.

Marriott, McKim, and Ronald B. Inden. "Caste Systems." In *Encyclopedia Britannica,* 15th ed., 3:982–991.

———. "Toward an Ethnosociology of South Asian Caste Systems." In *The New Wind*, ed. Kenneth David. The Hague: Mouton, 1977.

Matsubara, Mitsunori. "The Early Pāñcaratra with Special Reference to the Ahirbudhnya Samhitā." Ph. D. diss., Harvard University, 1973.

Mencher, Joan P. "Namboodiri Brahmans—An Analysis of a Traditional Elite in Kerala." In *Journal of Asian and African Studies* 1, pp. 183–196.

Menon, C. A. *Kālī-worship in Kerala*. Madras, 1959, second edition.

Monier-Williams, M. *Religious Thought and Life in India: Vedism, Brahmanism and Hinduism*. Reprint editon, New Delhi: Oriental Books, reprint, 1974.

Mookerjee, A. *Tantra Art: Its Philosophy and Physics*. New Delhi, 1968.

Müller-Ortega, Paul Eduardo. "Exploring Textbooks: Introductions to Hinduism." In *Critical Review of Books in Religion 1988*, ed. Beverly Roberts Gaventa. Atlanta: *Journal of the American Academy of Religion and The Journal of Biblical Studies*, 1988, pp. 61ff.

———. *The Triadic Heart of Śiva*. Albany: State University of New York Press, 1987.

Nandi, R. N. *Religious Institutions and Cults in the Deccan (c.* A.D. 600–A.D. 1000). New Delhi, 1973.

Needham, Rodney. "Polythetic Classification: Convergence and Consequences." In *Man* vol. 10, no. 3, 1975, pp. 349–369.

———. *Belief, Language and Experience*. Oxford: Basil Blackwell, 1972.

Neusner, Jacob. "Comparing Judaisms." In *History of Religions*, 18 (November 1978):177–199.

———, ed. *Take Judaism, for Example*. Chicago and London: University of Chicago Press, 1983.

———. *Judaism in the American Humanities*. Brown Judaic Studies 28. Chico, California: Scholars Press, 1981.

———. "The Study of Religion as the Study of Tradition: Judaism." In *History of Religions*, February 1975, vol. 14, no. 3, pp. 191–206.

———. "Thinking about the 'Other' in Religion: It is Necessary but is it Possible?" In *Modern Theology* 6:3, April 1990, pp. 273–285.

O'Flaherty, Wendy Doniger. *Asceticism and Eroticism in the Mythology of Śiva*. Oxford: Clarendon Press, 1973.

Oldenberg, H. *Die Religion des Veda*. Stuttgart-Berlin, 1917, second edition.

Padoux, A. "A Survey of Tantric Hinduism for the Historian of Religions,"

Review article of *Hindu Tantrism* by Sanjukta Gupta, Dirk Jan Hoens, and Teun Goudriaan. In *History of Religions*, 1981.

———. "Contributions a l'étude du Mantraśāstra. I: La selection des mantra (*mantroddhara*)." In *BEFEO*, 65, 1978, pp. 65–85.

———. "Un japa tantrique: Yoginīhṛdaya 3. 170–190." In *Tantric and Taoist Studies in Honor of R. Stein*, vol. 1, ed. M. Strickman. Brussels: Institut Belge des Hautes Etudes Chinoises, 1981, pp. 141–154.

———. *Recherches sur la symbolique et l'Énergie de la parole dans certains textes tanriques*. Paris: Institut de Civilisation Indienne, 1964.

———. *Vāc, The Concept of the Word In Selected Hindu Tantras*, trans. Jacques Gontier. Albany: State University of New York Press, 1990.

Palaniappan, K. *The Great Temple of Madurai*. Madurai: Śrī Meenakshisundareswarar Temple Renovation Committee, 1970.

Pandey, K. C. *Abhinavagupta, An Historical and Philosophical Study*. Varanāsī: Chaukhanba Publication, reprint 1963, second edition.

Parpola, Asko. "The Pre-vedic Indian Background of the Śrauta Rituals." In *Agni: The Vedic Altar of Fire*, ed. Frits Staal. Berkeley: Asian Humanities Press, 1983, II:41–75.

Payne, E. J. *The Śāktas*. Calcutta: Y.M.C.A. Publishing House and London: Oxford University Press, 1933.

Peirce, Charles S. *Writings of Charles S. Peirce: A Chronological Edition*. Bloomington: Indiana University Press, vol. 1, 1857–1866.

Pillai, J. M. Somasundaram. *Tiruchendur: The Sea-shore Temple of Subrahmanyam*. Madras: Addison Press, 1948.

Penner, Hans H. "Creating a Brahman: A Structural Approach to Religion." In *Methodological Issues in Religious Studies*, ed. Robert D. Baird. Chico, Cal. : New Horizons, 1975, pp. 49–66.

———. *Impasse and Resolution. A Critique of the Study of Religion*. Toronto Studies in Religion, ed. Donald Wiebe. New York: Peter Lang, 1989.

———, and Edward Yonan. "Is a Science of Religion Possible?" in *The Journal of Religion* 52, 1972, pp. 107–33.

Pensa, C. "Considerazioni sul tema della bipolarita nelle religioni indianne." In *Gururājamañjarikā, Studi in onore di Giuseppi Tucci*. Vol. 2, Naples, 1974, pp. 379–409.

Pope, G. U. trans. and ed. *The Tiruvacāgam or 'Sacred utterances' of the Tamil poet, saint and sage Manikka-vacagar*. Oxford: Clarendon Press, 1900.

Pott, P. H. *Yoga en Yantra in hunne beteenkenis voor de Indische archaelogie*. Leiden: E. J. Brill, 1946. English version: *Yoga and Yantra. Their Interrelation and Their Significance for Indian Archeology*. The Hague: E. J. Brill, 1966.

Pratyagātmānanda, Swami. "Tantra as a Way of Realization." In *CHI*, vol. IV, second revised edition. Calcutta: Ramakrishna Mission Institute of Culture, 1953–1962, pp. 227–240.

Proudfoot, Wayne. "Religion and Reduction." In *Union Seminary Quarterly Review* 37 (Fall–Winter 1981–1982):13–25.

———. *Religious Experience*. Berkeley: University of California Press, 1986.

Raghavan, V. "Methods of Popular Religious Instruction in South India." In *The Cultural History of India*, ed. Haridass Bhattacharyya. 4 Vols. Second revised edition, Calcutta: Ramakrishna Mission Institute of Culture, 1953–1962. Vol. IV, pp. 503–514.

———. *The Present Position of Vedic Recitation and Vedic Sākhās*. Kumbhakonam: Veda Dharama Paripalana Sabha, 1962.

Raman, K. V. *Śrī Varadarājaswāmī Temple—Kāñchi: A Study of Its History, Art and Architecture*. New Delhi: Abhivava Publications, 1975.

Rao, T. A. Gopinath. *Elements of Hindu Iconongraphy*. 2 Vols. Madras: Law Printing House, 1914. Reprinted Delhi: Motilal Banarsidass, 1985.

Rastogi, N., *Krama Tantricism of Kashmir. Historical and General Sources, Vol. 1*. Delhi: Motilal Banarsidass, 1981.

Rawson, P. *The Art of Tantra*. London, 1973.

Redfield, Robert. *The Primitive World and Its Transformations*. Ithaca, N. Y. : Cornell University Press, 1953.

Renou, L. *Études Védiques et Paninéennes*. 17 Vols. Paris: de Boccard, 1955–1967. Publications de l'Institut de Civilisation Indienne fasc. 1, 2, 4, 6, 9, 10, 12, 14, 16, 17, 18, 20, 22, 23, 26, 27, 30.

Ricoeur, Paul. *The Conflict of Interpretations: Essays in Hermeneutics*. Evanston, Ill. : Northwestern University Press, 1974.

Rorty, Richard. *Philosophy and the Mirror of Nature*. Princeton: Princeton University Press, 1979.

Sahlins, Marshal. "Colors and Cultures." In *Semiotica* 16, 1976, pp. 1–22.

———. *Culture and Practical Reason*. Chicago: University of Chicago Press, 1976.

Sanderson, Alexis. "Purity and Power Among the Brahmins of Kashmir." In *The Category of the Person: Anthropological and Philosophical Perspectives*, eds. Michael Carrither, Steven Collins, Steven Lukes. Cambridge: Cambridge University Press, 1985.

———. "Maṇḍala and Āgamic Identity in the Trika of Kashmir." In *Mantras et diagrammes rituels dans l'Hindouisme*, ed. Andre Padoux. Paris, 1986.

Sastri, H. Krishna. *South-Indian Images of Gods and Goddesses*. Madras: Govt. Press, 1916.

Sastri, K. A. Nilakanta. *Development of Religion in South India*. Bombay: Orient Longman, 1963.

Sastry, T. V. Kapali. *Sidelights on the Tantra*. Pondicherry, 1971.

de Saussure, Ferdinand. *Course in General Linguistics*, eds. Charles Bally and Albert Sechehaye with Albert Reidlinger. Translated by Wade Baskin. New York: Philosophical Library, 1959.

Schomerus, H. W. *Der Caiva-Siddhānta, eine Mystik Indiens*. Leipzig, 1912.

Schrader, F. O. *Introduction to the Pāñcaratra and the Ahirbudhnya Samhitā*. Adyar, Madras: Adyar Library, 1916.

Shankaranaryanam, S. *Śrī Chakra*. Pondicherry: Dipti Publications, 1970.

Sharma, Dasharatha "Verbal Similarities between the Durgā-Sapta-Śatī and the Devī-Bhāgavata-Purāṇa and other Considerations bearing on their Date." In *Purāṇa* V, 1, January, 1963, pp. 90–103.

Sharma, P. Kumar. *Śakti Cult in Ancient India (with Special Reference to the Puranic Literature)*. Varanāsī: Bharatiya Publishing House, 1974.

Shulman, David Dean. *Tamil Temple Myths: Sacrifice and Divine Marriage in the South Indian Śaiva Tradition*. Princeton: University Press, 1980.

Silburn, L. *Le Bhakti, Le Stavacintāmani de Bhaṭṭanārāyana*. Paris: Institut de Civilisation Indienne, 1979.

———. *Le Mahārthamañjarī de Maheśvarānanda avec des extraits du Parimala*. Paris: Editions E. De Boccard, 1968.

———. *Le Vijñāna Bhairava*. Paris: Editions E. De Boccard, 1961.

Silverstein, Micheal. "Shifters, Linguistic Categories, and Cultural Description." In *Meaning in Anthropology*, ed. Keith H. Basso and Henry A. Selby. Albuquerque: University of New Mexico Press, 1976.

Sinha, Jadunath. *Shakta Monism: The Cult of Shakti*. Calcutta: Sinha Publishing House Pvt. Ltd., 1966.

Singer, Milton. *When a Great Tradition Modernizes*. London: Pall Mall, 1972.

Sircar, D. C. *The Śākta Pīthas*. Calcutta: University Press, 1973, second edition; reprint edition, Delhi: Motilal Banarsidass, 1981.

———. ed., *The Śakti Cult and Tārā*. Calcutta: University Press, 1967.

———. text and translation, *Tantrasāradhrta dhyānamālā*. In *JAIH*, Vol. VI parts 1–2, 1972–1973. Calcutta.

Smith, Brian K. "Exorcising the Transcendent: Strategies for Defining Hinduism and Religion." In *History of Religions* 27 (August 1987):32–55.

———. "Gods and Men in Vedic Ritualism: Toward a Hierarchy of Resemblence." In *History of Religions* 24 (May 1985):291–307.

———. "Ritual, Knowledge, and Being: Initiation and Veda Study in Ancient India." In *Numen* 33 (1986):65–89.

———. "The Unity of Ritual: The Place of Domestic Sacrifice in Vedic Ritualism." In *Indo-Iranian Journal* 28 (1985):79–96.

Smith, Jonathan Z. "Connections," unpublished address to the annual meeting of The American Academy of Religion, Anaheim, 1989, forthcoming in *The Journal of the American Academy of Religion.*

———. *Imagining Religion. From Babylon to Jonestown*. Chicago: University of Chicago Press, 1982.

———. *Map is Not Territory. Studies in the History of Religions*. Leiden: E. J. Brill, 1978.

———. *To Take Place. Towards Theory in Ritual*. Chicago: University of Chicago Press, 1982.

———. "What a Difference a Difference Makes." In *"To See Ourselves as Other See Us" Christians, Jews, "Others" in Late Antiquity*, eds. Jacob Neusner and Ernest S. Frerichs. Chico, Calif. : Scholars Press, 1985.

Smith, W. C. *Faith and Belief*. Princeton: Princeton University Press, 1979.

———. *The Meaning and End of Religion: A New Approach to the Religious Traditions of Mankind*. New York: Mentor Books, New American Library, 1964, first published New York: Macmillan, 1963.

———. "The True Meaning of Scripture: An Empirical Historian's Nonreductionist Interpretation of the Qur'an." In *International Journal of Middle East Studies*, 1980, 11:487–505.

Sperber, Dan. *Rethinking Symbolism*. Cambridge: Cambridge University Press, 1975.

Srinivas, M. N. *Social Change in Modern India*. Berkeley: University of California Press, 1966.

Staal, Frits "The Meaninglessness of Ritual." In *Numen* 26:1:2–22.

———. "Ritual Syntax." In *Sanskrit and Indian Studies. Essays in Honor of Daniel H. H. Ingalls*, ed. M. Nagatomi, et al. Leiden: E. J. Brill, 1983.

———. "Ritual Structure." In *Agni. The Vedic Ritual of the Fire Altar*. Delhi: Motilal Banarsidass, 1981.

———. *The Science of Ritual*. Poona: The Bhandharkar Oriental Research Institute, 1982.

Subrahmaniam, K. *Brahman Priest of Tamil Nādu*. New York: John Wiley, 1974.

Sundaramoorthy, G. *Aruṇopaniṣad with the Commentary of Lakṣmīdhara*. Madurai: Śrīvidya Educational Trust, 1990.

———. *Śaivism. (Based on Tamil Tradition)*. Kuala Lampur: Malaysia Hindu Sangam.

———. *Caiva Camayam (Tamil Marapai Ottiyatu)*. Madurai: Sarvotaya Ilakkiyap Pannai, 1977. (In Tamil)

———. *Vadamoli Nurkalil Caiva Cittāntam*. Madurai: Sarvotaya Ilakkiyap Pannai, 1977. (In Tamil)

Tiwari, Jagdish Narain. *Goddess Cults in Ancient India*. Delhi: Āgam Prakāśhan, 1986.

Tracy, David. "Is a Hermeneutics of Religion Possible?." In *Religious Pluralism*, ed. L. Rouner, 1984, pp. 116–129.

Trautmann, Thomas R. *Dravidian Kinship*. Cambridge: University Press, 1981.

van Buitenen, J. A. B. *Yāmuna's Āgama Pramāṇyam, or treatise on the validity of Pāñcaratra*. Madras: Rāmānuja Research Society, 1968.

———. "Hindu Sacred Literature." In *Encyclopedia Britannica III*. Macropaedia, vol. 8, pp. 932–40.

van den Hoek, A. W. "The goddess of the northern gate: Cellatamman as the 'divine warrior' of Madurai." In *Asie du sud: traditions et changements*, edited by Marc Gaborieau and Alice Thorner. Paris: Editions du *CNRS*, 1979.

van der Leeuw, G. *Religion in Essence and Manifestation*. trans. J. E. Turner with Appendices to the Torchbook edition incorporating the addition of the second German edition by Hans H. Penner. 2 Vols. New York and Evanston: Harper and Row, 1963.

Venkataraman, K. R. "Śakti cult in South India." In *CHI*, Vol. IV, 1956, second edition, pp. 252–259.

Weber, Max. *The Religion of India*. New York: Free Press 1967.

Winternitz, M. *A History of Indian Literature*, vol. 1., trans. V. Srinivasa Sarma. Delhi: Motilal Banarsidass, 1981.

———, "Die Tantra und die Religion der sākta." In *Ostasiatische Zeitschrift*, IV, 1915/16, pp. 153–163.

———, "Notes on the Guhyasamāja-Tantra and the Age of the Tantras." In *IHQ* 9, 1933, pp. 1–10.

Woodroffe, Sir John (See also Avalon, Arthur). *Shakti and Shakta. Essays and Addresses on the Shakta Tantrashastra*. Madras: Ganesh and Co., reprinted eighth edition, 1975.

———. *Tantrarāja Tantra. A Short Analysis*, in *Tantrarāja Tantra and Kāmakalāvilāsa*. Madras: Ganesh and Co., 1971.

Zimmer, Heinrich. *Myths and Symbols in Indian Art and Civilisation*. Bollingen Series 6. Princeton: University Press, 1972 reprint.

———. *Kunst Form und Yoga im Indischen Kult Bild*. Reprinted Frankfurt-am-Main, 1976.

Zvelebil, K. V. *The Poets of the Powers*. London, 1973.

———. *Tamil Literature*. Wiesbaden: Otto Harrossowitz, 1974 (A History of Indian Literature, ed. Jan Gonda, Vol. X, fasc. 1).

———. *Tamil Literature*. Leiden: E. J. Brill, 1975 (*Handbuch der Orientalistik*, II–2–I).

INDEX

Abhinavagupta, 3, 18, 23, 39, 40, 41, 42, 203 n. 1; on definition of *kula*, 19, 20; on Trika, 21. *See also* Kashmiri Śaivism
Absolute, 77; as binary divinity, 60; as blissful, 101, 220 n.59 (see also *ānanda*); cosmology of, xix, 60, 99, 112, 117; as creator, 60, 91, 112; experience of, 125; *See also* Brahman
ācāra, 22, 42, 88, 106
ācārya. *See* guru
accomplishment, 86, 94; through Tantric practice, 110. See also *siddhi*
action, xix, 6. See also *kriyā*
adept, xix, 4; judgements of, xix; living in contrast to historical Tantrics, xvii, 8, 16, 205. *See also* Tantra
ādhāra (cakra). See *mūlādhara*
adharma, 154, 158
adhikāra, 6, 24, 62, 95; for Tantric practice, 93, 156-157; for *śrīcakra* worship, 24-25; for study of Tantric texts, 45; role in transmission of Tantric tradition, 57. *See also* qualification
ādhikya, 105. *See also* priority
ādirahasya, 11. *See also* original secret.
ādividyā, 104, 105
advaita, 16, 46, 48, 55, 73, 172. See also *kevalādvaita*; non-dualism
advija, 24; as impure persons, 151. *See also* non-twice-born
Āgama, 22, 29, 37, 55, 56, 203 n.16
Agastya, 45, 87
aghora, xvii, xviii, 17.
Agni, 87, 91, 120, 137, 185
agnicayana, 165, 170
agniṣṭoma, 170. *See also* ritual
agrahara, 54
ahaṃkāra, 98
aims of human existence. See *puruṣārtha*
aiśvarya, 49
Aiyar, N. Subrahmanya, 50
ājñā(cakra), 91
Akhilandeśvarī, 48, 72
akula, 23
Alper, Harvey, 19
Ambikā, 90, 92, 124; mentioned in Tantric texts, 124
āmnāya, 140
Amṛtānanda, xv, 23, 40, 42, 50, 51, 88, 89, 90, 105, 106, 123, 124, 131, 136, 137; on the *śrīpañcakam*, 22
anahāta, 90
ānanda, 122, 220 n.59; as goal of Tantric practice, 158, 171, 185. *See also* bliss
ānandabhairava, 137, 139
Ānandalaharī, 47, 48. See also *Saundaryalaharī*
Ānandārṇava Tantra, 43
aniconic, xviii
antaḥkaraṇa, 98
antaryāga, 24, 81, 160, 171; according to Bhāskararāya, 39. *See also* ritual
anthropological study, xiv, xvi
anthropomorphic image, xvii, xviii, 71. See *sthūla*

Padmapurāṇa, 72, 75, 76
pāduka, 23
pañcadaśākṣarī, 45, 86, 90, 96, 109. See also *śrīvidyā*
pañcadaśī, 86, 87, 97, 105, 108, 111. See also *śrīvidyā*
pañcamakāra, 18, 176, 186; and Tantric classification, 20; as external ritual elements, 19, 24, 155; restrictions on, 161; and Samaya, 24, 25, 49, 58, 180; and Śāktism,; mentioned in Tantric texts, 43, 50, 53 . *See also* five m's
Pāñcarātra Vaiṣṇavism, 67
Pandey, K. C., 20, 21, 39
Pāṇini, 5, 102
parā, xviii, 74, 90, 92, 109; mentioned in Tantric texts, 78, 89, 107, 124. *See also* goddess; *śrīcakra*; transcendent
Paramānanda Tantra, 43, 110
paramparā, 52, 88: and the guru, 22; as locus of Tantric tradition, 11. *See also* lineage; guru
parāśakti, 30, 60
Paraśurāma, 53
Paraśurāma Kalpasūtra (*PKS*), 22, 52-53, 61, 77, 89, 110, 140, 173; critique of Vedas, 97; as ritual text, 104
Parimala, 51
parināma, 48, 92, 99, 123, 244 n.26. *See also* Brahman; transformation
Pārvatī, 61
paśyantī, 78, 90, 124, 137; mentioned in Tantric texts, 78, 107, 124
path: three types of, 78. See also *mārga*
peaceful aspect. See *śānta*
peak, 31, 81. See also *kūṭa*; mantra
Peirce, Charles Sanders, xviii, 82
Penner, Hans, 147, 148, 156, 250 n.3
pilgrimage, 59
piṅgala, 42, 91
pīṭha, 45, 48, 126
pleasure, 182. *See also* desire; *kāma*
power: acquisition of, 17, 95, 98, 136, 142, 143; definition of, 149; dispositional, 81, 84, 95, 154; divine forms of, 81, 112, 113, 117, 133, 149, 152, 154; episodic, 84, 85, 95, 152, 154; and the guru, 50, 102, 110, 112; and impurity, 151, 152-153, 155; of mantras, 61-62, 81, 84, 86, 90, 94, 95, 99, 102, 112; miraculous, 86, 133-134; as claim to privilege and prosperity, 142, 171, 188; reality as, xix, 69, 129; and ritual, xix, 98, 109, 112, 117, 147 *passim*; of signs, 14, 82, 95; social and religious, 147 *passim*; and substances, 150 superhuman, 142; symbolism of, xix, 127; as *tapas*, 67. See also *śakti*
practice. See *sādhana*
Practitioners of Convention. *See* Samaya
pradhāna, 77
prakāśa, 60, 89, 91, 98, 122, 123, 131, 132. *See also* illumination
prakaṭa, 142. *See also* exoteric
prakṛti, 47, 100, 138, 160
pramāṇa (and related forms), 22
praṇava, 90, 92, 93, 112. See also *AUM*, *Om*
prapañca, 60, 127. *See also* expansion
Prapañcasāra (*PS*), 44, 77
prasāda, 84
Pratapatarudra Gajapati, xv
pratibimba, 115. See also *bimba*; reflection
pratinidhi: use among contemporary adepts, 15. *See also* ritual
pratyabhijñā, 21; as a school of Kashmiri Śaivism, 19. *See also* re-cognition
Pravarasena, 47
Prayāg, 59
prayāścitta, 175, 181. *See also* expiation
priest. *See* brahman
priority, 105. See also *ādhikhya*
privilege, 188. *See also* power
prohibited substances. See *pañcamākara*

LaVergne, TN USA
17 December 2010
209183LV00003B/58/A

9 780791 411469